International Financial Reporting Standards in Depth
Volume 1: Theory and practice

PUBLISHING

International Financial Reporting Standards in Depth

Volume 1: Theory and practice

Robert J. Kirk

ELSEVIER
BUTTERWORTH
HEINEMANN

AMSTERDAM • BOSTON • HEIDELBERG • LONDON • NEW YORK • OXFORD
PARIS • SAN DIEGO • SAN FRANCISCO • SINGAPORE • SYDNEY • TOKYO

CIMA Publishing
An Imprint of Elsevier
Linacre House, Jordan Hill, Oxford OX2 8DP
30 Corporate Drive, Burlington, MA 01803

First published 2005

Copyright © 2005 Elsevier Ltd. All rights reserved

British Library Cataloguing in Publication Data
A catalogue record for this book is available from the British Library

Library of Congress Cataloguing in Publication Data Control Number: 2005923930

ISBN 0 7506 64738 (Set)
ISBN 0 7506 67788 (Volume 1)
ISBN 0 7506 67796 (Volume 2)

For information on all Elsevier Butterworth-Heinemann publications
visit our website at http://books.elsevier.com

Typeset by Newgen Imaging Systems Pvt Ltd, Chennai, India

Printed and bound by CPI Group (UK) Ltd, Croydon, CR0 4YY
Transferred to Digital Print 2012

Working together to grow
libraries in developing countries

www.elsevier.com | www.bookaid.org | www.sabre.org

ELSEVIER   BOOK AID International   Sabre Foundation

This book is dedicated to the memory of my father

Contents

The author   *xi*

Introduction   *xiii*

1   The regulatory framework and the standard-setting process   1
   1.1   Introduction to the standard-setting process   1
   1.2   Trustees   2
   1.3   The International Accounting Standards Board (IASB)   3
   1.4   The Standards Advisory Council (SAC)   4
   1.5   The International Financial Reporting Interpretations
        Committee (IFRIC)   4
   1.6   Process of standard setting   4
   1.7   List of extant Financial Reporting Standards and
        International Standards   5
   1.8   Framework for the Preparation and Presentation of
        Financial Statements (1989)   6
   1.9   IFRS 1 *First Time Adoption of International Financial Reporting
        Standards* (July 2003)   11
   1.10   IAS 1 *Presentation of Financial Information* (revised
        December 2003)   13
   1.11   Examination questions   23

2   Asset valuation: accounting for tangible fixed assets   29
   2.1   IAS 16 *Property, Plant and Equipment* (revised December 2003)   29
   2.2   IAS 40 *Investment Property* (revised March 2004)   33
   2.3   IAS 20 *Accounting for Government Grants and Disclosure of
        Government Assistance* (1994)   40
   2.4   IAS 36 *Impairment of Assets* (revised March 2004)   43
   2.5   IAS 23 *Borrowing Costs* (revised December 2003)   57
   2.6   Examination questions   59

3   Asset valuation: accounting for intangible assets,
   inventories and construction contracts   72
   3.1   IAS 38 *Intangible Assets* (revised March 2004)   72
   3.2   IAS 17 *Leases* (revised December 2003)   84
   3.3   IAS 2 *Inventories* (revised December 2003)   90
   3.4   IAS 11 *Construction Contracts* (1978, revised 1993)   93
   3.5   Examination questions   96

4 Balance sheet: liabilities 105
   4.1 IAS 37 *Provisions, Contingent Liabilities and Contingent Assets*
        (May 1975, revised September 1998) 105
   4.2 Examination questions 115

5 Performance measurement 121
   5.1 IAS 33 *Earnings per share* (revised December 2003) 121
   5.2 IAS 8 *Accounting Policies, Changes in Accounting Estimates
        and Errors* (December 2003) 128
   5.3 IAS 18 *Revenue* (1993) 131
   5.4 IFRS 5 *Non-Current Assets Held for Sale and Presentation of
        Discontinued Operations* (March 2004) 133
   5.5 Examination questions 140

6 Cash flow statements 163
   6.1 IAS 7 *Cash Flow Statements* (revised 1992) 163
   6.2 Examination questions 168

7 Foreign trading 175
   7.1 IAS 21 *The Effects of Changes in Foreign Exchange Rates*
        (revised December 2003) 175
   7.2 IAS 29 *Financial Reporting in Hyperinflationary Economies*
        (December 2003) 180
   7.3 Examination questions 184

8 Taxation 188
   8.1 IAS 12 *Income Taxes* (revised 2000) 188
   8.2 Examination questions 201

9 Group accounting 207
   9.1 IAS 27 *Consolidated and Separate Financial Statements*
        (December 2003) 207
   9.2 IFRS 3 *Business Combinations* (March 2004) 212
   9.3 IAS 28 *Accounting for Investments in Associates* (December 2003) 222
   9.4 IAS 31 *Investments in Joint Ventures* (December 2003) 225
   9.5 Examination questions 231

10 Disclosure standards 258
   10.1 IAS 10 *Events After the Balance Sheet Date* (December 2003) 258
   10.2 IAS 14 *Segment Reporting* (1997) 261
   10.3 IAS 24 *Related Party Disclosures* (December 2003) 272
   10.4 Examination questions 275

11 Employee benefits, pension schemes and share-based payment 279
   11.1 IAS 19 *Employee Benefits* (December 1998, amended 2000) 279
   11.2 IAS 26 *Accounting and Reporting by Retirement Benefit Plans* (1994) 301

11.3	IFRS 2 *Share-Based Payment* (April 2004)	306
11.4	Examination questions	318

12 Financial instruments — 323
12.1	IAS 30 *Disclosures in Financial Statements of Banks and Similar Institutions* (reformatted 1994)	323
12.2	IAS 32 *Financial Instruments: Disclosure and Presentation* (revised 2003)	329
12.3	IAS 39 *Financial Instruments: Recognition and Measurement* (revised March 2004)	340
12.4	Examination questions	355

13 Sundry financial reporting standards — 358
13.1	IAS 34 *Interim Financial Reporting* (1998)	358
13.2	IAS 41 *Agriculture* (February 2001)	362
13.3	IFRS 4 *Insurance Contracts* (March 2004)	371
13.4	Examination questions	372

14 Exposure drafts and statements of the International Financial Reporting Interpretations Committee (IFRIC formerly SIC) — 375
14.1	IFRS 6 Exploration for and Evaluation of Mineral Resources (December 2004) (ED 6 January 2004)	375
14.2	Standards Interpretations Committee (extant interpretations)	377
14.3	IFRICs developed after 31st October 2004	384

The author

Robert Kirk BSc (Econ) FCA CPA qualified as a chartered accountant in 1976. He trained in Belfast with Price Waterhouse & Co, and subsequently spent two years in industry in a subsidiary of Shell (UK) and four further years in practice. In 1980 he was appointed a director of a private teaching college in Dublin, where he specialised in the teaching of professional accounting subjects. He later moved into the university sector, and is currently Professor of Financial Reporting in the School of Accounting at the University of Ulster.

He has been lecturing on the CIMA Mastercourses presentations *Recent Accounting Standards* and *Accounting Standards in Depth* since 1985. He has also presented continuing professional education courses for the Institute of Chartered Accountants in Ireland over the same period, specialising in the delivery of programmes on both national and international accounting standards.

His publications to date, in addition to numerous professional journal articles, include two books on company law in Northern Ireland, co-authorship with University College Dublin of the first Survey of Irish Published Accounts, a joint publication with Coopers & Lybrand on the legislation enacting the 7th European Directive into UK legislation, four editions of *Accounting Standards in Depth* and two Financial Reporting publications for the CIMA Study Packs.

Introduction

The pace of development in financial reporting has accelerated sharply during the last few years, especially since the advent of the Accounting Standards Board (ASB) in 1990. The pace of progress shows no sign of abating, and it has become increasingly difficult for both the student and the professionally qualified accountant to keep abreast of the changes.

International Financial Reporting Standards in Depth examines the standards in a unique and detailed way, and has been written with a broad readership in mind. Each chapter includes a brief summary of the relevant accounting standards in force, together with the proposed changes contained within outstanding exposure drafts. This is followed by a selection of questions which attempt to cover most of the major problem areas that students are likely to encounter. The questions have been carefully selected from two of the major accounting bodies in the United Kingdom – CIMA and ACCA. A number of illustrative examples taken from published accounts are included. These mainly cover the disclosure required in published accounts.

The questions in the book are reproduced as they were originally set in the professional examinations. The solutions, however – which are supplied in a companion text to this volume – are based on the most recent standards, which may not have been in existence at the time of devising of the question.

The book commences with an introduction to the standard-setting process. As well as looking at the development of the IASB it examines the *Framework for the Preparation and Presentation of Financial Statements*, which underpins the practice of financial accounting. Chapter 1 also covers the first-time adoption of IFRSs covered in IFRS 1, and the broad content and presentation of financial statements covered in IAS 1. The next three chapters, Chapters 2–4, cover the key accounting problems in the balance sheet, i.e. tangible fixed assets, intangible assets, inventories and liabilities. Chapter 5 concentrates on performance measurement, and Chapter 6 on the effects of taxation. Chapter 7 covers the important area of foreign exchange transactions and translation, whilst Chapter 8 investigates liquidity and viability by examining cash flow statements.

The longest chapter (Chapter 9) is reserved for the accounting aspects of groups, and this encapsulates accounting under the purchase method , the death of mergers, and both associated undertakings and joint ventures. Chapter 10 concentrates on the disclosure standards of post-balance sheet events, segment reporting and related party transactions.

Chapter 11 covers the difficult area of retirement benefits, but also incorporates other employee benefits as well as the content of pension scheme financial statements and the new standard on share-based payment. One of the most controversial aspects of financial reporting is the topic of financial instruments, and Chapter 12 is devoted entirely to that topic.

Chapters 13 and 14 sweep up standards not covered elsewhere, and include a discussion of topics such as agriculture, interim reporting and insurance contracts. In addition, the Standards Interpretation Committee statements are briefly covered in the final chapter.

The intention of the book is that the reader will be tested on basic numerical application, on an understanding of the underlying theory, and on presentation of financial statements under the international regulatory framework. The questions have been carefully chosen to test the readers's ability to write good practical reports, perform calculations, and present both extracts and full sets of financial statements.

Acknowledgements

Examination questions are reproduced by kind permission of The Association of Chartered Certified Accountants, London.

1

The regulatory framework and the standard-setting process

1.1 Introduction to the standard-setting process

The first *Statement of Standard Accounting Practice* (SSAP) was published in 1970 in the United Kingdom. Prior to this, there were relatively few financial reporting requirements for companies. It was the highly publicised scandals of the late 1960s, such as the GEC takeover of AEI, that brought the need for more extensive regulations and the instigation of a standards-setting body.

The International Accounting Standards Committee (IASC) was set up in 1973. Between 1973 and its demise in April 2001 it published 41 international accounting standards (IASs). These were largely drafted by part-time volunteer boards from a wide background of experience and range of countries. It resulted in a rather slow and protracted process of developing standards. Many of these offered a number of options, and thus were largely ignored by the major standard-setting countries. However, problems started to emerge with multinationals having to prepare a number of different sets of financial statements for different jurisdictions. It therefore became difficult to make comparisons across countries – for example, when Daimler Benz was first quoted in New York, the same set of financial statements disclosed a profit of 630DM in Germany but a loss of 1300DM using US rules. The International Organisation for Securities and Exchange Commissions (IOSCO), a loose federation of all the major stock exchanges in the world, therefore offered a challenge to the IASC to carry out a review of existing standards to ensure that many of the options be removed and the standards strengthened. If satisfactorily achieved, then IASs would become acceptable for cross-border listings. That challenge was taken up by the Secretary-General of the IASC, Sir Bryan Carsberg, and he largely achieved his objectives by the end of 2000.

The big push, however, for the development of international standards was the need to solve the problem of financial instruments. This could only be solved on an international basis, and a group of standard setters (known as G4 + 1) attempted to get agreement. In addition, they started to investigate leasing and reporting financial performance. They were well on their way to producing some very interesting international agreements on future standards. However, the European Commission forced the G4 + 1 group to dissolve when it announced that all listed companies in the EC must comply, for their consolidated financial statements, with international standards. The G4 + 1 group (basically the UK/Ireland, USA, Canada New Zealand and Australia, and the IASC as observer) agreed to put their

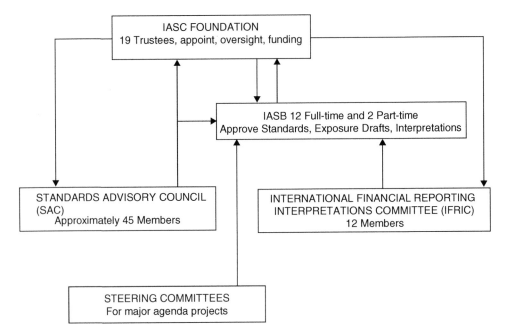

Figure 1.1   Revised structure of the IASC

support behind the development of a new Board to further improve existing international standards and to develop new standards. A new structure was finally set up in April 2001.

The principal body under the new structure is the International Accounting Standards Board (IASB), which has sole responsibility for establishing International Financial Reporting Standards (IFRSs). Other components of the structure are the Trustees of the IASC Foundation, the International Financial Reporting Interpretations Committee (IFRIC) and the Standards Advisory Council (SAC). The IASB held its first official meeting in London in April 2001, at which meeting it was resolved that all Standards and Interpretations issued by the IASC should continue to be applicable unless and until they are amended or withdrawn. It was agreed that new IASB standards would be called International Financial Reporting Standards (IFRSs).

When the term 'IFRSs' is used, it includes standards and interpretations approved by the IASB, and IAS and interpretations issued by the IASC.

The revised structure of the IASC is illustrated in Figure 1.1.

1.2   Trustees

The governance of the IASC Foundation rests with the Trustees. The initial nineteen Trustees include six from North America, seven from Europe, four from the Asia Pacific region, and one each from Africa and South America. They come from diverse functional backgrounds.

The Trustees have responsibility to:

• appoint the members of the Board, including those that will serve in liaison capacities with national standard setters, and establish their contracts of service and performance criteria;

- appoint the members of the IFRIC and the SAC;
- review annually the strategy of the IASC and its effectiveness;
- approve annually the budget of the IASC and its effectiveness;
- review broad strategic issues affecting accounting standards, promote the IASC and its work, and promote the objective of rigorous application of IFRS, provided that the Trustees shall be excluded from involvement in technical matters relating to accounting standards;
- establish and amend operating procedures for the Board, the IFRIC and the SAC.

The Trustees act by simple majority vote, except for amendments to the Constitution, which require a 75% majority.

1.3   The International Accounting Standards Board (IASB)

The IASB is the principal body under the new structure. The Board has fourteen members, of whom twelve serve full time and two part time. The Board's principal responsibilities are to:

- develop and issue IFRSs and Exposure Drafts; and
- approve Interpretations developed by the IFRIC.

The key qualification for Board membership is technical expertise. The Trustees must also ensure that the Board is not dominated by any particular constituency or regional interest. To achieve a balance of perspectives and experience, at least five members must have backgrounds as practising auditors, at least three as financial statement preparers, at least three as users of financial statements, and at least one as an academic.

Seven of the fourteen board members have direct liaison responsibility with one or more national standard setters. The Board has full discretion over its technical agenda. It may outsource detailed research or other work to national standard setters or other organisations. The Board will normally form Steering Committees or other types of specialist advisory groups to give advice on major projects. The Board is required to consult the Standards Advisory Council on major projects, agenda decisions and work priorities.

Before issuing a final Standard, the Board must publish an Exposure Draft for public comment. Normally, it will also publish a Draft Statement of Principles or other discussion document for public comment on major projects.

The Board will normally issue bases for conclusions within IFRS and Exposure Drafts. Although there is no requirement to hold public hearings or to conduct field tests for every project, the Board must, in each case, consider the need to do so.

The publication of an Exposure Draft, IFRS or final Interpretation of the IFRIC requires approval by eight of the fourteen members of the Board. Other decisions of the Board, including the publication of a Draft Statement of Principles or discussion paper, require a simple majority of the members of the Board present at a meeting.

The IASB generally meets monthly (except August) for three to five days. It holds several meetings each year with representatives of its liaison standard-setting bodies, and generally three meetings each year with the Standards Advisory Council.

1.4   The Standards Advisory Council (SAC)

The Standards Advisory Council currently has 49 members, and provides a forum for organisations and individuals with an interest in international financial reporting to participate in the standard-setting process. Members are appointed for a renewable term of 3 years, and have diverse geographical and functional backgrounds. The Chairman of the IASB is also the Chairman of the SAC.

The SAC will normally meet three times each year at meetings open to the public to:

- advise the Board on priorities in the Board's work;
- inform the Board of the implications of proposed standards for users and preparers of financial statements; and
- give other advice to the Board or to the Trustees.

1.5   The International Financial Reporting Interpretations Committee (IFRIC)

The International Financial Reporting Interpretations Committee (IFRIC) (until 2002 known as the Standing Interpretations Committee) has twelve members appointed by the Trustees for terms of 3 years. IFRIC members are not salaried, but their expenses are reimbursed. The IFRIC is chaired by a non-voting Chair who can be one of the members of the IASB, the Director of Technical Activities, or a member of the IASB's senior technical staff. (In fact, the Director of Technical Activities was appointed the Chair of the IFRIC.) The IFRIC's responsibilities are to:

- interpret the application of IFRS and provide timely guidance on financial reporting issues not specifically addressed in IFRS in the context of the IASB's Framework, and undertake other tasks at the request of the Board;
- publish Draft Interpretations for public comment and consider comments made within a reasonable period before finalising an Interpretation; and
- report to the Board and obtain Board approval for final Interpretations.

A Draft or final Interpretation is approved by the IFRIC when not more than three voting members of the IFRIC vote against the Draft or final Interpretation. By allowing the IFRIC to develop Interpretations on financial reporting issues not specifically addressed in an IFRS, the new IASB constitution has broadened the IFRIC's mandate beyond that of the former Standing Interpretations Committee.

1.6   Process of standard setting

The process of development of an IFRS will generally include the following:

- IASB staff work to identify and review all the issues related to a topic and study other national accounting standards and practices;
- a Steering Committee or advisory group may be formed to give advice on major projects;
- a Draft Statement of Principles or similar discussion document will be developed and published on major projects;

- following receipt of comments on the initial discussion document, if any, the IASB will develop and publish an Exposure Draft; and
- following receipt of comments on the Exposure Draft, the IASB will approve all IFRSs.

1.7 List of extant Financial Reporting Standards and International Standards

The extant financial Reporting Standards and International Standards are listed in Table 1.1.

Table 1.1 Extant financial reporting standards and international standards

UK Accounting Standards (SSAPs and FRSs)	International Accounting Standards (IFRSs and IASs)
SSAP 4 Accounting for Government Grants	IAS 20 Accounting for Government Grants and Disclosure of Government Assistance
SSAP 5 Accounting for Value Added Tax	–
SSAP 9 Stocks and Long Term Contracts	IAS 2 Inventories
	IAS 11 Construction and Service Contracts
SSAP 13 Accounting for Research and Development	IAS 38 Intangible Assets
FRS 21 Events after the Balance Sheet Date	IAS 10 Events After the Balance Sheet Date
SSAP 19 Investment Properties	IAS 40 Investment Properties
FRS 23 The Effect of Change in Foreign Exchange Rates	IAS 21 The Effect of Changes in Foreign Exchange Rates
FRS 24 Financial Reporting in Hyperinflationary Economies	IAS 29 Financial Reporting in Hyperinflationary Economies
SSAP 21 Accounting for Leases and Hire Purchase Contracts	IAS 17 Leases
SSAP 25 Segmental Reporting	IAS 14 Segment Reporting
FRS 1 Cash Flow Statements	IAS 7 Cash Flow Statements
FRS 2 Accounting for Subsidiary Undertakings	IAS 27 Consolidated and Separate Financial Statements
FRS 3 Reporting Financial Performance	IAS 8 Account Policies, Changes in Accounting Estimates and Errors
	IFRS 5 Non Current Assets Held for Sale and Presentation of Discontinued Operations
FRS 26 Financial Instruments: Measurement	IAS 39 Financial Instruments: Recognition and Measurement
FRS 5 Reporting the Substance of Transactions	–
FRS 6 Acquisitions and Mergers	IFRS 3 Business Combinations
FRS 7 Fair Values in Acquisition Accounting	IFRS 3 Business Combinations
FRS 8 Related Party Disclosures	IAS 24 Related Party Disclosures
FRS 9 Associates and Joint Ventures	IAS 28 Investments in Associates
	IAS 31 Financial Reporting of Interests in Joint Ventures
FRS 10 Goodwill and Intangible Assets	IFRS 3 Business Combinations
FRS 11 Impairments of Fixed Assets and Goodwill	IAS 36 Impairment of Assets

Table 1.1   *(Continued)*

UK Accounting Standards (SSAPs and FRSs)	International Accounting Standards (IFRSs and IASs)
FRS 12 Provisions, Contingent Liabilities and Contingent Assets	IAS 37 Provisions, Contingent Liabilities and Contingent Assets
FRS 25 Financial Instruments: Disclosure and Prevention	IAS 32 Financial Instruments: Disclosure and Presentation
FRS 22 Earnings Per Share	IAS 33 Earnings Per Share
FRS 15 Tangible Fixed Assets	IAS 16 Property, Plant and Equipment
	IAS 23 Borrowing Costs
FRS 16 Current Tax	IAS 12 Income Taxes
FRS 17 Retirement Benefits	IAS 19 Employee Benefits
FRS 18 Accounting Policies	IAS 1 Presentation of Financial Statements
	IAS 8 Accounts Policies, Changes in Accounting Estimates and Errors
FRS 19 Deferred Tax	IAS 12 Income Taxes
FRS 20 Share Based Payment	IFRS 2 Share Based Payment
AN G FRS 5 Reporting the Substance of Transactions: Revenue Recognition	IAS 18 Revenue
SORP Retirement Benefit Plans	IAS 26 Accounting and Reporting by Retirement Benefit Plans
–	IAS 30 Disclosures in the Financial Statements of Banks and Similar Financial Institutions
SBP Interim Accounts	IAS 34 Interim Financial Reporting
–	IAS 41 Agriculture
	IFRS 1 First Time Adoption of Financial Reporting Standards
–	IFRS 4 Insurance Contracts
	IFRS 6 Explorations For and Evaluations of Mineral Resource

1.8   Framework for the Preparation and Presentation of Financial Statements (1989)

Background

One of the main problems that faced standard-setting bodies in their quest to develop authoritative accounting standards was their failure to publish standards that were consistent with each other. There was no firm foundation on which they could be built. As a result, the actual standards were produced in an *ad hoc* manner with very little logical thought behind their publication. The Framework is an attempt to put this right by introducing the core principles that should govern financial reporting.

Objective of financial statements

This section of the Framework argues that there are several users of financial reporting and that the Annual Report is the main vehicle of communicating with users. The information should largely be directed towards meeting their needs. These needs are twofold – to ensure the reporting entity has performed adequately (the stewardship function), and to ensure that the user has sufficient information on which to make decisions about the future (i.e. the decision-making function). In order to provide information that may be helpful to users it is recommended that the entity provide information about the *financial position, performance* and *changes in financial position* of the organisation. The financial statements should be prepared under both the accruals and going concern bases.

Qualitative characteristics

This section of the Framework identifies the key primary qualitative characteristics that should make the information in the Annual Report useful to users. There are four principal characteristics, two relating to the content of the Report and two in relation to its presentation; these are described below.

Relevance

The information must be relevant, i.e. up to date and current, and actually used by the reader. Included within this characteristic is the concept of materiality. It provides a threshold or cut-off judgement rather than a primary qualitative characteristic.

Reliability

The reader must have faith in the information provided, and it must be free from material error and represent faithfully what it is supposed to represent. It must be free from bias, and the information must be complete within the bounds of materiality.

This characteristic tends to come into conflict with that of relevance, since relevance would favour the adoption of current subjective values whereas reliability would gravitate towards the adoption of historic and more objective costs. Where the two do clash, the International Accounting Standards Board (IASB) favours relevance.

Transactions should also be accounted for in accordance with their substance and not merely their legal form. A degree of caution (prudence) must also be exercised in making estimates under conditions of uncertainty.

Comparability

This is really the former consistency concept, and insists that information must be comparable from period to period and within like items in the same period. It also requires sufficient disclosure for a user to appreciate the significance of transactions. However, it does not mean uniformity, and accounting policies must be reviewed when more relevant and reliable alternatives exist.

Understandability

This concept insists that the information being provided by the reporting entity be presented in such a way that it is as understandable as possible to the user. However, this does not mean that it is so simple that the information being provided becomes meaningless.

The elements of financial statements

This chapter of the Framework contains the key elements in a set of financial statements. It defines the balance sheet elements first, and then argues that the income statement should pick up any residuals – e.g. a gain is either an increase in an asset or a decrease in a liability. The main definitions are as follows:

Financial position:

- Asset: 'Resource controlled by the enterprise as a result of a past events and from which future economic benefits are expected to flow to the enterprise'
- Liability: 'A present obligation of the enterprise arising from past events, the settlement of which is expected to result in an outflow from the enterprise of resources embodying economic benefits'
- Equity: 'The residual interest in the assets of the enterprise after deducting all of its liabilities'.

Financial performance:

- Incomes: 'Increases in economic benefits during the accounting period in the form of inflows or enhancements of assets or decreases in liabilities that result in increases in equity, other than contributions from equity participants'
- Expenses: 'Decreases in economic benefits during the accounting period in the form of outflows or depletions of assets that result in decreases in equity, other than distributions to equity participants'.

Clearly this section of the Framework puts the balance sheet on a pedestal, with its concentration on getting the assets and liabilities right first before looking at the income statement. This represents a cultural swing for the UK from its former profit and loss and accruals based preference. The accruals concept is now clearly downgraded in importance in that expenditure cannot be matched against future income unless it can meet the definition of an asset in the first place. Similarly the prudence concept has been given a 'knock', as a liability can only be created if there is either a legal or constructive obligation in place. A mere intention to expend monies in the future is not sufficient on its own.

Recognition of the elements of financial statements

Even if a transaction meets the definition of an asset/liability, it will not be recorded on the balance sheet unless it meets the following two recognition criteria:

1. Is there sufficient evidence that a change in assets or liabilities has occurred?
2. Can it be measured at cost or value with sufficient reliability?

If these cannot be passed initially then the transactions must be written off directly to income. If one of the criteria is subsequently failed, then the asset/liability must then be removed or derecognised from the balance sheet. It is possible that the asset/liability will need to be remeasured where there is sufficient evidence that the amount has changed, and the new amount measured with sufficient reliability.

Measurement of the elements of financial statements

Measurement is the process of determining the monetary amounts at which the elements are to be recognised in the balance sheet and income statement.

A number of different measurement bases are employed to different degrees and in various combinations in financial statements. They include the following:

1. *Historic cost.* Assets recorded at cash paid at date of acquisition. Liabilities are recorded at the amount of proceeds received in exchange for the obligation or the amount of cash expected to be paid to satisfy the liability, e.g. taxation.
2. *Current cost.* Assets recorded at cash that would have to be paid to acquire the same or equivalent asset. Liabilities are carried at the undiscounted amount of cash required to settle the obligation.
3. *Realisable value.* Assets recorded at cash that would be obtained by selling the asset in an orderly disposal. Liabilities are carried at their settlement values, i.e. the undiscounted amounts of cash expected to be paid to satisfy the liabilities in normal course of business.
4. *Present value.* Assets recorded at the present discounted value of future net cash inflows that the item is expected to generate in the normal course of business. Liabilities are carried at the present discounted value of the future net cash outflows that are expected to be required to settle the liabilities in the normal course of business.

The most popular basis is historic cost, but it is usually combined with other bases – e.g. inventories at lower of cost and net realisable value, marketable securities at market value, and pension liabilities at present value.

Some entities adopt current cost accounting to cope with the inability of historic cost accounting to deal with the effects of changing prices.

Concepts of capital and capital maintenance

The following concepts exist:

1. *Financial capital maintenance.* Profit is only earned if the financial amount of net assets at the end of the period exceeds the financial amount of net assets at the start of the period after excluding distributions to and contributions from owners during the period. It can be measured in either nominal or in purchasing power units.
2. *Physical capital maintenance.* Profit is earned only if the physical productive capacity of the entity at the end of the period exceeds the physical productive capacity at the start of the period after excluding distributions to and contributions from owners during the period.

Capital maintenance links the concepts of capital and the concepts of profit, as it provides a reference by which profit is measured. Only inflows of assets in excess of amounts needed to maintain capital may be regarded as profit. Profit is the residual amount that remains after expenses have been deducted from income. If expenses exceed income, the residual amount is a net loss.

Physical capital maintenance requires the adoption of the current cost basis of measurement. The financial capital maintenance concept does not require the use of a particular basis of measurement. Selection of appropriate basis is dependent on the type of financial capital that the entity is seeking to maintain.

The main difference between the two types of capital maintenance is on the effects of changes in the prices of assets and liabilities of the entity. Generally, capital is maintained if an entity has as much capital at the end of the period as at the start. Any amount over and above that is profit.

Under financial capital maintenance, where capital is defined in nominal terms, profit is the increase in nominal money capital over the period. Holding gains are therefore included in profit, but only when disposed. Under the current purchasing power approach, profit represents the increase in purchasing power over the period. Thus only that part of the increase in prices of assets that exceeds the increase in the general level of prices is regarded as profit; the rest is a capital maintenance adjustment and therefore part of equity.

Under physical capital maintenance, where capital is defined in terms of productive capacity, profit represents the increase in that capital over the period. All price changes are viewed as changes in the measurement of the physical productive capacity of the entity, and thus are treated as capital maintenance adjustments that are part of equity.

The choice of model will depend on the different degrees of relevance and reliability available, and management must seek an appropriate balance between the two. The Framework is applicable to a range of accounting models, and provides guidance on preparing and presenting the financial statements constructed under the chosen model. The IASB is not at present intending to prescribe a particular model other than in exceptional circumstances, e.g. hyperinflationary economies (IAS 29), but this intention will be reviewed in the light of world developments.

Summary

The Framework was published in late 1989 in the form of a statement of best practice which will form the cornerstone of all future standard-setting procedures.

The Framework has set out the concepts that underlie the preparation and presentation of financial statements for external users. The purpose of the Framework is to:

- assist the IASB in developing future IFRSs and reviewing existing IFRSs;
- assist the IASB to promote harmonisation;
- assist national standard setters to develop national standards;
- assist preparers to apply IFRSs and in dealing with topics not covered by an IFRS;
- assist auditors in forming an opinion as to whether or not financial statements conform with IFRSs;
- assist users in interpreting information in financial statements;
- provide those with an interest in the work of the IASB about its approach to formulating IFRSs.

It is not an IFRS itself, but where an IFRS conflicts with the Framework the IFRS prevails. However, this is likely to be rare and to diminish over time. The Framework will be revised from time to time, with experience.

The financial statements should include a balance sheet, income statement, a statement of changes in financial position, and back-up notes. Supplementary information (e.g. segment reporting) is also included, but not Directors' Reports, Discussion and Analysis Statements or Chairman's Reports. The Framework should be applied to all commercially reporting entities.

Users and their needs are specifically covered in the Framework:

1. *Investors.* Concerned about risk and return provided by their investments. Need information to determine buy, hold or sell decisions, and to assess the entity's ability to pay dividends.
2. *Employees.* Concerned about the stability and profitability of their employers and assessing the ability of the entity to provide remuneration, retirement benefits etc. to employees.
3. *Lenders.* Concerned about whether or not their loans and interest can be repaid.
4. *Suppliers and other trade creditors.* Concerned about whether or not they will be paid when due.
5. *Customers.* Concerned about the continuance of the business, especially if they have a long term involvement with the entity.
6. *Governments and their agencies.* Interested in the allocation of resources and information on taxation policies, national statistics etc.
7. *Public.* Can provide information about the local economy, numbers employed, environmental issues etc.

There are common needs of users, and financial statements should meet most of those needs. Information for management purposes is specialised, although published statements may be used by them in assessing financial performance, position and changes in financial position of the entity.

1.9 IFRS 1 *First Time Adoption of International Financial Reporting Standards* (July 2003)

Key points

The objective of the IFRS is to ensure that an entity's first IFRS statements and interim accounts contain high quality information that:

- is transparent over all periods concerned;
- provides a suitable starting point for accounting under IFRSs; and
- can be generated at a cost that does not exceed the benefits to users.

Entities must apply the IFRS in:

- their first IFRS financial statements; and
- each interim report under IAS 34 for part of the period covered by its first IFRS statements.

The first IFRS statements are the first annual statements in which the entity adopts IFRSs by an explicit and unreserved statement of compliance.
    However, IFRS 1 does not apply to an entity when:

- an entity stops applying national Gaap when presenting both national and international sets of financial statements in the same year; or
- an entity presented statements in the previous year under national Gaap and they also contained an explicit statement of compliance with IFRSs; or

- an entity presented statements in previous year with a statement of unreserved compliance, even if qualified by the auditors.

In addition, IFRS 1 does not apply to changes in accounting policies. These are subject to:

- IAS 8; and
- specific transitional requirements in other IFRSs.

An entity must prepare an opening IFRS balance sheet at the date of transition to IFRSs, and must adopt the same accounting policies in its opening IFRS balance sheet throughout all periods presented in its first IFRS statements. They should comply with each effective IFRS at the reporting date for its first financial statements. A new IFRS may be applied that is not yet mandatory if it may be permitted to be adopted early (see Example 1.1).

Example 1.1
Consistent application of latest version of IFRSs

Background
The reporting date for A's first IFRS accounts is 31.12.2005. It has opted for only 1 year's comparatives, thus its date of transition to IFRSs is 1.1.2004.

Application of requirements
Entity A is required to apply the IFRSs for periods ending on 31.12.2005 in:

- preparing its opening IFRS balance sheet at 1.1.2004; and
- preparing and presenting its balance sheet for 31.12.2005, income statement, statement of changes in equity and cash flow statement for the year to 31.12.2005 and disclosures (including 2004 comparatives).

If a new IFRS is not yet mandatory but is permitted, entity A is permitted but not required to apply that IFRS in its first IFRS statements.

An entity shall, in its opening balance sheet:

- recognise all assets and liabilities required by IFRSs;
- not recognise assets and liabilities if IFRSs do not permit such recognition;
- reclassify items under previous Gaap but are different under IFRSs; and
- apply IFRSs in measuring all recognised assets and liabilities.

The accounting policies adopted may differ from those adopted using previous Gaap. The resulting adjustments must be charged directly to retained earnings.

The IFRS establishes two categories of exceptions to the principle that an entity's opening balance sheet comply with each IFRS:

1. Certain paragraphs grant exemptions from some requirements of other IFRSs
2. Certain paragraphs prohibit retrospective application of some aspects of other IFRSs.

The first category includes business combinations, employee benefits, cumulative translation differences, compound financial instruments as well as fair value as deemed cost and assets and liabilities of subsidiaries, associates and joint ventures. These cover the right to use merger accounting for past combinations, to use a previous valuation for property to be a deemed cost subsequently if the entity moves back to historic cost accounting and to provide for all actuarial gains/losses in full rather than the current 'corridor approach' adopted in IAS 19.

The second group prohibits retrospection to the recognition of financial assets and liabilities, to hedge accounting and to estimates.

The standard is only applicable for first-time adoption of IFRSs, so it will be relatively short lived in its application in practice.

1.10   IAS 1 *Presentation of Financial Information* (revised December 2003)

Key points

The objective of IAS 1 is to prescribe the basis for presentation of general purpose financial statements. It sets out the overall framework and responsibilities for the presentation of financial statements, guidelines for their structure, and minimum requirements for the content of financial statements. IAS 1 applies to all general purpose financial statements prepared in accordance with International Financial Reporting Standards. General purpose financial statements are defined as those intended to serve users who do not have the authority to demand financial reports tailored for their own needs.

Content of financial statements

The financial statements should comprise the following:

1. Balance sheet
2. Income statement
3. Statement of changes in equity or statement of non-owner changes in equity
4. Cash flow statement
5. Explanatory notes including a summary of significant accounting policies.

There is no prescribed standard format, although examples of the minimum headings are provided in the Appendix. It does, however, set out minimum disclosures to be made on the face of the financial statements as well as in the notes. For example, an analysis of income and expenditure using a classification based on their nature or function must be disclosed. The standard also requires comparatives to be provided for all items unless a particular accounting standard specifically exempts that requirement.

The reporting currency should generally be that of the country in which the enterprise is domiciled. If a different reporting currency is adopted or a change in reporting currency made, then the reasons must be disclosed.

A reporting enterprise complying with the requirements of IFRSs is considered as providing a fair presentation of the financial statements. A statement that the financial statements comply with IFRSs and SIC interpretations is required. No statement is now permitted stating that compliance with IFRSs has been undertaken with certain specified exemptions. Full compliance is essential.

Overall considerations

Fair presentation and compliance with IFRSs

Financial statements should present fairly the financial position, performance and cash flows of the entity, and the entity should provide an explicit and unreserved statement that the statements are in compliance with IFRSs.

Inappropriate policies are not rectified either by disclosure or by notes.

Entities can, in rare circumstances, depart from an IFRS (if it is regarded as misleading), but the following must be disclosed in those cases:

- management has concluded that the financial statements give a fair presentation;
- that it has complied with IFRSs etc. except from a particular requirement to achieve fair presentation;
- the title of the IFRS, nature of departure and why the normal treatment was not adopted; and
- the financial impact for each period of the departure.

If departure is not permitted, the entity should reduce the perceived misleading aspects by disclosing:

- the title of the standard, the nature of issue and the reason why it was misleading;
- the adjustments management has concluded would be appropriate.

Going concern   Management must assess the ability of an entity to continue as a going concern. If there are doubts over that concept, disclosure should be made of the underlying uncertainties; however, if it is more serious, the financial statements should be prepared on a break up basis but that fact must be disclosed.

Offsetting   Assets and liabilities and income and expenses should not be offset unless required or permitted by a standard or SIC.

Comparative information   This should be disclosed for the previous period for all amounts disclosed in the financial statements. If the current period has been reclassified so should the comparatives, unless that is impracticable. If practical, the following should be disclosed:

- the nature of the reclassification;
- the amount of each item or class of items reclassified; and
- the reason for the reclassification.

Where it is found to be impractical, the following should be disclosed:

- the reason for not reclassifying; and
- the nature of the adjustments that would have been made.

Structure and content

Identification of the financial statements   The financial statements should be clearly identified and distinguished from other information in the same published document.

Each component should be clearly identified. In addition, the following information should be displayed prominently:

- the name of the reporting entity and any change from the preceding year;
- whether the statements cover an individual or group of entities;

- the balance sheet date or period covered;
- the presentation currency;
- the level of rounding adopted.

Reporting period   There is a presumption that financial statements will be prepared annually, at a minimum. If the annual reporting period changes and financial statements are prepared for a different period, the entity should disclose the reason for the change and a warning that the corresponding amounts shown may not be comparable.

Balance sheet

The standard specifies minimum headings to be presented on the face of the balance sheet, and guidance is provided for the identification of additional line items.

Entities should present the balance sheet by separating current from non-current assets and liabilities unless a presentation based on liquidity provides information that is more reliable and relevant. If the latter, assets and liabilities must be presented broadly in order of their liquidity (or reverse order), without a current/non-current distinction.

In either case, if an asset/liability category combines amounts that will be received/settled after twelve months with assets/liabilities that will be received/settled within twelve months, note disclosure is required that separates the longer-term amounts from the amounts due to be received/settled within twelve months.

Current assets
An asset is classified as current when it satisfies any of the following criteria:

- it is expected to be realised in the entity's normal operating cycle; or
- it is held primarily for trade; or
- it is expected to be realised within twelve months; or
- it is cash or a cash equivalent.

Non-current assets incorporate tangible, intangible and financial assets of a long-term nature.

Current liabilities
A liability is classified as current when it satisfies any of the following criteria:

- it is expected to be settled in the entity's normal operating cycle; or
- it is held primarily for trade; or
- it is due to be settled within twelve months; or
- the entity does not have an unconditional right to defer settlement for at least twelve months.

Information to be presented on the face of the balance sheet
As a minimum, the following should be disclosed on the face of the balance sheet:

- property, plant and equipment;
- investment property;
- intangible assets;

- financial assets;
- investments accounted under the equity method;
- biological assets;
- inventories;
- trade and other receivables;
- cash and cash equivalents;
- trade and other payables;
- provisions;
- financial liabilities;
- current tax;
- deferred tax;
- minority interest;
- capital and reserves.

Additional items may be presented, if relevant to an understanding of the entity's financial position. Deferred tax may not be reclassified as a current asset/liability if an entity adopts the current/non-current approach.

The standard does not prescribe the order or format of the balance sheet – it is merely a list of items warranting separate disclosure.

Information to be presented either on the face of the balance sheet or in the notes

Further subclassifications may be provided in the notes or on the face of the balance sheet:

- for each class of share capital: number of authorised shares, number of issued shares, par value per share, reconciliation of number outstanding over the year, any rights or restrictions, any treasury shares held and any shares reserved for options including terms and conditions;
- a description of the nature and purpose of each reserve.

Any entity without share capital or a trust should provide equivalent information to the above.

Income statement

All items of income and expense recognised in a period should be included in the income statement unless a standard or SIC requires otherwise (e.g. IAS 8, 16, 21).

IAS 1 specifies the minimum headings that must be presented on the face of the income statement, and provides guidance for the identification of additional line items. There is no particular format or order of presentation mandated.

Information to be presented on the face of the income statement

As a minimum, the following should be disclosed on the face of the income statement for the period:

- revenue;
- finance costs;
- share of profit/loss of associates and joint ventures;

- pre-tax gain or loss recognised on the disposal of assets or settlement of liabilities attributable to discontinuing operations;
- tax expense;
- profit or loss.

The following items should be disclosed on the face of the income statement as allocations of profit:

- minority interest;
- profit/loss attributable to equity holders of the parent.

Additional items should be presented when such presentation is relevant to understanding the entity's financial performance. However, extraordinary items are no longer permitted to be disclosed in the statement or in the notes.

Information to be presented either on the face of the income statement or in the notes

Where material, the nature and amount of income and expenses should be disclosed separately. Examples include inventory writedowns, restructurings, disposals of plant etc., discontinuing operations, litigation settlements etc.

Income and expenses should not be offset unless another IAS requires or permits such offset, or the amounts to be offset arise from the same events and are not material.

Expenses should be analysed either by nature (raw materials, staff costs, depreciation etc.) or by function (cost of sales, selling, administration etc.) either on the face of the income statement or in the notes. If an entity categorises by function, additional information on the nature of expenses, including depreciation, amortisation and employee benefit expense, should be disclosed. The choice of method should the one that provides the most reliable and relevant information to the entity.

An entity should disclose, either on the face of the income statement or the statement of changes in equity, or in the notes, the amount of dividends recognised as distributions to equity holders during the period, and the related amount per share.

Statement of changes in equity

IAS 1 requires the presentation of a statement of changes in equity as a separate component of the financial statements, showing:

- the profit or loss for the period;
- each item of income or expense, and gain or loss, that is recognised directly in equity and the total of those items; and
- the effects of changes in accounting policies or material errors in accordance with IAS 8.

Either within this statement or separately in the notes, the entity is required to disclose:

- capital transactions;
- the balance of accumulated profits at the beginning and at end of the period, and the movements for the period; and

- a reconciliation between the carrying amount of each class of equity capital, share premium and each reserve at the beginning and end of the period, disclosing each movement.

Cash flow statement

IAS 1 refers to IAS 7 *Cash Flow Statements* (1992) for presenting the cash flow statement.

Notes

Structure
The notes should:

- present information about the basis of preparation of the financial statements and the specific accounting policies adopted;
- disclose information required by IFRSs not included on the face of the primary statements; and
- provide additional information that is relevant to understanding the financial statements.

Notes should be presented in a systematic manner, and each item cross-referenced to the primary statements.

Accounting policies
The notes, as a minimum, should disclose the significant accounting policies adopted; narrative descriptions or detailed analyses of items shown on the face of the financial statements; information required or encouraged by other IASs; and other disclosures necessary for an understanding and the fair presentation of the financial statements.

The accounting policies section should describe the measurement basis adopted in preparing the financial statements and each specific accounting policy that is necessary for an understanding of the financial statements.

An entity should disclose, in the summary of significant accounting policies or other notes, the judgements, apart from those involving estimates, that management has made in the process of applying the entity's accounting policies that have the most significant effect on the amounts recognised in the financial statements.

Key sources of estimation uncertainty   An entity should disclose in the notes information about the key assumptions concerning the future and other key sources of estimation uncertainty at the balance sheet date that have a significant risk of causing a material adjustment to the carrying amounts of assets and liabilities. Details of their nature and carrying amount at the balance sheet date should also be provided.

Other disclosures
In the notes, disclosures should include:

- dividends proposed or declared before the accounts have been authorised and related amounts per share;
- the amount of any cumulative preference dividends not recognised.

If not disclosed elsewhere, the following should be included:

- the domicile and legal form of the entity; country of incorporation and address of registered office if different from the principal place of business;
- a description of the nature of the entity's operations and principal activities;
- the name of the parent and ultimate parent of the group.

Review of performance and financial position   IAS 1 encourages the management to include a review of the financial performance and position of the enterprise and to discuss the principal uncertainties that it faces. Such a review would be similar in content to the Management Discussion & Analysis (MD&A) in the United States, and the Operating and Financial Review (OFR) in the United Kingdom and Ireland. The review would include a discussion of dividend policy, changes in the operating environment, funding and risk management policies.

SIC 29 Disclosure – Service Concession Arrangements   Comprehensive disclosures are required in respect of service concession arrangements both in the financial statements of the concession operator and the concession provider. These are similar to the rules on PFI contracts that are covered in the ASB's accounting standard on reporting substance (FRS 5).

Guidance on implementing IAS 1

This guidance accompanies, but is not part of, IAS 1.

Illustrative financial statement structure

The standard sets out the components of financial statements and minimum requirements for disclosure on the face of the balance sheet and the income statement as well as for the presentation of changes in equity. It also describes further items that may be presented either on the face of the relevant financial statement or in the notes. This guidance provides simple examples of ways in which the requirements of the standard for the presentation of the balance sheet, income statement and changes in equity might be met. The order of presentation and the descriptions used for line items should be changed, when necessary, in order to achieve a fair presentation in each entity's particular circumstances.

The illustrative balance sheet shows one way in which a balance sheet distinguishing between current and non-current items may be presented. Other formats may be equally appropriate, provided the distinction is clear.

Two income statements are provided, to illustrate the alternative classifications of income and expenses, by nature and by function. Two possible approaches to presenting changes in equity are also illustrated.

The examples are not intended to illustrate all aspects of IFRSs; nor do they comprise a complete set of financial statements, which would also include a cash flow statement, a summary of significant accounting policies and other explanatory notes.

Part A – Illustrative financial statement structure
XYZ GROUP – BALANCE SHEET AS AT 31 DECEMBER 2002
(in thousands of currency units)

	2002	2001
ASSETS		
Non-current assets		
Property, plant and equipment	X	X
Goodwill	X	X
Other intangible assets	X	X
Investments in associates	X	X
Available-for-sale investments	X	X
	X	X
Current assets		
Inventories	X	X
Trade receivables	X	X
Other current assets	X	X
Cash and cash equivalents	X	X
	X	X
Total assets	X	X
EQUITY AND LIABILITIES		
Equity attributable to equity holders of the parent		
Share capital	X	X
Other reserves	X	X
Retained earnings	X	X
	X	X
Minority interest	X	X
Total equity	X	X
Non-current liabilities		
Long-term borrowings	X	X
Deferred tax	X	X
Long-term provisions	X	X
Total non-current liabilities	X	X
Current liabilities		
Trade and other payables	X	X
Short-term borrowings	X	X
Current portion of long-term borrowings	X	X
Current tax payable	X	X
Short-term provisions	X	X
Total liabilities	X	X
Total equity and liabilities	X	X

XYZ GROUP – INCOME STATEMENT FOR THE YEAR ENDED 31 DECEMBER 2002

(illustrating the classification of expenses by function)
(in thousands of currency units)

	2002	2001
Revenue	X	X
Cost of sales	(X)	(X)
Gross profit	X	X
Other income	X	X
Distribution costs	(X)	(X)
Administrative expenses	(X)	(X)
Other expenses	(X)	(X)
Finance costs	(X)	(X)
Share of profit of associates	X	X
Profit before tax	X	X
Income tax expense	(X)	(X)
Profit for the period	X	X
Attributable to:		
Equity holders of the parent	X	X
Minority interest	X	X
	X	X

XYZ GROUP – INCOME STATEMENT FOR THE YEAR ENDED 31 DECEMBER 2002

(illustrating the classification of expenses by nature)
(in thousands of currency units)

	2002	2001
Revenue	X	X
Other income	X	X
Changes in inventories of finished goods and work in progress	(X)	X
Work performed by the entity and capitalised	X	X
Raw material and consumables used	(X)	(X)
Employee benefits expense	(X)	(X)
Depreciation and amortisation expense	(X)	(X)
Impairment of property, plant and equipment	(X)	(X)
Other expenses	(X)	(X)
Finance costs	(X)	(X)
Share of profit of associates	X	X
Profit before tax	X	X
Income tax expense	(X)	(X)
Profit for the period	X	X
Attributable to:		
Equity holders of the parent	X	X
Minority interest	X	X
	X	X

XYZ GROUP – STATEMENT OF CHANGES IN EQUITY FOR THE YEAR ENDED 31 DECEMBER 2002

(in thousands of currency units)

	Share capital	Other reserves	Translation reserve	Retained earnings	Total	Minority interest	Total equity
	Attributable to equity holders of the parent						
Balance at 31 December 2000	X	X	(X)	X	X	X	X
Changes in accounting policy				(X)	(X)	(X)	(X)
Restated balance	X	X	(X)	X	X	X	X
Changes in equity for 2001							
Gain on property revaluation		X			X	X	X
Available-for-sale investments:							
Valuation gains/(losses) taken to equity		(X)			(X)		(X)
Transferred to profit or loss on sale		(X)			(X)		(X)
Cash flow hedges:							
Gains/(losses) taken to equity		X			X	X	X
Transferred to profit or loss for the period		X			X	X	X
Transferred to initial carrying amount of hedged items		(X)			(X)		(X)
Exchange differences on translating foreign operations			(X)		(X)	(X)	(X)
Tax on items taken directly to or transferred from equity		(X)	X		(X)	(X)	(X)
Net income recognised directly in equity		X	(X)		X	X	X
Profit for the period				X	X	X	X
Total recognised income and expense for the period		X	(X)	X	X	X	X
Dividends				(X)	(X)	(X)	(X)
Issue of share capital	X				X		X
Equity share options issued		X			X		X
Balance at 31 December 2001 carried forward	X	X	(X)	X	X	X	X

XYZ GROUP – STATEMENT OF RECOGNISED INCOME AND EXPENSE FOR THE YEAR ENDED 31 DECEMBER 2002

(in thousands of currency units)

	2002	2001
Gain/(loss) on revaluation of properties	(X)	X
Available-for-sale investments:		
Valuation gains/(losses) taken to equity	(X)	(X)
Transferred to profit or loss on sale	X	(X)
Cash flow hedges:		
Gains/(losses) taken to equity	X	X
Transferred to profit or loss for the period	(X)	X
Transferred to the initial carrying amount of hedged items	(X)	(X)
Exchange differences on translation of foreign operations	(X)	(X)

Tax on items taken directly to or transferred from equity	X	(X)
Net income recognised directly in equity	(X)	X
Profit for the period	X	X
Total recognised income and expense for the period	X	X
Attributable to:		
Equity holders of the parent	X	X
Minority interest	X	X
	X	X
Effect of changes in accounting policy:		
Equity holders of the parent		(X)
Minority interest		(X)
		(X)

1.11   Examination questions

Question 1.1: Vincible (ACCA Diploma in International Financial Reporting and Auditing)

(The first question requires students to prepare three of the primary statements required by IAS 1 – the income statement, balance sheet, and statement of changes in equity. Although not stated as required in the question, the solution adopts a current/non-current format for the balance sheet and analysis by function in the income statement. There is not sufficient information to prepare a note re analysis by nature as required by IAS 1.

In addition, students are required to integrate final accounts preparation with an application of IFRSs – in particular, IAS 33 Earnings Per Share and IAS 31 Financial Reporting of Interests in Joint Ventures, although impairment (IAS 36), taxation (IAS 12) and revaluation of property (IAS 16) are also covered.)

The following list of account balances relates to Vincible at 30 September 2002:

	$000	$000
Sales revenue		473,300
Purchases	310,500	
Operating expenses	18,400	
Loan stock interest	5,000	
Dividends paid	15,500	
Leasehold building at cost (note (ii))	200,000	
Plant and equipment at cost (note (ii))	124,800	
Deferred development expenditure (note (iii))	75,000	
Joint venture (note (iv))	62,000	
Depreciation at 1 October 2001 – leasehold		56,000
– plant and equipment		48,800
– development expenditure		15,000
Trade receivables	49,200	
Inventory – 1 October 2001	27,500	
Bank	12,100	
Trade payables		82,200
Ordinary shares of 25 cents each		100,000
10% Convertible loan stock – issued 2000 (note (vi))		100,000
Deferred tax at 1 October 2001 (note (v))		11,400
Profit and loss reserve at 1 October 2001		13,300
	900,000	900,000

The following notes are relevant:

(i) The cost of the inventory at 30 September 2002 was $37.7 million (excluding joint venture inventory – see note (iv)).

(ii) Non-current assets:
- On 1 October 2001 Vincible's leasehold building was revalued at $270 million by an independent surveyor. The lease was for a 25-year period when Vincible acquired it. The directors wish to incorporate the revalued amount in Vincible's financial statements. The revaluation reserve will be deemed to be realised in line with the remaining life of the lease.
- Plant is depreciated at 20% per annum on the reducing balance basis.
- All depreciation is charged to cost of sales.

(iii) The deferred development expenditure relates to a new product. The project was successfully completed on 1 October 2000, and sales of the new product commenced on that date. The development costs are being depreciated on a straight-line basis over the expected product life of 5 years. Early in the current year, a review of the sales figures for the new product showed that they were disappointing. In view of this, Vincible has estimated that the present value of the expected net future cash flows from sales of the new product is $30 million; however Vincible has been approached by a rival company with an offer of $40 million for the rights to the product. At this stage, Vincible intends to continue to market and sell the product.

(iv) On 1 October 2001 Vincible entered into a joint venture with two other companies. Each venturer contributes its own assets and pays its own expenses, The agreement stipulates that the joint venture will be terminated on 30 September 2005. Vincible is entitled to 30% of the joint venture's total revenues. The joint venture is not a separate entity.

Details of Vincible's joint venture transactions are:

	$000
Plant and equipment at cost	70,000
Share of joint venture sales revenues (30% of total sales revenues)	(18,000)
Inventory	2,500
Related cost of sales excluding depreciation	8,000
Accounts receivable 30 September 2002	3,500
Accounts payable 30 September 2002	(4,000)
Net balance included in the above list of balances	62,000

Plant should be depreciated on a straight-line basis. It is not expected to have any residual value at the end of joint venture.

(v) The directors have estimated the required provision for income tax for the year to 30 September 2002 is $15 million. The deferred tax provision at 30 September 2002 is to be adjusted to reflect the tax base of the company's assets being $70 million less than their carrying values. $28.8 million of this $70 million is attributable to the revaluation of the leasehold. Vincible's rate of income tax is 25%.

(vi) The convertible loan stock is redeemable at par on 31 March 2004, or at the option of the stockholders, it can be exchanged for ordinary shares on the basis of 60 new shares in Vincible for each $100 of loan stock.

(vii) In June 2000 the directors and senior staff of Vincible were given options to purchase 50 million ordinary shares (in total) in the company. The options are exercisable on

1 July 2004 at a price of $2.40 per share. The stock market price of Vincible's ordinary shares over the current year has been $4.00.

(viii) The directors have proposed a final ordinary dividend of 6 cents per share. Vincible discloses proposed dividends as part of shareholders' funds.

Required

(a) Prepare for Vincible, in accordance with International Accounting Standards as far as the information permits:
(i) the income statement
(ii) the statement of changes in equity for the year to 30 September 2002, and
(iii) a balance sheet as at 30 September 2002.
Notes to the financial statements are not required.
(b) Next, calculate the basic and diluted earnings per share for Vincible for the year to 30 September 2002.

Question 1.2: Stilson (ACCA Accounting and Audit Practice)

(The second question is very similar to the first in its basic requirement to publish an income statement, balance sheet and statement of changes in equity in accordance with IAS 1. However, it also incorporates the need to implement other account-ing standards, particularly IAS 11 Construction Contracts, IAS 16 Property, Plant and Equipment and IAS 18 Revenue.)

The summarised list of account balances of Stilson, a publicly listed company, at 31 March 2001 is as follows:

	$000	$000
Land and building – at cost (land $2 million) (note (i))	10,000	
Plant and equipment – at cost	4,480	
Depreciation 1 April 2000: – building		3,200
– plant		2,400
Trade receivables and prepayments	8,620	
Inventory – 31 March 2000	1,900	
Cash and bank	4,180	
Trade payables and accruals		3,540
Equity shares of 25c each		5,000
8% Loan Note (issued in 1999)		5,000
Accumulated profits 1 April 2000		580
Purchases	16,000	
Construction contract costs to 31 March 2001 (note (iii))	1,900	
Construction contracts progress billings received (note (iii))		2,000
Sales		26,750
Interest paid	200	
Property rental	1,250	
Profit on sale of property (note (i))		3,400
Operating expenses	1,340	
Interim dividend	2,000	–
	51,870	51,870

The following notes are relevant:

(i) One of the company's buildings was sold on 1 April 2000. The disposal has been recorded leaving a profit on sale of $3.4 million, which is included in the balances above. On the same date the company's only remaining property was revalued at $12 million ($3 million is attributable to the land). The building had an estimated life of 25 years when it was acquired on 1 April 1990, and this has not changed as a result of the revaluation. The directors of Stilson wish to incorporate this value in the financial statements for the year ended 31 March 2001. Plant is depreciated at 20% per annum on cost.

(ii) Included in the sales revenues is an amount of $3 million relating to sales made under a special promotion in March 2001. These goods were sold with an accompanying voucher equal to the selling price. Five years after the sale, these vouchers will be exchanged for goods of the customer's choosing. The profit margin on these goods is expected to be 30% of selling price, and market research estimates that 50% of the vouchers will be redeemed. The present value (at 31 March 2001) of $1 at the time the vouchers will be exchanged can be taken as 60c.

(iii) The figures in respect of contract balances relate to a 3-year contract entered into on 1 July 2000. Details relating to this contract are:

	$000
Contract price	10,000
Estimated total contract costs	6,000
Agreed value of work completed and billed at 31 March 2001	3,000

Stilson's policy is to recognise profits on long-term construction contracts from the point that they become more than 20% complete. The percentage of completion is deemed to be the agreed value of the work completed to date as a percentage of the total contract price. Contract revenue is taken as the agreed value of the work completed to date.

(iv) A provision for income tax for the year to 31 March 2001 of $2,400,000 is required. The directors declared a final dividend of 15c per share on 25 March 2001.

(v) Inventory, other than that relating to the construction contract, at 31 March 2001 was valued at a cost of $2.8 million.

Required

Prepare the income statement, the statement of changes in equity and balance sheet for Stilson for the year to 31 March 2001.

Question 1.3: S (CIMA)

S, a car dealer with a number of outlets, has expanded rapidly in recent years, but cash flow problems worsened in the year to March 2003. On 1 April 2003, the management of S decided to make three major changes to its activities.

A trainee management accountant prepared a set of draft financial statements for the year ended 31 March 2004, but unfortunately did not appreciate the need to apply the concept of 'substance over form' in the treatment of the various transactions involved.

Required

(a) Explain the meaning of the accounting concept of substance over form. You should refer to relevant International Accounting Standards in your answer.

The three major changes made by S on 1 April 2003, and the way in which they have been treated in the draft financial statements for the year ended 31 March 2004, are as follows:

1. *Change 1*: S sold all of its land and buildings on a sale and leaseback agreement to P on 1 April 2003. The terms were as follows:
   - the annual rental was agreed at $7.5 million
   - the agreed selling price was $50 million with an option for S to repurchase the land and buildings at any time in the next 10 years
   - the repurchase price was set at $50 million plus interest at bank rate plus 5% per annum from the date of the sale.

   At the time of the sale, the land and buildings had a net book value (and current market value) of $80 million. The draft financial statements have treated the transaction as a disposal of the land and buildings and record a loss on disposal of $30 million in the draft income statement.

2. *Change 2*: S decided to acquire new cars direct from the manufacturer on consignment. The terms of the trading are:
   - on delivery of the cars to S they are invoiced at 50% of the purchase price
   - the balance of the purchase price is payable when the cars are sold
   - if a car remains unsold for three months, it must be paid for or returned to the manufacturer
   - when a car is returned, the manufacturer refunds the deposit less a 20% administration fee.

   At 31 March 2004, S had 500 new cars in its inventories; all had been in inventories less than three months. The combined purchase price of the cars was $6 million. The draft financial statements omit the new cars from inventories, as they have been treated as the inventory belonging to the manufacturer. The 50% of the purchase price paid has been debited to prepayments in the draft balance sheet.

3. *Change 3*: S replaced the computerised equipment used in its repair workshops. The previous equipment was purchased outright, and had no value on disposal. The new equipment was acquired on a lease, with the following terms:
   - lease term 6 years
   - useful economic life of the equipment 5–7 years
   - six annual payments of $1.5 million paid in advance commencing on 1 April 2003 and annually thereafter
   - the interest rate implicit in the lease is 7% per annum
   - the fair value of the equipment at the inception of the lease was $7,650,296
   - S will insure and maintain the equipment in good working order.

The draft financial statements record the lease payment of $1.5 million as an expense in the draft income statement.

Required

(b) For each of the changes above, explain how S should treat each transaction in its income statement for the year ended 31 March 2004 and its balance sheet at that date. Justify your answer by reference to relevant International Accounting Standards. Prepare any journal entries that are required to adjust the draft financial statements.

2

Asset valuation: accounting for tangible fixed assets

2.1 IAS 16 *Property, Plant and Equipment* (revised December 2003)

Objective

IAS 16 prescribes the accounting treatment for property, plant and equipment. Key issues include the initial recognition of cost, the determination of their carrying amounts, and their related depreciation and impairment charges.

Key definitions

Property, plant and equipment: tangible assets that are held by an entity for use in the production or supply of goods or services, for rental to others, for administrative purposes and are expected to be used during more than one period.

Depreciation: the systematic allocation of the depreciable amount of an asset over its useful life.

Accounting treatment

Initial measurement

Whether acquired or self-constructed, property, plant etc. should initially be recorded at cost. Only those costs that are directly attributable to bringing an asset into *working condition* for its *intended use* are permitted to be capitalised. Capitalisation of costs is also only permitted for the period in which activities are in progress (see IAS 23 *Borrowing Costs*).

Capitalisation of interest is permitted, but the policy must be applied consistently and all finance costs directly attributable to the construction of a tangible fixed asset should be capitalised, provided that they do not exceed the total finance costs incurred during the period.

The amount recognised should not exceed an asset's recoverable amount.

Subsequent expenditure should normally be expensed (maintenance), but may be capitalised if:

- a component of an asset has been treated as a separate asset and is now replaced or restored (e.g. Ryanair's splitting up of aircraft into different components and BAA's policy of separating runway surfaces from runway beds); or
- the expenditure enhances the economic benefits of the asset in excess of the original assessed standard of performance; or
- it relates to a major overhaul or inspection whose benefits have already been consumed in the depreciation charge.

Subsequent cost or valuation

An entity should choose either the cost model or the revaluation model and apply that policy to the entire class of property, plant and equipment.

Cost model

Property etc. should be carried at cost less any accumulated depreciation and impairment losses to date.

Revaluation model

Property etc. should be carried at fair value at date of revaluation less any subsequent accumulated depreciation and impairment losses. Revaluations should occur sufficiently regularly so that the amount does not differ materially from the fair value at the balance sheet date.

Revaluations   The fair value of land and buildings is usually its market value, normally appraised by professionally qualified valuers. The fair value of plant is usually its market value. If there is no evidence of market values due to its specialised nature or if it is rarely sold, then plant should be valued at depreciated replacement cost.

The frequency of revaluations depends upon their movements. Some items of property may experience significant and volatile movements in fair value, thus necessitating annual revaluation. For those assets with insignificant movements, then a revaluation every 3 or 5 years may be sufficient.

When an item of property is revalued, any accumulated depreciation at the date of the revaluation is either:

- restated proportionately with the change in the gross carrying value; or
- eliminated against the gross carrying amount of the asset and the net amount restated to the revalued amount of the asset (often adopted for buildings).

When an item of property is revalued, the entire class of property must be revalued. A class of property is a grouping of assets of a similar nature and use in an entity's operations. Examples include land, land and buildings, machinery, ships, aircraft, motor vehicles, furniture and fixtures, and office equipment.

A class of assets may be revalued on a rolling basis provided the revaluation is completed within a short period of time and the revaluations are kept up to date.

Any increase in valuation must be recognised directly in equity except to the extent that it reverses a revaluation decrease of the same asset previously recognised as an expense. In that case, it should be recognised in the income statement. A decrease shall be recognised in equity until the carrying amount reaches its depreciated historical cost, and thereafter in the income statement.

The revaluation surplus may be transferred directly to retained earnings when the asset is derecognised – i.e. disposed of, or the asset used up. Transfers are not made through the income statement.

The effects on taxes on income re the revaluation should be recognised in accordance with IAS 12.

Depreciation

Each part of an item of property, plant and equipment with a significant cost in relation to total cost should be depreciated separately, e.g. airframe, engines (component accounting).

The depreciable amount of property etc. should be allocated on a systematic basis over its useful life, and the method adopted should reflect the pattern in which the asset's future economic benefits are expected to be consumed. Depreciation should normally be recognised as an expense.

The useful life and residual value should be reviewed at each year end and adjusted as a change in accounting estimate as per IAS 8.

Depreciation is recognised even if the value of the asset exceeds its carrying amount. The charge for depreciation should be reflected in the income statement unless included in the carrying amount of the asset. Depreciation usually begins when an asset is ready for use, but does not cease when idle or retired from active use. However, if classified as held for sale under IFRS 5 and transferred to current assets, it should not be depreciated. The residual value and the useful life of an asset should be reviewed at least at each year end and, if expectations of previous estimates are judged incorrect, the adjustment should be accounted for as a change in an accounting estimate in accordance with IAS 8. Depreciation could be zero under some methods if based on nil production units.

Future economic benefits are principally consumed through the use of an asset, but other factors such as technical or commercial obsolescence and wear and tear must be considered.

All the following factors must be considered in determining the useful life of an asset:

- the expected usage of the asset – capacity/output
- the expected physical wear and tear
- technical or commercial obsolescence
- legal limits on the use of the asset, such as expiry dates of related leases.

The useful life is defined in terms of the asset's expected utility to the entity. The asset management policy may involve the disposal of assets after a specified time or after consumption of a proportion of future benefits. It can be shorter than its economic life.

Land and buildings must be treated as separable assets. With certain exceptions, such as quarries and landfill sites, land has an unlimited useful life and is therefore not depreciated. Buildings are depreciable assets. If the cost of land includes site dismantling/restoration costs, these may be depreciated over the period of benefits obtained by incurring these costs.

The depreciable amount of an asset is after deducting its residual value. In practice, the value is often insignificant and immaterial. If it is material, its value should be reviewed at each balance sheet date. Any change should be accounted for prospectively as an adjustment to future depreciation. An estimate of an asset's residual value is based on the amount recoverable from disposal, at the date of the estimate of similar assets that have reached the end of their useful lives and under similar operating conditions. This could lead to the reintroduction of 'nil' depreciation, particularly in relation to buildings which have very high residual values.

Subsequent developments

- *Revision of useful economic life.* Useful economic life should be reviewed on a regular basis and, if necessary, the life of the fixed asset adjusted to recognise depreciation over the asset's remaining economic useful life.
- *Change in method of depreciation.* The method of depreciation can be changed if it would present a truer and fairer view of the financial statements. The net book value should be written off over its estimated remaining useful life. This is not a change in accounting policy but merely a change in estimate, and therefore no prior year adjustment is required. IAS 16 encourages the use of methods based on the expected patttern of consumption of future economic benefits.
- *Policy of non-depreciation.* All property etc., with the exception of land, should be depreciated, per IAS 16. Even buildings are expected to be depreciated over their economic useful lives with the exception of investment properties. There has grown up a practice, however, of non-depreciation of certain buildings which interface with the public – e.g. supermarkets, hotels, public houses, etc. This policy was confirmed in the United Kingdom by the Financial Reporting Review Panel in the test case of Forte plc. However, it was subsequently rejected, for industrial buildings, by the Panel in the case of SEP Industrial Holdings plc. IAS 16, however, still permits this policy, but insists that an annual impairment review be carried out (under IAS 36) on such assets to ensure that they are not recorded above their recoverable amount.

Specific disclosures are required with regard to depreciation policies, and changes in those policies and, in particular, a tangible fixed asset schedule should be published giving details of the full movement for the year in cost/value and in accumulated depreciation.

Disclosure

For each class of property the following should be disclosed:

1. The measurement bases adopted; where more than one basis is used, the gross carrying value for each basis adopted shall be disclosed
2. The depreciation methods used
3. The useful lives or depreciation rates used
4. The gross carrying amount and accumulated depreciation at start and end of the year

5. A reconciliation of the carrying amount at start and end of the period showing:
   - additions
   - disposals
   - acquisitions through business combinations
   - revaluations
   - impairment losses
   - impairment losses reversed
   - depreciation
   - net exchange differences re translation of functional currency into a different presentation currency
   - other changes
6. The existence and amounts of restrictions on title and property etc. pledged as securities
7. The amount of expenditures capitalised in course of construction
8. The amount of contractual commitments for the acquisition of property etc.
9. If not disclosed separately on the face of the income statement, the amount and compensation from third parties included in the income statement.

The selection of the depreciation method and estimate of useful life are matters of judgement. Disclosure of the methods adopted is useful information to users and to allow users to review the policies selected. For similar reasons, it is necessary to disclose the following:

1. Depreciation during the period
2. Accumulated depreciation at the end of the period.

An entity should disclose the nature and effect of a change in accounting estimate with respect to residual values, estimated costs of dismantling or restoring property etc., useful lives, and depreciation method in accordance with IAS 8.

When items of property etc. are revalued, the following should be disclosed:

1. The effective date of the revaluation
2. Whether an independent valuer was involved
3. The methods and significant assumptions applied in estimating the assets' fair values
4. The extent to which the assets' fair values were determinable to observable prices in an active market or recent market transactions at arm's length or estimated using other valuation techniques
5. For each revalued class of property, the carrying amount at historic cost
6. The revaluation surplus, indicating the movement for the period and any restrictions on distribution.

2.2   IAS 40 *Investment Property* (revised March 2004)

Objective

IAS 40 prescribes the accounting treatment for investment properties and their related disclosure. It is effective for accounting periods starting on or after 1 January 2005.

Investment property is defined as property held to earn rentals or for capital appreciation or both, rather than for use in production, administration or sale in the ordinary course of business.

IAS 40 permits entities to choose between either:

- fair value reporting with changes recognised in the income statement; or
- cost.

Whichever model is chosen must be used for all investment properties. A change from one model to another is only permitted if it gives a fairer presentation – which is highly unlikely. If an entity adopts the fair value model but cannot get clear evidence of the fair value of an investment property, then cost must be used until the asset is disposed.

Key definition

Investment property: property held to earn rentals or for capital appreciation or both, rather than for:

- use in the production or supply of goods or services or for administration purposes; or
- sale in the ordinary course of business.

Investment properties are acquired to earn rentals or for capital appreciation or both, and thus their cash flows are largely independent of those from other assets held by the enterprise. The following are examples:

- land held for long-term capital appreciation;
- land held for a currently undetermined future use;
- a building owned and leased out under an operating lease;
- a vacant building which is to be leased under an operating lease.

However, the following are NOT investment properties:

- property held for sale in the ordinary course of business or in the course of construction for such sale (see IAS 2);
- property being constructed for third parties (see IAS 11);
- owner occupied properties (see IAS 16);
- property that is being constructed or developed for future use as an investment property (see IAS 16); and
- property that is leased to another entity under a finance lease.

Mixed properties, if sold separately, should be accounted for separately. If not, the property is only classified as investment if an insignificant portion is held for use for production or for administrative purposes. Similarly, properties providing ancillary services should be treated as investment properties if the services are a relatively insignificant portion of the whole. Judgement is needed to determine whether a property qualifies or not.

Recognition

Investment property should be recognised as an asset when, and only when:

* it is probable that the future economic benefits associated with the asset will flow to the entity;
* the cost of the investment property can be measured reliably.

The former requires an assessment of the degree of certainty attaching to the flows based on available evidence, and the second should normally be satisfied at the time of acquisition. Costs of day-to-day servicing should be expensed immediately, as repairs and maintenance. Replacement costs should only be capitalised if they meet the recognition criteria.

Measurement at recognition

Investment properties should be initially measured at cost with transaction costs included. That includes their purchase price and any directly attributable expenditure, such as legal and professional fees and property taxes.

Cost is cost when construction is complete. Until that date, IAS 16 applies. Normally, start-up costs, initial operating losses, abnormal wastage of materials or labour etc. would not be included.

If payment is deferred, the cost is the cash price equivalent and any difference is treated as an interest expense over the period of credit.

Measurement after recognition

Accounting policy

Either the fair value model or the cost model should be chosen and the same model applied to all investment properties. If fair value is chosen, an entity is encouraged (but not required) to determine fair value on the basis of a valuation by an independently qualified valuer.

It is highly unlikely that a change from one model to another could result in a more appropriate policy under IAS 8.

Fair value model   After initial recognition, if fair value is adopted, entities must measure all investment properties at that value with any gains/losses being included in net profit/loss for the period in which it arises.

Fair value is usually its market value but excluding any special terms. Any selling costs must not be deducted in arriving at fair value.

When a property interest held by a lessee under an operating lease is classified as an investment property, the fair value model should be applied.

The fair value should reflect the actual market state at the balance sheet date, not of the past or the future. It also assumes simultaneous exchange and completion of the contract between knowledgeable and willing parties.

Fair value should reflect any rental income from current leases, and be based on reasonable and supportable assumptions about the market's view on rental income from future leases in the light of current market conditions. Both parties are assumed to be able to buy and sell at the best price possible, and not eager or forced to buy or sell.

The best evidence of fair value is normally provided by current prices on an active market for similar property in the same location and condition. In the absence of this, an entity should consider information from a variety of sources, including:

- current prices on an active market for properties of different nature, condition or location, adjusted to reflect those differences;
- recent prices on less active markets, with adjustments to reflect any changes in economic conditions since the date of the transactions that occurred at those prices; and
- discounted cash flow projections based on reliable estimates of future cash flows supported by external evidence and adopting discount rates reflecting current market assessments of the uncertainty in the amount and timing of the cash flows.

In some cases, a different conclusion as to the fair value of an investment property may be suggested using the above. The reasons for those differences must be considered in order to arrive at the most reliable estimate of fair value. Where the variability in the range of fair values is so great and probabilities are so difficult to assess then the fair value may not be determined reliably on a continuing basis.

Fair value is not the same as value in use. It does not reflect any:

- additional value derived from the creation of a portfolio of properties in different locations;
- synergies between investment property and other assets;
- legal rights or restrictions that are specific to the current owner; and
- tax benefits or tax burdens specific to the current owner.

Care must also be taken not to double count assets or liabilities that are recognised separately – for example:

- equipment such as elevators or air conditioning;
- furniture in a furnished lease;
- prepaid or accrued rental income; and
- the fair value of investment property held under a lease reflects expected cash flows thus there is the need to add back any recognised lease liability to arrive at the fair value of the investment property.

Fair value should also not reflect future capital expenditure that will enhance or improve the property. Moreover, any expected excess expenditure over receipts should be accounted for under IAS 37.

In exceptional cases, where there is clear evidence that the entity will not be able to determine the fair value of an investment property reliably on a continuing basis, an entity should measure the property according to the benchmark treatment in IAS 16 with an assumed residual value of zero. The entity must continue to apply IAS 16 until the property is disposed. However all other investment properties should be measured at fair value.

If an entity has measured investment properties at fair value, it must continue to do so until disposal or unless the property becomes owner occupied, even if comparable market transactions become less frequent or market prices less readily available.

Cost model If an entity adopts the cost model, it should measure all of its investment properties in accordance with IAS 16 – i.e. at cost less accumulated depreciation and impairment losses.

Transfers

Transfers to or from investment property should be made when, and only when, there is a change in use, evidenced by:

- commencement of owner occupation;
- commencement of development with a view to resale via inventories;
- end of owner occupation and transfer to investment property;
- commencement of an operating lease, for a transfer from inventories to investment property; or
- end of construction for a transfer to investment property.

When an entity adopts the cost model, transfers do not change the carrying amounts of those assets or the cost of that property for disclosure purposes.

When an entity transfers a fair value investment property to owner-occupied property or inventories, the property's cost for subsequent periods should be its fair value at the date of change in use.

If an owner-occupied property becomes an investment property, an entity should apply IAS 16 up to the date of change in use. Any difference between the carrying amount of the property under IAS 16 and its fair value should be accounted for as a revaluation as per IAS 16. That is:

1. Any decrease should be recognised in net income for the period but, to the extent that a revaluation surplus exists on that asset, the decrease should first be charged against that surplus.
2. Any resulting increase in the carrying amount should, to the extent it reverses a previous impairment loss, appear in net income but restored to the amount that would have been determined had no impairment been recognised.
3. Any remaining part of the increase in the carrying amount should be credited directly to equity (revaluation surplus). On disposal, the surplus may be transferred to retained earnings but not through net income.

For transfers between inventories and investment properties (fair value), any difference between the fair value of the property at that date and its previous carrying value should be recognised in net income for the period (i.e. same as sale of inventories).

For transfers from construction to investment properties at fair value, any difference between fair value at that date and its previous carrying amount should be recognised in net income.

Disposals

An investment property should be derecognised on disposal or when the property is permanently withdrawn from use and no future economic benefits are expected to be derived from its disposal. The creation of a finance lease would be one example.

Gains or losses arising from retirement or disposal represent the difference between the net disposal proceeds and the carrying amount of the asset, and should be recognised as profits or losses in the income statement in the period of that retirement or disposal.

Consideration initially should be at fair value and, if deferred, at the cash price equivalent, with any difference in the latter being treated as interest revenue (as per IAS 18) using the effective interest method.

Compensation from third parties for investment properties that have been impaired, lost or given up should be recognised in profit or loss when the compensation becomes receivable. The following should be separately disclosed:

- impairments recognised in accordance with IAS 36;
- retirements/disposals recognised in accordance with IAS 40;
- compensation from third parties recognised in profit and loss when it becomes receivable;
- the cost of assets restored, purchased or constructed as replacements in accordance with IAS 40.

Disclosure

Fair value and cost models

An entity should disclose:

1. Whether it applies the fair value or the cost model
2. If it applies the fair value model, whether, and in what circumstances, property interests held under operating leases are classified and accounted for as investment property
3. The criteria to distinguish investment property from owner-occupied property from property held for normal resale
4. The methods and significant assumptions applied in determining fair value, including a statement supported by market evidence or based on other factors
5. The extent to which the fair value of an investment property is based on a valuation by an independent valuer holding a recognised qualification with recent experience in the location and category of the investment property being valued; if none, that fact should be disclosed
6. The amounts included within income for:
   - rental income
   - direct operating expenses arising from investment properties generating rental income
   - direct operating expenses arising from investment properties not generating rental income
7. The existence and amounts of restrictions on realisability or remittance
8. Contractual obligations to purchase, construct or develop investment properties, or for repairs, maintenance or enhancements.

Fair value model

In addition to the above, a reconciliation of the carrying amount of investment property from the start to the end of the period is required showing the following:

1. Additions, disclosing acquisitions separately from capitalised subsequent expenditure
2. Additions from business combinations

3. Disposals
4. Net gains/losses from fair value adjustments
5. Net exchange differences on translation of a foreign entity
6. Transfers to/from inventories and owner-occupied property
7. Other movements.

When a valuation obtained for investment property is adjusted significantly, e.g. to avoid double counting of assets/liabilities, the entity should disclose a reconciliation between the valuation obtained and the adjusted valuation included in the financial statements, showing separately the aggregate amount of any recognised lease obligations that have been added back, and any other significant adjustments.

In exceptional cases, when using the cost model, the reconciliation shown above in (1) to (7) should be provided separately for that investment property from any others. In addition, the following should also be disclosed:

1. A description of the investment property
2. An explanation of why fair value cannot be reliably measured
3. If possible, the range of estimates within which fair value is highly likely to lie
4. On disposal of an investment property not carried at fair value:
   • the fact that it has disposed of such a property
   • the carrying amount of the investment property at the date of sale
   • the amount of the gain or loss recognised.

Cost model

In addition to the disclosure required in the joint section above, an entity should also disclose:

1. The depreciation methods used
2. The useful lives or depreciation rates adopted
3. The gross carrying amount and accumulated depreciation and impairment at start and end of period
4. A reconciliation of the carrying amount of the investment property at the start and end of the period showing:
   • additions separately from capitalised subsequent expenditure
   • additions from business combinations
   • disposals
   • depreciation
   • impairment losses recognised in the period
   • net exchange differences
   • transfers to/from inventories and owner occupied property
   • other movements
5. The fair value of investment property, but when it cannot be reliably determined the following should be disclosed:
   • a description of the investment property
   • an explanation of why fair value cannot be determined reliably
   • if possible, the range of estimates within which fair value is highly likely to lie.

2.3   IAS 20 *Accounting for Government Grants and Disclosure of Government Assistance* (1994)

Objective

The objective of IAS 20 is to prescribe the accounting for and disclosure of government grants and other forms of government assistance.

Scope

The following are exempt:

- special problems where changing prices affect government grants;
- income tax holidays, accelerated depreciation allowances (i.e. tax benefits);
- government participation in the ownership of the enterprise;
- government grants covered by IAS 41.

Key definitions

Government assistance: action by government to provide an economic benefit specific to an enterprise or range of enterprises qualifying under certain criteria. It does not include provision of infrastructure development or imposition of trading constraints.

Government grants: assistance by government in the form of transfers of resources to an enterprise in return for past or future compliance with certain conditions relating to the operating activities of the enterprise.

Government grants

Government grants, including non-monetary grants at fair value, should not be recognised until there is reasonable assurance that:

- the enterprise will comply with the conditions attached to them; and
- the grants will be received.

The receipt of grant, by itself, does not provide evidence that the conditions attaching to the grant have been or will be fulfilled. Also, the accounting treatment is the same whether the grant is in the form of cash or a non-monetary form.

Once the grant is recognised, any related contingent liability or asset should be treated in accordance with IAS 37.

Government grants should be recognised as income over the periods necessary to match them with the related costs which they are intended to compensate on a systematic basis. They should not be credited directly to reserves.

In most cases the periods over which the enterprise recognises the costs related to a government grant are readily ascertainable, and thus grants in recognition of specific expenses are recognised as income in the same period as the relevant expense – e.g. capital grants are released to income as the assets are depreciated.

A government grant that becomes receivable for expenses already incurred should be recognised as income in the period it becomes receivable.

Non-monetary government grants

A grant could be the transfer of land or other resources for the use of the enterprise. The fair value of the non-monetary asset should be assessed, and both the grant and the asset accounted for at that fair value. An alternative would be to record both asset and grant at a nominal amount.

Presentation of grants related to assets

These should be presented either by setting up a deferred income reserve or by deducting the grant in arriving at the carrying amount of the asset. The former requires the income to be recognised as income on a systematic and rational basis over the useful life of the asset, whilst the latter automatically achieves that by reducing the depreciation charge.

Presentation of grants related to income

These are sometimes presented as a credit in the income statement, either separately or under the general heading of 'other income'. Alternatively, they may be deducted in reporting the related expense. The former method enables better comparison with other expenses not affected by a grant, but it could be argued that the expense would not have been incurred unless the grant was available.

Both methods are therefore acceptable, but disclosure of the grant may be necessary for a proper understanding of the financial statements.

Repayment of government grants

A government grant that becomes repayable should be accounted for as a revision of an accounting estimate (see IAS 8). Repayment of a revenue grant should be applied first against any unamortised deferred credit balance and any excess recorded as an expense. Repayment of a capital-based grant should be recorded by increasing the carrying amount of the asset or reducing the deferred income reserve by the amount payable. The cumulative additional depreciation that would have to be recognised to date as an expense in the absence of the grant should be recognised as an expense immediately.

Consideration should also be given to a possible impairment review of the asset.

Government assistance

Excluded from the definition of government grants are certain forms of government assistance which cannot reasonably have a value placed upon them, and also transactions with government which cannot be distinguished from normal trading transactions.

Examples of the former include free technical advice and the provision of guarantees. An example of the latter would be a government procurement policy that is responsible for a portion of the enterprise's sales. Any attempt to segregate the trading activities from government assistance would be purely arbitrary.

Disclosure of the benefit, however, may be necessary in order that the financial statements may not be misleading. Loans at nil or low interest are a form of government assistance, but the benefit is not quantified by the imputation of interest.

Government assistance does not include the provision of infrastructure (e.g. transport facilities, communications network, water or irrigation systems), as these benefit the whole community.

Disclosure

The following should be disclosed:

1. The accounting policy adopted
2. The nature and extent of government grants recognised in the financial statements and an indication of other forms of government assistance from which the enterprise has directly benefited
3. Unfulfilled conditions and other contingencies attached to government assistance that has been recognised.

Application

Job creation grant

£100,000 provided to create 100 jobs in 4 years. The jobs have been created as follows:

Year		Profit and loss (grant released) £
1	20	20,000
2	30	30,000
3	20	20,000
4	10	10,000
	80	80,000

The £20,000 in the deferred grants reserve is now effectively a liability, as it will have to be paid back to government. It should therefore be transferred from the deferred grants reserve to current liabilities.

Purchase of equipment

£80,000 with attached grant of 20% and estimated useful life of 4 years.

Net of cost method		Deferred income reserve method	
Cost	£80,000	Cost	£80,000
Grant (20%)	£16,000	Capital grants reserve*	£16,000
	£64,000		
Depreciation straight line over 4 years	£16,000 p.a.		£20,000 p.a.
Release of grant to profit and loss			£(4,000) p.a.

*Recorded on the balance sheet outside shareholders' funds.

It is likely that IAS 20 will be changed in order to bring it closer to the IASB's conceptual framework. New Zealand is currently preparing an international draft standard which will probably require all capital-based grants to be recorded immediately in income and not spread over the useful life of the fixed assets.

2.4   IAS 36 *Impairment of Assets* (revised March 2004)

Objective

The objective of IAS 36 is to prescribe the procedures an entity should apply to ensure that its assets are carried at no more than their recoverable amount. If the asset value is above its future use or sale value it is said to be impaired, and an impairment loss should be recognised immediately. IAS 36 also covers situations when an impairment should be reversed, as well as disclosures.

Scope

IAS 36 applies to the impairment of all assets other than:

- inventories – see IAS 2;
- deferred tax assets – see IAS 12;
- employee benefit assets – see IAS 19;
- financial assets – see IAS 39;
- investment properties – see IAS 40;
- biological assets – see IAS 41.

However, it does apply to subsidiaries as defined in IAS 27, associates as defined in IAS 28 and joint ventures as defined in IAS 31. It also applies to revalued assets governed by IAS 16. In the latter case, if the fair value is its market value the only difference is the direct incremental costs of disposal, and if these are negligible then no impairment has occurred. If the disposal costs are substantial, then IAS 36 applies. If the asset is valued at other than market value, then IAS 16 only should be applied after the revaluation adjustments have been applied to determine whether or not it has been impaired.

Key definitions

Recoverable amount: the higher of an asset's net selling price and its value in use.

Value in use: the present value of future cash flows expected to be derived from the asset or cash generating unit (CGU).

Net selling price: the amount obtainable from the sale of an asset or CGU in an arms length transaction less costs of disposal.

Costs of disposal: incremental costs directly attributable to the disposal of an asset but excluding finance costs and income tax.

Impairment loss: the amount by which the carrying amount of an asset or CGU exceeds its recoverable amount.

Cash generating unit (CGU): the smallest identifiable group of assets that generates cash flows that are largely independent of cash inflows from other assets or groups of assets.

Identifying an asset that may be impaired

IAS 36 is structured in four stages as follows:

1. Measuring recoverable amount
2. Recognising and measuring impairment losses
3. Reversing impairment losses
4. Information to be disclosed.

An asset is impaired when the carrying amount of an asset exceeds its recoverable amount. Except for intangible assets with indefinite lives and goodwill, a formal estimate of recoverable amount does not occur annually unless there is an indication of a potential impairment loss. At each balance sheet date, however, an entity should assess whether or not there are indications of impairment losses.

In making an assessment of whether or not there are indications of impairment an entity, as a minimum, should consider the following.

1. External sources:
   - a significant decline in an asset's market value
   - significant changes with an adverse effect on the entity that have taken place during the period or in the near future – in the technological, economic or legal environments
   - market interest rate increases during the period which have affected the discount rate
   - whether the carrying amount of the net assets in the entity is more than its market capitalisation.
2. Internal sources:
   - evidence of obsolescence or physical damage
   - plans to discontinue or restructure the operation to which the asset belongs, or plans to dispose of the asset or reassess its useful life
   - evidence that economic performance is worse than expected.

The list is not intended to be exhaustive, and there may be other indications that are equally important.

Evidence from internal reporting of impairment includes the following:

- cash flows for operating and maintaining the asset are considerably higher than budgeted;
- actual cash flows are worse than budgeted;
- a significant decline in budgeted cash flows or operating profit; or
- operating losses.

Intangible assets with infinite lives or not yet in use, as well as goodwill, should be tested for impairment on an annual basis. Materiality, however, applies, and if interest rates have increased during the period an asset's recoverable amount need not be formally estimated if the discount rate is unlikely to be affected or if previous sensitivity analysis makes it unlikely that a material decrease has occurred or has resulted in a material impairment loss.

If an asset is impaired, depreciation should also be reviewed and adjusted as the remaining useful life may be considerably shorter.

Measuring recoverable amount

Recoverable amount is the higher of net selling price and value in use. Both need not necessarily be determined. If either exceeds the NBV, then the asset is not impaired.

If it is not possible to determine net selling price as there is no reliable estimate, then value in use should be adopted instead. Also, if there is no reason to believe that an asset's value in use is materially different from its net selling price then the asset's recoverable amount will be its net selling price.

Recoverable amount is determined for individual assets unless the asset does not generate cash flows that are largely independent of those from a group of assets. If the latter, then recoverable amount is determined for the CGU to which the asset belongs unless either:

- the asset's net selling price is higher than its NBV; or
- the asset's value in use can be determined to be close to its net selling price.

In some cases averages may provide a reasonable approximation of the detailed computations.

Measuring the recoverable amount of an intangible asset with an indefinite useful life
This must be measured at the end of each reporting period, but a previous detailed calculation in a preceding period may be adopted provided all of the following criteria are met:

- the intangible asset does not generate cash inflows largely independent from other assets and is therefore tested as part of an CGU whose assets and liabilities have largely remain unchanged since the last calculation;
- the most recent recoverable amount resulted in an amount that exceeded the assets NBV by a considerable amount;
- based on an analysis of events since the last valuation, the likelihood that a current recoverable amount would be less than the asset's NBV is remote.

Net selling price
Best evidence is a binding sale agreement at arm's length, adjusted for incremental costs directly attributable to disposal of the asset.

If there is no binding sale agreement but it is traded on an active market, net selling price is the asset's market price less costs of disposal. The price should be the current bid price or the price of the most recent transaction. If none exists it should be based on the best information available to reflect what would be received between willing parties at arm's length, but it should not be based on a forced sale. Costs of disposal include legal costs, stamp duty and other direct incremental costs, but not reorganisation or termination benefits.

Value in use

The following elements should be reflected in the calculation of value in use:

- an estimate of future cash flows to be derived from the asset;
- expectations about possible variations in the amount or timing of such flows;
- the time value of money;
- the price for bearing the uncertainty inherent in the asset; and
- other factors, including poor liquidity, that market participants would reflect in pricing expected future cash flows.

This requires estimating the future cash flows to be derived from continuing use of the asset and from its ultimate disposal, as well as applying the appropriate discount rate to those flows. Either cash flows or the discount rate can be adjusted to reflect the above five elements.

Basis for estimates of future cash flows   Cash flows should be based on reasonable and supportable assumptions that represent management's best estimate of a range of economic conditions that exist over the life of the asset and take into account the past ability of management to forecast cash flows accurately.

Greater weight should be given to external evidence and cash flows should be based on the most recent financial forecasts approved by management covering a normal maximum period of 5 years. If a longer period is justified, budgets/forecasts should be extrapolated using a steady or declining growth rate that should not exceed the long-term average growth rate for the products, industries or countries in which the entity operates, unless a higher rate is justified. If appropriate, the growth rate should be zero or negative.

Composition of estimates of future cash flows   These shall include:

- projections of cash inflows from continuing use of the asset;
- projections of cash outflows necessarily incurred to generate the cash inflows and that can be directly attributed to the asset;
- net cash flows to be received for the disposal of the asset at the end of its useful life.

Estimates should reflect consistent assumptions about price increases due to general inflation, and should include future overheads that can be directly attributed or allocated to the asset. If the asset is not in use yet, all expected future costs to get it ready should be included within future cash outflows.

Cash flows do not include either cash inflows from assets that generate cash inflows largely independent of the cash inflows from the asset, nor cash outflows related to obligations already recognised as liabilities.

Future cash flows should be estimated for the asset in its current condition and should not include cash inflows from restructuring (under IAS 37) or from future capital expenditure that will enhance or improve the asset's performance.

Estimates of future cash flows shall not include:

- cash inflows from financing activities; or
- income tax receipts or payments.

This will avoid double counting of the interest cost and ensure that the discount rate is determined on a pre-tax rate basis.

Estimates of net cash flows to be received from disposal are those expected to be obtained on an arm's length basis after deducting disposal costs. It should be based on prices prevailing at the date of the estimate for assets operating under similar conditions and should reflect the effect of future price increases (general and specific).

Discount rate   This should be a pre-tax rate that reflects both the time value of money and the specific risks attached to the asset. The latter is the return that investors would require if they were to choose an investment that would generate cash flows equivalent to those expected to be derived from the asset. Where an asset specific rate is not directly available then surrogates may be adopted.

Recognising and measuring impairment losses

Assets other than goodwill

Only if the recoverable amount of an asset is less than its NBV should the asset be reduced to its recoverable amount and an impairment loss created. That should then be expensed in the income statement unless the asset has been carried at a revalued amount under IAS 16, in which case it is treated as a revaluation decrease.

A revaluation loss is charged to income to the extent that the loss exceeds the amount held in the revaluation reserve for the same asset. Where the impairment loss is greater than the NBV, a liability should be recognised only if required by another standard. After recognition of the impairment loss, depreciation must be adjusted in future periods to allocate the asset's revised book value to be spread over the asset's remaining useful life. Any related deferred tax assets or liabilities are determined under IAS 12 by comparing the revised NBV of the asset with its tax base.

Cash generating units and goodwill

Identification of the CGU to which an asset belongs   If there is any indication that an asset may be impaired, the recoverable amount shall be estimated for that individual asset. If it is not possible to estimate the recoverable amount of the individual asset, then the entity should determine the recoverable amount of the CGU to which the asset belongs (the CGU).

This occurs when an asset's value in use cannot be estimated to be close to net selling price and the asset does not generate cash inflows from continuing use that are largely independent of those from other assets. In such cases the value in use and thus recoverable amount must be determined only for the asset's CGU. IAS 36 offers a few examples (see Examples 2.1 and 2.2).

Example 2.1
Identification of CGU in a mining company

A mine owns a private railway to support its mining activities. It could only be sold for scrap and does not generate independent cash flows from those of the mine.

The CGU, in this case, is therefore the mine as a whole, including the railway, as the railway's value in use cannot be independently determined and would be very different from its scrap value.

Identification of an asset's CGU involves judgement and should be the lowest aggregation of assets that generate largely independent cash inflows from continuing use.

Example 2.2
Identification of CGU in a bus company

A bus company has a contract to provide a minimum service on five separate routes. Cash flows can be separately identified for each route.

Even if one route is operating at a loss, the entity has no option to curtail any one route and the lowest independent level is the group of five routes together. The CGU is therefore the bus company itself.

Cash inflows should be from outside parties only and should consider various factors, including how management monitors the entity's operations.

If an active market exists for the asset's or group of assets' output, then they should be identified as a CGU, even if some of the output is used internally. If this is the case, management's best estimate of future market prices shall be used:

- in determining the value in use of the CGU when estimating the future cash inflows relating to internal use; and
- in determining the value in use of other CGUs of the entity, when estimating future cash outflows that relate to internal use of the output.

CGUs must be identified consistently from period to period unless a change is justified.

Recoverable amount and carrying amount of a CGU   The recoverable amount of a CGU is the higher of its net selling price and value in use. The carrying amount shall be determined consistently with the way recoverable amount is determined.

The carrying amount of a CGU includes the carrying amount of only those assets that can be attributed directly or allocated on a reasonable and consistent basis to the CGU, and does not include the carrying amount of any recognised liability unless the recoverable amount of the CGU cannot be determined without its consideration.

The CGU should exclude cash flows relating to assets that are not part of a CGU. However, all assets that generate cash flows for the CGU should be included. In some cases, e.g. goodwill and head office assets, future cash flows cannot be allocated to the CGU on a reasonable and consistent basis. This is covered later. Also, certain liabilities may have to be considered – e.g. on disposal of a CGU, if a buyer is forced to take over a liability. In that case the liability must be included as per the example provided in IAS 36 (see Example 2.3).

Example 2.3
Recoverable amount of a CGU

A company must restore a mine by law, and has provided for the cost of restoration of 500 which is equal to the present value of restoration costs. The CGU is the mine as a whole. Offers of 800 have been received to buy the mine, and disposal costs are negligible. The value in use is 1,200 excluding restoration costs and the carrying amount 1,000.

Net selling price	800
Value in use	700 (1,200 less 500)
Carrying amount of CGU	500 (1,000 less 500)

The recoverable amount of 800 exceeds its carrying amount of 500 by 300 and there is no impairment.

Goodwill

Allocating goodwill to CGUs   Goodwill should be allocated to one or more CGUs, and the CGUs should represent the smallest CGU to which a portion of the carrying amount of goodwill can be allocated on a reasonable and consistent basis. It is capable of being allocated only when a CGU represents the lowest level at which management monitors the return on investment in assets that include the goodwill. The CGU should not be larger than a segment based on IAS 14.

Goodwill does not generate cash flows independently, the benefits are not capable of being individually identified and separately recognised and they often contribute to multiple CGUs. If the initial allocation of goodwill cannot be completed before the end of the first annual reporting period in which the business combination occurs, it must be completed before the end of the first annual reporting date beginning after the acquisition date.

If provisional values are adopted, the acquirer must initially adopt those provisional figures and then adjust within twelve months to final. Additional information must be disclosed about the adjustments.

If a CGU is disposed, which includes goodwill previously allocated, the goodwill associated with the disposal shall be:

- included in the NBV of the operation when determining the gain or loss on disposal; and
- measured on the basis of relative values of the operation disposed of and the portion of the CGU retained (see Example 2.4).

Example 2.4
Allocating goodwill if a CGU is disposed

An entity sells for 100 an operation that was part of a CGU to which goodwill was allocated. The recoverable amount of part of CGU retained is 300.

Of the goodwill allocated, 25% is included in the NBV of operation that is sold.

If an entity reorganises so that changes in composition of one or more CGUs (to which goodwill has been allocated) occur, the goodwill shall be reallocated to units affected by adopting a relative value approach similar to that used when an entity disposes of an operation within a CGU (see Example 2.5).

Example 2.5
Allocating goodwill if an entity reorganises

Goodwill was previously allocated to CGU A, but A will now have to be divided into three other CGUs.

Goodwill allocated to A is reallocated to B, C and D based on the relative values of the three portions of A before those portions are integrated with B, C and D.

Testing CGUs with goodwill for impairment   When goodwill cannot be allocated on a reasonable and consistent basis, the unit should be tested for impairment whenever there is an indication of impairment by comparing its NBV excluding goodwill with its recoverable amount.

If a CGU includes an intangible asset that has an indefinite useful life or is not yet in use, then the asset can be tested for impairment only as part of the CGU.

A CGU to which goodwill has been allocated shall be tested for impairment annually, and whenever there is an indication that it may be impaired its NBV (including goodwill) should be compared with its recoverable amount. If the NBV exceeds its recoverable amount, the entity shall:

1. Determine whether goodwill allocated to CGU is impaired by comparing the implied value of goodwill with its carrying amount;
2. Recognise any excess of the carrying value of goodwill immediately in profit and loss as an impairment loss;
3. Recognise any remaining excess as an impairment loss first against goodwill allocated to the CGU and then to other assets on a pro rata basis (per NBVs).

Implied value of goodwill   The implied value of goodwill should be measured as the excess of:

• the recoverable amount of the CGU to which goodwill is allocated, over
• the net fair value of identifiable assets, liabilities and contingent liabilities the entity would recognise if it acquired the CGU in a business combination on the date of the impairment test.

Minority interest   Under IAS 36 goodwill is based on parent's ownership interest, and thus goodwill attributable to minority interest is not recognised. If there is a minority interest in a CGU to which goodwill has been allocated, the carrying amount of that CGU comprises:

• both the parent's interest and the minority interest in the identifiable net assets of the CGU; and
• the parent's interest in goodwill.

However, part of the recoverable amount of the CGU will be attributable to the minority interest in goodwill. For impairment testing the carrying amount of the CGU should be notionally adjusted by grossing up goodwill to include that attributable to minority interest. This is then compared with the recoverable amount to determine whether the CGU is impaired. If it is, the entity must allocate the impairment loss as per (1) to (3) above.

The implied value of goodwill allocated to a CGU with a minority interest includes goodwill attributable to both the parent and minority interests. This implied value is then compared with the notionally grossed up carrying value of goodwill to determine whether goodwill is impaired. Any impairment loss is apportioned between parent and minority, but only the parent's share is recognised.

If the total impairment loss relating to goodwill is less than the amount by which the notionally adjusted carrying amount of the CGU exceeds its recoverable amount, any excess must be accounted for as an impairment loss (see Example 2.6).

Example 2.6
Impairment testing CGUs with goodwill and minority interests

Background
Entity X acquires 80% of Entity Y for 1,600 on 1.1.2003. Y's identifiable net assets at that date have a fair value of 1,500. X recognises:

- goodwill $1,600 - 80\% \times 1500 = 400$;
- Y's identifiable net assets at fair value of 1,500;
- minority interest of $20\% \times 1500 = 300$.

The assets of Y are the smallest group of independent assets; thus it is a CGU. Because it includes goodwill, it must be tested for impairment annually or more frequently if there is an indication of impairment.

At the end of 2003, X determines that the recoverable amount of Y is 1,000. Assume X adopts straight-line depreciation with a life of 10 years for all its identifiable net assets.

Testing Y for impairment

End of 2003	Goodwill	Identifiable net assets	Total
Gross carrying amount	400	1,500	1,900
Accumulated depreciation	–	(150) 10%	(150)
Carrying amount	400	1,350	1,750
Unrecognised minority interest	100 (400 × 20/80)	–	100
Notionally adjusted carrying amount	500	1,350	1,850
Recoverable amount (800 + 200)			1,000
Impairment loss			850

The impairment loss of 850 is allocated by first examining whether goodwill is impaired. That occurs if its carrying amount exceeds its implied value. If X determines that the fair value of the identifiable assets it would recognise if it had acquired Y at the date of the test is 800, the implied value of goodwill is 200. This implied value includes goodwill attributable to both X and minority interest.

Thus, 300 of the 850 impairment loss is attributable to goodwill (i.e. 500 − 200). However, because goodwill is only recognised to the extent of X's 80% ownership in Y, X only recognises 80% of the loss (i.e. 240). The remaining loss of 550 is used to reduce the carrying amount of Y's identifiable assets.

End of 2003	Goodwill	Identifiable net assets	Total
Gross carrying value	400	1,500	1,900
Accumulated depreciation	–	(150)	(150)
Carrying amount	400	1,350	1,750
Impairment loss	(240)	(550)	(790)
Carrying amount after impairment loss	160	800	960

Timing of the impairment test

The test can be carried out at any time during the year provided it is at the same time every year. Different CGUs may be tested for impairment at different times. However, if some of the goodwill was acquired in a business combination during the year, that CGU shall be tested for impairment before the end of the current reporting period.

If other assets or smaller CGUs are tested at the same time as the larger unit, they shall be tested for impairment before the larger unit.

The most recent detailed calculation made in a preceding reporting period may be adopted for the test provided all of the following criteria are met:

- the assets and liabilities have not changed significantly since the most recent recoverable amount calculation;
- the most recent recoverable amount calculation resulted in an amount substantially in excess of the CGU's carrying amount; and
- based on an analysis of events and changed circumstances, the likelihood that a current recoverable amount would be less than the current carrying amount of the CGU is remote.

If the carrying amount of a CGU exceeds its recoverable amount but the entity has not completed its determination of whether goodwill is impaired or not, it may use its best estimate of any probable impairment loss. Any adjustment shall be recognised in the succeeding reporting period.

Corporate assets

These include headquarters buildings, research centres etc. Their key characteristics are that they do not generate independent cash flows, and therefore their recoverable amount cannot be determined. Thus if there is an indication that a corporate asset may be impaired, recoverable amount is determined for the CGU to which the corporate asset belongs compared with the carrying amount of this CGU and any impairment loss recognised (see Example 2.7).

If a portion of the carrying amount of a corporate asset can be allocated on a reasonable and consistent basis, then the entity shall compare the carrying amount of the CGU (including corporate asset) with its recoverable amount and any losses recognised.

If a portion of the carrying amount of a corporate asset cannot be allocated on a reasonable and consistent basis, then the entity shall:

- compare the carrying amount of the CGU, excluding the corporate asset, with its recoverable amount and recognise any impairment loss;
- identify the smallest CGU to which a portion of the corporate asset can be allocated on a reasonable and consistent basis; and
- compare the carrying amount of the larger CGU including a portion of the corporate asset with its recoverable amount. Any impairment loss shall be recognised.

Example 2.7
Allocation of corporate assets

Background
Entity M has three CGUs – A, B and C. They do not include goodwill. At the end of 2000 the carrying amounts are 100, 150 and 200.

Corporate assets have a carrying amount of 200 (buildings 150, research centre 50). The remaining useful life of CGU A is 10 years and of CGUs is B and C 20 years. The entity adopts a straight-line basis for depreciation.

There is no basis to calculate net selling price for each CGU, thus recoverable value is based on value in use using a 15% pre-tax discount rate.

Identification of corporate assets
The carrying amount of headquarters building can be allocated on a reasonable and consistent basis. The research centre cannot be allocated on such a manner.

Allocation of corporate assets

End of 2000	A	B	C	Total
Carrying amount	100	150	200	450
Useful life	10 years	20 years	20 years	
Weighting based on useful life	1	2	2	
Carrying amount after weighting	100	300	400	800
Pro rata allocation of building	12%	38%	50%	100%
Allocation of carrying amount of building	19	56	75	(150)
Carrying amount after allocation	119	206	275	600

Determination of recoverable amount and calculation of impairment losses
The recoverable amount of each individual CGU must be compared with its carrying amount, including the portion of the headquarters, and any impairment loss recognised. IAS 36 then requires the recoverable amount of M as a whole to be compared with its carrying amount, including the headquarters and the research centre.

Calculation of A, B, C and M's value in use at the end of 2000:

A	Future cash flows for 10 years discounted at 15%	199
B	Future cash flows for 20 years discounted at 15%	164
C	Future cash flows for 20 years discounted at 15%	271
M	Future cash flows for 20 years discounted at 15%	720

Impairment testing A, B and C:

End of 2020	A	B	C
Carrying amount after allocation of building	119	206	275
Recoverable amount	199	164	271
Impairment loss	0	(42)	(4)

Allocation of impairment losses for CGUs B and C:

		B	C
To headquarters building	$(42 \times 56/206)$	(12)	(1) $(4 \times 75/275)$
To assets in CGU	$(42 \times 150/206)$	(30)	(3) $(4 \times 200/275)$
		(42)	(4)

Because the research centre could not be allocated on a reasonable and consistent basis to A, B and C's CGUs, M compares the carrying amount of the smallest CGU to which the carrying amount of the research centre can be allocated (i.e. M as a whole) to its recoverable amount.

Impairment testing the 'larger' CGU (i.e. M as a whole):

End of 2020	A	B	C	Building	Research centre	M
Carrying amount after allocation of building	100	150	200	150	50	650
Impairment loss (first step)	–	(30)	(3)	(13)	–	(46)
Carrying amount (after first step)	100	120	197	137	50	(604)
Recoverable amount						720
Impairment loss for the larger CGU						0

Thus, no additional impairment loss results from the application of the impairment test to the 'larger' CGU. Only the 46 uncovered in the first step is recognised.

Impairment loss for a CGU

An impairment loss should be recognised only if its recoverable amount is less than its carrying amount. The impairment loss is allocated to reduce the carrying amount of the assets:

- first, against goodwill to its implied value; and
- then to other assets on a *pro rata* basis based on the carrying amount of each asset in the unit.

These are treated as impairment losses on individual assets. In allocating the loss, an asset should not be reduced below the highest of:

- its net selling price (if determinable);
- its value in use (if determinable); and
- zero.

The amount of the loss that would otherwise have been allocated to the asset shall be allocated to the other assets on a *pro rata* basis.

If the recoverable amount of each individual asset in a CGU cannot be estimated without undue cost or effort, IAS 36 requires an arbitrary allocation between assets of the CGU other than goodwill.

If the recoverable amount of an individual asset cannot be determined:

- an impairment loss is recognised for the asset if its carrying value is greater than the higher of its net selling price and the results of procedures described above;
- no impairment loss is recognised if the related CGU is not impaired even if its net selling price is less than its carrying amount.

Reversing impairment losses

An entity shall assess at each balance sheet date whether there is any indication that an impairment loss recognised in prior periods, other than goodwill, may no longer exist. If such exists, the entity shall estimate the recoverable amount of that asset.

In assessing whether or not there is a reversal, the entity should consider the following indications, as a minimum.

1. External sources of information:
   - whether the asset's market value has increased significantly during the period
   - significant changes with a favourable impact in the technological, market, economic or legal environment in which the entity operates
   - whether market interest rates have decreased and are likely to affect the discount rate and the recoverable amount.
2. Internal sources of information:
   - any significant changes with a favourable effect during the period or in the near future; this includes capital expenditure that enhances an asset's standard of performance
   - evidence that indicates that economic performance is better than expected.

An impairment loss in prior periods, for assets other than goodwill, shall be reversed only if there is a change in estimate used to determine the asset's recoverable amount since the loss was recognised.

Examples of changes in estimate include:

- a change in the basis for recoverable amount;
- if the recoverable amount was based on value in use, a change in amount or timing of cash flows or in the discount rate;
- if the recoverable amount was based on net selling price, a change in components of net selling price.

An impairment loss, however, is not reversed merely because of the passage of time.

Reversal of an impairment loss for an individual asset

The increased carrying value of an asset (other than goodwill) due to a reversal shall not exceed the carrying amount that would have existed had the asset not been impaired in prior years.

Any increase in the carrying amount, above the carrying amount had no impairment taken place, would have been a revaluation.

A reversal shall be recognised immediately in profit and loss unless the asset is carried at a revalued amount under another standard. Any reversal of an impairment loss on a revalued asset shall be treated as a revaluation reserve increase, and credited directly to equity. However, to the extent a loss was previously recognised in profit and loss, a reversal is also recognised in profit and loss.

After a reversal, the depreciation charge should be adjusted in future periods to allocate its revised carrying amount over its remaining useful life.

Reversal of an impairment loss for a CGU

A reversal of an impairment loss for a CGU should be allocated to the assets in the unit, except for goodwill, on a *pro rata* basis with the carrying amount of those assets.

In allocating a reversal for a CGU, the carrying amount of an asset should not be increased above the lower of:

- its recoverable amount (if determinable);
- the carrying amount that would be determined had no impairment taken place.

The amount of the reversal of the impairment loss that would otherwise have been allocated to the asset shall be allocated on a *pro rata* basis to the other assets of the CGU, except for goodwill.

Reversal of an impairment loss for goodwill

An impairment loss recognised for goodwill shall not be reversed in subsequent periods, as IAS 38 expressly forbids the creation of internally generated goodwill.

Information to be disclosed

An entity should disclose the following for each class of assets:

1. The amount of impairment losses recognised in profit and loss during the period
2. The amount of reversals of impairment losses recognised in profit and loss during the period
3. The amount of impairment losses recognised directly in equity during the period
4. The amount of reversals of impairment losses recognised directly in equity during the period.

The information may be included in a reconciliation of the carrying amount of property, plant and equipment as required by IAS 16.

The following should be disclosed for each material impairment loss recognised or reversed during the period for an individual asset, including goodwill, or a CGU.

1. The events and circumstances that led to the recognition or reversal of the impairment loss
2. The amount of the impairment loss recognised or reversed
3. For an individual asset:
   - the nature of the asset
   - the reportable segment to which the asset belongs, if applicable
4. For a CGU:
   - a description of the CGU
   - the amount of the impairment loss recognised or reversed by class of asset and, if applicable, by reportable segment under IAS 14
   - if the aggregation of assets for identifying the CGU has changed since the previous estimate of the CGU's recoverable amount, a description of the current and former way of aggregating assets and the reasons for changing the way the CGU is identified
5. Whether the recoverable amount of the asset (CGU) is its net selling price or its value in use
6. If recoverable amount is net selling price, the basis used to determine net selling price
7. If recoverable amount is value in use, the discount rate used in the current and previous estimates of value in use.

An entity shall disclose the following information for the aggregate impairment losses and the aggregate reversals of impairment losses recognised during the period for which no information is disclosed above:

1. The main classes of assets affected by impairment losses and the main classes of assets affected by reversals of impairment losses
2. The main events and circumstances that led to the recognition of these impairment losses and reversals of impairment losses.

An entity is encouraged to disclose key assumptions used to determine the recoverable amount of assets (CGUs) during the period, but required to do so when goodwill or intangible assets with indefinite useful lives are included in a CGU.

If goodwill has not been allocated to a CGU, the amount shall be disclosed together with reasons for non-allocation.

If an entity recognises the best estimate of a probable impairment loss for goodwill the following should be disclosed:

1. The fact that the impairment loss recognised for goodwill is an estimate, not yet finalised
2. The reasons why the impairment loss has not been finalised.

In the immediate succeeding period, the nature and amount of any adjustments shall be disclosed.

There are also considerable additional disclosures for segments.

2.5   IAS 23 *Borrowing Costs* (revised December 2003)

Objective

The objective of IAS 23 is to prescribe the accounting treatment for borrowing costs. Generally it requires immediate expending, but there is an allowed alternative to permit capitalisation of borrowing costs that are directly attributable to the acquisition, construction or production of a qualifying asset.

Scope

The standard should be applied in accounting for borrowing costs, but it does not cover the actual or imputed costs of equity.

Key definitions

Borrowing costs: interest and other costs incurred by an enterprise in connection with borrowing of funds.

Qualifying asset: an asset which takes a substantial period of time to get ready for its intended use or sale.

Borrowing costs include interest on bank overdrafts, amortisation of discounts, amortisation of ancillary costs and finance lease charges.

Examples of qualifying assets include inventories requiring a substantial period of time to bring to a saleable condition, power generation facilities, and investment properties. Assets that are ready for their intended use are not qualifying assets.

Borrowing costs – benchmark treatment

Recognition

Borrowing costs should be expended in the period that they are incurred.

Disclosure

The accounting policy adopted for borrowing costs should be disclosed.

Borrowing costs – allowed alternative treatment

Recognition

Borrowing costs should be expended in the period they are incurred except to the extent that they are capitalised. However, borrowing costs that are directly attributable to the acquisition, construction or production of a qualifying asset should be capitalised as part of the cost of that asset. That can occur when it is probable that they will result in future economic benefits to the enterprise and the costs can be measured reliably.

Borrowing costs eligible for capitalisation

These are those borrowing costs that would have been avoided if the expenditure on the qualifying asset had not been made. When an enterprise borrows funds specifically to obtain a particular asset, the borrowing costs can be readily identified.

It may be difficult to identify a direct relationship – e.g. central coordination of finance, use of a range of debt instruments, loans in foreign currencies, operations in highly inflationary economies or from fluctuations in exchange rates. The exercise of judgement is required to determine the amount of borrowing costs to capitalise.

The FRS requires the use of actual borrowing costs less any temporary investment income where funds are borrowed specifically. To the extent that funds are borrowed generally, then the amount capitalised should be determined by applying a weighted average capitalisation rate to the borrowings outstanding during the period. However, the amount of borrowing costs capitalised during a period should not exceed the amount of borrowing costs incurred during that period.

Excess of the carrying amount of the qualifying asset over recoverable amount

When the carrying amount of the qualifying asset exceeds its recoverable amount or net realisable value, the carrying amount is written down. In certain circumstances the amount can be written back.

Commencement of capitalisation

Capitalisation should commence when:

- expenditures for the asset are being incurred;
- borrowing costs are being incurred; and
- activities to prepare the asset for intended use are in progress.

Only those expenditures that result in payments of cash, transfers of other assets or assumption of interest-bearing liabilities may be capitalised. These are reduced by any progress payments and grants received. The average carrying amount of the asset during a period should normally be a reasonable approximation of the expenditure to which the capitalisation rate is applied in that period.

The activities necessary to prepare the asset encompass more than the physical construction of the asset. They include technical and administrative work prior to the commencement of physical construction. This excludes holding costs, e.g. borrowing costs incurred while land acquired for building is held without any associated development activity.

Suspension of capitalisation

Capitalisation should be suspended during extended periods in which active development is interrupted. Capitalisation of borrowing costs is not normally suspended during a period when substantial technical and administrative work is being carried out, nor when a temporary delay is necessary to get an asset ready for intended use or sale – e.g. high water levels delaying construction of a bridge.

Cessation of capitalisation

Capitalisation should cease when substantially all the activities necessary to prepare the qualifying asset for its intended use or sale are complete. Normally when physical construction is complete but minor modifications are all that is outstanding, this would indicate that substantially all activities are complete.

When the construction of a qualifying asset is completed in parts and each part is capable of being used, then capitalisation should cease when substantially all the activities necessary to prepare that part for use are completed – e.g. each building in a business park but not an industrial plant involving several processes carried out in sequence.

Disclosure

The following should be disclosed:

1. The accounting policy adopted for borrowing costs
2. The amount of borrowing costs capitalised in the period
3. The capitalisation rate used.

2.6   Examination questions

The first batch of questions cover the accounting treatment required by IAS 16. Broadoak Plc concentrates on the costs that may be capitalised as property etc., both initially and subsequently. The second question covers the process of revaluation. The third question links IAS 16 with IAS 37 on provisions and the final question covers nil depreciation and component accounting.

Question 2.1: Broadoak (ACCA)

The broad principles of accounting for tangible non-current assets involve distinguishing between capital and revenue expenditure, measuring the cost of assets, determining how they should be depreciated, and dealing with the problems of subsequent measurement and subsequent expenditure. IAS 16 *Property, Plant and Equipment* has the intention of improving consistency in these areas.

Required

(a) Explain:
   (i) how the initial cost of tangible non-current assets should be measured, and
   (ii) the circumstances in which subsequent expenditure on those assets should be capitalised.
(b) Explain IAS 16's requirements regarding the revaluation of non-current assets and the accounting treatment of surpluses and deficits on revaluation and gains and losses on disposal.

Broadoak has recently purchased an item of plant from Plantco, the details of this are:

	$	$
Basic list price of plant		240,000
trade discount applicable to Broadoak		12.5% on list price
Ancillary costs:		
shipping and handling costs		2,750
estimated pre-production testing		12,500
maintenance contract for 3 years		24,000
site preparation costs		
electrical cable installation	14,000	
concrete reinforcement	4,500	
own labour costs	7,500	26,000

Broadoak paid for the plant (excluding the ancillary costs) within four weeks of order, thereby obtaining an early settlement discount of 3%.

Broadoak had incorrectly specified the power loading of the original electrical cable to be installed by the contractor. The cost of correcting this error of $6,000 is included in the above figure of $14,000.

The plant is expected to last for 10 years. At the end of this period there will be compulsory costs of $15,000 to dismantle the plant and $3,000 to restore the site to its original use condition.

Required

(c) Calculate the amount at which the initial cost of the plant should be measured (ignore discounting).

Broadoak acquired a 12-year lease on a property on 1 October 1999 at a cost of $240,000. The company policy is to revalue its properties to their market values at the end of each year. Accumulated amortisation is eliminated and the property is restated to the revalued amount. Annual amortisation is calculated on the carrying values at the beginning of the year. The market values of the property on 30 September 2000 and 2001 were $231,000 and $175,000 respectively. The existing balance on the revaluation reserve at 1 October 1999 was $50,000. This related to some non-depreciable land whose value had not changed significantly since 1 October 1999.

Required

(d) Prepare extracts of the financial statements of Broadoak (including the movement on the revaluation reserve) for the years to 30 September 2000 and 2001 in respect of the lease-hold property.

Question 2.2: L (CIMA)

(The second question covers the rationale behind the revaluation of property etc. rather than adopting historic costing. This is followed by a short practical example of how to account for revaluations.)

L has never revalued its property. The directors are unsure whether they should adopt a policy of doing so. They are concerned that IAS 16 *Property, Plant and Equipment* has an 'all or nothing' approach which would impose a duty on them to maintain up-to-date valuations in the balance sheet for all property into the indefinite future. They are also concerned that the introduction of current values will make the accounting ratios based on their balance sheet appear less attractive to shareholders and other users of the finan-cial statements.

Required

(a) Explain why IAS 16 requires those companies who revalue non-current assets to revalue all of the assets in the relevant classes, and why these valuations must be kept up to date.
(b) Explain whether it is logical for IAS 16 to offer companies a choice between showing all assets in a class at either cost less depreciation or at valuation.
(c) Calculate the figures that would appear in L's financial statements below in respect of property if the company opts to show the factories at their valuation. You should indicate where these figures would appear, but do NOT prepare any detailed notes in a form suitable for disclosure.

The directors have commissioned an independent valuation of the property at 30 June 2001. The findings from this report are summarised below:

	Cost	Depreciation to date	Valuation	Comments
	$m	$m	$m	
Factory A	250	70	160	This factory has been well maintained, but is located in an area where prices have been depressed by market conditions
Factory B	150	60	120	This factory is an area that has benefited from growth in the local economy driving up prices
Factory C	134	48	40	This factory has been badly maintained for several years and its valuation reflects the deterioration that has arisen because of this

Question 2.3: K (CIMA)

(This question is similar to the first in the series. However, it is also combined with the link with IAS 37 and how to deal with provisions for decommissioning costs.)

K is a CIMA member who has recently established an enterprise which specialises in biotechnology applications. The enterprise has just reached the end of its first year of trading. K is working through the accounting records prior to drafting the enterprise's first annual report. The non-current assets section of the balance sheet is causing him some difficulty. The enterprise has invested heavily in sophisticated equipment, and K is checking whether the associated costs have been accounted for in accordance with the requirements of IAS 16 *Property, Plant and Equipment.*

K is reviewing the file relating to a sophisticated oven that is used to heat cell cultures to a precisely controlled temperature:

		$
(i)	List price paid to supplier	50,000
(ii)	Wages and materials costs associated with testing and calibrating oven, up to start of operations	800
(iii)	Ongoing wages and materials costs associated with calibrating oven since start of operations	2,000
(iv)	Expected costs of disposing of oven at the end of its useful life	16,000

The oven is used to heat cell cultures to a temperature range that must be closely controlled. The oven's controls will have to be regularly checked and calibrated throughout its working life.

The oven will have to be dismantled and sterilised by an expert contractor at the end of its life and then disposed of at a special facility. K has already provided $16,000 against these costs, in accordance with the requirements of IAS 37 *Provisions, Contingent Liabilities and Contingent Assets.*

The machine's expected useful life is 5 years. K is planning to adopt the straight-line basis of depreciation. The market value/value in use of the machine at the year end is $28,000. This decrease in value from new is partly because the oven has been used to culture dangerous organisms, and so it is much less valuable. K is unsure whether to value equipment at cost less depreciation or at valuation. This decision will be based on an analysis of the resulting figures in terms of two of the qualitative characteristics of accounting statements (those of relevance and reliability) contained in the International Accounting Standards Committee's (IASC's) *Framework for the Preparation and Presentation of Financial Statements* (Framework).

Required

(a) Calculate the cost of the oven, applying the requirements of IAS 16. Explain your treatment of items (ii), (iii) and (iv).
(b) Calculate the figures that will appear in respect of the oven in the income statement for the enterprise's first year and the balance sheet at the year end under both the historical cost and valuation bases, then discuss the relevance and reliability of both sets of figures you have calculated in the answer.

Question 2.4: Aztech (ACCA)

(The final question on IAS 16 covers the topic of depreciation and whether or not a 'nil' depreciation policy is acceptable. It also covers the important adoption of component accounting as an alternative policy to providing for major overhauls.)

IAS 16 *Property, Plant and Equipment* deals with accounting for tangible non-current assets. However, when accounting for tangible non-current assets, it is important to consider the requirements of IAS 36 *Impairment of Assets* and IAS 37 *Provisions, Contingent Liabilities and Contingent Assets*.

Required

(a) Explain briefly why it is important to consider the requirements of IAS 36 and IAS 37, in addition to those of IAS 16, when accounting for tangible non-current assets.

Aztech, a public limited company manufactures and operates a fleet of small aircraft. It draws up its financial statements to 31 March each year.

Aztech also owns a small chain of hotels (book value $16m), which are used in the sale of holidays to the public. It is the policy of the company not to provide depreciation on the hotels as they are maintained to a high standard and the economic lives of the hotels are long (20 years remaining life). The hotels are periodically revalued, and on 31 March 2000 the value in use was determined to be $20 million, the replacement cost of the hotels was $16 million and the market value was $19 million. One of the hotels included above is surplus to the company's requirements as at 31 March 2000 and has been removed from use and is currently up for sale. This hotel had a carrying amount of $3 million, a value in use of $2 million and a market value of $25 million, before expected agent's and solicitor's fees of $200,000. Aztech wishes to revalue the hotels as at 31 March 2000. There is no indication of any impairment in value of the hotels which are still in use.

The company has recently finished manufacturing a fleet or five aircraft to a new design. These aircraft are intended for use in its own fleet for domestic carriage purposes. The company commenced construction of the assets on 1 April 1998, and wishes to recognise them as non-current tangible assets as at 31 March 2000. The aircraft were completed on 1 January 2000, but their exterior painting was delayed until 31 March 2000.

The costs (excluding finance costs) of manufacturing the aircraft were $28 million and the company has adopted a policy of capitalising the finance costs of manufacturing the aircraft. Aztech had taken out a 3-year loan of $20 million to finance the aircraft on 1 April 1998. Interest is payable at 10% per annum, but is to be rolled over and paid at the end of the 3-year period together with the capital outstanding. Income tax is 35%.

During the construction of the aircraft, certain computerised components used in the manufacture fell dramatically in price. The company estimated that at 31 March 2000 the net selling price of the aircraft was $30 million and their value use was $29 million.

The engines used in the aircraft have a 3-year life and the body parts have an 8-year life: Aztech has decided to depreciate the engines and the body parts over their different useful lives on the straight-line basis. The cost of replacing the engines on 31 March 2003 is estimated to be $15 million. The engine costs represent 30% of the total cost of manufacture.

The company has decided to revalue the aircraft annually on the basis of their market value. On 31 March 2001, the aircraft have a value in use of $22 million, market value of $21 million and a net selling price of $18 million. On 31 March 2002, the aircraft have a value in use of $20 million, a market value of $19.6 million and a net selling price of $19.0 million. Revaluation surpluses or deficits are apportioned between the engines and the body parts on the basis of their year-end book values before the revaluation.

Required

(b) Describe how the hotels should be valued in the financial statements of Aztech on 31 March 2000, and explain whether the current depreciation policy relating to the hotels is acceptable under IAS 16 *Property, Plant and Equipment*.
(c) Show the accounting treatment of the aircraft fleet in the financial statements on the basis of the above scenario for the financial years ending:
  (i) 31 March 2000
  (ii) 31 March 2001, 2002
  (iii) 31 March 2003 before revaluation.

Question 2.5: Low Paints (ACCA)

(Although the following question is largely concerned with the calculation of earnings per share under IAS 33, it also includes the accounting treatment of government grants under IAS 20 and leasing contracts under IAS 17.)

On 1 November 2000, the chief executive of Low Paints, Mr Low, retired from the company. The ordinary share capital of $1 at the time of his retirement was $6 million. Mr Low owns 52% of the ordinary shares of Low Paints, and the remainder is owned by employees. As an incentive to the new management Mr Low agreed to a new executive compensation plan, which commenced after his retirement. The plan provides cash bonuses to the board of directors when the company's earnings per share exceeds the 'normal' earnings per share which has been agreed at $0.50 per share.

The cash bonuses are calculated as being 20% of the profit generated in excess of that required to give an earnings per share figure of $0.50. The new board of directors has reported that the compensation to be paid is $360,000 based on earnings per share of $0.80 for the year ended 31 October 2001. However, Mr Low is surprised at the size of the compensation as other companies in the same industry were either breaking even or making losses in the period. He was anticipating that no bonus would be paid during the year as he felt that the company would not be able to earn the equivalent of the normal earnings per share figure of $0.50.

Mr Low, who had taken no active part in management decisions, decided to take advantage of his role as non-executive director and demanded an explanation of how the earnings per share figure of $0.80 had been calculated. His investigations revealed the following information:

(i) The company received a grant from the government of $5 million towards the cost of purchasing a non-current asset of $15 million. The grant had been credited to the income statement in total and the non-current asset had been recognised at $15 million in the balance sheet and depreciated at a rate of 10% per annum on the straight-line basis. The directors explained that current thinking by the International Accounting Standards Board was that the accounting standard on government grants was conceptually wrong because it mis-states the assets and liabilities of the company and hence they were following the approach that had recently been advocated in a discussion paper.

(ii) Shortly after Mr Low had retired from the company, Low Paints made an initial public offering of its shares. The sponsor of the issue charged a fee of $300,000. The fee on 1 January 2001 was paid by issuing 100,000 $1 shares at a market value of $120,000 and by cash of $180,000. The directors had charged the cash paid as an expense in the income statement. Further, they had credited the value of the shares issued to the sponsor in the income statement as they felt that the shares were issued for no consideration and that, therefore, they should offset the cash paid by the company. The public offering was made on 1 January 2001 and involved vesting four million ordinary (exclusive of the sponsor's shares) shares of $1 at a market price of $1.20. Mr Low and other current shareholders decided to sell three million of their shares as part of the offer, leaving one million new shares to be issued. The costs of issuing shares are to be regarded as an element of the net consideration received.

(iii) The directors sold, on 1 November 2000, a property under a 20-year lease to a company, Highball, which the bank had set up to act as a vehicle for investments and special projects. The consideration for the lease is $4.5 million. Low Paints has signed an unconditional agreement to repurchase the lease of the property after 4 years for a fixed amount of $5.5 million. The property has been taken off the balance sheet and the profit on the transaction, which has been included in the income statement, is $500,000. The profit has been calculated by comparing the carrying value of the property with the consideration received. Depreciation on the property is charged at 5% per annum on the carrying value of the asset.

(iv) Low Paints had made a one for four rights issue on 30 November 2001. The cost of the shares was $1.60 per share and the market price was $2.00 per share before the rights issue. The directors had ignored this transaction because it occurred after the balance sheet date, but they intend to capitalise accumulated profit to reflect the bonus element of the rights issue in the financial statements for the year ending 31 October 2002. The financial statements are not yet approved for the current year.

(v) The directors had calculated earnings per share for the year ended 31 October 2001 as follows:

Net profit	$4.8 million
Ordinary shares of $1	6,000,000
Earnings per share	$0.80

(vi) Mr Low was concerned over the way that earnings per share had been calculated by the directors, and also he felt that some of the above accounting practices were at best unethical and at worst fraudulent. He therefore asked your technical and ethical advice on the practices of the directors.

Required

(a) Advise Mr Low as to whether earnings per share has been accurately calculated by the directors showing a revised calculation of earnings per share.
(b) Discuss whether the directors may have acted in an unethical manner in the way they have calculated earnings per share.

Question 2.6 Shiplake (ACCA)

(The next batch of questions looks at the complicated world of impairment accounting under IAS 36. The first question, Shiplake, covers the definition of an impairment and outlines indications where possible impairment might occur. The theory of impairment is then applied to goodwill, plant, and research assets separately. Finally a calculation of impairment via a CGU and its associated loss allocation across various assets is investigated.) It is generally recognised in practice that non-current assets should not be carried in a balance sheet at values that are greater than they are 'worth'. In the past there has been little guidance in this area, with the result that impairment losses were not recognised on a consistent or timely basis or were not recognised at all. IAS 36 *Impairment of Assets* was issued in June 1998 on this topic.

Required

(a) Define an impairment loss and explain when companies should carry out a review for impairment of assets.
(b) Describe the circumstances that may indicate that a company's assets may have become impaired.

Shiplake is preparing its financial statements to 31 March 2002. The following situations have been identified by an impairment review team.

(i) On 1 April 2001 Shiplake acquired two subsidiary companies, Halyard and Mainstay, in separate acquisitions. Consolidated goodwill was calculated as:

	Halyard $000	Mainstay $000
Purchase consideration	12,000	4,500
Estimated fair value of net assets	(8,000)	(3,000)
Consolidated goodwill	4,000	1,500

A review of the fair value of each subsidiary's net assets was undertaken in March 2002. Unfortunately, both companies' net assets had declined in value. The estimated value of Halyard's net assets as at 1 April 2001 was now only $7 million. This was due to more detailed information becoming available about the market value of its specialised properties. Mainstay's net assets were estimated to have a fair value of $500,000 less than their carrying value. This fall was due to some physical damage occurring to its plant and machinery. Shiplake amortises all goodwill over a 5-year life.

(ii) Shiplake has an item of earth-moving plant, which is hired out to companies on short-term contracts. Its carrying value, based on depreciated historical cost, is $400,000. The estimated selling price of this asset is only $250,000, with associated selling expenses of $5,000. A recent review of its value in use based on its forecast future cash flows was estimated at $500,000. Since this review was undertaken there has been a dramatic increase in interest rates that has significantly increased the cost of capital used by Shiplake to discount the future cash flows of the plant.

(iii) Shiplake is engaged in a research and development project to produce a new product. In the year to 31 March 2001 the company spent $120,000 on research that concluded that there were sufficient grounds to carry the project on to its development stage, and a further $75,000 had been spent on development. At that date management had decided that they were not sufficiently confident in the ultimate profitability of the project and wrote off all the expenditure to date to the income statement. In the current year further direct development costs have been incurred of $80,000 and the development work is now almost complete, with only an estimated $10,000 of costs to be incurred in the future. Production is expected to commence within the next few months. Unfortunately, the total trading profit from sales of the new product is not expected to be as good as market research data originally forecast and is estimated at only $150,000. As the future benefits are greater than the remaining future costs, the project will be completed, but due to the overall deficit expected, the directors have again decided to write off all the development expenditure.

(iv) Shiplake owns a company called Klassic Kars. Extracts from Shiplake's consolidated balance sheet relating to Klassic Kars are:

	$000
Goodwill	80,000
Franchise costs	50,000
Restored vehicles at cost	90,000
Plant	100,000
Other net assets	50,000
	370,000

The restored vehicles have an estimated realisable value of $115 million. The franchise agreement contains a 'sell back' clause, which allows Klassic Kars to relinquish the franchise and gain a repayment of $30 million from the franchiser. An impairment review at 31 March 2002 has estimated that the value of Klassic Kars as a going concern is only $240 million.

(c) Explain with numerical illustrations where possible how the information in (i) to (iv) above would affect the preparation of Shiplake's consolidated financial statements to 31 March 2002.

Question 2.7: Nettle (ACCA)

(The second question in the batch covers a number of accounting standards including IFRS 2 Share Based Payment, but it also covers the change from the old IASC to the new IASB and finally how impairment should be calculated when a major new competitor enters a market.)

The directors of Nettle, a public limited company, are currently preparing the financial statements for the year ending 30 September 2001 and have requested a meeting with your firm in order to discuss the implications of certain events which have recently occurred. They are concerned about the impact that these events may have on the current and future financial statements of Nettle. Nettle has to prepare group accounts, as it has one subsidiary company.

Additionally, they wish to be advised of the steps that they should take to ensure that the company is adequately prepared to deal with the potential effects of these events.

(i) The International Accounting Standards Board (IASB) has recently restructured its organisation. The directors have only recently approved the use of International Accounting Standards and are worried by the reorganisation. Their view is that entities only reorganise when there are problems, and they are concerned that the public standing of International Accounting Standards may be damaged by the changes, with the result that the credibility of the standards may be put into question.

(ii) Nettle had granted share options to its employees on 1 October 2000. The options are vested in instalments over a 2-year period, and are based upon the performance of the employees. On 30 September 2001 the employees can potentially receive two million ordinary shares of $1, and on 30 September 2002 a further three million ordinary shares of $1 could be vested in the employees. The options due to vest on 30 September 2002 relate to the performance of the employees over the period 1 October 2000 to 30 September 2002.

In the year to 30 September 2001, 90% of employees achieved the performance targets and became eligible for shares. In the period to 30 September 2002 it is hoped that 96% of employees will achieve their performance targets.

The following table sets out price information relating to the ordinary shares:

As at	Market price	Fair value of option at 30 September 2001
	($)	($)
30 September 2001	9	2
30 September 2002 (projected)	10	3

The options can be exercised at $7 per share during the 12-month period following the financial year ends of 30 September 2001 and 2002. The market price of the shares on 1 October 2000 was $7 per share.

The directors are unsure as to the impact of the share options on the financial statements for the year ending 30 September 2001 if they were accounted for in accordance with the Discussion Paper *Share Based Payment* issued originally by the IASC.

(iii) Nettle had acquired a competitor organisation, Leaf, on 1 October 1999 for $150 million. The fair value of the net assets at that date was $130 million and the acquired business was combined with Nettle's existing business and did not retain its separate identity. At the time of the acquisition the fair value of the net assets of Nettle was $240 million, the value in use was $250 million and their carrying amount was $180 million. Goodwill is written off over 5 years. At 30 September 2001, the combined entity's net tangible assets had a carrying value of $310 million. There is no reliable estimate of the net selling price of the assets, but the directors have estimated that the cash flows for the year ended 30 September 2002 would be $19 million and for the year ended 30 September 2003 would be $26 million. They feel that there would be steady growth in cash flows of 2% thereafter, after eliminating the effect of inflation. (Assume inflation of 2%, a pre tax discount rate of 12% and pre tax discount rate adjusted to reflect growth in cash flows and inflation of 8%.) The directors feel that the market in which they operate has changed significantly because of the entrance of a major competitor which has adversely affected the company's profitability. They are wondering whether they should review their assets for impairment, as the first year review carried out on 30 September 2000 indicated that future cash flows would meet their target amounts and that there was no impairment of the company's assets.

Required

Advise the directors of the implications of the above three events, setting out the potential effects on the financial statements.

Question 2.8: COM (CIMA)

(The final question deals with an impairment of a previous acquisition and the need to write off goodwill first followed by intangibles and a pro rata allocation of impairment against tangible assets. It also covers the disclosure required under IAS 24 Related Party Disclosures.)

You are the management accountant of Com, a listed company with a number of subsidiaries. Your assistant has prepared the first draft of the consolidated financial statements of the group for the year ended 31 January 2001. These are prepared from the individual draft financial statements of the companies in the group plus other relevant information supplied to your assistant by the companies. The draft consolidated financial statements show a group profit before taxation of $35 million. Your assistant has queried the treatment of two complex transactions that have arisen during the year. Details of the transactions are given below.

Transaction 1

On 15 August 1999, the company acquired a new 100% subsidiary, Novel, for an immediate cash payment of $60 million. Group policy is to write off goodwill on acquisition over 10 years, with a full year's write off in the year of acquisition. No fair value adjustments were necessary in order to record the acquisition of Novel in the consolidated financial statements. The balance sheets of Novel at 15 August 1999 and 31 January 2001 were as follows:

	15 August 1999 $000	31 January 2001 $000
Non-current assets:		
Property, plant and equipment	50,000	55,000
Development expenditure	1,000	1,500
	51,000	56,500
Current assets	29,000	21,000
	80,000	77,500
Capital and reserves:		
Issued capital	30,000	30,000
Reserves	20,000	13,500
	50,000	43,500
Non-current liabilities	20,000	25,000
Current liabilities	10,000	9,000
	80,000	77,500

The additional information provided to your assistant shows that the value in use of Novel at 31 January 2001 was $40 million. The company is treated as a single cash-generating unit for the purposes of computing value in use. The information also states that the development expenditure had a net realisable value of $100,000 at 31 January 2001. The net realisable value of all the current assets of the company is above cost. There was no information that any other assets of Novel had suffered a specific decline in value. Your assistant has ignored this additional information, as she is unsure how it affects the financial statements.

Transaction 2

During the year another subsidiary, Beta, sold goods to Gamma, a company outside the group that was controlled by one of the directors of Beta. This director also exercises a very powerful and persuasive influence over the operating and financial policies of Beta. The goods were sold at their normal market price of $10 million. Gamma experienced cash flow problems during the year, and had not paid for any of the goods at 31 January 2001. Because of the cash flow problems, Beta decided to accept payment of $8 million for the goods. This decision was communicated to Gamma on 20 January 2001. Gamma paid the agreed amount of $8 million on 27 March 2001. Your assistant has written off $2 million of the original amount of $10 million owing by Gamma. The $2 million has been charged as part of administration expenses in the draft financial statements. No details of the transaction between Beta and Gamma have been included in the notes to the financial statements, because Com, the parent, was not directly involved in it. There were no other transactions between Beta and Gamma during the year.

Required

Draft a reply to your assistant that clearly explains the effect Transactions 1 and 2 will have on the consolidated financial statements of Com for the year ended 31 January 2001. Your reply should refer to relevant Accounting Standards and, in the case of Transaction 2, should comment on the treatment adopted by the assistant in the draft consolidated financial statements.

Asset valuation: accounting for intangible assets, inventories and construction contracts

3.1 IAS 38 *Intangible Assets* (revised March 2004)

Objective

The objective of IAS 38 is to prescribe the accounting treatment for intangible assets and identify how to recognise an intangible asset if, and only if, certain criteria are met. It also specifies how to measure the carrying amount of intangible assets and requires certain disclosures.

Scope

IAS 38 should be applied to all intangible assets, except:

- intangible assets covered by another standard, e.g. those for sale in ordinary course of business, deferred tax assets, leases under IAS 17, employee benefits under IAS 19, goodwill;
- financial assets as defined per IAS 32 and IAS 39;
- mineral rights and exploration for oil and gas expenditure (see IFRS 6);
- insurance contracts with policyholders (see IFRS 4).

Some intangibles may be contained in a physical asset, for example compact discs. Judgement is required to decide if IAS 16 or IAS 38 should be applied. Where software is not an integral part of related hardware, it is an intangible asset.

IAS 38 applies to advertising, training, start-up, and research and development. Licensing agreements, patents, copyrights etc. are excluded from IAS 17 and fall within the scope of IAS 38.

Key definitions

Intangible asset: an intangible asset is an identifiable non-monetary asset without physical substance.

Research: original and planned investigation undertaken with the prospect of gaining new scientific or technical knowledge and understanding.

Development: the application of research findings or other knowledge to a plan or design for the production of new or substantially improved materials, devices, products, processes, systems or services prior to the commencement of commercial production or use.

Intangible assets

Examples include computer software, patents, copyrights, motion picture films, customer lists, mortgage servicing rights, fishing licences, import quotas, franchises, customer or supplier relationships, customer loyalty, market share and marketing rights.

To be capitalised they must meet the definition of an intangible asset – i.e. identifiability, control over a resource and the existence of future economic benefits. If an asset fails to meet this definition, then expenditure should be expensed unless part of a business combination, when it should be treated as part of goodwill.

Identifiability

Goodwill, in a business combination, represents a payment in anticipation of future economic benefits from assets that are not capable of being individually identified and separately recognised.

An intangible asset meets the identifiability criterion in the definition of an intangible asset when it:

- is separable – i.e. capable of being separated or divided from the entity and sold, transferred, licensed, rented or exchanged, either individually or together with a related contract, asset or liability; or
- arises from contractual or other legal rights, regardless of whether those rights are transferable or separable from the entity or from other rights and obligations.

Control

An entity controls an intangible asset if it has the power to obtain future economic benefits and restrict the access of others to those benefits. Capacity to control is usually via legal rights, but that is not a necessary condition.

Market and technical knowledge may give rise to future economic benefits if it is protected by legal rights such as copyrights, a restraint of trade agreement, or by a legal duty on employees to maintain confidentiality.

Skilled staff and specific management or technical talent is unlikely to meet the definition of an intangible asset unless it is protected by legal rights and also meets the other parts of the definition. An entity has not sufficient control over customer loyalty and customer relationships and thus is also unlikely to meet the definition.

Future economic benefits

These can include revenue from the sale of products or services, cost savings or other benefits resulting from the use of the asset – e.g. use of intellectual property may reduce future production costs rather than increase future revenues.

Recognition and initial measurement of an intangible asset

Recognition of an intangible asset requires an entity to demonstrate that the item meets:

- the definition of an intangible asset; and
- the recognition criteria set out in IAS 38.

An intangible asset shall be recognised if, and only if:

- it is probable that the future economic benefits attributable to the asset will flow to the entity; and
- the cost of the asset can be measured reliably.

An entity shall assess the probability of future economic benefits using reasonable and supportable assumptions that represent management's best estimate of the set of economic conditions that will exist over the useful life of the asset. Greater weight will be put on external evidence when using judgement as to the degree of certainty attached to future cash flows.

An intangible asset shall be measured initially at cost.

Separate acquisition

The price an entity pays to acquire separately an intangible asset normally reflects expectations about the probability that the future economic benefits embodied in the asset will flow to the entity. Probability is already reflected in the cost of the acquired asset.

In addition, the cost of a separately acquired intangible asset can usually be measured reliably. That is especially the case if paid out in cash.

The cost of a separately acquired intangible asset comprises:

- its purchase price, including import duties but after deducting trade discounts and rebates; and
- any directly attributable expenditure on preparing the asset for its intended use, e.g. costs of employee benefits as per IAS 19, professional fees.

Costs incurred in using or redeploying intangible assets are excluded from the cost of those assets (e.g. costs incurred while the asset is capable of operating in the manner intended by management and initial operating losses).

Incidental operations are not necessary to bring an asset to its normal working condition, and thus they should be recognised immediately in the income statement and not included in the costs capitalised.

Acquisition as part of a business combination

Under IFRS 3 *Business Combinations*, the fair value of an intangible asset reflects market expectations about the probability that future economic benefits will flow to the entity. Probability is already reflected in the fair value measurement, and thus the probability criterion is always satisfied for acquired intangible assets.

A non-monetary asset without physical substance must be identifiable to meet the definition of an intangible asset – i.e. when an asset is separable or arises from contractual or other legal rights. Sufficient evidence must exist to measure reliably a fair value that is separable from the entity.

It is unlikely that a workforce and its related intellectual capital would be measured with sufficient reliability to be separately recognised.

IAS 38 requires, at acquisition date, that an acquirer recognises all of the acquiree's intangible assets (excluding assembled workforces) separately from goodwill, irrespective of whether those assets had been recognised in the acquiree's financial statements before the business combination. Research and development projects that meet the definition should be recognised separately.

Measuring the fair value of an intangible asset acquired in a business combination

Quoted market prices are the most reliable estimates of fair values of intangible assets. The market price is usually the current bid price or, if not available, the price of the most recent similar transaction, provided no significant change in the economic circumstances occurred between the transaction date and the date of fair value.

If no active market exists, fair value is the amount that an entity would have paid for the asset, at acquisition date, in an arm's length transaction. Recent transactions should help in this situation.

Certain entities that are regularly involved in the purchase and sale of unique intangible assets have developed techniques for estimating their fair values indirectly. These techniques may be used to calculate the initial measurement of an intangible asset if their objective is to estimate fair value for that purpose.

Acquisition by way of a government grant

Some intangible assets could be acquired for free or for a nominal consideration, e.g. landing rights, import licences, licences to operate radio stations etc. Under IAS 20, an entity may choose to recognise both the asset and the grant at fair value initially. If it chooses not to do that, the entity must recognise the asset initially at a nominal amount including any expenditure that is directly attributable to preparing the asset for its intended use.

Exchanges of assets

The cost of such an asset is measured at the fair value of the asset given up, adjusted by the amount of any cash or cash equivalents transferred. The fair value of the asset received is used to measure its cost if this is more clearly evident than the fair value of the asset given up.

The cost of an intangible asset acquired in exchange for a similar asset is measured at the carrying amount of the asset given up when the fair value of neither of the assets exchanged can be determined reliably.

Internally generated goodwill

Internally generated goodwill shall not be recognised as an asset. It is not an identifiable resource (i.e. it is not separable nor does it arise from contractual or other legal rights) controlled by the entity that can be measured reliably at cost.

Differences between the market value of an entity and the carrying amount of its identifiable net assets may capture a range of factors that affect the value of the entity.

Such differences cannot be considered to represent the cost of intangible assets controlled by the entity.

Internally generated intangible assets

It is difficult to assess whether or not an identifiable internal intangible asset exists or not. Thus, in addition to ensuring that there are probable economic benefits flowing to the entity and measuring cost reliably, an entity must also classify the generation of the asset into its research and development phases. If it cannot separate between the two, it must be classified as research.

Research phase

No intangible asset can arise from the research phase, and thus it must be written off as an expense. No demonstration of probable future economic benefits can exist. Examples include:

- activities aimed at obtaining new knowledge;
- the search for, evaluation and final selection of, applications of research findings;
- the search for alternatives for materials, devices, products, processes, systems or services;
- the formulation, design, evaluation and final selection of possible alternatives for new or improved materials, products, devices, processes, systems or devices.

Development phase

This should be recognised but if, and only if, an entity can demonstrate all of the following:

- the technical feasibility of completing the intangible asset so that it will be available for use or sale;
- its intention to complete the intangible asset and use or sell it;
- its ability to use or sell the intangible asset;
- how the intangible asset will generate probable future economic benefits – it shall demonstrate the existence of a market for the output of the intangible asset or, if used internally, its usefulness;
- the availability of adequate technical, financial and other resources to complete the development and to use or sell the intangible asset; and
- its ability to reliably measure the expenditure attributable to the intangible asset during its development phase.

These could be verified by an internal business plan or by lenders providing external finance for the project. Internal costing systems can often measure reliably the cost of generating an intangible asset internally, such as salary and other expenditure in securing copyrights or licences or developing computer software.

Examples of development activities are:

- the design, construction and testing of pre-production or pre-use prototypes and models;
- the design of tools, jigs, moulds and dies involving new technology;
- the design, construction and operation of a pilot plant that is not of a scale economically feasible for commercial production; and
- the design, construction and testing of a chosen alternative for new or improved materials, devices, products, processes, systems or services.

Internally generated brands, mastheads, publishing titles, customer lists and items similar in substance shall not be recognised as intangible assets. They cannot be distinguished from the cost of developing the business as a whole.

Cost of an internally generated intangible asset

Reinstatement of expenditure recognised as an expense in previous years may not occur.

The cost of an internally generated intangible asset comprises all expenditure that can be directly attributable and is necessary to create, produce and prepare the asset for it to be capable of operating in the manner intended by management. The cost includes, if applicable:

- expenditure on materials and services used or consumed in generating the intangible asset;
- the salaries, wages and other employment related costs of personnel directly engaged in generating the asset; and
- any expenditure directly attributable to generating the asset, such as fees to register a legal right and the amortisation of patents and licences.

The following are not included:

- selling, administration and other general overheads unless directly attributable to the asset;
- clearly identified inefficiencies and initial operating losses; and
- expenditure on training staff to operate the asset.

Example 3.1 provides an illustration.

Example 3.1
Cost of an internally generated intangible asset

An entity is developing a new production process. During 2004, expenditure incurred was 1,000, of which 900 was incurred before 1.12.2004 and 100 was incurred in December. At 1.12.04 the production process met the criteria for recognition as an intangible asset.

At the end of 2004 an intangible asset of 100 should be recorded with 900 being expensed (pre-criteria).

During 2005 expenditure incurred is 2,000. At the end of 2005 the recoverable amount of knowhow is estimated to be 1,900.

At the end of 2005, the cost of the production process is 2,100 (100 + 2,000). An impairment loss of 200 needs to be recorded, which may be reversed in a subsequent period if the requirements in IAS 36 are met.

Recognition of an expense

Expenditure on an intangible item shall be expensed when incurred unless:

- it forms part of the cost of an intangible asset that meets the recognition criteria; or
- the item is acquired in a business combination and cannot be recognised as an intangible asset, in which case it forms part of goodwill.

Research is always expensed when incurred. Other examples include costs of start-up activities unless included as a fixed asset under IAS 16, training expenditure, advertising, and relocation and reorganisation expenses.

Expenditure initially expensed in previous years may not be reinstated as part of an asset at a later date.

Subsequent expenditure

Subsequent expenditure shall be expensed when incurred unless:

- it is probable that the expenditure will increase future economic benefits beyond that originally assessed prior to the expenditure taking place; and
- the expenditure can be attributed to the asset and can be reliably measured.

If both conditions are met, any subsequent expenditure should be added to the cost of the intangible asset. Normally the nature of such an asset is that it is not possible to determine whether or not the subsequent expenditure is likely to enhance or maintain future economic benefits, and only rarely will it fulfil the two criteria above.

Subsequent expenditure on brands, mastheads, customer lists, publishing titles etc. should always be expensed to avoid the recognition of internally generated goodwill.

Research and development that:

- relates to an in process research or development project acquired separately or in a business combination and recognised as an intangible asset; and
- is incurred after the acquisition of that project

should be accounted for as above. Effectively that means that subsequent expenditure should be expensed if it is in the nature of research expenditure, expensed if it is development but fails to satisfy the criteria as an intangible asset, and added to the asset if it satisfies the recognition criteria.

Measurement subsequent to initial recognition

Benchmark treatment

An intangible asset shall be carried at cost less accumulated amortisation and impairment losses.

Allowed alternative treatment

An intangible asset shall be carried at a revalued amount, being its fair value at the date of the revaluation less any subsequent accumulated amortisation and impairment losses. Fair value should refer to an active market. Revaluations should be carried out with sufficient regularity so that the carrying values are not materially different from the fair value at the balance sheet date.

It is uncommon to find an active market in intangible assets but this can occur – for example, with taxi licences, fishing licences, production quotas etc. However, it cannot exist for brands, newspaper mastheads, music and film publishing rights, patents or trademarks, because each asset is unique and transactions are infrequent.

The frequency of revaluations depends on the volatility of the fair values, and if they are significant an annual valuation may be necessary.

If an intangible asset is revalued, any accumulated amortisation at the date of revaluation is either:

- restated proportionately with change in the gross carrying amount of the asset so that the carrying amount of the asset after revaluation equals its revalued amount; or
- eliminated against the gross carrying amount of the asset and the net amount restated to the revalued amount of the asset.

If an intangible asset is revalued, all the other assets in that class shall also be revalued unless there is no active market for those assets. This is to prevent selective revaluation and reporting of a mixture of costs and values as at different dates.

If there is no active market then the class of asset must be carried at cost less accumulated amortisation and impairment losses. Also if the fair value can no longer be determined by reference to an active market, the carrying amount of the asset shall be its revalued amount at the date of the last revaluation less accumulated amortisation and impairment losses. The fact that there is no active market should also trigger off an impairment review.

Any increase on a revaluation should normally be credited directly to equity, but to income to the extent it reverses a revaluation decrease of the same asset that has previously been recognised as an expense.

Any decrease on a revaluation should be expensed unless there is a previous revaluation surplus on the same asset, in which case it should be used to reverse the surplus first. Any excess is then expensed.

The cumulative revaluation surplus included in equity may be transferred directly to retained earnings when the surplus is realised – i.e. on retirement or disposal of the asset.

Useful life

An entity shall assess whether the useful life of an intangible asset is indefinite or finite. An indefinite life is one where there is no foreseeable limit to the period over which the asset is expected to generate net cash inflows for the entity.

An intangible asset with a finite life shall be amortised, but not an intangible asset having an indefinite life.

Many factors must be considered in determining the useful life, including:

- the expected usage of the asset and whether it can be managed efficiently;
- typical product life cycles;
- technical, technological, commercial or other types of obsolescence;
- the stability of the industry in which the asset operates and changes in market demand;
- expected actions by competitors;
- the level of maintenance expenditure required to obtain future benefits;
- the period of control over the asset;
- whether the useful life is dependent on the useful life of other assets in the entity.

Illustrations of the determination of useful life for different intangible assets and their subsequent accounting are provided by the standard, and are listed in Example 3.2.

Example 3.2
Determination of useful life for different intangible assets and their subsequent accounting

An acquired customer list
A direct mail company acquires a customer list and expects to derive benefit for at least 1 year but no more than 3 years. The customer list would be amortised over best estimate of useful life – say 18 months. Even the intention to add customer names to the list must be ignored as the asset relates only to the list of customers that existed at the date it was acquired. It should also be reviewed for impairment under IAS 36.

An acquired patent that expires in 15 years
The patent is protected for 15 years. There is a commitment to sell the patent after 5 years to a third party for 60% of the fair value of the patent at the date it was acquired.

The patent should be amortised over 5 years with a residual value of 60% of the present value of the patent's fair value at the date it was acquired. It should also be reviewed for impairment under IAS 36.

An acquired copyright that has a remaining legal life of 50 years
Assume an analysis of consumer habits provides evidence that there are only 30 years left of future benefits. The asset must now be amortised over the new expected remaining estimated useful life of 30 years as well as reviewing the asset for impairment.

An acquired broadcast licence that expires in 5 years
The licence is renewable every 10 years but can be renewed indefinitely at little cost and the entity intends to renew the licence. The technology is not expected to be replaced in the foreseeable future.

The licence would be treated as having an indefinite useful life, thus the licence would not be amortised until its useful life is determined to be finite. The licence would be tested for impairment at the end of each annual reporting period and whenever there is an indication of impairment.

A broadcast licence is revoked
Assume the licensing authority will no longer renew the licence but decides to auction it. There are 3 years before the licence expires. The useful life is no longer infinite and must be amortised over the remaining useful life of 3 years as well as being tested for impairment.

An acquired airline route authority between two major cities expires in 3 years
The route authority may be renewed every 5 years; these authorities are routinely granted at minimal cost and historically have been renewed. The acquiring entity expects to service the route indefinitely and cash flow analysis supports that view. The intangible asset therefore has an indefinite life and should not be amortised until its useful life is determined to be finite. It must, however, be tested annually for impairment and whenever there is an indication of an impairment.

An acquired trademark used to identify and distinguish a leading consumer product that has been a market leader for the past 8 years
A trademark has a legal life of 5 years but is renewable every 10 years at little cost and the entity intends to renew. This asset has an indefinite life and should not be amortised until useful life is determined to be definite. It should also be tested for impairment annually or when there is an indication of impairment.

A trademark acquired 10 years ago that distinguishes a leading consumer product
Unexpected competition has emerged which will reduce future sales by 20% but management expects that the 80% will continue indefinitely. An impairment must be recognised immediately to recoverable amount, but would continue to be subject to annual impairment although not amortised.

A trademark for a line of products acquired several years ago in a business combination
This is a well-established product, going for 35 years. There was an expectation that there would be no limit to period of time it would contribute to cash flows, thus it has not been amortised. Management has recently decided that the product line will be discontinued over the next 4 years. It must now be tested for impairment and subsequently amortised over the next 4 years.

The term 'indefinite' does not mean infinite. A conclusion that the useful life is indefinite should not depend on planned future expenditure in excess of that required to maintain the asset at that standard of performance.

Computer software is susceptible to changes in technology, and should be written off over a short useful life.

The useful life may be very long, but uncertainty justifies estimating the useful life on a prudent basis – but it does not justify an unrealistically short life.

The useful life of an intangible asset that arises from contractual or other legal rights should not exceed the period of the legal or contractual rights, but may be shorter. The useful life may include a renewal period, but only if there is evidence to support renewal by the entity without significant cost. If there are both legal and economic factors influencing the useful life of an intangible asset, then economic factors determine the period over which benefits will be received but legal factors may restrict the period over which the entity controls access to those benefits. The useful life is the shorter of the periods determined by these factors.

Intangible assets with finite useful lives

Amortisation period and amortisation method

The depreciable amount of an intangible asset should be allocated over its useful life. Amortisation should be allocated on a systematic basis over its useful life from the day it is available for use. It should reflect the pattern of economic benefits being consumed, but straight line should be adopted if it cannot be determined reliably. The standard requires it to be expensed unless permitted by another standard to be capitalised, e.g. IAS 2 *Inventories*.

The method should be applied consistently, but it would be rare for persuasive evidence to support a method that would result in lower amortisation than that achieved by straight line.

Residual value

This should be assumed to be zero unless:

. There is a commitment by a third party to purchase the asset at the end of its useful life; or

2. There is an active market for the asset, and
   - residual value can be determined by reference to the market, and
   - it is probable that such a market will exist at the end of the asset's useful life.

The depreciable amount is determined after deducting residual value, but the latter is based on prices prevailing at the date of the estimate and is reviewed at each balance sheet date. Any change in that value is treated as an adjustment to future amortisation.

Review of amortisation period and amortisation method

The amortisation period and method shall be reviewed at the end of each annual reporting period. If the expected useful life is different from previous estimates, the amortisation period shall be changed. If there is a change in the expected pattern of consumption of future benefits the amortisation period shall be accounted for as a change in accounting estimates as per IAS 8 – for example, it may become apparent that the diminishing balance method is more appropriate than straight line.

Intangible assets with indefinite useful lives

An intangible asset with an indefinite useful life shall not be amortised. However, it is required to be tested annually for impairment and whenever there is an indication of an impairment.

Review of useful life assessment

The useful life of an intangible asset should be reviewed each period to determine whether events and circumstances support an indefinite useful life. If not, the change should be treated as a change in accounting estimate by amortising the asset over its remaining useful life.

A reassessment of useful life is a sign that the asset should be tested for impairment. Any excess of the carrying amount over the recoverable amount should be treated as an impairment loss.

Recoverability of the carrying amount – impairment losses

To determine whether an intangible asset is impaired an entity applies IAS 36, which explains when and how an entity reviews the carrying amount of its assets, how it determines the recoverable amount of an asset, and when it recognises or reverses an impairment loss.

Retirements and disposals

An intangible asset should be derecognised on disposal or when no future economic benefits are expected from its use or disposal.

Gains or losses should be calculated as the difference between the net disposal proceeds and the carrying amount of the asset, and shall be recognised as income/expenses in the period in which the retirement or disposal occurs. The date of disposal should be determined by applying IAS 18, and the consideration should be valued initially at fair value. If the latter is deferred, then it should be recognised at the cash price equivalent.

The difference between the nominal amount of the consideration and the cash price equivalent is recognised as interest revenue under IAS 18 according to the effective yield on the receivable. However, IFRS 5 will require a transfer to current assets on the disposal decision.

Amortisation should not cease on temporary idleness unless already fully depreciated.

Disclosure

General

The following should be disclosed for each class of intangible assets – split between internally generated and other intangible assets:

1. Whether the useful lives are indefinite or finite and, if the latter, their useful lives or amortisation rates used
2. The amortisation methods adopted
3. The gross carrying amount and accumulated amortisation at start and end of the period
4. The line item of the income statement in which the amortisation charge is included
5. A reconciliation of the carrying amount at start and end of the period showing:
   - additions, split between internal, acquired and via business combinations
   - retirements and disposals
   - revaluations
   - impairment losses
   - impairment losses reversed
   - amortisation during the period
   - net exchange differences
   - other changes in carrying amount.

A class of intangible assets may include:

1. Brand names
2. Mastheads and publishing rights
3. Computer software
4. Licences and franchises
5. Copyrights, patents and other industrial property rights
6. Recipes, formulae, models, designs and prototypes
7. Intangible assets under development.

Further disaggregation may be required if it involves providing more relevant information. The financial statements shall also disclose:

1. If an intangible asset has an indefinite useful life, the carrying amount and the reasons supporting the assessment of that life; the significant factors should be described
2. A description, the carrying amount and remaining amortisation period of any individual intangible asset that is material to the entity as a whole
3. For acquired intangibles via grant, the initial fair value, their carrying amount, and whether carried under the benchmark or allowed alternative treatment for subsequent measurement

4. The existence and carrying amounts of intangibles whose title is restricted or pledged for security
5. The amount of contractual commitments for the acquisition of intangibles.

Intangible assets carried under the allowed alternative treatment

The following shall be disclosed:

1. By class of intangible assets:
   - the effective date of the revaluation
   - the carrying amount and
   - the carrying amount had the benchmark treatment been adopted (historic cost)
2. The amount of the revaluation surplus at start and end of period indicating any changes and any restrictions on distribution
3. The methods and significant assumptions applied in estimating the asset fair values.

Research and development expenditure

The aggregate amount of research and development expenditure expensed during the period should be disclosed.

Other information

An entity is encouraged to disclose the following:

1. A description of any fully amortised intangible asset that is still in use
2. A brief decription of significant intangible assets controlled by the entity but not recognised as assets as they failed to meet the recognition criteria in IAS 38 or were generated prior to IAS 38 being made effective.

SIC 32 *Intangible Assets – Website Costs* (January 2003)

Issue

A website arising from internal development should be recognised as an asset if, and only if, the general conditions for recognition of an internally generated intangible asset are satisfied. Costs incurred on a website developed solely or primarily for promoting and advertising the entity's products should be expensed as incurred, since the entity will be unable to demonstrate that such a website will generate probable future economic benefits.

3.2 IAS 17 *Leases* (revised December 2003)

Objective

The objective of IAS 17 is to prescribe, for lessees and lessors, the appropriate accounting policies and disclosures to apply to both operating and finance leases.

Scope

The standard should apply to all leases other than:

- leases to explore for minerals, oil, natural gas etc.;
- licensing agreements for motion pictures, videos, plays, manuscripts, patents and copyrights.

There is also an exemption to the measurement of investment properties held by lessees under finance leases and *vice versa* to investment properties let out as operating leases by lessors as well as those relating to biological assets governed by IAS 41.

Key definitions

Lease: an agreement whereby the lessor conveys to the lessee the right to use an asset in return for a payment or series of payments for an agreed period of time.

Finance lease: a lease that transfers substantially all the risks and rewards attached to an asset to a lessee. Title may or may not eventually be transferred (incident to ownership).

Operating lease: a lease other than a finance lease.

Net investment in the lease: the gross investment in the lease less unearned finance income.

Interest rate implicit in the lease: the discount rate that, at the inception of the lease, causes the present value of (a) the minimum lease payments and (b) the unguaranteed residual value to be equal to the sum of the fair value of the leased asset and any initial direct costs of the lessor.

Classification of leases

This is based on the extent to which risks and rewards incident to ownership lie with the lessee or lessor. Risks include idle capacity losses, obsolescence, variations in returns etc., and rewards include expectation of future profits and appreciation in the value of the residual value.

A lease is classified as finance if it transfers substantially all the risks and rewards, and an operating lease if *vice versa*.

There should be consistent treatment between lessor and lessee, but the application of common definitions could still result in the same lease being classified differently by both parties.

The decision as to whether or not there is a finance lease depends on the substance of the transaction rather than its legal form. Normally a finance lease results where:

- the lease transfers ownership of the asset to the lessee at the end of the lease term;
- the lessee has the option to purchase the asset at a price sufficiently lower than the fair value at the date the option becomes exercisable such that, at the inception of the lease, it is reasonably certain that the option will be exercised;
- the lease term is for a major part of the asset's economic life;
  at the inception of the lease, the present value of the minimum lease payments amounts to substantially all of the fair value of the leased asset; and

- the leased assets are of a specialised nature such that only the lessee can use them without major modifications being made.

Indicators of situations that individually or in combination could also lead to a lease being classified as a finance lease are:

- if the lessee can cancel the lease and the losses of cancellation are borne by the lessee;
- if gains/losses from fluctuations in fair values of the residual values fall to the lessee – e.g. rent rebate equal to most of the sale proceeds at the end of the lease;
- if the lessee has the ability to continue the lease for a secondary period at a rent substantially lower than market rent.

The decision is made at the inception of the lease, but if both parties substantially alter the terms of the lease in a manner that would have resulted in a different classification then the revised agreement should be treated as a new agreement.

Leases of land and buildings should be classified in the same way. However, land has an indefinite life and if title does not change hands then the lessee does not have substantially all the risks and rewards incident to ownership. In that case a premium paid for such a leasehold represents pre-paid lease payments which are amortised over the lease term in accordance with the pattern of benefits provided.

Accounting for leases in the financial statements of lessees

Finance lease

This should be recognised as an asset and a liability in the balance sheet of a lessee at amounts equal, at the inception of the lease, to the fair value of the leased property, net of grants and any tax credits receivable by the lessor. However, if the present value of the minimum lease payments is lower, that value should be adopted.

The discount rate adopted should be the implicit rate of return in the lease, if practicable, or if not, the lessee's incremental borrowing rate.

By capitalising finance leases, the substance of the transaction is recognised and thus financial ratios such as gearing are not distorted. It is not appropriate to net off finance lease assets and liabilities.

Initial direct costs are included as part of the amount recognised as an asset under the lease.

Lease payments should be apportioned between the finance charge and the reduction of the outstanding liability. The finance charge should be allocated to periods during the lease term so as to produce a constant rate of interest on the remaining balance of the liability for each period. Some form of approximation, however, is acceptable.

A finance lease gives rise to a depreciation charge as well as a finance cost for each period. The depreciation policy should be consistent with purchased assets and as per IAS 16 and IAS 38. If there is no reasonable certainty that the lessee will obtain ownership by the end of the lease term, the asset should be fully depreciated over the shorter of the lease term or its useful life.

It would be rare for the sum of the depreciation charge and finance cost to be the same as the lease payments made, thus the asset and related liability are unlikely to be equal after the inception of the lease. If a leased asset appears to be impaired, IAS 36 should be applied.

Disclosures

The following disclosures must be made:

1. For each class of asset, the net carrying amount at the balance sheet date
2. A reconciliation between the total of minimum lease payments (MLPs) at the balance sheet date and their present value; in addition, the total of MLPs at the balance sheet date and their present value for each of the following periods:
   - not later than 1 year
   - later than 1 year but not later than 5 years
   - later than 5 years
3. Contingent rents recognised in income for the period
4. The total of future minimum sublease payments expected to be received under non-cancellable subleases at the balance sheet date
5. A general description of the lessee's significant leasing arrangements including, but not limited to, the following:
   - the basis on which contingent rent payments are determined
   - the existence and terms of renewal or purchase options and escalation clauses, and
   - restrictions imposed by lease arrangements, such as those concerning dividends, additional debt, and further leasing.

Operating leases

Lease payments should be recognised as an expense in the income statement on a straight-line basis over the lease term unless another systematic basis is representative of the time pattern of the user's benefit.

Disclosures

The following disclosures should be made:

1. The total of future minimum lease payments under non-cancellable operating leases for each of the following periods:
   - not later than 1 year
   - later than 1 year and not later than 5 years
   - later than 5 years
2. The total of future minimum sublease payments expected to be received under non-cancellable subleases at the balance sheet date
3. Lease and sublease recognised in income for the period, with separate amounts for minimum lease payments, contingent rents, and sublease payments
4. A general description of the lessee's significant leasing arrangements including, but not limited to, the following:
   - the basis on which contingent rent payments are determined
   - the existence and terms of renewal or purchase options and escalation clauses, and
   - restrictions imposed by lease arrangements, such as those concerning dividends, additional debt, and further leasing.

Accounting for leases in the financial statements of lessors

Finance leases

Lessor should recognise these as receivables in their balance sheet at amounts equal to the net investment in the lease.

The recognition of finance income should be based on a pattern reflecting a constant periodic rate of return on the lessor's net investment outstanding in respect of the finance lease.

Any lease payments should be applied against the gross investment in the lease to reduce both the principal and the unearned finance income. Estimated unguaranteed residual values are reviewed regularly, and if a reduction occurs the income allocation over the lease term is revised and any reduction in respect of amounts already accrued is recognised immediately.

Initial direct costs such as commissions and legal fees can be either recognised immediately in income or allocated against income over the lease term.

Manufacturer/lessors

Manufacturer or dealer lessors should recognise their selling profit/loss in income in accordance with normal sales. If artificially low rates of interest are quoted, selling profit should be restricted to that which would apply if a commercial rate were charged. Initial direct costs should be expensed in the income statement at the inception of the lease.

These contracts lead to the creation of two types of income:

- profit/loss equivalent to outright sale; and
- the finance income over the lease term.

The difference between the sales revenue (i.e. fair value of the asset) and the cost of sale (i.e. cost or carrying amount of the leased property less present value of the unguaranteed residual value) is selling profit, which should be accounted as per the normal policy for sales.

Manufacturer or dealer lessors sometimes quote artificially low rates of interest in order to attract customers. The use of such a rate would result in an excessive portion of the total income from the transaction being recognised at time of sale. If artificially low rates of interest are quoted, selling profit would be restricted to that which would apply if a commercial rate were charged. Initial costs are immediately expensed, as they relate mainly to earning the manufacturer's/dealer's profit.

The following should be disclosed:

1. A reconciliation between the total gross investment in the lease at the balance sheet date and the present value of MLPs at the balance sheet date; in addition, the total gross investment in the lease and the present value of MLPs receivable at the balance sheet date, for each of the following periods:
   - not later than 1 year
   - later than 1 year and not later than 5 years
   - later than 5 years
2. Unearned finance income
3. The unguaranteed residual values accruing to the benefit of the lessor
4. The accumulated residual values accruing to the benefit of the lessor
5. The accumulated allowance for uncollectible MLPs receivable
6. Contingent rents recognised in income
7. A general description of the lessor's significant leasing arrangements.

Operating leases

Lessors should record assets in balance sheets according to their nature.

Lease income should be recognised on a straight-line basis unless a more systematic basis would be more representative of the time pattern in which the benefits deriving from the asset are diminished.

Initial direct costs are either deferred and allocated to income over the lease term in proportion to rent income, or are recognised as expenses in the income statement in the period they are incurred.

Depreciation should be on a basis consistent with the lessor's normal depreciation policy for similar assets, and calculated as per IAS 16. If the asset becomes impaired, IAS 36 must be applied.

No selling profit is recognised, as the agreement is not the equivalent of a sale.

Lessors should disclose the following:

1. The future MLPs under non-cancellable operating leases, in aggregate, and for each of the following periods:
   - not later than 1 year
   - later than 1 year but not later than 5 years
   - later than 5 years
2. Total contingent rents recognised in income
3. A general description of the lessor's significant leasing arrangements.

Sale and leaseback transactions

The lease payment and the sale price are usually interdependent as they are negotiated as a package. The accounting treatment depends on the type of lease involved.

Finance lease

Any excess of sales proceeds over carrying value should not be immediately expensed, but instead deferred and amortised over the lease term. Effectively, the lessor provides finance to the lessee with the asset as security, thus it is not appropriate to regard an excess of sales proceeds over the carrying amount as income. Such excess is deferred and amortised over the lease term.

Operating lease

Any profit/loss should be recognised immediately. If the sale price is below fair value, any profit/loss should be recognised immediately except that if the loss is compensated by future lease payments at below market price, it should be deferred and amortised in proportion to the lease payments over the period for which the asset is expected to be used. If the sale price is above fair value, the excess over fair value should be deferred and amortised over the period for which the asset is expected to be used. It is effectively a normal sale transaction, and any profit/loss is recognised immediately.

If the fair value at the time of sale and leaseback is less than the carrying amount of the asset, a loss equal to the amount of the difference between the carrying amount and fair value should be recognised immediately.

Disclosures for lessees/lessors should be the same as for other lease disclosures for lessees and lessors.

SIC 15 *Operating Leases – Incentives* (July 1999)

Issue

In negotiating a new or renewed operating lease, the lessor may provide incentives for the lessee to enter into the agreement. Examples include upfront cash to the lessee, or the reimbursement or assumption by the lessor of costs to the lessee (e.g. relocation costs, leasehold improvements etc.). Alternatively, initial periods of the lease term may be agreed to be rent free or at a reduced rent.

The issue is how incentives in an operating lease should be recognised in the financial statements of both lessor and lessee.

Consensus

All incentives for the agreement of a new or renewed operating lease should be recognised as an integral part of the net consideration agreed for the use of the leased asset, irrespective of the incentive's nature or form or timing of payments.

The lessor should recognise the aggregate cost of incentives as a reduction of rental income over the lease term, on a straight-line basis unless another systematic basis is representative of the time pattern over which the benefit of the leased asset is diminished.

The lessee should recognise the aggregate benefit of incentives as a reduction in rental expense over the lease term, on a straight-line basis unless another systematic basis is representative of the time pattern of the lessee's benefit from the use of the leased asset.

Costs incurred by the lessee, including costs in connection with a pre-existing lease, should be accounted for by the lessee in accordance with IASs applicable to those costs, including costs which are effectively reimbursed through an incentive arrangement.

SIC 27 *Evaluating the Substance of Transactions in the Legal Form of a Lease*

This SIC outlines the approach that must be taken, when assessing an arrangement involving the legal form of a lease, to determine whether, in substance, the arrangement results in a lease under IAS 17. Where the arrangement does not meet the definition of a lease, IAS 17 is not applicable and the principles of the Framework for the Preparation and Presentation of Financial Statements, and other relevant standards, should be used to determine the appropriate accounting for this arrangement.

3.3   IAS 2 *Inventories* (revised December 2003)

Objective

The objective of IAS 2 is to prescribe the accounting treatment for inventories and to determine the cost to be recognised as an asset which will be subsequently expended. I also provides guidance on cost formulas to adopt, and when to write down inventories to net realisable value.

Scope

The standard applies only to inventories. It does not apply to:

- work in progress arising in construction and service contracts (see IAS 11);
- financial instruments (see IAS 39);
- biological assets related to agricultural activity (see IAS 41);
- inventories of agricultural and forest products and mineral ores to the extent that they can be measured at NRV i.e. crops harvested (see IAS 41);
- commodity broker traders who measure inventories at NRV e.g. active market, sale assumed under forward contracts.

Key definitions

Inventories: assets

- held for sale in the ordinary course of business;
- in the process of production; or
- in the form of materials, supplies to be consumed in production or rendering of services.

Net realisable value: the estimated selling price in the ordinary course of business less estimated costs of completion and estimated selling costs.

Examples of inventories include retail merchandise, land held for resale and finished goods.

Measurement of inventories

Inventories should be measured at the lower of cost and net realisable value.

1. *Cost of inventories.* This includes all costs of purchase, costs of conversion and other costs in bringing the inventories to their present location and condition.
2. *Costs of purchase.* These comprise the purchase price, import duties, transport and handling costs. However, trade discounts and rebates must be deducted.
3. *Costs of conversion.* These include direct labour and a systematic allocation of overheads, both fixed and variable, incurred in converting materials into finished goods.

   Fixed overheads (maintenance, depreciation, factory management costs) should be allocated on the basis of normal capacity – i.e. that which could be achieved on average over a number of periods or seasons. The actual may be adopted if it approximates normal activity. Unallocated overheads are expended. In abnormally high production periods the allocation should be decreased so that inventories are not measured above cost.

   Variable production overheads are allocated on the basis of the actual use of the production facilities.

   Where joint products are being produced a suitable allocation method should be adopted – e.g. relative sales value. By-products should be measured at NRV and deducted from the cost of the main product.
4. *Other costs.* These are only permitted if bringing inventories to their present location and condition – e.g. cost of specific designing of products for customers. Examples of

specific exclusions are:
- abnormal costs (e.g. wasted materials, labour)
- storage costs
- administration overheads
- selling costs.

However, borrowing costs are included provided they meet the criteria in IAS 23.

5. *Costs of a service provider.* These should primarily be labour and personnel costs plus attributable overheads. Selling and administrative costs are not included. No profit margins may be included either. Costs of agricultural produce harvested from biological assets – as per IAS 41 – are valued at fair value less costs of sale at harvest.

6. *Costs of agricultural produce harvested from biological assets.* These are measured initially at their fair value less estimated point of sale costs at the point of harvest.

7. *Techniques for the measurement of cost.* Standard cost and the retail gross margin method may be adopted if their results approximate cost. They must, however, be regularly reviewed and revised, if necessary. The retail method must be careful to deduct gross margins, but care is particularly required in cases of marked down inventories not to reduce stocks below cost where clearly they are worth more.

Cost formulas

Costs should be specifically identified to specific projects, where possible. That, however, is not appropriate where there are large numbers of items of inventories that are ordinarily interchangeable. In those cases the method selected should be FIFO or weighted average.

The same formula should be adopted for all inventories having a similar nature and use to the entity. A difference in geographical location, by itself, would not be sufficient to justify the use of different cost formulas.

FIFO results in inventory valuations being up to date. LIFO would not be an acceptable method, as inventories tend to be valued at out-of-date prices.

Net realisable value (NRV)

Where the cost of inventories may not be recoverable (e.g. damaged, obsolete, selling prices declined etc.), then inventories should not be carried in excess of the amounts expected to be realised from their sale or use.

Inventories are usually written down to NRV on an item-by-item basis. It is not appropriate to write down inventories based on a general classification (e.g. finished goods, or all inventories in a particular industry).

Estimates of NRV are based on the most reliable evidence of amounts expected to realise, and should take into account price fluctuations post-balance sheet date to the extent that they can confirm conditions at that date.

If inventories are for a specific contract reference should be made only to the contract price of that specific contract, but if for sale generally then to general selling prices.

Materials are not written down below cost provided the finished products in which they will be incorporated are expected to be sold at or above cost. However, if a decline in material prices indicates that the cost of finished goods exceeds NRV then the materials should be written down to NRV using replacement cost as the best available measure.

NRV should be reviewed in every subsequent period, and if circumstances reveal that the writedown is no longer appropriate, it should be reversed.

Recognition as an expense

When inventories are sold, they should be expended in the period when the revenue is recognised. Any writedowns or reversals should be recorded in the period they occur.

If some inventories are used in the construction of property, plant etc., they should be capitalised and expended over the useful life of the fixed assets created.

Disclosure

The financial statements should disclose the following:

1. The accounting policies adopted in measuring inventories, including cost formulas
2. The total carrying amount of inventories broken into appropriate classifications
3. The carrying amount at fair value less costs to date
4. The amount expended in the period
5. The amount of any writedowns of inventories
6. The amount of any reversal of any writedowns
7. The circumstances or events that led to the writedown(s)
8. The carrying amount of inventories pledged as security for liabilities.

Common classifications include retail merchandise, production supplies, materials, work in progress and finished goods.

3.4   IAS 11 *Construction Contracts* (1978, revised 1993)

The basic principle of IAS 11 is that when the outcome of a construction contract can be estimated reliably, contract revenue and associated costs with the construction contract should be recognised as revenue and expenses respectively by reference to the stage of completion of the contract activity at the balance sheet date. An expected loss on the construction contract should be recognised as an expense immediately.

Objective

The objective of IAS 11 is to prescribe the accounting treatment of revenue and costs associated with construction contracts.

Key definition

Construction contracts: a construction contract is a contract specifically negotiated for the construction of an asset or group of inter-related assets. Construction contracts include contracts for architectural, engineering, demolition, and other services related to the construction of an asset.

Under IAS 11, if a contract covers two or more assets, the construction of each asset should be accounted for separately if:

- separate proposals were submitted for each asset;
- the portions of the contract relating to each contract were negotiated separately; and
- the costs and revenues of each asset can be measured.

Otherwise, the contract should be accounted for in its entirety. Two or more contracts should be accounted for as a single contract if they were negotiated together and the work is inter-related.

If a contract gives the customer an option to order one or more additional assets, the construction of each additional asset should be accounted for as a separate contract if either (a) the additional asset differs significantly from the original asset(s), or (b) the price of the additional asset is separately negotiated.

Contract revenue and costs

Contract revenue

Contract revenue should comprise:

1. The initial amount of revenue agreed in the contract; and
2. Variations in contract work, claims and incentive payments:
   - to the extent that it is probable that they will result in revenue, and
   - they are capable of being reliably measured.

Contract costs

Contract costs should comprise:

1. Costs that relate directly to the specific contract
2. Costs that are attributable to contract activity in general and can be allocated to the contract
3. Such other costs as are specifically chargeable to the customer under the terms of the contract.

Costs that relate directly to a specific contract include:

1. Site labour costs, including supervision
2. Costs of materials used in construction
3. Depreciation of plant used on the contract
4. Costs of moving plant and materials to and from the contract
5. Costs of hiring plant
6. Costs of design and technical assistance directly attributable to the contract
7. The estimated costs of rectification and guarantee work, including expected warranty costs
8. Claims from third parties.

Borrowing costs may be capitalised under IAS 23.

Determining when contract revenue and expenses may be recognised

Fixed price contracts

In the case of a fixed price contract, the outcome of a construction contract can be estimated reliably when all the following conditions are satisfied:

- the total contract revenue can be measured reliably;
- it is probable that the economic benefits associated with the contract will flow to the enterprise;
- both the contract costs to complete and the stage of completion at the balance sheet date can be measured reliably;
- the contract costs attributable to the contract can be clearly identified and measured reliably so that actual contract costs incurred can be compared with prior estimates.

Cost plus contracts

In the case of a cost plus contract, the outcome of a construction contract can be estimated reliably when both the following conditions are satisfied:

- it is probable that the economic benefits associated with the contract will flow to the enterprise;
- the contract costs attributable to the contract, whether or not specifically reimbursable, can be clearly identified and measured reliably.

The stage of completion of a contract may be determined in a variety of ways. The enterprise uses the method that measures reliably the work performed. Depending on the nature of the contract, the methods may include:

- the proportion that contract costs incurred for work performed to date bear to the estimated total contract costs;
- surveys of work performed;
- completion of a physical proportion of the contract work.

Progress payments and advances from customers often do not reflect the work performed. When the stage of completion is determined by reference to the contract costs incurred to date, only those contract costs that reflect work performed are included in costs incurred to date. Examples of contract costs which are excluded are:

- contract costs that relate to future activity on the contract such as costs of materials that have been delivered to a contract site or set aside for use in a contract but not yet installed, used or applied during contract performance, unless the materials have been made specifically for the contract; and
- payments made to sub contractors in advance of work performed under the sub-contract.

When the outcome of a construction contract cannot be estimated reliably:

- revenue should be recognised only to the extent of contract costs incurred that it is probable will be recoverable; and
- contract costs should be recognised as an expense in the period in which they are incurred.

An expected loss on the construction contract should be recognised as an expense immediately.

Expected losses on contract

When it is probable that total contract costs will exceed total contract revenue, the expected loss should be recognised as an expense immediately.

Disclosure

An enterprise should disclose:

1. The amount of contract revenue recognised as revenue in the period
2. The methods used to determine the contract revenue recognised in the period
3. The methods used to determine the stage of completion of contracts in progress.

An enterprise should disclose each of the following for contracts in progress at the balance sheet date:

1. The aggregate amount of costs incurred and recognised profits less recognised losses to date
2. The amount of advances received
3. The amount of retentions.

Retentions are amounts of progress billings which are not paid until the satisfaction of conditions specified in the contract for the payment of such amounts or until defects have been rectified. Progress billings are amounts billed for work performed on a contract whether or not they have been paid by the customer. Advances are amounts received by the contractor before the related work is performed.

An enterprise should present:

1. The gross amount due from customers for contract work as an asset
2. The gross amount due to customers for contract work as a liability.

3.5   Examination questions

Question 3.1: Satellite (ACCA)

(This question investigates four separate accounting issues which could affect the publication of the final consolidated balance sheet. These cover:

1. *Provisions under IAS 37 for onerous leases*
2. *Whether or not an intangible asset may be recognised under IAS 38*
3. *The use of forward rate contracts in hedging contracts under IAS 32*
4. *How to account for contingent consideration in the calculation of goodwill under IFRS 3.*

The balance sheet then has to be redrawn in order to comply with the above standards.)

Satellite, a public limited company, has produced the following draft consolidated balance sheet as at 30 November 2000:

Group Balance Sheet as at 30 November 2000

	$000
Non-current assets	
Intangible assets	5,180
Tangible assets	38,120
	43,300
Net current assets	27,900
Total assets less current liabilities	71,200
Capital and reserves:	
Called up share capital	16,100
Share premium account	5,000
Accumulated profits	27,400
	48,500
Minority interest	9,100
Non-current liabilities – interest bearing borrowings	12,700
Provisions for liabilities and charges	900
	71,200

The group accountant has asked your advice on several matters. These issues are set out below, and have not been dealt with in the draft group financial statements:

(i) Satellite has buildings under an operating lease. A requirement of the operating lease for the corporate offices is that the asset is returned in good condition. The operating lease was signed in the current year and lasts for 6 years. Satellite intends to refurbish the building in 6 years' time at a cost of $6 million in order to meet the requirements of the lease. This amount includes the cost of renovating the exterior of the building and is based on current price levels. Currently there is evidence that due to severe and exceptional weather damage the company will have to spend $1.2 million in the next year on having the exterior of the building renovated. The company feels that this expenditure will reduce the refurbishment cost at the end of the lease by an equivalent amount. There is no provision for the above expenditure in the financial statements.

An 80% owned subsidiary company, Universe, has a leasehold property (depreciated historical cost $8 million at 30 November 2000). It has been modified to include a sports facility for the employees. Under the terms of the lease, the warehouse must be restored to its original state when the lease expires in 10 years' time or earlier termination. The present value of the costs of reinstatement are likely to be $2 million and the directors wish to provide for $200,000 per annum for 10 years. The lease was signed and operated from 1 December 1999. The directors estimate that the lease has a recoverable value of $9.5 million at 30 November 2000, and have not provided for any of the above amounts.

Additionally, Satellite owns buildings at a carrying value of $20 million, which will require repair expenditure of approximately $6 million over the next 5 years. No provision has been made for this amount in the financial statements and depreciation is charged on leasehold buildings at 10% per annum and on owned buildings at 5% per annum, on the straight-line basis.

(ii) Universe has developed a database during the year to 30 November 2000 and it is included in intangible non-current assets at a cost of $3 million. The asset comprises the internal and external costs of developing the database. The cost of all intangible assets is amortised over 5 years, and 1 year's amortisation has been charged. The database is used to produce a technical accounting manual, which is used by the whole group and sold to other parties. Net revenue of $2 million is expected from sales of the manual over its 4-year life. It has quickly become a market leader in this field. Any costs of maintaining the database and the technical manual are written off as incurred. The technical manual requires substantial revision every 4 years.

(iii) On 1 December 1999, Satellite entered into an agreement with a wholly owned overseas subsidiary, Domingo, to purchase components at a value of 2.1 million unos on which Domingo made a profit of 20% on selling price. The goods were to be delivered on 31 January 2000 with the payment due on 31 March 2000. Satellite took out a foreign currency contract on 1 December 1999 to buy 2.1 million unos on 31 March 2000 at the forward rate of $1 = 1.4 unos.

At 30 November 2000, Satellite had two-thirds of the components in inventory. The spot rates were as follows:

	$1 equivalent
1 December 1999	1.3 unos
31 January 2000	1.46 unos
31 March 2000	1.45 unos
30 November 2000	1.35 unos

The initial purchase of the inventory had been recorded on receipt at the forward rate and the forward rate had been used for the year end valuation of inventory. The directors are unsure as to how to treat the items above both for accounting and disclosure purposes, but they have heard that the simplest method is to translate the asset and liability at the forward rate and they wish to use this method.

(iv) Satellite purchased a wholly owned subsidiary company, Globe, on 1 December 1998. The vendors commenced a legal action on 31 March 2000 over the amount of the purchase consideration which was based on the performance of the subsidiary. An amount had been paid to the vendors and included in the calculation of goodwill, but the vendors disputed the amount of this payment. The court made a decision on 30 November 2000 which requires Satellite to pay an additional $8 million to the vendors within 3 months. The directors do not know how to treat the additional purchase consideration and have not accounted for the item. Goodwill is written off over 5 years with no time apportionment in the year of purchase.

(Assume that the effect of the time value of money is not material.)

Required

(a) Discuss how the above four issues should be dealt with in the group financial statements of Satellite, stating the nature of the accounting entries required.

(b) Prepare a revised Group Balance Sheet at 30 November 2000 taking into account the four issues above.

Question 3.2: H (CIMA)

(This question reviews a more specialised aspect of IAS 38 and requires a discussion of whether or not research expenditure should be capitalised. It also requires a knowledge of the criteria in IAS 38 to permit capitalisation of development expenditure.)

H is a major electronics company. It spends a substantial amount of policy on research and development. The company has a policy of capitalising development expenditure, but writes off pure and applied research expenditure immediately in accordance with the requirements of IAS 38 *Intangible Assets*.

The company's latest annual report included a page of voluntary disclosures about the effectiveness of the company's research programme. This indicated that the company's prosperity depended on the development of new products and that this could be a very long process. In order to maintain its technical lead, the company often funded academic research studies into theoretical areas, some of which led to breakthroughs which H was able to patent and develop into new product ideas. The company claimed that the money spent in this way as a good investment because for every 20 unsuccessful projects there was usually at least one valuable discovery which generated enough profit to cover the whole cost of the research activities. Unfortunately, it was impossible to tell in advance which projects would succeed in this way.

A shareholder expressed dismay at H's policy of writing off research costs in this manner. He felt that this was unduly pessimistic given that the company earned a good return from its research activities. He felt that the company should depart from the requirements of IAS 38 in order to achieve a fair presentation.

Required

(a) Explain why it might be justifiable for H to capitalise its research costs.
(b) Explain why IAS 38 imposes a rigid set of rules which prevent the capitalisation of all research expenditure and make it difficult to capitalise development expenditure.
(c) Explain whether the requirements of IAS 38 are likely to discourage companies such as H from investing in research activities.
(d) Describe the advantages and disadvantages of offering companies the option of departing from the detailed requirements of International Accounting Standards in order to achieve a fair presentation.

Question 3.3: S (CIMA)

(This question covers the basics of IAS 17 Leases and explains the impact of choosing operating as opposed to finance leases on accounting ratios. It also requires students to discuss the opportunities still available for the creative accountant to influence the profit and loss account and balance sheet position.)

S is a large manufacturing company. The company needs to purchase a major piece of equipment which is vital to the production process. S does not have sufficient cash available to buy this equipment. It cannot raise the necessary finance by issuing shares because it would not be cost-effective to have a share issue for the amount involved. The directors are also unwilling to borrow because the company already has a very high level of debt in its balance sheet.

C Bank has offered to lease the equipment to S. The bank has proposed a finance package in which S would take the equipment on a 2-year lease. The intention is that S will take out a second 2-year lease at the conclusion of the initial period and a third at the conclusion of that one. By that time the equipment will have reached the end of its useful life.

C Bank will not require S to commit itself in writing to the two secondary lease periods. Instead, S will agree in writing to refurbish the equipment to a brand new condition before returning it to C Bank. This condition will, however, be waived if the lease is subsequently extended to a total of 6 years or more. Once the equipment is used, it would be prohibitively expensive to refurbish it.

S's directors are very interested in the arrangement proposed by C Bank. They believe that each of the 2-year contracts could be accounted for as an operating lease because each covers only a fraction of the equipment's expected useful life.

Required

(a) Explain how the decision to treat the lease as an operating lease rather than a finance lease would affect S's income statement, balance sheet and any accounting ratios based on these.
(b) Explain whether S should account for the proposed lease as an operating lease or as a finance lease.
(c) It has been suggested that forcing companies to disclose liabilities in respect of finance leases in their balance sheets has an adverse effect on their gearing ratios. Explain whether the classification of a lease as a finance lease can actually affect a company.
(d) It has been suggested that the rules governing the preparation of financial statements leave some scope for the preparers of financial statements to influence the profit figure or balance sheet position. Explain whether you agree with this suggestion.

Question 3.4: Leese (ACCA)

(Following on from the previous question, Leese *requires the student to explain why the IASB is likely to abolish the distinction between operating and finance leases and force all leases on to the balance sheet of the user. It also tests the ability of students to redraft the income statement and balance sheet and to reflect those changes and impact on performance ratios.)*

Leese, a public limited company and a subsidiary of an American holding company, operates its business in the services sector. It currently uses operating leases to partly finance its usage of land and buildings and motor vehicles. The following abbreviated financial information was produced as at 30 November 2000:

Income Statement for the year ending 30 November 2000

	$m
Revenue	580
Profit on ordinary activities before taxation	88
Taxation on profit on ordinary activities	(30)
Profit on ordinary activities after taxation	58

Balance Sheet as at 30 November 2000

Non-current assets	200
Net current assets	170
	370

Share capital	200
Accumulated profits	120
	320
Non-current liabilities (interest free loan from holding company)	50
	370

Notes:

Operating lease rentals for the year – paid 30 November 2000

	$m
Land and buildings	30
Motor vehicles	10

Future minimum operating lease payments for leases payable on 30 November each year were as follows:

Year	Land and buildings $m	Motor vehicles $m
30 November 2001	28	9
30 November 2002	25	8
30 November 2003	20	7
Thereafter	500	–
Total future minimum operating lease payments (non-cancellable)	573	24

The company is concerned about the potential impact of bringing operating leases onto the balance sheet on its profitability and its key financial ratios. The directors have heard that the International Accounting Standards Board (IASB) is moving towards this stance and wish to seek advice on the implications for the company.

The directors, for the purpose of determining the impact of the IASB's proposals, have decided to value current and future operating lease rentals at their present value.

The appropriate interest rate for discounting cash flows to present value is 5% and the current average remaining lease life for operating lease rentals after 30 November 2003 is deemed to be 10 years.

Depreciation on land and buildings is 5% per annum and on motor vehicles is 25% per annum with a full year's charge in the year of acquisition. The rate of income tax is 30%. Assume that operating leases payments are allowable for taxation purposes and that capitalised finance leases attract tax relief in respect of finance costs and depreciation of the lease. The operating lease agreements commenced on 30 November 2000.

Required

(a) Discuss the reasons why accounting standard setters are proposing to bring operating leases on to the balance sheets of companies.

(b) Show the effect on the Income Statement for the year ending 30 November 2000 and the Balance Sheet as at 30 November 2000 of Leese capitalising its operating leases.

(c) Discuss the specific impact on the key performance ratios and the general business impact of Leese capitalising its operating leases.

Question 3.5: Petroplant

(Petroplant is the first of two questions covering the issue of construction contracts. It takes the student through the life of one contract over a 3-year period and determines both income and balance sheet extracts. In addition, it incorporates a variation in the contract as well as possible incentive payments and how these should be incorporated in contract revenue.)

Petroplant is a large company whose activity is the construction of oil refineries. Petroplant prepares its financial statements to 30 September each year. On 1 April 2000 it was successful in securing a contract to construct an oil refinery for Oiltex.

The contract is scheduled for completion on 30 June 2002. The contract contains a completion clause whereby if the contract is completed within 1 month of the scheduled date, the agreed price of $1,500 million will be paid. However, if completion is more than one calendar month ahead of schedule then an incentive of 2% of the agreed price is payable by Oiltex. Conversely, if the contract is more than 1 month late then Oiltex will deduct a penalty on equivalent terms to the incentive.

In addition to the completion clause, the contract contains a cost escalation clause whereby a 3% increase in the contract price will be paid if labour costs rise by more than 10% from the start of the contract (as measured by a government index). This occurred in May 2002.

During the construction of the oil refining plant the price of crude oil increased dramatically and Oiltex negotiated a variation to the design and construction of the plant such that it would be suitable to produce petrol from coal instead of crude oil. Oiltex agreed a price of a further $200 million for the variation. Petroplant estimated the cost of adapting the plant would be $120 million. The incentive/penalty clause does not apply to the variation nor does the labour escalation clause. No adjustment was made to the scheduled completion date as a result of the variation.

The following details relate to the progress of the contract. All estimates are at the end of the relevant year and can be taken as being reliable.

Year to 30 September	2000 $ million	2001 $million	2002 $ million
Estimated total cost (original contract)	1,200	1,230	
Actual costs to date (original contract)	300	740	1,265
Estimated variation costs		120	
Actual variation cost to date		70	115
Estimated date of completion	On time	6 weeks early	Completed 10 August 2002
Agreed value of work completed:			
original contract	330	800	1,250
variation		60	150
cumulative progress billings received	280	1,100	Paid in full

Petroplant determines the stage of completion of its contracts by the proportion that the cost incurred to date bears to the total estimated contract costs. Contract revenues should include the appropriate proportion of cost escalations and incentives/penalties from the time they are reasonably foreseeable. The variation i considered to be part of the original contract (from the date it was agreed), and not a separate contract.

No profit is recognised on contracts until they are at least 20% complete.

Question 3.6: S (CIMA)

(The final question in the chapter investigates two construction contracts. The first (deep-sea fishing boat) is a typical profit maker and requires revenues and costs to be recorded as the contract progresses. However, the second (ferry) is an example where the contract is clearly a loss maker and there is the need therefore, under IAS 11, to provide in full immediately for all estimated losses to the end of that contract.)

S is a shipbuilder which is currently working on two contracts:

	Deep-sea fishing boat $000	Small passenger ferry $000
Contract price (fixed)	3,000	5,000
Date work commenced	1 October 2000	1 October 2001
Proportion of work completed during the year ended 30 September 2001	30%	Nil
Invoiced to customer during year ended 30 September 2001	900	Nil
Cash received from customer during year ended 30 September 2001	800	Nil
Costs incurred during year ended 30 September 2001	650	Nil
Estimated cost to complete at 30 September 2001	1,300	
Proportion of work completed during the year ended 30 September 2002	25%	45%
Invoiced to customer during year ended 30 September 2002	750	2,250
Cash received from customer during year ended 30 September 2002	700	2,250
Costs incurred during year ended 30 September 2002	580	1,900
Estimated cost to complete at 30 September 2002	790	3,400

S recognises revenue and profit on long-term contracts in relation to the proportion of work completed.

Required

(a) Calculate the figures that will appear in S's income statement for the year ended 30 September 2002 and its balance sheet at that date in respect of each of these contracts.

(b) The IASB's *Framework for the Preparation and Presentation of Financial Statements* (Framework) effectively defines losses on individual transactions in such a way that they are associated with increases in liabilities or decreases in assets. A liability is defined as 'a present obligation of the enterprise arising from past events, the settlement of which is expected to result in an outflow from the enterprise of resources embodying economic benefits'. Explain how the definition of losses contained in the Framework could be used to justify the requirement of IAS 11 *Construction Contracts* to recognise losses in full on long-term contracts as soon as they can be foreseen.

Balance sheet: liabilities

4.1 IAS 37 *Provisions, Contingent Liabilities and Contingent Assets* (May 1975, revised September 1988)

Objective

IAS 37 prescribes the accounting and disclosure for all provisions, contingent liabilities and contingent assets, except for those listed below.

Scope

The following are exceptions:

- those financial instruments carried at fair value (see IAS 39);
- executory contracts (neither party performed nor both partially performed), except where onerous;
- insurance enterprises from contracts with policyholders (see IFRS 4);
- those covered by another IAS, e.g. IAS 11, 12, 17, 19, nor any revenue covered by IAS 18;
- reduction in asset values e.g. depreciation, doubtful debts.

The objective of IAS 37 is to ensure that appropriate recognition criteria and measurement bases are applied to provisions, contingent liabilities and contingent assets, and that sufficient information is disclosed in the notes to enable users to understand their nature, timing and amount.

Restructuring provisions are included in IAS 37, but additional disclosures may be required by IFRS 5 on discontinuing operations.

Key definitions

Provision: a liability of uncertain timing or amount.

Legal obligation: an obligation that derives from a contract, legislation or other operation of law.

Constructive obligation: an obligation that derives from an enterprise's actions where:

- by an established pattern of past practice, published policies or a sufficiently specific current statement, the enterprise has indicated to other parties that it will accept certain responsibilities; and
- as a result, the enterprise has created a valid expectation on the part of those parties that it will discharge those responsibilities.

Contingent liability:

- a possible obligation that arises from past events and whose existence will be confirmed only by the occurrence or non-occurrence of one or more uncertain future events not wholly within the control of the enterprise; or
- a present obligation that arises from past events but is not recognised because either it is not probable that an outflow of resources embodying economic benefits will be required to settle the obligation; or the amount of the obligation cannot be measured with sufficient reliability.

Contingent asset: a possible asset that arises from past events and whose existence will be confirmed only by the occurrence or non-occurrence of one or more uncertain future events not wholly within the control of the enterprise.

Provisions and other liabilities

What distinguishes provisions from other liabilities is uncertainty about the timing or amount of future expenditure. Trade payables are certain liabilities to pay for goods or services received, and accruals are certain liabilities for goods or services received not invoiced or formerly agreed as due to employees/suppliers.

Provisions, due to their uncertain nature, are reported separately, whereas accruals are reported as part of trade and other payables.

Relationship between provisions and contingent liabilities

The key difference between provisions and contingencies is that the latter are not recognised because their existence will be confirmed only by the occurrence or non occurrence of one or more uncertain future events not wholly within the entity's control or else they fail to meet the recognition criteria for liabilities.

Provisions

These represent either a legal or a constructive obligation, but also they must result in a probable outflow of resources to another party.

Contingent liabilities

Contingent liabilities consist of possible obligations or those that fail to pass recognition criteria – i.e. it is not probable that an outflow of resources embodying economic benefits will be required to settle the obligation, or the amount of the obligation cannot be measured with sufficient reliability.

Recognition

Provisions

A provision should be recognised when:

- an enterprise has a legal or constructive obligation;
- it is probable that an outflow of resources will be required to settle the obligation; and
- a reliable estimate can be made of the obligation.

In rare cases where it is not clear whether or not there is an obligation, a past event is deemed to give rise to a present obligation if it is more likely than not that a present obligation exists at the balance sheet date. All available evidence should be considered, including the opinion of experts.

The financial statements deal with the financial position at the period end, not with the future. No provision can be recognised for costs that need to be incurred in the future. It must only be those that existed at the balance sheet date.

However, provisions are required for penalties, clean-up costs and decommissioning costs, as these are legal obligations. In contrast, expenditure to operate in a future way by fitting smoke filters would not be permitted as the entity could change its method of operation to avoid the liability.

For a liability to be created it is not necessary to know the identity of the party to whom the liability is owed – it may be to the public at large. A board decision, by itself, does not result in a constructive obligation unless that decision has been communicated before the balance sheet date to those affected by it.

An event may not immediately give rise to an obligation, but may do so in the future because of a change in law or statement to make the obligation constructive. If a new law has yet to be finalised, an obligation only arises when the legislation is virtually certain to be enacted.

An entity should be able to determine a range of possible outcomes and therefore make an estimate of the obligation that is sufficiently reliable to use when recognising a provision. In extremely rare cases where no reliable estimate can be made, a liability exists that cannot be recognised. Instead, it should be disclosed as a contingent liability.

Contingent liabilities

An enterprise should not recognise a contingent liability. Instead it should be disclosed unless the possibility of an outflow of resources is remote.

Where an entity is jointly and severally liable for an obligation, that part that is expected to be met by other parties is treated as a contingent liability. This must be assessed continually to determine whether an outflow has become probable. If that is the case, it will become a provision in the year in which the change in probability occurs.

Contingent assets

An entity should not recognise a contingent asset since this may result in the recognition of income that may never be realised. However, when realisation is virtually certain, then the related asset should be recognised.

A contingent asset should be disclosed where an inflow of benefits is probable.

Contingent assets are not recognised since this may result in recognition of income that may never be realised. However, when realisation is virtually certain then the related asset is not a contingent asset and should be recognised. Contingent assets should be continually assessed to ensure that they are appropriately accounted for.

Measurement

Best estimate
The amount recognised as a provision should be a best estimate of the expenditure required to settle the present obligation at the balance sheet date.

It is the amount an entity would rationally pay to settle at the balance sheet date or to transfer it to a third party. Often that amount would be prohibitive to settle. However, the estimate that would rationally be paid would be the best estimate of expenditure required to settle.

The estimates of outcomes and financial effect should be determined by the judgement of management supplemented by experience of similar transactions and independent experts (see Example 4.1). That should include any additional evidence discovered in the post balance sheet period.

Where a large population is involved the obligation should be estimated by weighing up all possible outcomes by their associated probabilities, i.e. expected value. Where there is a continuous range of possible outcomes and each point in that range is as likely as any other, the midpoint of the range is used.

Example 4.1
Best estimate

An entity sells goods with a warranty that covers defects within first 6 months after purchase. If minor defects were detected, repair costs of £1 m would be incurred; if major, £4 m. Past experience and future expectations indicate that 75% of goods sold will have no defects, 20% minor and 5% major.

The expected value of cost of repairs is therefore 75% × Nil + 20% × £1 m + 5% × £4 m = £400,000.

Where a single obligation is being measured, the most likely outcome should be chosen. However, an entity must consider other outcomes – e.g. if it must rectify a serious fault and assumes the most likely outcome to be £1,000, a provision for a larger amount is made if there is a significant chance that further attempts to rectify the fault will be necessary.

The provision should be measured before tax. Any tax consequences are dealt with in IAS 12.

Risks and uncertainties
The risks and uncertainties surrounding events should be considered in reaching the best estimate of a provision. Risk describes the variability of outcomes. A risk adjustment may require an increase in a liability. However, the existence of uncertainty does not justify the creation of excessive provisions.

Disclosure of the uncertainties surrounding the amount of the expenditure is required.

Present value

Where the time value of money is material, the amount of a provision should be its present value. The discount rate should be a pre-tax rate that reflects the risks for which future cash flow estimates have been adjusted.

Future events

Future events that may affect the amount required to settle an obligation should be reflected in the amount of a provision where there is sufficient evidence that they will occur.

It is appropriate to include expected cost reductions associated with past experience in applying existing technology but not to anticipate the development of new technology unless that is supported by objective evidence.

The effect of possible new legislation is considered when measuring an existing obligation, if the legislation is virtually certain to be enacted. Evidence is required both of what the legislation will demand and of whether or not it is virtually certain to be enacted and implemented. In many cases sufficient objective evidence will not exist until the new legislation is actually enacted.

Expected disposal of assets

Gains from the expected disposal of assets should not be taken into account in measuring a provision. Instead an entity recognises gains on disposal at the time specified in more specific IASs, when dealing with the assets concerned.

Reimbursements

Where some of the expenditure is expected to be reimbursed by another party, the reimbursement should be recognised when, and only when, it is virtually certain that reimbursement will be received if the entity settles the obligation. It should be treated as a separate asset. The reimbursement should not exceed the provision.

In the income statement, the expense relating to a provision may be presented net of the amount recognised for a reimbursement.

Changes in provisions

Provisions should be reviewed at each balance sheet date and adjusted to reflect the current best estimate. If it is no longer probable that an outflow of resources embodying economic benefits will be required to settle, the provision should be reversed.

Where discounting is used, the carrying amount of the provision increases each period to reflect the passage of time and the increase is recognised as a borrowing cost.

Use of provisions

A provision should be used only for expenditures for which the provision was originally recognised. There should be no virement across provisions.

Application of the recognition and measurement rules

Future operating losses

Provisions should not be recognised for future operating losses. They do not meet the definition of a liability, nor the general recognition criteria. However, there may be an indication for impairment testing under IAS 36.

Onerous contracts

A provision should be made for any contract which is onerous. Where certain rights and obligations make a contract onerous, a liability should be recognised. Executory contracts fall outside the scope of the standard.

It is onerous when, in a contract, any unavoidable costs of meeting the obligations under the contract exceed any economic benefits. The former represent the least net cost of exiting from the contract – i.e. the lower of fulfilling it or the penalties from failure to fulfil.

Any impairment losses must be recognised first, however, under IAS 36.

Restructuring

The following are examples of events that may fall under the definition of restructuring:

- sale or termination of a line of business;
- the closure or relocation of business activities;
- changes in management structure;
- fundamental reorganisations having a material effect on the nature and focus of an entity's operations.

A constructive obligation only arises when an entity:

- has a detailed formal plan for restructuring identifying at least: the part of business concerned; the principal locations affected; the location, function and number of employees being terminated; the expenditures to be undertaken; and when the plan will be implemented
- has raised a valid expectation in those affected that it will carry out the restructuring by starting to implement the plan or announcing its main features to those affected by it.

Commencement could be evidenced by selling off assets, dismantling plant, or the public announcement of its main features. For a constructive obligation the implementation should take place as soon as possible and be completed in a timeframe that makes significant changes unlikely to the plan. Long delays are unlikely to achieve that objective.

A board decision to restructure, before the balance sheet date, does not give rise to a constructive obligation unless the entity has:

- started to implement the restructuring plan; or
- announced its main features sufficiently well to those affected that it will clearly result in a valid expectation that the entity will carry out the restructuring.

Any post-balance sheet disclosure may be disclosed under IAS 10 *Events after the Balance Sheet Date* as a non-adjusting event.

Some countries have a two-tiered board system with employees on the secondary board; if they are informed, then a constructive obligation could exist.

No obligation arises for the sale of an operation until the entity is committed to the sale – i.e. there is a binding sale agreement.

A restructuring provision should only include the direct expenditures arising from the restructuring which are those that are both:

- necessarily entailed by the restructuring; and
- not associated with the ongoing activities of the enterprise.

It does not include retraining costs, marketing, or investment in new systems. These relate to the future. Future operating losses are also excluded unless they are related to an onerous contract.

Disclosure

For each class of provision, the following must be disclosed:

1. The net book value at start and end of the period
2. Additional provisions made in the period, including increases to existing provisions
3. Amounts used during the period
4. Unused amounts reversed during the period
5. The increase during the period in the discounted amount arising from the passage of time and any change in the discount rate.

Comparatives are not required.

In addition, an entity should disclose the following:

1. A brief description of the nature of the obligation and expected timing of any resulting outflows of economic benefits
2. An indication of the uncertainties about the timing or amount of any outflows including the major assumptions adopted
3. The amount of any expected reimbursement, stating the amount of any asset recognised for that expected reimbursement.

For all possible contingent liabilities the following should be disclosed together with a brief description of the nature of the contingent liability:

1. An estimate of its financial effect
2. An indication of the uncertainties relating to the amount or timing of any outflow
3. The possibility of any reimbursement.

Disclosures may be aggregated provided their nature is sufficiently similar for a single statement to fulfil the above requirements.

Where an inflow of economic benefits is probable an entity should disclose a brief description of the nature of the contingent asset at the balance sheet date and, if practicable, an estimate of its financial effect.

Where any of the above disclosure is not practicable, that fact should be disclosed. In extremely rare cases disclosure may seriously prejudice the entity in a dispute with other parties. In that case an entity need not disclose the information but should instead disclose the general nature of the dispute together with the fact that, and reason why, the information has not been disclosed.

IAS 37 provides a number of illustrations that demonstrate how to apply the standard (see Example 4.2).

Example 4.2
Illustrations of how to apply IAS 37

1. Warranties
A manufacturer gives warranties to its customers. Under the terms of the contract it promises to remedy any defects that become apparent within 3 years from the date of sale. On past experience, it is probable that there will be some claims under the warranties.

Present obligation as a result of a past obligating event: the sale of the product gives rise to a legal obligation.

Outflow of resources: probable for warranties as a whole.

Conclusion: a provision is recognised for the best estimate of the costs of making good under warranty products sold before the balance sheet date.

2. Contaminated land – legislation virtually certain to be enacted
An oil company causes contamination. In one country there is no legislation requiring cleaning up, but contamination has occurred for several years. At 31 December 2000 it is virtually certain that a draft law will be enacted shortly after the year end.

Present obligation as a result of a past obligating event: the obligating event is the contamination of the land because of virtual certainty of clean-up.

Outflow of resources: probable.

Conclusion: a provision is recognised for the best estimate of the costs of clean-up.

3. Contaminated land and constructive obligation
An oil company causes environmental damage in a country with no legislation to clean up, but the entity has a widely published environmental policy in which it undertakes to clean up all contamination that it causes. It normally honours that pledge.

Present obligation as a result of a past obligating event: the obligating event is the contamination of the land giving rise to a constructive obligation to clean up.

Outflow of resources: probable.

Conclusion: a provision for the best estimate of the costs of clean-up.

4. Offshore oilfield
An agreement requires the removal of an oil rig and the restoration of the seabed; 90% of the costs relate to the removal of the rig and restoration of damage and 10% to the extraction of oil. At year end the rig was constructed but no oil extracted.

Present obligation as a result of a past obligating event: construction of oil rig creates a legal obligation. At the balance sheet date, however, there is no obligation to rectify the damage caused by the extraction of oil.

Outflow of resources: probable.

Conclusion: a provision is recognised for the best estimate of 90% of the eventual costs that relate to the removal of the oil rig. These costs are included as part of the cost of the oil rig. The 10% are recognised as a liability as the oil is extracted.

5. Refunds policy
A retail store has a policy of refunding purchases by dissatisfied customers and this is generally known.

Present obligation as a result of a past obligating event: the obligating event is the sale of the product – constructive obligation – with the valid expectation by customers that the store will refund purchases.

Outflow of resources: probable, a proportion of goods are returned for refund.

Conclusion: a provision is recognised for the best estimate of the costs of the refunds.

6. Closure of a division – no implementation before balance sheet date

Assume in December 2004 the board of an entity decides to close down a division. Before the year end (31.12.04) the decision was not communicated to any of those affected.

Present obligation as a result of a past obligating event: there has been no obligating event and so no obligation.

Conclusion: No provision is recognised.

7. Closure of a division – communication/implementation before balance sheet date

Assume in December 2004 the board of an entity decides to close down a division. Before the year end (31.12.04) a detailed plan for closing down the division was agreed by the board and letters sent to customers warning them to seek an alternative source of supply. Redundancy notices were also sent to employees.

Present obligation as a result of a past obligating event: the obligating event is the communication of the decision to customers and staff – constructive contract.

Outflow of resources: probable.

Conclusion: a provision should be recognised for the best estimate of the costs of closing the division.

8. Legal requirements to fit smoke filters

Under new legislation an entity is required to fit smoke filters by 30 June 2004. It has not fitted these.

* At 31 December 2003: there is no obligation as no obligating event either for costs of fitting the filters or for fines; no provision is recognised.
* At 31 December 2004: there is still no obligation for fitting the filters, but there could be for fines. There is therefore the need to assess the probability of incurring fines and penalties by non-compliance, and thus a provision is recognised for the best estimate of any fines and penalties that are more likely than not to be imposed.

9. Staff retraining as a result of changes in the income tax system

A number of changes to the tax systems resulted in a need to retrain a large proportion of its administrative and sales workforce to ensure compliance with financial services regulations. No retraining had taken place by the year end.

Present obligation as a result of a past obligating event: no obligation because no obligating event (retraining) has taken place.

Conclusion: No provision is recognised.

10. An onerous contract

During December 2004 the entity relocates to a new factory. The lease on the old factory continues for the next 4 years, and cannot be cancelled or re-let.

Present obligation as a result of a past obligating event: the obligating event is the signing of the lease contract – a legal obligation.

Outflow of resources: when the lease becomes onerous, an outflow is probable.

Conclusion: a provision is recognised for the best estimate of the unavoidable lease payments.

11. A single guarantee
During 2002, A guarantees certain borrowings of B. During 2005 B's financial condition deteriorates, and in June 2005 it files for protection from creditors.

- At 31 December 2004: the obligating event is the giving of the guarantee – legal obligation. No outflow of benefits is probable. No provision is recognised. The guarantee is a contingent liability unless probability of outflow is remote.
- At 31 December 2005: the obligating event is the giving of the guarantee – legal obligation. Probable an outflow of resources will occur. Provision is recognised for the best estimate of the obligation.

12. A court case
Ten people died after a wedding, of food poisoning, possibly from goods sold by the company. Legal proceedings have started but are being disputed by the company. In 2004 the legal advisors felt that the loss was not probable, but during 2005 they have changed their mind.

- At 31 December 2004: no obligation exists and thus no provision should be created. It is disclosed as a contingent liability, unless liability is remote.
- At 31 December 2005: there is a present obligation. It is probable, and a provision should be made for the best estimate of the amount to settle the obligation.

13. Repairs and maintenance
Where a major overhaul is required, IAS 16 permits component accounting.

- No legislative requirement: no obligation exists even if, for example, a furnace needs to be relined every 5 years. No provision is permitted as this still only an intention. Instead, the relining costs should be capitalised when incurred and depreciated over the subsequent 5 years.
- Legislative requirement: an airline is required by law to overhaul its aircraft every 3 years. There is no obligation and no provision as there is still only an intention. The company can avoid the expenditure by selling the aircraft. Once again depreciation should be accelerated via component accounting and subsequent overhaul costs capitalised.

A number of illustrations of disclosure are also provided by IAS 37 (see Example 4.3).

Example 4.3
Illustrations of disclosure

1. Warranties
A manufacturer gives warranties at the time of sale to purchasers of its three product lines. Under the terms of the warranty, the manufacturer undertakes to repair or replace items that fail to perform satisfactorily for 2 years from the date of sale. At the balance sheet date, a provision of 60,000 has been recognised. The provision has not been discounted, as the effect of discounting is not material. The following information is disclosed:

A provision of 60,000 has been recognised for expected warranty claims on products sold during the last three financial years. It is expected that the majority of this expenditure will be incurred in the next financial year, and all will be incurred within 2 years of the balance sheet date.

Decommissioning costs
In 2002, an entity involved in nuclear activities recognises a provision for decommissioning costs of 300 million. The provision is estimated using the assumption that decommissioning

will take place in 60–70 years' time. However, there is a possibility that it will not take place until 100–110 years' time, in which case the present value of the costs will be significantly reduced. The following information is disclosed:

A provision of 300 million has been recognised for decommissioning costs. These costs are expected to be incurred between 2060 and 2070; however, there is a possibility that decommissioning will not take place until 2100–2110. If the costs were measured based upon the expectation that they would not be incurred until 2100–2110, the provision would be reduced to 136 million. The provision has been estimated using existing technology, at current prices, and discounted using a real discount rate of 2%.

4.2 Examination questions

Question 4.1: Genpower (ACCA)

(The first question requires students to explain the need for a unique accounting standard on provisions. The next part of the question describes the principles in IAS 37 and how they fit in with the recognition and measurement criteria contained in the Framework.)

IAS 37 *Provisions, Contingent Liabilities and Contingent Assets* was issued in September 1998 and became effective for accounting periods beginning on or after 1 July 1999. It supersedes certain parts of IAS 10 in respect of contingencies.

Required

(a) Explain the need for an accounting standard in respect of provisions.
(b) Describe the principles in IAS 37 of accounting for provisions. Your answer should refer to definitions and recognition and measurement criteria.

Genpower is a company involved in the electricity generating industry. It operates some nuclear power stations for which environmental clean-up costs can be a large item of expenditure. The company operates in some countries where environmental costs have to be incurred as they are written into the licensing agreement, and in other countries where they are not a legal requirement. The details of a recent contract Genpower entered into are as follows.

A new nuclear power station has been built at a cost of $200 million and was brought into commission on 1 October 1999. The licence to produce electricity at this station is for 10 years. This is also the estimated economic life of the power station. The terms of the licence require the power station to be demolished at the end of the licence. It also requires that the spent nuclear fuel rods (a waste product) have to be buried deep in the ground and the area 'sealed' such that no contamination can be detected. Genpower will also have to pay for the cost of cleaning up any contamination leaks that may occur from the water cooling system that surrounds the fuel rods when they are in use.

Genpower estimates that the cost of the demolition of the power station and the fuel rod 'sealing' operation will be $180 million in 10 years' time. The present value of these costs at an appropriate discount rate is $120 million. From past experience there is a 30% chance of a contaminating water leak occurring in any 12-month period. The cost of cleaning up a leak varies between $20 million and $40 million, depending on the severity of the contamination.

Extracts from the company's draft financial statements to 30 September 2000 relating to the contract after applying the company's normal accounting policy for this type of power station are:

	$ million
Income Statement charge:	
Non-current asset depreciation (power station) 10% × $200 million	20
Provision for demolition and 'sealing' costs 10% × $180 million	18
Provision for cleaning up contamination due to water leak	
(30% × an average of $30 million)	9
	47
Balance sheet:	
Tangible non-current assets:	
Power station at cost	200
Depreciation	(20)
	180
Non-current liabilities:	
Provision for environmental costs ($18 + $9 million)	27

Note: no contamination from water leakage occurred in the year to 30 September 2000.

Genpower is concerned that its current policy does not comply with IAS 37 *Provisions, Contingent Liabilities and Contingent Assets*, and has asked for your advice.

Required

(c) Comment on the acceptability of Genpower's current accounting policy, and redraft the extracts of the financial statements in line with the regulations of IAS 37. *Note:* your answer should ignore the 'unwinding' of the discount to present value.
(d) Assume Genpower was operating the nuclear power station in a country that does not legislate in respect of the above types of environmental costs. Explain the effect this would have on your answer to (c) above.

Question 4.2: L (CIMA)

(A similar question is found in the CIMA examinations. It takes a specific product, selling gaming cards, and looks at the possible claims that can arise from such sales e.g. packaging error, possible forgery etc. It concentrates mainly on the distinction between provisions and contingent liabilities.)

L is an enterprise which sells gaming cards to retailers, who then resell them to the general public. Customers who buy these cards scratch off a panel to reveal whether they have won a cash prize. There are several different ranges of cards, each of which offers a different assortment of prizes.

Prizewinners send their winning cards to L and are paid by cheque. If the prize is major, then the prize-winner is required to telephone L to register the claim and then send the winning card to a special address for separate handling.

All cards are printed and packaged under conditions of high security. Special printing techniques make it easy for L to identify forged claims, and it is unusual for customers to make false claims. Large claims are, however, checked, using a special chemical process that takes several days to take effect.

The directors are currently finalising their financial statements for the year ended 31 March 2002. They are unsure about how to deal with the following items:

(i) A packaging error on a batch of 'Chance' cards meant that there were too many major prize cards in several boxes. L recalled the batch from retailers, but was too late to prevent many of the defective cards being sold. The enterprise is being flooded with claims. L's lawyers have advised that the claims are valid and must be paid. It has proved impossible to determine the likely level of claims that will be made in respect of this error because it will take several weeks to establish the success of the recall and the number of defective cards.

(ii) A prize-winner has registered a claim for a $200,000 prize from a 'Lotto' card. The financial statements will be finalised before the card can be processed and checked.

(iii) A claim has been received for $100,000 from a 'Winner' card. The maximum prize offered for this game is $90,000, and so the most likely explanation is that the card has been forged. The police are investigating the claim, but this will not be resolved before the financial statements are finalised. Once the police investigation has concluded, L will make a final check to ensure that the card is not the result of a printing error.

(iv) The enterprise received claims totalling $300,000 during the year from a batch of bogus 'Happy' cards that had been forged by a retailer in Newtown. The police have prosecuted the retailer and he has recently been sent to prison. The directors of L have decided to pay customers who bought these cards 50% of the amount claimed as a goodwill gesture. They have not, however, informed the lucky prizewinners of this yet.

Required

(a) Identify the appropriate accounting treatment of each of the claims against L in respect of (i) to (iv) above. Your answer should have due regard to the requirements of IAS 37 *Provisions, Contingent Liabilities and Contingent Assets*.

(b) It has been suggested that readers of financial statements do not always pay sufficient attention to contingent liabilities even though they may have serious implications for the future of the enterprise.
  (i) Explain why insufficient attention might be paid to contingent liabilities.
  (ii) Explain how IAS 37 prevents enterprises from treating as contingent liabilities those liabilities that should be recognised in the balance sheet.

Question 4.3: Clean (CIMA)

The next question explains the logic behind the decision of the Directors to create a provision for the reduction of the level of pollution that a company has incurred and thus requires a student to create the required provision bearing in mind the time value of money. The breakdown of the charge to income is then split into its component parts – depreciation and finance costs. The last section of the question covers the application of IASs to environmental policies.)

Clean is a company that prepares its financial statements in accordance witl International Accounting Standards. On 25 June 2000, Clean made a public announce ment of a decision to reduce the level of emissions of harmful chemicals from its facto ries. The average useful economic lives of the factories on 30 June 2000 (the accountin₤ reference date of the company) was 20 years. The depreciation of the factories is com puted on a straight-line basis and charged to cost of sales. The directors formulated th₤ proposals for emission reduction following agreement in principle earlier in the year.

The directors prepared detailed estimates of the costs of their proposals, and thes₤ showed that the following expenditure would be required:

- $30 million on 30 June 2001
- $30 million on 30 June 2002
- $40 million on 30 June 2003.

All estimates were for the actual anticipated cash payments. No contracts were entere₤ into until after 1 July 2000. The estimate proved accurate as far as the expenditure du₤ on 30 June 2001 was concerned. When the directors decided to proceed with this pro ject, they used discounted cash flow techniques to appraise the proposed investment. The annual discount rate they used was 8%. The company has a reputation of fulfillin₤ its financial commitments after it has publicly announced them. Clean included a provi sion for the expected costs of its proposal in its financial statements for the year ende₤ 30 June 2000.

Required

(a) Explain the decision of the directors of Clean to recognise the provision in the balance sheet at 30 June 2000. You should refer to the provisions of relevant International Accounting Standards.

(b) Compute the appropriate provision in the balance sheets in respect of the proposed expenditure at 30 June 2000 AND 30 June 2001.

(c) Compute the two components of the charge to the income statement in respect of the proposal for the year ended 30 June 2001. You should explain how each component arises and identify where in the income statement each component is reported.

(d) Evaluate the extent to which financial statements prepared in accordance with International Accounting Standards give useful information regarding the environmental policies of the reporting entity.

Question 4.4: Z (CIMA)

(This question concentrates on the definition of contingent liabilities but it then applies that definition ₤ a number of mini case studies. It also requires the student to distinguish between those liabilities that a₤ probable and must be accrued, and those that are merely disclosed in the notes as genuine continger liabilities.)

IAS 37 *Provisions, Contingent Liabilities and Contingent Assets* requires contingencies to b classified as remote, possible, probable and virtually certain. Each of these categorie should then be treated differently, depending on whether it is an asset or a liability.

The Chief Accountant of Z, a construction enterprise, is finalising the work on the financial statements for the year ended 31 October 2002. She has prepared a list of all of the matters that might require some adjustment or disclosure under the requirements of IAS 37.

(i) A customer has lodged a claim against Z for repairs to an office block built by the enterprise. The roof leaks and it appears that this is due to negligence in construction. Z is negotiating with the customer and will probably have to pay for repairs that will cost approximately $100,000.

(ii) The roof in (i) above was installed by a subcontractor employed by Z. Z's lawyers are confident that the enterprise would have a strong claim to recover the whole of any costs from the subcontractor. The Chief Accountant has obtained the subcontractor's latest financial statements. The subcontractor appears to be almost insolvent with few assets.

(iii) Whenever Z finishes a project, it gives customers a period of 3 months to notify any construction defects. These are repaired immediately. The balance sheet at 31 October 2001 carried a provision of $80,000 for future repairs. The estimated cost of repairs to completed contracts as at 31 October 2002 is $120,000.

(iv) During the year ended 31 October 2002, Z lodged a claim against a large firm of electrical engineers which had delayed the completion of a contract. The engineering enterprise's Directors have agreed in principle to pay Z $30,000 compensation. Z's Chief Accountant is confident that this amount will be received before the end of December 2002.

(v) An architect has lodged a claim against Z for the loss of a laptop computer during a site visit. He alleges that the enterprise did not take sufficient care to secure the site office and that this led to the computer being stolen while he inspected the project. He is claiming for consequential losses of $90,000 for the value of the vital files that were on the computer. Z's lawyers have indicated that the enterprise might have to pay a trivial sum in compensation for the computer hardware. There is almost no likelihood that the courts would award damages for the lost files because the architect should have copied them.

Required

(b) Explain how each of the contingencies (i) to (v) above should be accounted for. Assume that all amounts stated are material.

Question 4.5: Stonemaster (CIMA)

IAS 37 *Provisions, Contingent Liabilities and Contingent Assets* was issued in July 1998 and became effective for accounting periods from 1 July 1999 onwards. The standard's main objective is to specify when provisions should, and should not be made. Prior to its introduction there had been widespread inconsistencies in the use, and some would say, the abuse of provisioning.

Required

(a) Describe the circumstances where a provision should, and should not, be made. Give two examples of the previous abuse of provisioning, and explain how the requirements of IAS 37 are intended to prevent them occurring in the future.

Stonemaster has recently acquired a 10-year licence to mine stone from land that it owns. Stonemaster has constructed some temporary buildings on the site and transferred some heavy plant to be used in the quarrying. A condition of the licence is that at the end of quarrying Stonemaster has to remove the building and plant and restore the land to an environmentally satisfactory condition through a landscaping scheme. Due to the weight of the vehicles that will be used to transport the stone, Stonemaster expects to have to pay various amounts of compensation on an annual basis for damage done to public roadways.

Required

(b) Describe how, if at all, Stonemaster should provide for the above restoration costs and roadway damage. Explain how your answer might differ if the government attached no conditions to the granting of the licence.

Performance measurement

5.1   IAS 33 *Earnings per Share* (Revised December 2003)

Background

One of the key financial ratios adopted by financial analysts has been the price/earnings ratio (P/E ratio). It is a widely used performance indicator and is published in the *Financial Times* on a daily basis. If the P/E ratio starts to veer away from the 'norm' for the industrial sector concerned, analysts may well advise their fund managers to sell shares in the company, resulting in a fall in the share price of that company and its over-all value to shareholders.

The P/E ratio is defined as:

$$\frac{\text{Current market share price}}{\text{earnings per share}} \quad \text{e.g.} \quad \frac{580 \text{ p}}{72.5 \text{ p}} = 8$$

In the example above it would take an investor 8 years of current earnings of 72.5 p to recover the initial investment of 580 p.

IAS 33 was published in order to clarify and standardise the calculation of the bottom line of that ratio, earnings per share (EPS), which is published at the foot of the income statement for every listed company in their annual report. This should serve to enhance comparability across listed companies. It only applies to listed companies, although if published by unlisted companies, the calculations must be the same.

Key definitions

Basic earnings per share should be calculated by dividing the net profit or loss for the period attributable to ordinary shareholders by the weighted average number of ordinary shares outstanding during the period.

IAS 33 also permits the adoption of alternative EPS figures based on other versions of profits. If adopted, a listed company must reconcile the alternative EPS back to the official EPS by itemising and quantifying the adjustments. The additional version must not be disclosed on the face of the income statement.

A further alternative EPS may be calculated based on the first *Statement of Investment Practice* published by the Institute of Investment Management and Research (IIMR),

which excludes non-trading items such as the profits/losses on termination of a discon
tinued operation, profits/losses on the sale of fixed assets and any permanent diminu
tions in the value of fixed assets from the calculation of earnings. It is therefore now
possible to calculate three different basic versions of EPS – the *official EPS*, the *alternative*
EPS and the *IIMR EPS*. Only the former is permitted to be discussed at the foot of the
income statement.

Basic earnings per share – problems

Preference dividends unpaid

Deduct if cumulative or if participating (fixed proportion).

The discount/premium on any increasing rate preference shares should be included
as part of the finance cost for non-equity shares (see Example 5.1).

Example 5.1
Increasing rate preference dividends

An entity issued non-convertible, non-redeemable class A cumulative preference shares of 100
par value on 1 January 2001. They are entitled to a 7% annual dividend, starting in 2004.

The market rate dividend yield, in 2001, was 7%. To compensate for no dividend for 3 years
the shares are issued at 81.63 (a discount of 18.37 – present value of 100 discounted at 7%
over 3 years).

The discount is amortised to profit and loss and treated as a preference dividend. The following imputed dividend is deducted:

	Carrying value 1 January 2001	Imputed dividend	Carrying value 31 December	Dividend paid
2001	81.63	5.71	87.34	
2002	87.34	6.12	93.46	
2003	93.46	6.54	100.00	
Thereafter	100.00	7.00	107.00	(7.00)

Losses

Losses per share should still be calculated in the same manner as earnings.

Changes in share capital

Changes in share capital may occur because of:

1. Issue at full market price
2. Capitalisation or bonus issue
3. Share-for-share exchange
4. Rights issue at less than market price.

1. Issue at full market price

Where new equity shares are issued for cash at full market price the new shares should
be included on a weighted average time basis on the grounds that the cash received will
generate earnings only for the period after the cash is received.

For example:

Earnings year 2	£10m	1 : 5 Full market price issue @ £2/share on 30.6.04
Number of shares prior to issue	5m	
Earnings per share	£2	1m × 1/2 year = 0.5m + 5m = 5.5m

Assume earnings of £10m incorporates additional earnings boosted by the cash received for the second half of the year.

Earnings £10m/5.5m = £1.81 per share

2.   Capitalisation or bonus issue

Where new equity shares are issued by way of conversion of reserves into equity capital, no increase in earnings has occurred but the bottom line has increased. To ensure comparability with prior years both the current and prior year are boosted *in full* by the issue of shares regardless of the date of issue.

For example:

Earnings year 2	£10m	1 : 5 bonus issue on 30.6.04
Number of shares prior to issue	5m	
Earnings per share	£2	1m × full year = 1m + 5m = 6m

Assume earnings of £10m are unaffected by the issue of shares as no cash has been received.

Earnings £10m/6m = £1.67 per share.

Assuming prior year EPS was £1.8, then prior year EPS is restated to £1.8 × 5/6 = £1.5.

3.   Share-for-share exchange

Where shares are exchanged in an acquisition for shares in the acquiree the shares are assumed to be included on a weighted average basis from the period from which the profits of the acquiree are included in the consolidated accounts.

For example:

Earnings year 2	£10m	Original shares	5m
Earnings of acquiree		Shares in exchange	
(1.4 to 31.12 only)	4m	(4m × 3/4)	3m
	£14m		8m

Earnings per share £14m/8m shares = £1.75 per share.

4.   Rights issue

Where shares are issued at a discount from their normal market price, the issue of shares is really a mixture of a full market price issue and a free bonus issue, i.e. a mixture of (1) and (2) above.

For example:

Earnings year 2	£10m	1 : 5 rights issue on 31.03.04 @ £4 per share (i.e. discount of 20% from market price of £5 per share)
Number of shares pre-rights issue	5m	
Earnings per share	£2	

Number of shares pre-rights	5m @	£5 cum	£25m
Rights issue (1 : 5)	1m @	£4	£4m
Total shares	6m @	£4.83	£29m

Adjustment factor £5/£4.83 = 1.035

Pre-rights	5m × 1.035 × 1/4 year = 1.294m
Post-rights	6m × 3/4 year = 4.500m
	5.794m

Earnings per share £10m/5.794m = £1.73 per share
Prior year (say £9m/5m) adjusted £9m/(5m × 1.035) = £1.74 per share.

Diluted earnings per share – problems

If a company has issued a separate class of equity shares which do not rank immediately for dividends in the current period (but will do so in the future), or if it has certain types of convertible loans or warrants which have the right to convert into ordinary shares at some future date, then these may well dilute earnings per share in the future. Users of financial statements should therefore be made aware of their likely impact.

As a result a second version of EPS is required to be disclosed on the face of the income statement, if the diluted EPS is either equal or below the basic EPS. It is not disclosed above basic EPS as it is argued that it will not happen because it would not be in the interests of the holders of those securities to exercise their rights.

There are three main types of diluting instrument:

1. Convertible preference shares
2. Convertible loan stock
3. Share options or warrants.

1. Convertible preference shares

There will be a saving in preference dividends and holders are assumed to transfer at the best conversion rate.

For example:

Basic earnings per share (assume)	£1.50	10% convertible preference shares	1m
Basic share structure (assume)	2m	(convertible 0.5 ordinary for every £1 ordinary)	
Basic earnings	£3m		

Diluted earnings per share £3m + £0.1m = £3.1m/(2m + 0.5m) = £1.24 per share, which is dilutive and therefore must be disclosed.

2. Convertible loan stock

There will be a saving in interest payments but because these are tax allowable the company will also lose the tax relief that it is currently saving. The net interest to be saved is therefore added back to basic earnings.

The bottom line will be increased by the maximum shares which the loan holders can earn if they convert into equity.

For example:

Basic earnings (as above)	£3.00m	£4m 8% convertible loan stocks convertible as
Add net interest saved	£2.24m	follows (assume tax at 30%):
	£5.24m	1.0m Year 5
		1.2m Year 6
		1.5m Year 7
		2.0m Year 8
Basic shares (assume)	2m	
Add convertible loans	2m	
(£4m × Year 8 = 2m)	4m	

Basic earnings per share   £3m/2m = £1.50 per share
Diluted earnings per share   £5.24m/4m = £1.31 per share, a dilution and therefore
     disclosable.

3.   Share options

The company is assumed to have to pay out shares to their employees/directors at an exercise price which is lower than current market, thus resulting in a dilution in earnings for existing shareholders. No dividends or interest are currently being paid to option holders so no adjustment is made to the top line of the ratio.

The bottom line is assumed to be increased by the discounted element of the number of shares to be issued.

For example:

Assume there are 5m of share options. Option holders can exercise their rights at a price of £2 per share. Currently the shares have a market value of £3 each.

Basic and adjusted earnings		£3m
Basic shares (assume)	2m	
Share options 5m × 1/3rd	1.67m	
Total shares		3.67m

Basic earnings per share   £3m/2m = £1.50 per share
Diluted earnings per share   £3m/3.67m = £0.82 per share, a dilution and therefore
     disclosable.

IAS 33 also provides guidance on the order in which to include dilutive securities in he calculation of the weighted average number of shares (see Example 5.2).

Example 5.2
Determining the order in which to include dilutive securities in the calculation of weighted average number of shares

Earnings

Net profit attributable to continuing operations	16,400,000
Less preference dividends	(6,400,000)
Profit from continuing operations attributable to ordinary shareholders	10,000,000
Loss from discontinued operations	(4,000,000)
Net profit attributable to ordinary shareholders	6,000,000

Ordinary shares outstanding	2m
Average market price of one ordinary share during year	75

Potential ordinary shares

Options	100,000 with exercise price of 60
Convertible preference shares	800,000 convertible 2 : 1,
	8 per share cumulative dividend

5% Convertible bond	
ordinary shares	100m each 1,000 convertible into 20
Tax rate	40%

Increase in earnings attributable to ordinary shareholders on conversion of potential ordinary shares

	Increase in earnings	Increase in number of ordinary shares	Earnings per incremental share
Options			
Increase in earnings	Nil		
Incremental shares			
100,000 × (75 − 60)/75		20,000	Nil
Convertible preference shares			
Increase in earnings			
8 × 800,000	6,400,000		
Incremental shares			
2 × 800,000		1,600,000	4
5% Convertible bonds			
Increase in earnings			
100m × 5% × 0.6	3,000,000		
Incremental shares		2,000,000	1.50

Ranking – (1) options, (2) convertible loans, (3) convertible preference shares.

Computation of diluted earnings per share

	Net profit attributable	Ordinary shares	Per share
As reported	10,000,000	2,000,000	5.00
Options	–	20,000	
	10,000,000	2,020,000	4.95 dilutive
5% Convertible bonds	3,000,000	2,000,000	
	13,000,000	4,020,000	3.23 dilutive
Convertible preference shares	6,400,000	1,600,000	
	19,400,000	5,620,000	3.45 antidilutive

The convertible preference shares are ignored in calculating the dilutive earnings per share as they are antidilutive.

Computation of basic and diluted earnings per share

	Basic	Diluted
Profit from continuing operations	5.00	3.23
Loss from discontinued operations	*(2.00)	**(0.99)
Net profit	3.00	2.24

*4,000,000/2m = 2.00
**4,000,000/4.02m = 0.99

Note also the need, under IAS 33, to disclose both basic and diluted earnings per share on an inclusive and exclusive basis of discontinued operations.

Presentation

Basic and diluted EPS should be presented on the face of the income statement with equal prominence given to both ratios. If diluted EPS is necessary then it must be provided for all periods presented.

The basic and diluted EPS for a discontinued operation, for both basic and diluted, should be disclosed either on the face of the income statement or in the notes.

The standard requires an entity to present basic and diluted EPS, even if the amounts are negative (i.e. loss per share).

Disclosure

An entity shall disclose the following:

1. Amounts used in the numerators and a reconciliation to net profit/loss
2. The weighted average number of ordinary shares used as the denominator in calculating basic and diluted EPS and a reconciliation to each other
3. Instruments that could potentially dilute basic EPS but were not included in the diluted EPS as antidilutive at present
4. A description of ordinary share transactions that occurred after the balance sheet date but before the issue of the financial statements that would significantly change the number of ordinary shares outstanding at the end of the period had they occurred before the end of the reporting period.

Examples included in (4) would include:

- an issue of shares for cash
- the issue of shares as part of a repayment of debt or preference shares
- the redemption of ordinary shares outstanding
- the conversion or exercise of potential ordinary shares into ordinary
- the issue of warrants, options or convertible securities
- the achievement of conditions that would result in the issue of contingently issuable shares.

The disclosure of terms and conditions should be encouraged as they may determine whether any potential ordinary shares are dilutive.

If an entity discloses amounts per share in addition to basic and dilutive EPS required by IAS 33 they should be calculated using the weighted average number of ordinary shares. Equal prominence should be presented for basic and diluted amounts per share and presented in the notes. An entity should indicate the basis on which the numerator is determined and if a component is used that is not reported as a line item. A reconciliation should be provided between the component and the line item in the income statement.

5.2   IAS 8 *Accounting Policies, Changes in Accounting Estimates and Errors* (December 2003)

Objective

The objective of IAS 8 is to prescribe the criteria for selecting and changing accounting policies together with the disclosure and accounting treatment of changes in accounting policies, accounting estimates and corrections of errors. It is also to enhance the relevance and reliability of financial statements and their comparability.

Scope

The standard should be applied in selecting and applying accounting policies, and accounting for changes in accounting policies, changes in accounting estimates and corrections of prior period errors.

Key definitions

Accounting policies: the specific principles, bases, conventions, rules and practices applied by an entity in preparing and presenting financial statements.

Change in accounting estimate: an adjustment to the carrying amount of an asset/liability or the amount of the periodic consumption of an asset that results from the assessment of the present status of, and expected future benefits and obligations associated with, assets and liabilities. These are not errors; they are caused by new information or developments.

Prior period errors: omissions or misstatements for one or more prior periods due to a failure to use or a misuse of reliable information that:

- was available when financial statements for those periods were authorised; and
- could have reasonably been obtained and taken into account when preparing and presenting those financial statements.

These include mathematical mistakes, mistakes in applying policies, oversights and fraud

Accounting policies

Selection and application of accounting policies

The appropriate standard should be applied if it applies specifically to a transaction. In the absence of an IFRS/IAS/SIC, management must use their judgement in developing and applying an accounting policy that results in information that is:

- relevant to the economic decision making needs of users; and
- reliable, as it purports faithfully the financial statements, reflects their substance, is neutral, prudent and complete in all material respects.

Management must consider the IFRSs etc. first and then the Framework in deciding the most appropriate policies. They are also encouraged to look to other standard setter.

having the same framework, accounting literature and accepted industry practice in making their choice.

Consistency of accounting policies

Consistent accounting policies must be adopted for similar transactions unless an IFRS/IAS requires a more specific policy to be adopted.

Changes in accounting policies

An accounting policy can only be changed if:

- required by an IFRS or IAS; or
- it results in financial statements providing more reliable and relevant information about the effects of transactions on the entity's financial position, performance or cash flows.

The following are not changes in accounting policies:

- the application of accounting policies for transactions that differ in substance from those previously undertaken; and
- the application of new policies that did not occur previously or were immaterial.

Applying changes in accounting policy

On first application of a standard the change must be applied retrospectively unless specific transitional arrangements in the IFRS/IAS apply.

Opening reserves should be adjusted for the earliest prior period presented as if the new policy had always applied (retrospective application).

If it is impracticable to apply retrospective application to prior periods, the entity should apply the new policy to the carrying amounts of assets and liabilities as at the start of the earliest period for which retrospective application is practicable. That may be the current period.

Disclosure

An entity should disclose the following (unless it is impracticable to determine the amount of the adjustment) on a change of accounting policy:

1. The title of the standard or SIC
2. That the change in policy is made in accordance with any transitional provisions (if applicable)
3. The nature of the change in accounting policy
4. A description of the transitional provisions, if applicable
5. The transitional provisions if they have an effect on future periods, if applicable
6. For current and prior periods, the amount of the adjustment for each item effected as well as its impact on EPS
7. For periods prior to those presented, the impact, if practicable
8. If retrospective application is impracticable, the circumstances causing that condition and how the change in policy has been applied.

When a voluntary change in policy affects the current or any prior period but it i
impracticable to determine its amount, an entity should disclose:

1. The nature of the change in accounting policy
2. The reasons why applying the new policy provides more reliable and relevan
   information
3. For the current and each prior period, to extent practicable, the amount of th●
   adjustment for each line item effected as well as its impact on EPS
4. For periods prior to those presented, the impact, if practicable
5. If retrospective application is impracticable, the circumstances causing that conditio●
   and how change in policy has been applied.

When an entity has not applied a new **IFRS** or **SIC** that is published but not effective
the entity should disclose that fact and estimate the possible impact that its applicatio●
will have on its financial statements.

Changes in accounting estimates

Many items in financial statements cannot be measured with precision but must be esti
mated. These involve judgements based on the latest available information. Example
where this would be applied include bad debts, inventory obsolescence, useful lives, war
ranty obligations etc.

Estimates need to be revised if circumstances change as a result of new informatio●
or experience. A change in measurement base is, however, a change in policy. If it is dif
ficult to distinguish between a policy and an estimate change, the change should b
treated as a change in estimate.

A change in estimate is charged prospectively in the income statement in the current an●
future years. Any related asset/liability should equally be adjusted in the period of change

Disclosure

The nature and amount of a change in accounting estimate and its effect on both cur
rent and future periods should be disclosed unless the amount is impracticable to esti
mate. If the amount of the effect on future years is not disclosed, due to impracticality
that fact must be disclosed.

Errors

Material prior period errors should be corrected retrospectively as soon as discovered by

- restating the comparatives for the prior periods presented; or
- if the error occurred before the earliest period presented, by adjusting the openin
  balances of assets, liabilities and equity for the earliest period presented.

Limitations on retrospective restatement

An error should be corrected retrospectively unless impracticable. If that is the case, th
entity must restate the opening balances of assets, liabilities and equity for the earlie
period for which retrospective restatement is practicable.

If impracticable to determine the cumulative impact for all prior periods, the entity shall restate the comparative information to correct the error prospectively from the earliest date practicable.

The corrections of prior period errors are not included in arriving at the profit or loss for the year.

Disclosure of prior period errors

The following should be disclosed:

1. The nature of the prior period error
2. For each prior period presented, to the extent practicable, the amount of the correction for each line item affected and for EPS
3. The amount of the correction at the start of the earliest period presented
4. If retrospective application is impracticable, the circumstances that led to the existence of that condition and a description of how and from when the error has been corrected.

This is only required in the year of discovery. It is not required in future years.

5.3   IAS 18 *Revenue* (1993)

Objective

IAS 18 deals with the bases for recognition of revenue in the income statements of enterprises, particularly from:

- the sale of goods;
- the rendering of services; and
- the use of resources yielding interest, royalties and dividends.

Scope

The following specialised aspects are excluded:

- dividends received under the equity method (see IAS 28);
- revenue arising from construction contracts (see IAS 11);
- revenue arising from lease agreements (see IAS 17);
- revenue arising from government grants (see IAS 20);
- revenue of insurance companies (see IFRS 4).

Revenue also does not include realised and unrealised gains from selling/holding non-current assets, unrealised holding gains due to changes in the value of current assets, natural increases in agricultural and forest products, changes in foreign exchange rates, discharges of obligations at less than their carrying amount, and unrealised gains from restating the carrying amount of obligations.

Key definitions

Revenue: gross inflow of cash, receivables or other consideration arising in the course of the ordinary activities of an enterprise from the sale of goods, from the rendering of services and from the use by others of enterprise resources yielding interest, royalties and dividends. It excludes third party collections such as VAT. In an agency relationship, revenue is the amount of the commission.

Completed contract method: recognises revenue only when the sale of goods or the rendering of services is complete or substantially completed.

Percentage of completion method: recognises revenue proportionately with the degree of completion of goods and services.

Revenue recognition

Revenue from sales or service transactions should be recognised when performance is satisfied. However, if it is unreasonable to expect ultimate collection then it should be postponed.

Sale of goods

Performance will be achieved if the following conditions are satisfied:

1. The seller has transferred the significant risks and rewards of ownership to the buyer; and
2. No significant uncertainty exists regarding:
   - the consideration to be derived from the sale of goods
   - the associated costs incurred in producing/purchasing the goods
   - the extent to which the goods may be returned.

If a seller retains significant risks it is not appropriate to recognise a sale. However, if a non-significant risk is retained by a seller this will not normally preclude the recognition of revenue (e.g. collectability of the debt).

In most cases the transfer of legal title coincides with the transfer of risks, but in other cases they may occur at different times. Each transaction must be examined separately.

In certain specific industries, e.g. harvesting of crops or extraction of mineral ores, performance may be substantially complete prior to the execution of the transaction generating revenue.

Rendering of services

In rendering services, performance should be measured under either the completed contract method or the percentage of completion method. Performance is achieved if no significant uncertainty exists regarding:

- the consideration that will be derived from rendering the service; and
- the associated costs.

Use by others of enterprise resources yielding interest, royalties and dividends

Revenues yielding interest, royalties and dividends should only be recognised when no significant uncertainty exists as to their measurability or collectability. They are recognised as follows:

- interest – on a time proportion basis;
- royalties – on an accruals basis in accordance with the terms of the agreement;
- dividends – when a right to receive payment is established.

In foreign countries revenue recognition may need to be postponed if exchange permission is required and a delay in remittance is expected.

Effect of uncertainties on revenue recognition

Recognition of revenue requires that revenue is measurable. Where the ability to assess the ultimate collection with reasonable certainty is lacking, revenue recognition is postponed. In such cases it may be appropriate to recognise revenue only when cash is collected.

If the uncertainty relates to collectability, a more appropriate approach would be to make a separate provision for bad debts.

Uncertainties may involve doubt over the collectability of the consideration, costs or returns, and in all cases revenue recognition should be postponed if they cannot be adequately measured.

Non-monetary consideration

The fair value of assets/services is normally used to determine the amount of revenue involved.

Disclosure

In addition to normal accounting policy notes, an enterprise should also disclose the circumstances in which revenue recognition has been postponed pending the resolution of significant uncertainties.

5.4   IFRS 5 *Non-Current Assets Held for Sale and Presentation of Discontinued Operations* (March 2004)

Objective

The objective of this IFRS is to improve the information about assets and disposal groups that are about to be disposed of and discontinued operations. It does this by specifying:

the measurement, presentation and disclosure of non-current assets and disposal groups; and
the presentation and disclosure of discontinued operations.

Scope

The IFRS applies to all recognised non-current assets except:

- deferred tax assets (see IAS 12);
- contractual rights under IFRS 4;
- assets arising from employee benefits (see IAS 19);
- financial assets included within the scope of IAS 39; and
- non-current assets under the fair value model in IAS 40.

A disposal group could be a group of cash generating units (CGUs) or part of a CGU. It is really the disposal of a group of assets and liabilities as part of a single transaction.

Classification of non-current assets as held for sale

Assets will be classified as held for sale if the asset will be recovered principally through a sale rather than through continuing use. Such a classification is only required when certain criteria are met:

1. Management are committed and have the authority to approve the action to sell
2. The asset or disposal group are available for immediate sale in their present condition subject to the usual terms (see Example 5.3(1)–(3))
3. An active programme to locate a buyer is initiated
4. The sale is highly probable and is expected to qualify for recognition as a completed sale within 1 year from the date of classification as 'held for sale' (see Example 5.3 (4)–(6))
5. The asset or disposal group is being actively marketed for sale at a reasonable price in relation to its fair value
6. Actions required to complete the plan indicate that it is unlikely that significant changes to the plan will be made or the plan withdrawn.

Example 5.3
Classification of non-current assets as held for sale

1. *An entity is committed to a plan to sell its HQ and has initiated action to find a buyer.*
(a) The entity intends to transfer the building to a buyer after it vacates the building. The time to vacate is normal. The criterion is met at the plan commitment date.
(b) The entity will continue to use the building until a new HQ is built. The building will not be transferred until construction is completed. The delay demonstrates that the building is not available for immediate sale and thus the criterion is not met even if a firm purchase commitment is obtained earlier.

2. *An entity is committed to a plan to sell a manufacturing facility and has initiated action to locate a buyer but there is a backlog of customer orders.*
(a) The entity intends to sell the manufacturing facility with its operations. Any uncompleted orders will transfer to the buyer. The criterion will be met at plan commitment date.
(b) The entity intends to sell the manufacturing facility but without its operations. It does not intend to transfer until it eliminates the backlog of orders. The delay means that the

facility is not available for immediate sale and thus the criterion is not met until the operations cease even if a firm purchase commitment were obtained earlier.

3. *An entity acquires a property via foreclosure comprising land and buildings that it intends to sell.*
(a) The entity does not intend to sell until it completes renovations. The delay means the property is not available for immediate sale until the renovations are completed.
(b) After renovations are completed and the property classified as held for sale, the entity is aware of environmental damage. The property cannot be sold until remediation takes place. The property is thus not available for immediate sale and the criterion would not be met. It would have to be reclassified.

4. *An entity in the power generation industry is committed to plan to sell a disposal group that represents a significant portion of its regulated operations.*
The sale requires regulatory approval which could extend beyond 1 year. Actions to obtain approval cannot be initiated until a buyer is located and a firm purchase commitment obtained. However, the commitment is highly probable and thus it may be classified as 'held for sale' even though it extends beyond 1 year.

5. *An entity is committed to sell a manufacturing facility.*
After a firm purchase commitment is obtained the buyer's inspection identifies environmental damage which must be made good, and this will extend beyond 1 year. However, the entity has initiated remediation and rectification is highly probable, thus it can still be classified as 'held for resale'.

6. *An entity is committed to sell a non-current asset and classifies the asset as held for sale at that date.*
During the initial 1-year period market conditions deteriorate, and the asset is not sold within the year and no reasonable offers are received. The asset continues to be actively marketed. At the end of the first year the asset would continue to be classified as 'held for sale'.

During the following year, market conditions deteriorate further and the asset is not sold. The sale price has not been reduced and thus, in the absence of a price reduction, the asset is not available for immediate sale, the criterion is therefore not met and the asset will need to be reclassified.

As can be seen from some of the illustrations in Example 5.3, events may extend the period to complete the sale beyond 1 year. An extension does not preclude an asset or disposal group from being classified as held for sale if the delay is caused by events beyond the entity's control and there is sufficient evidence that the entity remains committed to its plan to sell the asset. As a result an exception to the 1-year requirement shall therefore apply in the following situations:

1. At the date an entity commits itself to a plan to sell it reasonably expects that others will impose conditions on the transfer of the asset that will extend the period beyond 1 year, and:
   • actions cannot be initiated until after a firm purchase commitment is obtained, and
   • a firm purchase commitment is highly probable within 1 year.
2. An entity obtains a firm purchase commitment and a buyer unexpectedly imposes conditions to extend the period beyond 1 year, and:
   • timely actions necessary to respond have been taken, and
   • a favourable resolution of the delaying factors is expected.

3. During the initial 1-year period, circumstances arise which were previously considered unlikely and:
   - during the initial 1 year the entity took action to respond to change in circumstances, and
   - the non-current asset is being actively marketed given change in circumstances, and
   - the criteria in (1) to (6) above are met.

When an entity acquires a non-current asset exclusively with a view to subsequent disposal, it shall classify the non-current asset as held for sale at the acquisition date only if the 1-year criterion is met and it is highly probable that any other criteria that are not met will be met within a short period following the acquisition.

If the criteria are met after the balance sheet date but before they are authorised, an entity shall not classify a non-current asset as held for sale. However, the entity should disclose the information in the notes.

Impairment losses and subsequent increases in fair values less costs to sell of assets that were previously revalued

Any asset carried at a revalued amount under another IFRS shall be revalued under that IFRS immediately before it is classified as held for sale under this IFRS. Any impairment loss that arises on reclassification of the asset shall be recognised in the income statement.

Subsequent impairment losses

Any subsequent increases in costs to sell should be recorded in income. Any decreases in fair value should be treated as revaluation decreases in accordance with the IFRS under which the assets were revalued before their classification as held for sale.

Subsequent gains

Any subsequent decreases in costs to sell should be recognised in income. For individual assets that were revalued prior to classification under another IFRS, any subsequent increase should be treated as a revaluation increase. For disposal groups, any subsequent increases in fair value should be recognised to the extent that the carrying value of the non-current assets in the group after the increase has been allocated does not exceed their fair value less costs to sell. The increase should be treated as a revaluation increase in accordance with the IFRS under which the assets were revalued.

Non-current assets to be abandoned

These are not included as 'held for sale' as they will be recovered through use. However, if the disposal group to be abandoned is a component of an entity, the entity shall present the results and cash flows of the disposal group as discontinued on the date it ceases to be used.

A non-current asset that has been temporarily taken out of use as if abandoned should not be accounted for (see Example 5.4).

Example 5.4
Non-current assets to be abandoned

1. An entity ceases to use a manufacturing plant because demand has declined. However, the plant is maintained in workable condition and it is expected to be brought back into use if demand picks up. It is not therefore abandoned.

> 2. In October 2005 an entity decides to abandon all of its cotton mills (its major line of business). All work stops during 2006. For 2005 the results and cash flows should be treated as continuing operations, but in 2006 the entity discloses the information for discontinued operations including a restatement of any comparative figures.

Measurement of a non-current asset (or disposal group) classified as held for sale

An entity should measure a non-current asset (or disposal group) classified as 'held for sale' at the lower of its carrying amount and fair value less costs to sell.

If a newly acquired asset meets the criteria as 'held for sale', it should be measured initially at fair value less costs to sell.

Where, rarely, the sale takes more than 1 year to complete, it should be measured at present value.

The carrying amounts of any assets not covered by the IFRS but included in a disposal group should be measured in accordance with other IFRSs before the fair value less costs to sell is measured.

For assets that have not been revalued, an entity should recognise:

• an impairment loss for any initial writedown to fair value less costs to sell; and
• a gain for any subsequent increase in fair value less costs to sell but not in excess of the cumulative impairment loss recognised under this IFRS.

Changes to a plan of sale

If previously classified as 'held for sale' but now the criteria are no longer met, then the entity should cease to classify the asset or group as 'held for sale'.

On cessation as 'held for sale', a non-current asset should be valued at the lower of its:

• carrying amount before the asset or group was classified, as adjusted for depreciation that would have been recognised had the asset not been classified; and
• its recoverable amount at the date of the subsequent decision not to sell.

The entity should include, in income from continuing operations, any required adjustments to the carrying value of a non-current asset that ceases to be classified as held for sale.

Presentation and disclosure

Information should be presented to enable users to evaluate the financial effects of discontinued operations and disposals of non-current assets.

Presenting discontinuing operations

A component of an entity comprises operations and cash flows that can clearly be distinguished from the rest of the entity. It may be a CGU or any group of CGUs.

A discontinued operation is a component of an entity that has either been disposed of or is classified as 'held for sale' and:

represents a separate major line of business or geographical area of operations; or
is part of a single coordinated plan to dispose of a separate major line of business or geographical area of operations; or
is a subsidiary acquired exclusively with a view to resale.

An entity shall disclose for all periods presented:

1. A single amount on the face of the Profit and Loss comprising:
   - post-tax profit/loss of discontinued operations
   - post-tax gains/losses on measurement to fair value or on disposal of discontinued operations
2. Analysis of (1) into:
   - revenue, expenses and pre tax profits/losses of discontinued operations
   - related tax expense
   - gains/losses on measurement to fair value or on disposal of discontinued operations, and
   - related tax expense
3. The net cash flows attributable to the operating, investing and financing activities of discontinued operations.

The disclosures required by (1) must be on the face of the income statement, but the others may be presented in the notes or on the face of the income statement (see Example 5.5).

Prior periods for disclosures (1) to (3) are also required.

Adjustment to previous discontinued operations of prior periods should be classified separately – e.g. resolution of uncertainties.

Example 5.5
Presenting discontinuing operations

XYZ Group – Income Statement for the year ended 31 December 2002 (by function)

	2002	2001
Continuing operations		
Revenue	X	X
Cost of sales	(X)	(X)
Gross profit	X	X
Other income	X	X
Distribution costs	(X)	(X)
Administrative expenses	(X)	(X)
Other expenses	(X)	(X)
Finance costs	(X)	(X)
Share of profit of associates	X	X
Profit before tax	X	X
Income tax expense	(X)	(X)
Profit for the period from continuing operations	X	X
Discontinuing operations		
Profit for the period from discontinued operations*	X	X
Profit for the period	X	X
Attributable to:		
Equity holders of the parent	X	X
Minority interest	X	X

*The required analysis would be given in the notes.

Gains or losses relating to continuing operations

Any gain/loss on remeasurement of a non-current asset that does not meet the definition of a component shall be included in the profit/loss from continuing operations.

Presentation of a non-current asset or disposal group classified as held for sale

These should be separately disclosed from other assets. The liabilities of a disposal group classified as 'held for sale' shall be presented separately from other liabilities. These assets and liabilities shall not be offset but separately disclosed on the face of the balance sheet (see Example 5.6).

Example 5.6
Presenting discontinued operations

At the end of 2005 an entity decides to dispose of part of its assets and directly associated liabilities. This disposal which meets the criteria as held for sale takes the form of two disposal groups as follows:

NBV after classification as held for sale

	Disposal group 1	**Disposal group 2**
Property, plant and equipment	4,900	1,700
Asset for sale financial asset	1,400*	–
Liabilities	(2,400)	(900)
NBV of disposal group	3,900	800

*An amount of 400 relating to these assets has been recognised directly in equity.

The presentation in the entity's balance sheet of the disposal groups classified as held for sale can be shown as follows:

	2005	**2004**
Assets		
Non-current assets		
AAA	X	X
BBB	X	X
CCC	X	X
	X	X
Current assets		
DDD	X	X
EEE	X	X
	X	X
Non-current assets classified as held for sale	8,000	–
	X	X
Total assets	X	X

	2005	**2004**
Equity and liabilities		
Equity attributable to equity holders of the parent		
FFF	X	X

GGG	X	X
Amounts recognised directly in equity relating to non-current assets held for sale	$\underline{400}$	$\dfrac{\text{X}}{\text{X}}$
	X	
Minority interest	X	X
Total equity	$\underline{\text{X}}$	$\underline{\text{X}}$
Non-current liabilities		
HHH	X	X
III	X	X
JJJ	$\dfrac{\text{X}}{\overline{\underline{\text{X}}}}$	$\dfrac{\text{X}}{\overline{\underline{\text{X}}}}$
Current liabilities		
KKK	X	X
LLL	X	X
MMM	$\underline{\text{X}}$	$\underline{\text{X}}$
Liabilities directly associated with non-current assets classified as held for sale	$\underline{3,300}$	–
	X	X
Total liabilities	$\underline{\text{X}}$	$\underline{\text{X}}$
Total equity and liabilities	$\underline{\text{X}}$	$\underline{\text{X}}$

5.5   Examination questions

Question 5.1: Bosun (ACCA)

(The first question in the chapter covers a number of accounting standards but ends up by requiring the calculation of both basic and diluted earnings per share ratios, the latter incorporating share options. Other standards include IFRS 3, IAS 32 and IAS 17, and all require adjustments to be made to the draft financial statements.)

The summarised draft consolidated financial statements of Bosun to 31 March 2000 are shown below.

Bosun plc Profit and Loss Account year to 31 March 2000

	$000	$000
Sales revenue		2,800
Cost of sales		(1,750)
Gross profit		1,050
Operating costs		(344)
		706
Finance costs		(64)
Profit before tax		642
Taxation		(150)
Profit after tax		492
Minority interests		(20)
		472
Extraordinary item		(126)
		346
Dividends		(100)
Retained profit for year		246

Balance Sheet as at 31 March 2000

	$000	$000
Assets		
Non-current		
Property, plant and equipment		2,540
Investment in finance leases		900
		3,440
Current assets		1,000
Total assets		4,440
Equity and liabilities		
Capital and reserves		
Equity shares of $1 each		1,200
Reserves:		
Accumulated profit – b/f 1 April 1999	1,134	
– year to 31 March 2000	346	
– less dividends	(100)	1,380
		2,580
Minority interest		140
Non-current liabilities		
12% Redeemable Loan Note (2004)		200
Current liabilities		1,520
Total equity and liabilities		4,440

The above consolidated financial statements have been drafted by inexperienced accounting staff. The following information relates to issues that the accounting staff had particular difficulties with:

i) *Retail car sales.* In September 1999 Bosun held a 1-month promotion campaign aimed at increasing its retail sales of new cars. A special edition manufacturer's model called the 'Firefly' was sold during September. The promotion consisted of offering within the normal selling price:
- free lease finance over 2 years
- an extended 3-year warranty against mechanical failure.

In total, 100 of these cars were sold under the offer terms.
   Details relating to the finance of the cars sold under the offer are:

	$
Selling price included in turnover ($15,000 × 100)	1,500,000
Paid for by:	
Initial deposit paid in September 1999 ($3,000 × 100)	(300,000)
Initial investment in finance lease	1,200,000
Received 6 monthly payments of $500 × 100	(300,000)
Investment in finance leases at 31 March 2000	900,000
Receivable within 1 year 12 × $500 × 100	600,000
Receivable after more than 1 year 6 × $500 × 100	300,000

Applying the same finance rates as Bosun uses for normal leased car sales, the true finance cost of the promotional sales over the 2-year lease would be $1,200 per car. It has been calculated that this would normally be earned as follows.

In the year to:
31 March 2000 $500 per car
31 March 2001 $450 per car
31 March 2002 $250 per car

The manufacturer of the cars will reimburse any warranty claims in the first 12 months. From past experience, the second and third year's 'free' warranty will cost an average of $150 per car. Bosun has not provided any amount for warranty claims in the year to 31 March 2000, as they are covered by the manufacturer's warranty until September 2001.

(ii) *Business combination.* On 31 March 2000 Bosun issued 200,000 equity shares (market value $4 each) in a one-for-one share exchange to acquire the entire share capital of Capstan. The business combination has been accounted for as a uniting of interests. The summarised results of Capstan are:

Income Statement year to 31 March 2000

	$000
Sales revenue	600
Cost of sales	(350)
Gross profit	250
Operating costs	(90)
	160
Income tax	60
Profit after tax	100

No dividends have been paid by Capstan.

Summarised Balance Sheet as at 31 March 2000

	$000
Net assets	800
Equity shares $1 each	200
Accumulated profits	600
	800

The fair values of Capstan's net assets at the date of acquisition were equal to their book values.

Advice from the company's auditors in respect of the combination is that it does not meet the requirements of a uniting of interests under IAS 22 *Business Combinations* and should be treated using the purchase method (acquisition accounting). Capstan's trading on 31 March 2000 can be taken as negligible.

(iii) *Extraordinary item.* This represents the cost ($180,000 less tax relief of $54,000) incurred during the year of making the company's computer systems 'year 2000' compliant. As this cost will never recur it has been treated as an extraordinary item; however, the auditors have advised that this should be treated as ordinary expenditure.

(iv) *12% Redeemable Loan Note.* On 1 April 1999 a redeemable loan note with a nominal value of $200,000 was issued at a discount of 5% (i.e. at $95 per $100 nominal value). It is redeemable on 31 March 2004 at a premium of 10%. The inexperienced staff have treated the whole of the discount as a finance cost and ignored the premium on redemption. The company policy is to amortise (through the income statement) such discounts and premiums in a straight-line manner.

(v) *Directors' share options.* Four directors have each held options to buy 100,000 shares in Bosun at a price of $2.00 since 1997. The options become exercisable in the year 2003. The average fair value of the shares during the year to 31 March 2000 can be taken as $4.00.

Required

(a) Redraft the consolidated financial statements of Bosun for the year to 31 March 2000 to comply with the auditor's advice and relevant International Accounting Standards in relation to items (i) to (v) above.
(b) Calculate the basic and diluted Earnings Per Share for Bosun for the year to 31 March 2000 in accordance with IAS 33.

Question 5.2: Deltoid (ACCA)

(The second question in the chapter also requires the calculation of both basic and diluted earnings per share, the latter including the conversion of loan notes. The question also incorporates the need to amend draft financial statements in order to comply with IAS 16, IAS 17, IAS 32 and IAS 10.)

The following balance sheet has been extracted from the draft financial statements of Deltoid for the year to 31 March 2002.

Balance sheet as at 31 March 2002

	$000	$000
Non-current assets		
Property, plant and equipment		12,110
Current assets		
Inventory	3,850	
Trade accounts receivable	2,450	
Bank	250	6,550
Total assets		18,660
Equity and liabilities		
Capital and reserves		
Ordinary shares of 50 cents each		2,000
Reserves		
Share premium		1,000
Revaluation reserve		3,000
Accumulated profits b/f at 1 April 2001	2,500	
Profit after tax for year to 31 March 2002	2,000	4,500
		10,500
Non-current liabilities		
Environmental provision (note (iv))	1,200	
6% Convertible loan note (note (iii))	3,000	4,200
Current liabilities		
Trade accounts payable	2,820	
Taxation	1,140	3,960
Total equity and liabilities		18,660

The following additional information is available:

(i) The financial statements include an item of plant based on its treatment in the company's management accounts where plant is depreciated on a machine hour use basis. The details of this item of plant are:

Cost (1 April 2000)	$250,000
Estimated residual value	$50,000
Estimated machine hour life	8,000
Measured usage in year to: 31 March 2001	2,000
31 March 2002	800

In the financial statements the company policy is that plant and machinery should be written off at 20% per annum on the reducing balance basis.

(ii) The income statement includes a charge of $150,000, being the first two of ten payments of $75,000 each in respect of a 5-year lease of an item of plant. The payments were made on 1 April 2001 and 1 October 2001. The fair value of this plant at the date it was leased was $600,000. Information obtained from the finance department confirms that this is a finance lease and an appropriate periodic rate of interest is 10% per annum. Deltoid has treated the lease as an operating lease in the above financial statements. The company depreciates plant used under finance leases on a straight-line basis over the life of the lease.

(iii) On 1 April 2001 Deltoid issued a $3 million 6% convertible loan note at par. The loan note is redeemable at a premium of 10% on 31 March 2005, or it may be converted into ordinary shares on the basis of 50 shares for each $100 of loan note at the option of the holder. The interest (coupon) rate for an equivalent loan note without the conversion rights would have been 10%. In the draft financial statements Deltoid has paid and charged interest of $180,000 and shown the loan note at $3 million on the balance sheet.

The present value of $1 receivable at the end of each year, based on discount rates of 6% and 10% can be taken as:

	6%	10%
End of year 1	0.94	0.91
2	0.89	0.83
3	0.84	0.75
4	0.79	0.68

The draft financial statements contain an accumulating provision for the cost of restoring (landscaping) the site of a quarry that is being operated by Deltoid. The result of an environmental audit has concluded that the provision has been calculated on the wrong basis and is materially underprovided. A firm of environmental consultants has summarised the required revision:

	Current provision $000	Required provision $000
Income statement charge – year to 31 March 2002	180	245
Balance sheet liability – at 31 March 2002	1,200	2,150

The directors consider that the incorrect original estimate constitutes a fundamental error.

iv) Deltoid made a one-for-four bonus issue of shares on 1 March 2002 utilising the revaluation reserve. This has not yet been recorded in the above financial statements.
(v) The directors of Deltoid wish to propose a final dividend that will give an earnings yield of 4% to the ordinary shareholders. This is to be based on the current market price of Deltoid's shares of $2.00 each. The bonus shares in note (iv) will rank for the final dividend. No interim dividends have been paid during the year. Deltoid discloses proposed dividends as a note to the financial statements.

Required

(a) Redraft the balance sheet of Deltoid as at 31 March 2002 making appropriate adjustments for the items in (i) to (v) above. (*Note*: work to the nearest $000 and show separately your working for the accumulated profits included in the balance sheet.)
(b) Calculate the basic and diluted earnings per share for Deltoid for the year to 31 March 2002. Assume a tax rate of 25% and that only the actual loan interest paid is available for tax relief. Ignore deferred tax.

Question 5.3: Company X (ACCA)

This question breaks down into two distinct sections. The first covers, in narrative, the potential problems of placing undue emphasis on one ratio together with a general question on the reporting gap and how it might be eliminated.

The second part of the question requires the calculation of both basic and diluted earnings per share, but incorporates such features as discontinued operations, convertible loan stock and preference shares, warrants and the issue of ordinary shares at full market price.)

Accounting regulators believe that undue emphasis is placed on earnings per share (EPS), and that this leads to simplistic interpretation of financial performance. Many chief executives believe that their share price does not reflect the value of their company and yet are preoccupied with earnings based ratios. It appears that if the chief executives shared the views of the regulators then they might disclose more meaningful information than EPS to the market, which may then reduce the 'reporting gap' and lead to higher share valuations. The 'reporting gap' can be said to be the difference between the information required by the stock market in order to evaluate the performance of a company and the actual information disclosed.

Required

(a) Discuss the potential problems of placing undue emphasis on the earnings per share figure.
(b) Discuss the nature of the 'reporting gap' and how the gap might be eliminated.

Company X has a complex capital structure. The following information relates to the company for the year ending 31 May 2001:

(i) The net profit of the company for the period attributable to the preference and ordinary shareholders of the parent company was $14.6 million. Of this amount, the net profit attributable to discontinued operations was $3.3 million. The following details relate to the capital of the company:

(ii)   Ordinary shares of $1 in issue at 1 June 2000   6m
        Ordinary shares of $1 issued 1 September 2000 at full market price   1.2m

The average market price of the shares for the year ending 31 May 2001 was $10 and the closing market price of the shares on 31 May 2001 was $11. On 1 January 2001, 300,000 partly paid ordinary shares of $1 were issued. They were issued at $8 per share, with $4 payable on 1 January 2001 and $4 payable on 1 January 2002. Dividend participation was 50% until fully paid.

(iii) Convertible loan stock of $20 million at an interest rate of 5% per annum was issued at par on 1 April 2000. Half a year's interest is payable on 30 September and 31 March each year. Each $1,000 of loan stock is convertible at the holder's option into 30 ordinary shares at any time. $5 million of loan stock was converted on 1 April 2001 when the market price of the shares was $34 per share.

(iv) $1 million of convertible preference shares of $1 were issued in the year to 31 May 1998. Dividends are paid half-yearly on 30 November and 31 May at a rate of 6% per annum. The preference shares are convertible into ordinary shares at the option of the preference shareholder on the basis of two preference shares for each ordinary share issued. Holders of 600,000 preference shares converted them into ordinary shares on 1 December 2000.

(v)   Warrants to buy 600,000 ordinary shares at $6.60 per share were issued on 1 January 2001. The warrants expire in 5 years' time. All the warrants were exercised on 30 June 2001. The financial statements were approved on 1 August 2001.

(vi) The rate of taxation is to be taken as 30%.

Required

(c) Calculate the basic and diluted earnings per share for X for the year ended 31 May 2001 in accordance with IAS 33 *Earnings per Share*.

Question 5.4: G (CIMA)

G is a large manufacturing company. It is listed on its national stock exchange. The company's shares are widely held by a very large number of individual shareholders and its activities are heavily reported in the business press.

G's trial balance at 31 December 2000 is shown below.

	$ million	$ million
Administrative expenses	130	
Bank	10	
Cost of sales	240	
Deferred taxation		200
Dividend – interim paid	40	
Goodwill – net book value	1,900	
Interest	95	
Inventory at 31 December 2000	110	
Interest-bearing borrowings		1,100
Reserves – accumulated profits		1,875

Property, plant and equipment – net book value	2,400	
Revenue (sales)		1,000
Selling and distribution costs	100	
Share capital		500
Reserves – share premium		400
Tax		10
Trade and other payables		30
Trade and other receivables	90	
	5,115	5,115

Notes:

(i) The company has a funded, defined benefit pension scheme. The company makes regular payments to the insurance company that operates the scheme on its behalf. These payments are treated as an employment cost and included under cost of sales in the trial balance.

During the year ended 31 December 2000, G received a report on the fund. This indicated that it was under-funded by $20 million. The actuaries who prepared the report recommended that the company should pay an additional $5 million into the fund each year for the next 4 years. These payments would be in addition to the regular payments to the fund.

During the year ended 31 December 2000, G paid the first instalment of $5 million to supplement the pension fund. The company also paid $8 million as its routine annual contribution into the fund.

The actuaries who prepared the report estimated the average service life of the company's work force at 10 years. The directors have decided to amortise the actuarial loss of $20 million over that period. The figures in the trial balance have not yet been updated to reflect the actuaries' report.

Pension costs are included in the cost of sales figure.

(ii) The directors estimate the tax charge on the year's profits at $120 million. The balance on the taxation account represents the balance remaining after settling the amount due for the year ended 31 December 1999.

(iii) The balance on the provision for deferred taxation should be increased to $280 million.

(iv) The directors have proposed a final dividend of $60 million. The company did not pay a dividend during the year ended 31 December 1999.

(v) G's share capital is made up of $1 shares, all of which are fully paid up. The company issued 100 million shares on 29 February 2000. These were sold for their full market price of $1.40 per share. This sale has been included in the figures shown in the trial balance.

(vi) A major customer went into liquidation on 16 January 2001, owing G $8 million. G's directors are of the opinion that this amount is material.

(vii) A member of the public was seriously injured on 24 January 2001 while using one of G's products. The company lawyer is of the opinion that the company will have to pay $2 million in compensation. G's directors are of the opinion that this amount is material.

Required

(a) Prepare G's income statement for the year ended 31 December 2000 and its balance sheet at that date. These should be in a form suitable for publication, and should be accompanied by notes as far as you are able to prepare these from the information provided. Do NOT prepare a statement of accounting policies, a statement of total recognised gains and losses, a statement of changes in equity or calculate earnings per share.

(b) Calculate G's earnings per share (EPS) in accordance with the requirements of IAS 33 *Earnings per Share*.

(c) It has been suggested that the EPS ratio is unique in that its calculation is the subject of detailed Accounting Standards. Explain why it has been necessary to provide such detailed guidance on the calculation of EPS.

(d) Identify what is meant by 'diluted' earnings per share, and explain the reasons why companies should be required to disclose this figure.

Question 5.5: Myriad (ACCA)

(The second batch of questions in the chapter concentrates on the application of IAS 8 and, in particular, how to deal with changes in accounting policies. The second part of this question covers a topic covered in Chapter 2, i.e. the accounting treatment of investment properties under IAS 40.)

You have been asked to assist the financial accountant of Myriad in preparing the company's financial statements for the year to 30 September 2001. The financial accountant has asked for your advice in the following matters.

Myriad has recently adopted the use of International Accounting Standards and a review of its existing policy of prudently writing off of all development expenditure is no longer considered appropriate under IAS 38 *Intangible Assets*. The new policy, to be first applied for the financial statements to 30 September 2001, is to recognise development costs as an intangible asset where they comply with the requirements of IAS 38. Amortisation of all 'qualifying' development expenditure is on a straight-line basis over a 4-year period (assuming a nil residual value). Recognised development expenditure 'qualifies' for amortisation when the project starts commercial production of the related product. The amount of recognised development expenditure, and the amount qualifying for amortisation each year is as follows:

	$000 Amount recognised as an asset	$000 Amount qualifying for amortisation
In the year to 30 September 1999	420	300
In the year to 30 September 2000	250	360
In the year to 30 September 2001	560	400
	1,230	1,060

No development costs were incurred by Myriad prior to 1999.

Changes in accounting policies should be accounted for under the benchmark treatment in IAS 8 *Accounting Policies, Changes in Accounting Estimates and Errors.*

Required

(a) Explain the circumstances when a company should change its accounting policies.
(b) Prepare extracts of Myriad's financial statements for the year to 30 September 2001, including the comparatives figure to reflect the change in accounting policy. (*Note*: ignore taxation.)

Myriad owns several properties which are revalued each year. Three of its properties are rented out under annual contracts. Details of these properties and their valuations are:

Property type/life	Cost $000	Value 30 September 2000 $000	Value 30 September 2001 $000
A freehold/50 years	150	240	200
B freehold/50 years	120	180	145
C freehold/15 years	120	140	150

All three properties were acquired on 1 October 1999. The valuations of the properties are based on their age at the date of the valuation. Myriad's policy is to carry all non-investment properties at cost. Annual amortisation, where appropriate, is based on the carrying value of assets at the beginning of the relevant period.

Property A is let to a subsidiary of Myriad on normal commercial terms. The other properties are let on normal commercial terms to companies not related to Myriad. Myriad adopts the fair value model of accounting for investment properties in IAS 40 *Investment Properties* and the benchmark treatment for owner-occupied properties in IAS 16 *Property, Plant and Equipment*.

Required

(c) Describe the possible accounting treatments for investment properties under IAS 40 and explain why they may require a different accounting treatment to owner-occupied properties.
(d) Prepare extracts of the consolidated financial statements of Myriad for the year to 30 September 2001 in respect of the above properties assuming the company adopts the fair value method in IAS 40.

Question 5.6: Pailing (ACCA)

The following question requires a student to discuss the main reasons why multinational companies might wish to adopt IASs, and the problems in getting IASs accepted. The second part of the question requires the draft income statement and the capital and reserves section of the balance sheet to be redrafted in order to comply with extant accounting standards, particularly IFRS 3, IAS 12 and IAS 21.)

There is a wide variety of accounting practices adopted in different countries and it seems that no two countries have identical accounting systems. At present, overseas companies preparing financial statements utilising International Accounting Standards (IAS) can obtain a listing on many stock exchanges. However, some companies cannot use IAS to obtain an equivalent listing but have to use local Generally Accepted Accounting

Practice (GAAP). Many companies feel that there are several advantages in preparing financial statements in accordance with IAS which outweigh the disadvantages of changing from local GAAP.

Required

(a) Describe the main reasons why multinational companies might wish International Accounting Standards to be adopted as the only standards of accounting.

(b) Describe the problems with International Accounting Standards which may act as a barrier to their widespread acceptance.

Pailing, a public limited company, is a company registered in Europe. Under the local legislation, it has to prepare its financial statements using local accounting standards. Klese is considering buying the company but wishes to restate Pailing's group financial statements so that they are consistent with IAS before any decision is made, as the company is also considering the purchase of another company. Klese wishes to restate the financial statements as if IAS were being applied for the first time.

The Pailing group's net profit for the period drawn up, utilising local GAAP, is $89 million for the year ending 31 March 2000, and its group capital and reserves under local GAAP is $225 million as at 31 March 2000. The following accounting practices under local GAAP have been determined.

(i) A change in accounting policies has been dealt with by a cumulative catch-up adjustment which is included in the current year's income. During the year, depreciation on buildings was charged for the first time. The total cumulative depreciation charge for the buildings was computed at $30 million, of which $3 million relates to the current year.

(ii) Pailing had acquired a subsidiary company, Odd, on 31 March 2000. The minority interest (25%) stated in the balance sheet was based on the book value of the net assets of the subsidiary before any fair value adjustments. Pailing's interest was based on fair values. The fair value and the book value of the net assets of Odd at the date of acquisition were $28 million and $24 million respectively. Klese wishes to use the allowed alternative treatment in IAS 22 *Business Combinations* and not the benchmark treatment.

(iii) Pailing had paid $16 million for the subsidiary, Odd, on 31 March 2000. The negative goodwill did not relate to identifiable losses or expenses to be incurred and it had recognised all of the negative goodwill in the income statement in the current year. Klese writes off its depreciable non-monetary assets on average over a 5-year period. The fair value of the non-monetary assets is $7 million.

(iv) Pailing had sold a 100% owned overseas subsidiary on 1 April 1999 for $40 million resulting in a gain on sale of $8 million when comparing the sale proceeds with the cost of the investment. Pailing had excluded all of the results of the subsidiary from its financial statements other than reporting the gain on sale of $8 million in its group income statement. The net asset value of the subsidiary at the date of sale was $36 million. There was no goodwill arising on the original purchase of the subsidiary. The cumulative exchange gain held in the Group Exchange Reserve was $3 million on 31 March 1999, and this was left in the reserve on disposal.

(v) Pailing provided for deferred taxation using a method not allowable under IAS12 *Income Taxes*. The company had net temporary differences of $13 million and $6 million as at 31 March 2000 and 31 March 1999 respectively. The opening deferred tax provision under the method not allowable under IAS 12 was $0.3 million and the closing provision was $0.9 million. Assume taxation at 30%.

Required

(c) Restate the net profit for the year ending 31 March 2000 and the capital and reserves of Pailing as at 31 March 2000 in accordance with International Accounting Standards.

(d) Briefly, state the effect that the restatement of Pailing's financial statements might have on the decision to purchase the company.

Question 5.7: Transystems (ACCA)

(Transystems covers a number of accounting standards and requires a narrative report to be presented which explains how to apply those standards. It covers IAS 18 Revenue Recognition and, in particular, the need to apply USA standards as IAS 18 is now out of date and needs to be revamped for the 21st century. However, the question also covers the new accounting standard on business combinations (IFRS 3), the link between IAS 2 and IAS 38, IAS 16 and the presentation in the income statement under IAS 1.)

Transystems, a public limited company, designs websites and writes bespoke software. The company has a history of conflict with the auditors regarding its creative use of accounting standards. The following accounting practices are proposed by the directors:

(i) The company acquired the whole of the share capital of Zest Software, a public limited company on 28 February 2002 and merged Zest Software with its existing business. The directors feel that the goodwill ($10 million) arising on the purchase has an indefinite economic life, and therefore no amortisation has been provided as the goodwill is an inseparable part of the value of the business acquired. Additionally, Transystems has a 50% interest in a joint venture which gives rise to a net liability of $3 million. The reason for this liability is the fact that the negative goodwill ($6 million) arising on the acquisition of the interest in the joint venture has been deducted from the interest in the net assets ($3 million). Transystems is proposing to settle the liability of $3 million against a loan made to the joint venture by Transystems of $5 million, and show the resultant balance in tangible non-current assets. The equity method of accounting has been used to account for the interest in the joint venture. It is proposed to treat negative goodwill in the same manner as the goodwill on the purchase of Zest Software and leave it in the balance sheet indefinitely.

(ii) Transystems had itself disclosed in its financial statements $15 million of music and screen production rights which it had acquired via the purchase of another subsidiary. The group policy is to classify this intangible as current assets under inventory. Further, during the current financial period, the group has capitalised its domain names acquisition costs of $1 million within tangible non-current assets, and revalued the asset to $3 million.

(iii) The turnover of the group results mainly from the sale of software under licences which provide customers with the right to use these products. Transystems has stated that it follows emerging best practice in terms of its revenue recognition policy which it regards as US GAAP. It has stated that the International Accounting Standards Board has been slow in revising its current standards and the company has therefore adopted the US standard SAB101 *Revenue Recognition in Financial Statements*. The group policy is as follows:
- If services are essential to the functioning of the software (for example setting up the software) and the payment terms are linked, the revenue for both software and services is recognised on acceptance of the contract;
- fees from the development of customised software, where service support is incidental to its functioning, are recognised at the completion of the contract.

(iv) The group's tangible non-current assets are split into long leasehold properties (over 50 years) and short leasehold property. The group's accounting policy as regards long leasehold properties is not to depreciate them, on the grounds that their residual value is very high and the market value of the property is in excess of the carrying amount. Short leasehold properties are only depreciated over the final 10 years of the lease. The company renegotiates its short leaseholds immediately before the final 10 years of the lease, and thus no depreciation is required up to this point.

(v) Transystems uses a multi-column format in order to present its Income Statement. It wishes to use a 'boxed presentation' (see below) to highlight its exceptional items.

Transystems: Extract from Consolidated Income Statement

	Before Exceptional $m	Exceptional items $m	Total $m
Operating Profit	500	–	500
Disposal of non-current assets	–	(50)	(50)
Interest payable	(210)	–	(210)
Profit on ordinary activities before taxation	290	(50)	240

The group accountant has asked for your advice as to the acceptability of the above accounting practices under International Accounting Standards/International Financial Reporting Standards as he does not wish to suffer a qualification of the audit report or have any special comment in that report.

Required

Write a report to the group accountant advising him as to the acceptability of the above accounting practices utilised by Transystems plc.

Question 5.8: Sandown (ACCA)

(The following question is the first of three covering the thorny issue of how to account for discontinued operations under IFRS 5 (formerly IAS 35) and how to calculate and present such information. It also includes a section on deciding what costs may be incorporated within 'closure costs' under IFRS 5.)

IAS 35 *Discontinuing Operations* was approved by the IASC in April 1998 and published in June 1998. It is mainly a presentation and disclosure standard that expands on the requirements of IAS 8 *Net Profit or Loss for the Period, Fundamental Errors and Changes in Accounting Policies*. The IAS contains detailed requirements relating to discontinued operations. Many commentators feel that these requirements were prompted by a previous lack of a definition of such operations and inconsistencies in their accounting treatment, including the timing of their recognition.

Required

(a) Define a discontinuing operation and comment on the defining criteria.
(b) Describe how users of financial statements benefit from information relating to discontinuing operations; and summarise the main disclosures required in respect of discontinuing operations.

Sandown is a diversified public company. It has three main operating divisions: a chain of restaurants, a car rental agency, and the sale of computer equipment through an Internet website. In March 2001 the Board of Sandown held a meeting to consider the deteriorating performance of its Internet selling activities. The decision of the Board was that the continued losses could no longer be tolerated and the website would be closed down on 31 December 2001. In June 2001 a detailed closure plan was formulated, staff redundancy notices were issued, advertising and promotion of the website ceased and various notices to terminate contracts with service suppliers were issued.

Relevant details of Sandown's turnover and profit before taxation are:

Year to 30 September	2001 $ million	2000 $ million
Turnover	1,000	900
Cost of sales	(650)	(600)
Gross profit	350	300
Other operating expenses	(220)	(150)
Profit before tax	130	150

The following analysis of the Internet website operation has been obtained:

Year to 30 September	2001I $ million	2000 $ million
Turnover	80	50
Cost of sales	(50)	(70)
Gross profit	30	(20)
Other operating expenses	(140)	(30)
Profit/(loss) before tax	(110)	(50)

Required

(c) Prepare an analysis of the income statement into continuing and discontinuing operations as required by IAS 35 for Sandown for the year to 30 September 2001 including the comparative figures for 2000.

The 'other operating expenses' of the website for the year to 30 September 2001 were calculated as:

		$ million
Operating costs incurred		50
Provision for closure costs:		
Penalties on termination of contract	15	
Staff redundancy costs	10	
Retraining of retained staff	12	
Estimated losses on sale of net assets of the Internet site	25	
Estimated operating losses to date of closure (31 December 2001)	28	90
		140

Required

(d) Comment on the calculation of the closure costs of the website. Do not amend your answer to (c) as a result of your comments in part (d). Ignore taxation.

Question 5.9: Rationalise (ACCA)

(The next question in the batch on discontinued operations covers the presentation of discontinued operations but it also covers IAS 17 and the need to include proposed dividends as contingent liabilities. It covers IAS 39 briefly, the need to include preferred shares within debt, if redeemable, and their related dividends within interest payable. IAS 2 and the need to value inventories at the lower of their cost and NRV is also covered.)

Rationalise is a small publicly listed company whose activities consist of an engineering branch (also acting as the head office) and a paint shop branch producing specialist industrial coatings. The list of account balances of the two branches at 30 September 2000 are:

	Engineering (head office)		Paint shop	
	$	$	$	$
Equity shares of 25c each		500,000		
10% Preference shares		150,000		
Revaluation reserve		20,000		
Accumulated profits		90,000		
Land at valuation	210,000			
Buildings at cost	300,000			
Plant and equipment at cost	250,000		80,000	
Motor vehicles at cost	170,000		45,000	

Depreciation 1 October 1999:				
Buildings		80,000		
Plant and equipment		110,000		30,000
Motor vehicles		90,000		15,000
Inventories 1 October 1999	136,100		53,400	
Trade receivables	244,200		108,700	
Bank		33,100	16,000	
Trade payables		136,900		193,900
Income tax, over provision 1999		5,200		
Branch current account	81,500			
Head office current account				69,500
Sales revenue		893,000		550,000
Manufacturing expenses	545,900		461,600	
Operating expenses	151,100		93,700	
Bank interest	1,900			
Interim dividends – preference	7,500			
– equity	10,000	–	–	–
	2,108,200	2,108,200	858,400	858,400

The following information is relevant:

(i) During the year to 30 September 2000 the paint shop branch became unprofitable and the directors made the decision to close down the branch. The employees have been told of the closure and those employees who cannot be transferred to the engineering branch have been given redundancy/retrenchment notices. In addition the directors have written to all of the paint shop's customers informing them that no further orders will be accepted and the branch will formally close on 30 November 2000. The estimated direct costs of the closure, which have not yet been provided for, are:

	$
Employee related costs	10,000
Losses on disposal of branch net assets	15,000

In addition it is expected that the operating losses of the paint shop from 1 October to 30 November 2000 will be $5,000.

(ii) The inventories at 30 September 2000 were:

Head office at cost	$164,000
Paint shop at cost	$65,000

The inventories of the head office includes some goods that have a production cost of $16,000. These goods have a manufacturing defect that will cost $6,000 to correct. The normal selling price for these goods would be $25,000, but after the remedial work they will be sold through an agent as refurbished goods at a discount of 20% on the normal selling price. The agent will receive a commission of 10% of the reduced selling price.

(iii) Due to the increase in the head office's overdraft it requested a remittance of $12,000 from the branch in late September 2000. The branch had complied with the request and recorded the remittance. It had not been received by the head office at the year end.

(iv) No depreciation has been charged for the current year. The company policy is to charge a full year's depreciation on all assets held at the year end at the following rates:
- buildings – 2% per annum on cost, charged to cost of sales
- plant and equipment – 20% per annum on cost, charged to cost of sales
- motor vehicles – 25% per annum on a reducing balance basis, charged to operating expenses.

(v) The directors of Rationalise estimate that the company's provision for income tax on the operating profits for the year to 30 September 2000 of $19,000 will be comprised as follows:

On the head office profit	32,500
On the branch loss (relief)	(6,000)
On the estimated closure losses (relief)	(7,500)
	19,000

The current balance on the income tax account is the difference between the provision made in 1999 and the amount paid during the current year in settlement to the taxation authorities.

(vi) Deferred tax: at 30 September 2000 there were temporary differences of $20,000 relating to the plant and equipment of the head office of Rationalise. In addition to this, the head office building was revalued upwards by $20,000 during the year, There were no other temporary differences. Rationalise has not made any provision for deferred taxation. Assume an income tax rate of 30%.

(vii) On the 25 September 2000 the Directors declared the following dividends:
- the final preference dividend
- a final equity dividend of 1c per share.

These amounts have not yet been provided for.

Required

(a) Prepare the income statement of Rationalise for the year to 30 September 2000 treating the closure of the paint shop as a discontinued operation in accordance with IAS 35 *Discontinuing Operations*.
(b) Prepare the balance sheet of Rationalise at 30 September 2000.

Question 5.10: Halogen (ACCA)

(Although the following question is heavily directed to a business combination using the purchase or acquisition method, it does contain a second section covering IFRS 5 as well as disclosing whether or not a subsidiary could be excluded from consolidation under IAS 27. Consolidation adjustments mainly concern the elimination of inter-company profits, the calculation of minority interests and the need to freeze pre-acquisition profits and reserves.)

On 1 April 2000 Halogen acquired a controlling interest of 75% of Stimulus, a previously wholly owned subsidiary of Exowner. This date Halogen issued one new ordinary share valued at $5 and paid $1.40 in cash, for every two shares it acquired in Stimulus. The reserves of Stimulus at the date of acquisition were:

Accumulated profits	$180 million
Revaluation reserve	$40 million

The balance sheets of Halogen and Stimulus at 31 March 2001 were:

	Halogen		Stimulus	
Assets				
Non-current assets	**$ million**	**$ million**	**$ million**	**$ million**
Property, plant and equipment		910		330
Development expenditure		100		nil
Investments (including that in Stimulus)		700		60
		1,710		390
Current assets				
Inventory	224		120	
Trade receivables	264		84	
Bank	nil		25	
		488		229
Total assets		2,198		619
Equity and liabilities				
Capital and reserves:				
Equity shares of $1 each		1,000		200
Reserves:				
Share premium	300		nil	
Accumulated profits	480		240	
Revaluation reserve	60	840	40	280
		1,840		480
Non-current liabilities				
10% Debenture		nil		60
Current liabilities				
Trade payables	128		24	
Taxation	94		35	
Proposed dividends declared	50		20	
Bank overdraft	86	2,358	nil	79
Total equity and liabilities		2,198		619

The following information is relevant:

(i) At the date of acquisition the balance sheet of Stimulus included an intangible non-current asset of $8 million in respect of the development of a new medical drug. On this date an independent specialist assessed the fair value of this intangible asset at $28 million. Halogen had been developing a similar drug and shortly after the acquisition it was decided to combine the two development projects. All information and development work on Stimulus's project was transferred to Halogen in return for a payment of $36 million. The carrying value of Stimulus's development expenditure at the date of transfer was still $8 million. Stimulus has taken the profit on this transaction to its income statement. Approval to market the drug is expected in September 2001.

(ii) Both companies have a policy of keeping their land (included in property, plant and equipment) at current value. The balances on the revaluation reserves represent the revaluation surpluses at 1 April 2000. Neither company has yet recorded further increases of $10 million and $8 million for Halogen and Stimulus respectively for the year to 31 March 2001.

(iii) During the year to 31 March 2001 Halogen sold goods at a price of $26 million to Stimulus at a mark-up on cost of 30%. Half of these goods were still in inventory at the year end.

(iv) On 28 March 2001 Stimulus recorded a payment of $12 million to settle its current account balance with Halogen. Halogen had not received this by the year end. Inter-company current account balances are included in trade payables/receivables as appropriate.

(v) All goodwill is written off on a straight-line basis over a period of 5 years.

(vi) Halogen has not accounted for the proposed dividend receivable from Stimulus.

Required

(a) Prepare the consolidated balance sheet of Halogen as at 31 March 2001.

Included within the investments of Halogen is an investment in a wholly owned private limited company called Lockstart. Prior to the current year Halogen has consolidated the results of Lockstart. In recent years the profits of Lockstart have been declining and in the year to 31 March 2001 it made significant losses. In January of 2001 the management of Halogen held a board meeting where it was decided that the investment in Lockstart would be sold as soon as possible. No buyer had been found by 31 March 2001.

The directors of Halogen are aware that shareholders often use a company's published financial statements to predict future performance, and this is one of the reasons why IFRS 5 *Non-Current Assets Held for Sale and the Presentation of Discontinued Operations* requires the results of discontinuing operations to be separately identified. Shareholders are thus made aware of those parts of the business that will not contribute to future profits or losses.

In the spirit of the above, the management of Halogen have decided not to consolidate the results of Lockstart for the current year (to 31 March 2001), believing that if they were consolidated, it would give a misleading basis for predicting the group's future performance. They also note that a subsidiary company should only be consolidated when it is held as a long-term investment. They are therefore applying the rule in IAS 27 *Consolidated Financial Statements and Accounting for Investments in Subsidiaries* that a subsidiary may be excluded from consolidation where it is held with a view to resale.

Required

(b) Comment on the suitability of the Directors' treatment of Lockstart; and state how you believe Lockstart should be treated in the group financial statements of Halogen. (*Note:* you are not required to amend your answer to (a) in respect of this information.)

Question 5.11: Desolve (ACCA)

(The next question concentrates on the accounting consequences of closing down a subsidiary. It reveals the fact that there are a number of accounting standards that interface with IFRS 5 – IAS 37, IAS 36, IAS 19 and IAS 10 – and these are all covered in the question.)

Desolve, a public limited company, decided to significantly change the nature of its business and to refocus the Group's activities in two core areas: the production of carbon steel and steel alloy. In order to complete the refocusing, the directors planned and approved the closure of its glass-making activity, a 100% owned subsidiary company, Glass. This company generates 15% of the production of the Group. This decision was announced on 30 June 2001 and the subsidiary was closed down on 30 November 2001. The year end of the group is 31 July 2001 and the financial statements were approved on 10 December 2001. As a result of the closure of the operation, the following events took place:

(i) The employees of Glass were made redundant. As a result, a termination and severance agreement was drawn up by the company. All of the employees of the company were offered either employment in the refocused Group or compensation for loss of employment. Employees were told of the termination agreement in writing on 30 June 2001 and had to communicate their acceptance or otherwise by 31 August 2001. If all of the employees had accepted the severance pay, then it would have cost the Group $80 million in compensation. As at 31 July 2001 it was expected that 75% of employees would take the severance pay. The actual amount paid on 30 November 2001 was $56 million. As a result of the redundancy, the net present value of the obligation to the employees under the defined benefits retirement plan at 31 July 2001 had been reduced by $50 million, as the employees of the subsidiary affected by the redundancy would earn no further benefit beyond 30 November 2001. There was no change in the fair value of the plan assets at 31 July 2001 as a result of the redundancy.

(ii) Desolve wished to make a provision of $15 million at 31 July 2001 for the costs of closing the glass-making business. This amount has taken into account approximately $3 million for the potential profit on the disposal of the land and buildings of the subsidiary. Desolve has included this amount ($15 million) in non-current assets and not the income statement as the costs will be recoverable from the estimated disposal proceeds. The contracts for the sale of the land and buildings were signed on 1 November 2001 and were completed on 20 December 2001 for a price of $25 million at a profit of $4 million.

The equipment of the subsidiary was carried at a value of $10 million at 31 July 2001. It was anticipated that the equipment would generate cash flows of $7 million up to 30 November 2001 and that its net selling price at 31 July 2001 was $8 million. The equipment was sold on 30 November 2001 for $6 million.

iii) It was anticipated that between 31 July 2001 and 30 November 2001 the subsidiary would make operating losses of $20 million before it closed. Also there would be a cost of $5 million incurred in retraining and relocating the employees who accepted employment in the refocused Group.

iv) The directors of Desolve have indicated in the company's balance sheet at 31 July 2001 that there is a trade receivable of $8 million. This trade receivable is owed $7 million by Assess, and the trade receivable intended to offset these amounts against each other and pay Desolve the balance of $1 million. The trade receivable on hearing of the final closure of the subsidiary has decided to sue Desolve for the $7 million it is owed and has refused to pay the balance of $8 million to Desolve. The trade receivable decided to sue Desolve as it was thought that Desolve had the greater resources to repay the debt. The trade receivable is likely to go into liquidation if it does not receive the amounts that it is owed.

Required

Discuss how the above events relating to the closure of the subsidiary affected the financial statements of the Desolve Group in the year ending 11 July 2001.

Question 5.12: Zetec Group (ACCA)

(The final question in the chapter is all embracing. It requires the preparation of a consolidated income statement but it also encompasses standards covering foreign exchange translation under IAS 21, IAS 8, goodwill under IFRS 3 and intangible assets under IAS 38.)

Zetec, a public limited company, owns 80% of the ordinary share capital of Aztec, a public limited company which is situated in a foreign country. Zetec acquired Aztec on 1 November 2000 for $44 million when the retained profits of Aztec were 98 million Krams (Kr). Aztec has not issued any share capital, nor revalued any assets since acquisition. The following financial statements relate to Zetec and Aztec.

Balance Sheets at 31 October 2001

	Zetec $m	Aztec Kr m
Non-current assets		
Tangible assets (including investments)	180	380
Investment in Aztec	44	
Intangible assets		12
Net current assets	146	116
	370	508
Capital and reserves		
Ordinary shares of $1/1 Kr	65	48
Share premium	70	18
Revaluation reserves	–	12
Accumulated profits	161	110
	296	188
Non-current liabilities	74	320
	370	508

Income Statements for the year ended 31 October 2001

	Zetec $m	Aztec Kr m
Revenue	325	250
Cost of sales	(189)	(120)
Gross profit	136	130
Distribution and administrative expenses	(84)	(46)

Profit from operations	52	84
Interest payable	(2)	(20)
Profit before taxation	50	64
Income tax expense	(15)	(30)
Net profit on ordinary activities	35	34
Extraordinary items	–	(22)
Net profit for period	35	12

The directors of Zetec have not previously had the responsibility for the preparation of consolidated financial statements and are a little concerned as they understand that the financial statements of Aztec have been prepared under local accounting standards, which are inconsistent in some respects with International Accounting Standards (IAS). They wish you to prepare the consolidated financial statements on their behalf, and give you the following information about the financial statements of Aztec:

(i) Under local accounting standards, Aztec had capitalised 'market shares' under intangible assets. Aztec acquired a company in the year to 31 October 2001 and merged its activities with its own. This acquisition allowed the company to obtain a significant share of a specific market, and therefore the excess of the price paid over the fair value of assets is allocated to 'market shares'. The amount capitalised was Kr 12 million, and no amortisation is charged on 'market shares'.

(ii) Further, under local accounting standards, from 1 November 2000 Aztec classified revaluation gains and losses and the effects of changes in accounting policies as extraordinary items. During the year, the amounts classified as extraordinary items were as follows:

Revaluation loss	A non-current asset was physically damaged during the year and an amount of Kr9 million was written off its carrying value as an impairment loss. This asset had been revalued on 31 October 1999 and a credit of Kr6 million still remains in revaluation reserve in respect of this asset.
Changes in accounting policy	A change in the accounting policy for research expenditure has occurred during the period in an attempt to bring Aztec's policies into line with IAS. Prior to November 2000, research expenditure was capitalised. The amount included in extraordinary items was Kr13 million.

(iii) The fair value of the net assets of Aztec at the date of acquisition was Kr240 million after taking into account any necessary changes to align the financial statements with IAS. The directors have estimated that any goodwill arising on consolidation should be amortised over 4 years, but do not know how to calculate the amount of goodwill. The increase in the fair value of Aztec over the net assets carrying value relates to a stock market portfolio (included in tangible non-current assets) held by Aztec. The value of these investments (in Kr) has not changed materially since acquisition. Goodwill is to be treated as a dollar asset which does not fluctuate with changes in the exchange rate.

(iv) Zetec sold $15 million of components to Aztec on 31 May 2001, when the legal ownership of the goods passed to Aztec. The goods were received by Aztec on

30 June 2001 as there had been a problem in the shipping of the goods. Zetec made a profit of 20% on selling price on the components. All of the goods had been utilised in the production process at 31 October 2001, but none of the finished goods had been sold at that date. Aztec had paid for the goods on 31 July 2001. This was the only inter-company transaction in the year. Foreign exchange gains/losses on such transactions are included in cost of sales by Aztec.

(v) The following exchange rates are relevant to the financial statements:

Krams to the $	
31 October 1999	5
1 November 2000	6
1 April 2001	5.3
31 May 2001	5.2
30 June 2001	5.1
31 July 2001	4.2
31 October 2001	4
Weighted average for year to 31 October 2001	5

(vi) The directors have indicated that Aztec will operate as a separate entity with little management interference so that local profits will be maximised. Zetec utilises the benchmark treatment in IAS 8 *Net Profit or Loss for the Period, Fundamental Errors and Changes in Accounting Policies*, and intends to use the allowed alternative treatment in IAS 22 *Business Combinations* to allocate the cost of acquisition.

(vii) A dividend of $4 million had been paid by Zetec during the financial year.

Required

Prepare a consolidated income statement for the year ended 31 October 2001 and a balance sheet as at that date for the Zetec group.

6
Cash flow statements

6.1 IAS 7 *Cash Flow Statements* (revised 1992)

Objective

The income statement and the balance sheet of an enterprise show important aspects of its performance and position. However, users of financial statements are also interested in how the enterprise generates and uses its cash resources. In particular, users are concerned about the overall solvency and liquidity of the enterprise.

IAS 7 is designed to aid users in that regard, and requires a cash flow statement to be drawn up summarising the cash flows during a period classified into three separate sections:

1. Operating activities
2. Investing
3. Financing.

Operating activities

It is recognised that, although an enterprise may have generated a profit during the year and increased its assets, it may not necessarily create readily accessible cash, as the money could be tied up in stocks, debtors etc. Also, in arriving at profit a number of non-cash deductions and additions have been included – e.g. depreciation. These need to be taken into account when calculating the actual cash generated.

IAS 7 permits two methods of calculating operating cash flows – the direct and the indirect methods. The indirect method requires the profit to be reconciled to the cash flow being generated by operations. This is carried out as in the previous paragraph. The direct method, on the other hand, identifies the actual cash receipts from customers and the actual cash payments to suppliers and employees. Both methods lead to the same figure. The direct method is illustrated in Example 6.1, and the indirect as part of an overall specimen format:

Example 6.1
Direct method of calculating operating cash flows

As an alternative, the net cash flow from operating activities of 1,560 may be arrived at by
adopting the direct method as shown below:

Cash flows from operating activities

Cash receipts from customers	30,150
Cash paid to suppliers and employees	(27,600)
Cash generated from operations	2,550
Interest paid	(270)
Income taxes paid	(900)
Cash flow before extraordinary item	1,380
Proceeds from earthquake disaster settlement	180
Net cash from operating activities	1,560

Investing activities

Under this heading are included purchases and sales of long-term assets, and the
purchase and sales of investments not qualifying as cash equivalents.

Interest and dividends received may be classified under this heading, but they may
also be included under operating activities or financing. The specimen provided in the
IAS includes them as investing.

Only one figure for cash should be provided for subsidiaries acquired or disposed,
with disclosure by note of the assets and liabilities acquired/disposed.

Investing and financing transactions that do not require the use of cash or cash equivalents should be excluded from a cash flow statement. They should be disclosed elsewhere in the financial statements so that users have all the relevant information, but they
should not form part of the cash flow statement itself.

The following should be disclosed in aggregate for all acquisitions, and separately for
all disposals:

- the total purchase/disposal consideration;
- the portion of the consideration discharged via cash or cash equivalents;
- the amount of cash and cash equivalents in the acquisition/disposal;
- the amount of assets and liabilities other than cash or cash equivalents in the subsidiary acquired/disposed, summarised by each major category.

Financing activities

This should represent claims on future cash flows or sources of future cash flows, and
will include:

- cash proceeds from the issue of shares;
- cash payments to redeem/acquire the enterprise's shares;
- cash proceeds from the issue of debentures, loans etc.;

- cash repayments of loans etc.;
- cash payments by a lessee to repay principal of finance lease liabilities.

Cash and cash equivalents

The end product of the cash flow statement or balancing figure will be the increase or decrease in cash and cash equivalents. Cash equivalents are defined in IAS 7 as 'short-term, highly liquid investments that are readily convertible to known amounts of cash and which are subject to an insignificant risk of changes in value'.

An unusual feature which is required by IAS 7 is the need to provide a separate note to the financial statements detailing out the individual components of cash and cash equivalents and requiring a reconciliation to the amounts reported in the balance sheet. If there are any cash or cash equivalent balances held by the enterprise but that are not available for use by the group then these should be disclosed, together with a commentary by management.

Other issues

Foreign currency cash flows

Cash flows arising from transactions in a foreign currency should be recorded in an enterprise's reporting currency by applying to the foreign currency amount the exchange rate between the reporting currency and the foreign currency at the date of the cash flow.

On translation, the cash flows should be translated at the exchange rates between the reporting currency and the foreign currency at the dates of the cash flows.

Equity accounted investments

For associates, the only cash to be recorded are the actual dividends received and NOT the share of profit included in the income statement.

Proportionate consolidation

Joint ventures, reporting under IAS 31 *Financial Reporting of Interests in Joint Ventures* and that have adopted the policy of proportionate consolidation, should include their proportionate share of the jointly controlled entity's cash flows. However, an enterprise adopting the equity method should include the cash flows in respect of its investments in the jointly controlled entity only.

Reporting cash flows on a net basis

Cash flows arising from the following operating, investing or financing activities may be reported on a net basis:

a) Cash receipts and payments on behalf of customers when the cash flows reflect the activities of the customer rather than those of the enterprise
b) Cash receipts and payments for items in which the turnover is quick, the amounts are large, and the maturities are short.

Examples of cash receipts and payments referred to in (a) include:

- the acceptance and repayment of demand deposits of a bank;
- funds held for customers by an investment enterprise; and
- rents collected on behalf of, and paid over to, the owners of properties.

Examples of cash receipts and payments referred to in (b) are advances made for, and the repayment of:

- principal amounts relating to credit card customers;
- the purchase and sale of investments; and
- other short-term borrowings, for example those which have a maturity period of 3 months or less.

Segment information

The disclosure of segmental cash flows enables users to obtain a better understanding of the relationship between the cash flows of the business as a whole and those of its component parts and the availability and variability of segmental cash flows. An example of disclosure is provided in Note D of the specimen format.

Specimen format

Indirect method

Cash flows from operating activities		
Net profit before taxation, and extraordinary item	3,350	
Adjustments for:		
Depreciation	450	
Foreign exchange loss	40	
Investment income	(500)	
Interest expense	400	
Operating profit before working capital changes	3,740	
Increase in trade and other receivables	(500)	
Decrease in inventories	1,050	
Decrease in trade payables	(1,740)	
Cash generated from operations	2,550	
Interest paid	(270)	
Income taxes paid	(900)	
Cash flows before extraordinary item	1,380	
Proceeds from earthquake disaster settlement	180	
Net cash from operating activities		1,560
Cash flows from investing activities		
Acquisition of subsidiary X net of cash acquired (Note A)	(550)	
Purchase of property, plant and equipment (Note B)	(350)	
Proceeds from sale of equipment	20	
Interest received	200	
Dividends received	200	
Net cash used in investing activities		(480)

Cash flows from financing activities

Proceeds from issuance of share capital	250
Proceeds from long-term borrowings	250
Payment of finance lease liabilities	(90)
Dividends paid*	(1,200)
Net cash used in financing activities	(790)
Net increase in cash and cash equivalents	290
Cash and cash equivalents at beginning of period (Note C)	120
Cash and cash equivalents at end of period (Note C)	410

*This could also be shown as an operating cash flow.

Notes to the cash flow statement (direct and indirect methods)

A   Acquisition of subsidiary

During the period the group acquired subsidiary X. The fair value of assets acquired and liabilities assumed were as follows:

Cash	40
Inventories	100
Accounts receivable	100
Property, plant and equipment	650
Trade payables	(100)
Long-term debts	(200)
Total purchase price	590
Less: Cash of X	(40)
Cash flow on acquisition net of cash acquired	550

B   Property, plant and equipment

During the period, the group acquired property, plant and equipment with an aggregate cost of 1,250 of which 900 was acquired by means of finance leases. Cash payments of 350 were made to purchase property, plant and equipment.

C   Cash and cash equivalents

Cash and cash equivalents consist of cash on hand and balances with banks and investments in money market instruments. Cash and cash equivalents included in the cash flow statement comprise the following balance sheet amounts:

Cash on hand and balances with banks	40	25
Short-term investments	370	135
Cash and cash equivalents as previously reported	410	160
Effect of exchange rate changes	–	(40)
Cash and cash equivalents as restated	410	120

Cash and cash equivalents at the end of the period include deposits with banks of 100 held by a subsidiary which are not freely remittable to the holding company because of currency exchange restrictions.

The group has undrawn borrowing facilities of 2,000 of which 700 may be used only for future expansion.

D   Segment information

	Segment A	Segment B	Total
Cash flows from:			
Operating activities	1,700	(140)	1,560
Investing activities	(640)	160	(480)
Financing activities	(570)	(220)	(790)
	490	(200)	290

6.2   Examination questions

Question 6.1: Sundown (ACCA)

Shown below are the summarised financial statements of Sundown for the year to 30 September 2002, together with a comparative balance sheet:

Income statement	$ million
Sales revenue	662
Cost of sales	(396)
Gross profit	266
Operating expenses	(124)
Profit from operations	142
Interest payable	(6)
	136
Income tax	(48)
Profit for the period	88

Balance Sheet as at	30 September 2002			30 September 2001		
	$ million Cost/ valuation	$ million Depreciation	$ million NBV	$ million Cost/ valuation	$ million Depreciation	$ million NBV
Assets						
Property, plant and equipment	650	155	495	615	160	455
Current assets						
Inventory		86			72	
Trade accounts receivable		74			41	
Insurance claim		15			nil	
Bank		nil	175		12	125
Total assets			670			580
Total equity and liabilities						
Capital and reserves:						
Ordinary shares of $1 each			120			100
Reserves:						
Share premium		38			30	
Revaluation reserve		40			15	
Accumulated profits		294	372		256	301
			492			401

Non-current liabilities

Deferred tax	21		32	
10% Redeemable	30	51	50	82
preference shares				

Current liabilities

Trade accounts payable	74		65	
Provision for income tax	40		32	
Overdraft	13	127	nil	97
Total equity and liabilities		670		580

The following information is relevant:

(i) Non-current assets: depreciation of property, plant and equipment during the year was $45 million included in cost of sales. During the year, plant with a carrying value of $60 million was sold for $48 million. The loss was included in cost of sales.

(ii) Share capital: during the year some preference shares were redeemed at a premium of 10%. The company operates in a country where premiums on redemption of shares can be charged to an available share premium account. Sundown has taken advantage of this allowance. There was no issue of preference shares during the year. The increase in the ordinary share capital during the year was due to a cash issue.

(iii) Revaluation reserve: the revaluation reserve was increased during the year by the surplus on the revaluation of the company's head office. A transfer of $4 million was made from the revaluation reserve to accumulated realised profits representing the realisation of previous surpluses.

(iv) Ordinary dividends: the ordinary dividends paid during the year are part of the movement on the accumulated profits.

(v) Insurance claim: on 1 March 2002 an employee of Sundown suffered a serious accident. Sundown accepted responsibility for the accident and paid compensation of $18 million to the employee and his family. The company is partly insured against such liabilities and has agreed with the insurance company a settlement figure of $15 million (payable to Sundown). Sundown has accounted for the net cost of the claim as part of its operating expenses. It has not yet received the settlement from the insurance company, but it has recognised the $15 million receivable.

Required

(a) Prepare a cash flow statement for Sundown for the year to 30 September 2002 in accordance with IAS 7 *Cash Flow Statements*.

(b) IAS 7 encourages companies to disclose additional information on operating capacity cash flows (included as investing activities) and segment activity cash flows.

Question 6.2: Charmer (ACCA)

The summarised financial statements of Charmer for the year to 30 September 2001, together with a comparative balance sheet, are:

Income statement	$000
Sales revenue	7,482
Cost of sales	(4,284)
Gross profit	3,198
Operating expenses	(1,479)
Interest payable	(260)
Investment income	120
Profit before tax	1,579
Income tax	(520)
Profit for the period	1,059

Balance Sheet as at	30 September 2001			30 September 2000		
	$ million Cost/ valuation	$ million Depreciation	$ million NBV	$ million Cost/ valuation	$ million Depreciation	$ million NBV
Assets						
Property, plant and equipment	3,568	1,224	2,344	3,020	1,112	1,908
Investment			690			nil
			3,034			1,908
Current assets						
Inventory		1,046			785	
Trade accounts receivable		935			824	
Short-term treasury bills		120			50	
Bank		nil	2,101		122	1,781
Total assets			5,135			3,689
Total equity and liabilities						
Capital and reserves:						
Ordinary shares of $1 each			1,400			1,000
Reserves:						
Share premium		460			60	
Revaluation		90			40	
Accumulated profits						
B/f	162			147		
Net profit for the period	1,059			65		
Dividends	(500)			(50)		
C/f		721	1,271		162	262
			2,671			1,262
Non-current liabilities						
Deferred tax		439			400	
Government grants		275			200	
10% Convertible loan stock		nil	714		400	1,000

Current liabilities					
Trade accounts payable	644			760	
Accrued interest	40			25	
Provision for					
negligence claim	nil			120	
Proposed dividends	350			30	
Provision for income tax	480			367	
Government grants	100			125	
Overdraft	136	1,750		nil	1,427
Total equity and liabilities		5,135			3,689

The following information is relevant:

(i) Non-current assets: property, plant and equipment is analysed as follows:

	30 September 2001			30 September 2000		
	Cost/ valuation	**Depreciation**	**NBV**	**Cost/ valuation**	**Depreciation**	**NBV**
	$000	**$000**	**$000**	**$000**	**$000**	**$000**
Land and buildings	2,000	760	1,240	1,800	680	1,120
Plant	1,568	464	1,104	1,220	432	788
	3,568	1,224	2,344	3,020	1,112	1,908

On 1 October 2000 Charmer recorded an increase in the value of its land of $150,000. During the year an item of plant that had cost $500,000 and had accumulated depreciation of $244,000 was sold at a loss (included in cost of sales) of $86,000 on its carrying value.

(ii) Government grant: a credit of $125,000 for the current year's amortisation of government grants has been included in cost of sales.

(iii) Share capital and loan stocks: the increase in the share capital during the year was due to the following events:

- On 1 January 2001 there was a bonus issue (out of the revaluation reserve) of one bonus share for every 10 shares held
- On 1 April 2001 the 10% convertible loan stockholders exercised their right to convert to ordinary shares; the terms of conversion were 25 ordinary shares of $1 each for each $100 of 10% convertible loan stock
- The remaining increase in the ordinary shares was due to a stock market placement of shares for cash on 12 August 2001.

(iv) Dividends: the directors of Charmer always declare/propose a final dividend (if the company has made a profit) in the week preceding the company's year end. It is paid after the annual general meeting of the shareholders.

(v) Provision for negligence claim: in June 2001 Charmer made an out-of-court settlement of a negligence claim brought about by a former employee. The dispute had been in progress for 2 years and Charmer had made provisions for the potential liability in each of the two previous years. The unprovided amount of the claim at the time of settlement was $30,000, and this was charged to operating expenses.

Required

Prepare a cash flow statement for Charmer for the year to 30 September 2001 in accordance with IAS 7 *Cash Flow Statements*.

Question 6.3: Squire (ACCA)

(The third question in the chapter concentrates on the preparation of a group cash flow statement. It incorporates cash flows from associates and dividends paid out to minority interests. It also incorporates the cash flows to be taken into consideration when an acquisition takes place during the year.)

The following draft financial statements relate to Squire, a public limited company:

Draft Group Balance Sheet at 31 May 2002

	2002 $m	2001 $m
Non-current assets:		
Intangible assets	80	65
Tangible non-current assets	2,630	2,010
Investment in associate	535	550
	3,245	2,625
Retirement benefit asset	22	16
Current assets		
Inventories	1,300	1,160
Trade receivables	1,220	1,060
Cash at bank and in hand	90	280
	2,610	2,500
Total assets	5,877	5,141
Capital and reserves:		
Called up share capital	200	170
Share premium account	60	30
Revaluation reserve	92	286
Accumulated profits	508	505
	860	991
Minority interest	522	345
Non-current liabilities	1,675	1,320
Provisions for deferred tax	200	175
Current liabilities	2,620	2,310
Total equity and liabilities	5,877	5,141

Draft Group Income Statement for the year ended 31 May 2002

	$m
Revenue	8,774
Cost of sales	(7,310)
	1,464
Distribution and administrative expenses	(1,030)
Share of operating profit in associate	65
Profit from operations	499
Exchange difference on purchase of non-current assets	(9)
Interest payable	(75)
Profit before tax	415
Income tax expense (including tax on income from associate $20 million)	(225)
Profit after tax	190
Minority interests	(92)
Profit for period	98

Draft Group Statement of Recognised Gains and Losses for the year ended 31 May 2002

	$m
Profit for period	98
Foreign exchange difference of associate	(10)
Impairment losses on non-current assets offset against revaluation surplus	(194)
Total recognised gains and losses	(106)

Draft Statement of Changes in Equity for the year ended 31 May 2002

	$m
Total recognised gains and losses	(106)
Dividends paid	(85)
New shares issued	60
Total movements during the year	(131)
Shareholders' funds at 1 June 2001	991
Shareholders' funds at 31 May 2002	860

The following information relates to Squire:

(i) Squire acquired a 70% holding in Hunsten Holdings, a public limited company, on 1 June 2001. The fair values of the net assets acquired were as follows:

	$m
Tangible non-current assets	150
Inventories and work in progress	180
Provisions for onerous contracts	(30)
	300

The purchase consideration was $200 million in cash and $50 million (discounted value) deferred consideration which is payable on 1 June 2003. The provision for the onerous contracts was no longer required at 31 May 2002, as Squire had paid compensation of $30 million in order to terminate the contract on 1 December 2001. The group amortises goodwill over 5 years. The intangible asset in the group balance sheet comprises goodwill only. The difference between the discounted value of the deferred consideration ($50m) and the amount payable ($54 million) is included in 'interest payable'.

(ii) There had been no disposals of tangible non-current assets during the year. Depreciation for the period charged in cost of sales was $129 million.

(iii) Current liabilities comprised the following items:

	2002	2001
	$m	$m
Trade payables	2,355	2,105
Interest payable	65	45
Taxation	200	160
	2,620	2,310

(iv) Non-current liabilities comprised the following:

	2002 $m	2001 $m
Deferred consideration – purchase of Hunsten	54	–
Liability for the purchase of non-current assets	351	–
Loans repayable	1,270	1,320
	1,675	1,320

(v) The retirement benefit asset comprised the following:

Movement in year	$m
Surplus at 1 June 2001	16
Current and past service costs charged to income statement	(20)
Contributions paid to retirement benefit scheme	26
Surplus at 31 May 2002	22

Required

Prepare a group cash flow statement using the indirect method for Squire group for the year ended 31 May 2002 in accordance with IAS 7 *Cash Flow Statements*.

Foreign trading

7.1 IAS 21 *The Effects of Changes in Foreign Exchange Rates* (revised December 2003)

Objective

An entity may carry on foreign activities in two ways – transactions and translation. In addition, it may present its financial statements in a foreign currency. IAS 21 prescribes how transactions and foreign operations should be accounted, and how to translate financial statements into a presentation currency.

The principal issues are which exchange rates to use and how to report the effects of those changes in exchange rates.

Scope

The standard should be applied to:

- accounting for transactions and balances in foreign currencies;
- translating foreign operations in preparation for consolidation; and
- translating an entity's results into a different presentation currency.

The standard does not deal with hedge accounting (see IAS 39). It does not cover cash flows arising from transactions in a foreign currency, nor with the translation of cash flows of a foreign operation (see IAS 7).

Key definitions

Functional currency: currency of the primary economic environment in which the entity operates.

The following factors should be considered:

- the currency in which sales prices are denominated and settled;
- the country whose competitive forces and regulations mainly determine the sales prices of its goods/services;
- the currency in which labour and other costs are denominated and settled;
- the currency in which funds from financing activities are generated; and
- the currency in which receipts from operating activities are usually retained.

When the entity is a foreign operation, the following additional factors are considered:

- whether the activities of the foreign operation represent an extension of the reporting entity;
- whether transactions with the foreign entity are a high or a low proportion of the foreign operation's activities;
- whether the cash flows of the foreign operation directly affect the cash flows of the reporting entity;
- whether the cash flows of the foreign operation are sufficient to service existing and expected debt obligations.

Where the indicators are mixed, management must exercise judgement as to the functional currency to adopt that best reflects the underlying transactions.

Foreign currency: a currency other than the functional currency of the entity.

Presentation currency: the currency in which the financial statements are presented.

Exchange rate: the ratio of exchange for two currencies.

Spot exchange rate: the exchange rate for immediate delivery.

Closing rate: the spot exchange rate at the balance sheet date.

Exchange difference: difference resulting from translating one currency into another currency at different exchange rates.

Foreign operation: a subsidiary, associate, joint venture or branch whose activities are based in a country or currency other than those of the reporting entity.

Net investment in a foreign operation: the amount of the interest in the net assets of that operation. They include long-term receivables or loans, but do not include trade receivables or trade payables.

Monetary items: money and assets/liabilities held to be received/paid in fixed or determinable amounts. Examples include deferred tax, pensions, and provisions. The feature of a non-monetary item is the absence of a right to receive a fixed or determinable amount of money (includes prepayments, goodwill, intangible assets, inventories, property etc.)

Fair value: the amount for which an asset could be exchanged by willing parties in an arm's length transaction.

Summary of the approach required by this standard

Each entity must determine its functional currency as per the definition above. Many reporting entities are groups, and each individual entity should be translated into the currency in which the group statements are to be presented. The standard permits the presentation currency to be any currency. If the functional currency differs from the presentational currency, then the results and position should be translated in accordance with paras 20–37 and 49 of the standard (use of a presentation currency other than the functional currency).

The standard also permits a stand-alone entity to adopt a different presentation currency. The rules are in accordance with paras 38–49 (use of a presentation currency other than the functional currency).

Reporting foreign currency translation in the functional currency

Initial recognition

A foreign currency transaction is a transaction denominated or requiring settlement in a foreign currency, including:

- buying or selling of goods or services whose price is denominated in a foreign currency;
- borrowing or lending of funds in a foreign currency; or
- otherwise acquiring or disposing of assets denominated in a foreign currency.

A foreign currency transaction shall be recorded initially by applying the spot rate at the date of the transaction. For practical reasons, an average rate for a period may be adopted unless the rate fluctuates significantly.

Reporting at subsequent balance sheet dates

At each balance sheet date:

- monetary items should be translated at closing rate;
- non-monetary items measured at historic cost are translated at the exchange rate at the date of the transaction; and
- non-monetary items are measured at the fair value using the exchange rate when the value was determined.

The carrying amount is determined in accordance with other accounting standards – e.g. IAS 16, IAS 2 and, if an impairment, by IAS 36. When the asset is non-monetary, the carrying amount is determined by comparing the cost or carrying value and the NRV. The effect could be a write-down or *vice versa*.

When several exchange rates are available, the rate to be used should be that at which future cash flows could be settled. If exchangeability is temporarily lacking, the first subsequent rate at which exchanges could be made is used.

Recognition of exchange differences

IAS 39 deals with hedge accounting – for example, exchange differences that qualify as hedging instrument are recognised in equity to the extent that the hedge is effective.

Exchange differences on the settlement of monetary items should be expended in the period they arise with the exception of para 32 differences (see below).

Where a gain/loss on a non-monetary item is recognised directly in equity, any exchange component of that gain/loss shall also be recognised directly in equity. Conversely, when a gain/loss on a non-monetary item is recognised in profit or loss, any exchange component of that gain/loss shall be recognised in profit or loss.

Para 32 insists that exchange differences on a monetary item that forms part of an entity's net investment in a foreign operation be recognised as income/expense in the separate financial statements of the reporting entity or foreign operation, as appropriate. They should be recorded initially in a separate component of equity and then subsequently recognised in profit/loss on disposal of the net investment (i.e. they are recycled).

When a monetary item that forms part of an entity's net investment in a foreign operation is denominated in the functional currency of the reporting entity, an exchange difference should be recorded in equity. In addition, a monetary item that forms part of the net investment in a foreign operation may be denominated in a currency other than the functional currency. Exchange differences should be recognised in equity.

When an entity keeps its books in a currency other than its functional currency, all amounts are remeasured in the functional currency – i.e. monetary items at closing rate and non monetary at date of transaction.

Change in functional currency

When there is a change in functional currency, the translation procedures applicable to the new functional currency shall be applied from the date of the change. A change should only be made, however, if there is a change to those underlying transactions.

The effect is accounted for prospectively. All items are translated using the new functional exchange rate at the date of the change. The results are then treated as their historical cost. Exchange differences previously recognised in equity are not recognised as income or expenses until the disposal of the operation, and are then recycled through profits.

Use of a presentation currency other than the functional currency (paras 38–49)

Translation to the presentation currency

The financial statements may be presented in any currency. If the presentation currency differs from the functional, its results and financial position need to be translated into the presentation currency. The group, in particular, needs a common currency.

The results and position of an entity whose functional currency is not the currency of a hyperinflationary economy shall be translated into a different presentation currency as follows:

- assets and liabilities at closing rate;
- income and expenses at the exchange rates at the dates of the transactions; and
- all exchange differences in equity, as a separate component.

For practical reasons an average rate may be adopted unless exchange rates are likely to fluctuate significantly.

The exchange differences arise from:

- translating income and expenses at transaction rate and assets/liabilities at closing rate
- translating opening net assets at an exchange rate different from that previously reported.

These exchange differences are not recognised as income or expenses, as they have little or no direct effect on present and future cash flows from operations. If a foreign operation is not 100% owned, exchange differences should be attributable to minority interests.

The results and position of an entity whose functional currency is the currency of a hyperinflationary economy shall be translated as follows: all amounts at closing rate except that when amounts are being translated into the currency of a non-hyperinflationary economy, comparative amounts should be those that were presented as current year amounts in the relevant year (i.e. not adjusted for either subsequent changes in prices or exchange rates).

When the functional currency is that of a hyperinflationary economy, then its financial statements shall be restated under IAS 29 *Financial Reporting in Hyperinflationary Economies*. The accounts must be restated before the translation method is applied. Once it ceases to be hyperinflationary, it shall use the amounts restated to the price level at the date it ceases, as the historical costs for translation into the presentation currency.

Translation of a foreign operation

The incorporation of a foreign operation should follow normal consolidation procedures – e.g. elimination of inter-company balances (see IAS 27).

However, an intragroup monetary asset/liability cannot be eliminated against a corresponding intragroup asset/liability without showing the results of currency fluctuations in the consolidated accounts. Such exchange differences should continue to be recognised as income/expenses or in equity, as appropriate.

IAS 27 permits the use of different reporting dates as long as the difference is no greater than 3 months and adjustments are then made for the effects of any significant transactions between those dates. In such cases, the exchange rate to adopt is that at the balance sheet date of the foreign operation. The same approach should be applied to the equity method for associates and joint ventures.

Any goodwill and fair value adjustments shall be treated as assets and liabilities of the foreign operation. They therefore must be expressed in the functional currency of the foreign operation and translated at the closing rate.

Disposal of a foreign operation

Any cumulative exchange differences in equity shall be recognised as income or expenses when the gain or loss on disposal is recognised (i.e. they are all recycled through profits).

Tax effects of all exchange differences

Gains and losses on foreign currency transactions may have associated tax effects, and these should be accounted for under IAS 12.

Disclosure

All references are to the functional currency of the parent, if referring to a group.

An entity should disclose:

1. The amount of exchange differences included in profit or loss except those arising from IAS 39
2. Net exchange differences classified as a component of equity and a reconciliation at the start and end of the year
3. When the presentation currency is different from the functional currency, that fact shall be disclosed as well as disclosure of the functional currency and the reason for using a different presentation currency
4. When there is a change in the functional currency of either the reporting entity or a significant foreign operation, that fact and the reason for the change should be disclosed
5. When an entity presents its financial statements in a currency different from its functional, it should describe the statements as complying with IFRSs only if they comply with all of the requirements of each applicable standard and SIC including the translation method.

Where the requirements listed in (5) are not met, an entity should:

1. Clearly identify the information as supplementary
2. Disclose the currency in which the supplementary information is displayed
3. Disclose the entity's functional currency and method of translation used to determine the supplementary information.

7.2 IAS 29 *Financial Reporting in Hyperinflationary Economies* (December 2003)

Objective

The objective of IAS 29 is to establish specific standards for entities reporting in the currency of a hyperinflationary economy, so that the financial information provided is meaningful.

Scope

The standard should apply to the primary financial statements, including consolidated, of any entity whose functional currency is the currency of a hyperinflationary economy

In a hyperinflationary economy, reporting in local currency is not useful, as money loses purchasing power and therefore the accounts become misleading.

The standard does not establish an absolute rate. It is a matter of judgement when the standard becomes necessary, but the following characteristics should be reviewed:

- whether the general population prefers to invest in non-monetary assets or in a relatively stable currency
- whether the general population regards monetary amounts not in terms of local currency, but in terms of a relatively stable currency

- whether credit sales and purchases take place at prices adjusted for the expected loss in purchasing power, even if the credit period is short
- whether interest rates, wages and prices are linked to a price index
- whether the cumulative inflation rate over 3 years is approaching or exceeds 100%.

It is preferable that all enterprises in the same hyperinflationary economy apply the standard from the same date. It applies to the start of the reporting period in which hyperinflation is identified.

The restatement of financial statements

Prices change over time due to supply and demand, as well as general forces pushing up the general level of prices. In most countries, the primary statements are prepared on an historical cost basis except for the revaluation of property etc. Some enterprises, however, adopt a current cost approach using specific price increases.

In a hyperinflationary economy, financial statements must be expressed in terms of an up-to-date measuring unit if they are to be useful.

The financial statements of an entity whose functional currency is that of a hyper-inflationary economy, whether historic or current cost, must be restated in current measuring unit terms as well as corresponding figures for the previous period. The gain/loss on the net monetary position should be included within income and separately disclosed.

This approach must be consistently applied from period to period. That is more important than precise accuracy.

Historical cost financial statements

Balance sheet

Balance sheet amounts should be restated by applying a general price index. However, monetary items are not restated as they are already recorded in current monetary terms.

Index-linked bonds and loans are adjusted in accordance with the agreement. All other non-monetary assets must be restated unless they are already carried at NRV or market value.

Most non-monetary assets require the application of a general price index to their historic costs and accumulated depreciation from the date of acquisition to the balance sheet date. Inventory work in progress should be restated from the dates on which the costs of purchase and of conversion were incurred.

If detailed records of acquisition dates are not available or capable of estimation, then, in rare circumstances, an independent professional assessment may form the basis for their restatement.

If a general price index is not available, then an estimate should be based on movements in the exchange rate between the functional and a relatively stable foreign currency.

Some non-monetary assets are revalued. These need to be restated from the date of evaluation. Where fixed assets are impaired, they must be reduced to their recoverable amount and inventories to NRV.

An investee that is accounted for under the equity method may report in the currency of a hyperinflationary economy. The balance sheet and income statement are restated in accordance with this standard in order to calculate the investor's share of its net assets and results. If expressed in a foreign currency, they are translated at closing rates.

It is not appropriate both to restate the capital expenditure financed by borrowing and to capitalise that part of the borrowing costs that compensates for inflation during the same period. It should be expensed. Also, if undue effort or cost is needed to impute interest, such assets are restated from the payment date and not the date of purchase.

On first application of the standard, owner's equity must be restated by applying a general price index from the dates that different components of equity arose. Any revaluation surplus is eliminated.

At the end of the first period and subsequently, all components of owner's equity are restated by applying a general price index from the start of the period to date of contribution, and any movements disclosed as per FRS 3.

Income statement

All items must be expressed in terms of current measuring units at the balance sheet date – i.e. by being restated from the dates when initially recorded by the general price index.

Gain or loss on net monetary position

Any excess of monetary assets loses purchasing power and *vice versa*. The gain/loss is the difference resulting from the restatement of non-monetary assets, owner's equity and income statement items, and the adjustment of index-linked assets and liabilities. The gain/loss may be estimated by applying the change in a general price index to the weighted average for the period of the difference between monetary assets and monetary liabilities.

The gain or loss is included in net income. Other income statement items – e.g. interest, foreign exchange differences – are also associated with the monetary position. They should be presented together with the gain or loss on the net monetary position in the income statement.

Current cost financial statements

Balance sheet

Items stated at current cost are not restated, being already in current measurement units.

Income statement

All amounts need to be restated from their current cost at date of transactions to the balance sheet date by applying a general price index.

Gain or loss on net monetary position

This is accounted for in accordance with the historic cost approach.

Taxes

Restatement may give rise to deferred tax consequences – see IAS 12.

Cash flow statement

All items in the cash flow statement are expressed in current measuring units at the balance sheet date.

Corresponding figures

These are restated by applying a general price index so that comparative financial statements are presented in terms of current measuring units at the end of the reporting period.

Consolidated financial statements

Subsidiaries reporting in the hyperinflationary economy must be restated by applying a general price index, and if that is a foreign subsidiary then its restated financial statements should be translated at closing rates. If not in hyperinflationary economies, then they should report in accordance with IAS 21 *The Effects of Changes in Foreign Exchange Rates*.

  If adopting different reporting dates, these need to be restated into current measuring units at the date of the consolidated financial statements.

Selection and use of the general price index

All enterprises that report in the currency of the same economy should use the same index.

Economies ceasing to be hyperinflationary

When an economy ceases to be hyperinflationary and an entity discontinues using this standard, it should treat the amounts expressed at the end of the previous period as the basis for its subsequent financial statements.

Disclosures

The following should be disclosed:

. The fact that the financial statements and the corresponding periods have been restated for changes in general purchasing power and are restated in terms of current measurement units at the balance sheet date
. Whether the financial statements are based on historic cost or current cost
. The identity and level of the price index at the balance sheet date and the movement in the index during the current and previous reporting period.

7.3   Examination questions

Question 7.1: Shott (ACCA)

(The first of three questions in this chapter addresses the decision that reporting entities must make in relation to their investment in other companies – should they be regarded as totally integral to their own business and thus transaction accounting applied, or should they be treated as autonomous independent entities on their own account? The third section of the question then requires a student to demonstrate how to account for specific foreign currency transactions.)

Shott, a public limited company, set up a wholly owned foreign subsidiary company, Hammer, on 1 June 1999 with a share capital of 400,000 ordinary shares of 1 dinar. Shott transacts on a limited basis with Hammer. It maintains a current account with the company, but very few transactions are processed through this account. Shott is a multinational company with net assets of $1,500 million, and 'normal' profits are approximately $160 million. The management of Hammer are all based locally, although Shott does have a representative on the management board. The prices of the products of Hammer are determined locally, and 90% of sales are to local companies. Most of the finance required by Hammer is raised locally, although occasionally short-term finance is raised through borrowing monies from Shott. Hammer has made profits of 80,000 dinars and 120,000 dinars after dividend payments respectively for the 2 years to 31 May 2001. During the financial year to 31 May 2001, the following transactions took place:

(i)   On 30 September 2000, a dividend from Hammer of 0.15 dinars per share was declared. The dividend was received on 1 January 2001 by Shott.

(ii) Hammer sold goods of 24,000 dinars to Shott during the year. Hammer made 25% profit on the cost of the goods. The goods were ordered by Shott on 30 September 2000, were shipped free on board (fob) on 1 January 2001, and were received by Shott on 31 January 2001. Shott paid the dinar amount on 31 May 2001 and had not hedged the transaction. All the goods remain unsold as at 31 May 2001. (Goods shipped 'fob' pass the risks and rewards to the purchaser on shipment.)

(iii) Hammer borrowed 150,000 dinars on 31 January 2001 from Shott in order to alleviate its working capital problems. At 31 May 2001 Hammer's financial statements showed the amount as owing to Shott. The loan is to be treated as permanent and is designated in dollars.

The directors of Shott wish to translate the financial statements of Hammer as if it were a net investment in a foreign entity.

On 1 June 2001, Hammer was sold for 825,000 dinars and the proceeds were received on that day.

		Dinars to $1
Exchange rates:	1 June 1999	1.0
	31 May 2000	1.3
	30 September 2000	1.1
	1 January 2001	1.2
	31 January 2001	1.5
	31 May 2001	1.6
	1 June 2001	1.65
	Average rate for year to 31 May 2001	1.44

Required

(a) Discuss:
  (i) Whether the financial statements of Hammer should be translated as if the company was integral to the operations of Shott or as if Hammer were a net investment in a foreign entity
  (ii) The view that the choice of method used to translate the financial statements of an overseas company under IAS21 *The Effect of Changes in Foreign Exchange Rates* is based upon the economic relationship between the holding company and the foreign operation.
(b) Discuss how the above transactions should be dealt with in the consolidated financial statements of Shott, calculating the gain or loss on the disposal of Hammer on 1 June 2001 and stating how the cumulative exchange differences would be dealt with on the disposal.

Question 7.2: Leisure (CIMA)

(This question requires students to explain the factors that need to be taken into account when determining the appropriate method of translating a foreign subsidiary. It then goes on to discuss what impact a situation of hyperinflation would have on the accounting treatment adopted. Finally, assuming the adoption of the closing rate method, the computation of the carrying amount of a hotel complex has to be computed assuming both an economy having hyperinflation and one not.)
You are the management accountant of Leisure. On 1 January 1998, the company set up a subsidiary in Urep – a country whose currency is orbits. The investment by Leisure was 50 million orbits. The foreign subsidiary invested all the initial capital in a hotel complex, and this complex is effectively the sole asset of the subsidiary. The hotel complex is not being depreciated by the subsidiary. Relevant exchange rates at 1 January 1998 and 31 December 2000 – the accounting date for Leisure and its subsidiary – were as follows:

Date	Number of orbits per $
1 January 1998	25
31 December 2000	220

The retail price index in Urep was 100 on 1 January 1998 and 1000 on 31 December 2000.

Required

(a) Explain the factors that should be taken into account in determining the appropriate method for translating the results of an overseas subsidiary for consolidation purposes.
(b) Discuss the effects that hyperinflation can have on the usefulness of financial statements, and explain how companies with subsidiaries that are located in hyperinflationary economies should reflect this fact in their consolidated financial statements. You should restrict your discussion to financial statements that have been prepared under the historical cost convention.
(c) Assuming the closing rate method of translation is appropriate, compute the carrying value of the hotel complex in the consolidated financial statements of Leisure at 31 December 2000:
  • assuming the economy of Urep is not a hyperinflationary economy;
  • assuming the economy of Urep is a hyperinflationary economy.

Critically evaluate the results you have obtained.

Question 7.3: Ant (CIMA)

(The final question in the chapter covers a number of different accounting issues, including foreign currency translation. IAS 32's accounting for convertible loan notes and IAS 10's treatment of tax losses are also covered.)

You are the chief accountant of Ant, an enterprise that prepares financial statements in accordance with International Accounting Standards. Your assistant has prepared the first draft of the consolidated financial statements for the year ended 31 October 2003 and these show a profit after tax of $66 million, while the balance sheet shows owner-ship interest interests (i.e. total assets less total liabilities including minority interests) of $450 million.

Your assistant has identified the following issues that require your review:

Issue (a)

An overseas subsidiary has made a loss (adjusted for tax purposes and appropriately translated into $s) of $15 million for the year ended 31 October 2003. Local tax legisla-tion allows this loss to be relieved for tax purposes only against future profits of the same trade. Ant has no other subsidiaries in the same tax jurisdiction as this subsidiary. The loss is primarily due to a reduction in turnover caused by a reduction in demand for the product that the subsidiary produces. There is little indication that demand will be restored to its former levels in the foreseeable future.

Your assistant has recognised a deferred tax asset of $6 million in the draft financial statements, being the future tax consequences of the timing difference of $15 million, measured at the local tax rate of 40%. This deferred tax asset has been offset against deferred tax liabilities arising on timing differences originating in other tax jurisdictions.

Issue (b)

On 1 November 2002, Ant established a new subsidiary located in a jurisdiction where the unit of currency is the Franco. The initial investment was 40 million Francos (the ini-tial net assets of the subsidiary). The investment was financed by a loan of 40 million Francos from a German bank. No capital repayments of the loan are due until 31 October 2022.

The exchange rate at 1 November 2002 was 1.6 Francos to $1. On 31 October 2003 the exchange rate was 1.5 Francos to $1. Due to the large start-up costs, the subsidiary did not make a profit in the early months of trading and the net assets of the subsidiary at 31 October 2003 remained at 40 million Francos.

In preparing the draft consolidated financial statements, your assistant has translated both the loan and the financial statements of the subsidiary at 1.6 Francos to $1 on the basis that the financing of the subsidiary was obtained when the exchange rate was 1.6 Francos to $1. The subsidiary has its own distinct market presence and manufactures its products locally.

Issue (c)

On 1 November 2002, Ant issued two million $100 loan notes at $90 per note. A mer-chant bank received $4 million to underwrite the issue and Ant incurred other costs o

$500,000 relating to the issue of the notes. The notes pay no interest and are redeemable at $135 per note on 31 October 2007. As an alternative to redemption, the notes can be converted into 50 equity shares per $100 note on 31 October 2007. Your assistant has written off the issue costs of $4.5 million to the income statement for the year ended 31 October 2003 as an administrative expense and credited the proceeds of issue ($180 million) to a convertible loan notes account. He proposes to show this in the capital and reserves section of the balance sheet on the basis that the share price on 31 October 2007 is likely to be at least $4, so conversion, rather than repayment, is likely to be a near certainty.

Your assistant has been informed that, at 1 November 2002, the fair value of the options to convert the loan notes into shares on 31 October 2007 was $22.5 million. However, he does not consider this information to be relevant and so has ignored it.

Required

For each of the three issues, evaluate the treatment adopted by your assistant with reference to currently published Accounting Standards. Where you consider the treatment adopted to be incorrect, you should state the journal adjustment required to correct the error.

8
Taxation

8.1 IAS 12 *Income Taxes* (revised 2000)

Objective

The objective of IAS 12 is to prescribe the accounting treatment for income taxes, for both current and future tax consequences. These should be accounted for in the same way as the transactions and other events themselves – i.e. if transactions are recorded in the income statement, then so should be any related tax effect.

Scope

IAS 12 applies in accounting for income taxes, and this includes all domestic and foreign taxes based on taxable profits. It does not cover government grants. These are covered by IAS 20.

Key definitions

Accounting profit: net profit or loss for a period before deduction of tax.

Taxable profit: profit for the period determined in accordance with the rules established by the tax authorities upon which income taxes are payable.

Tax expense: the aggregate amount included in net profit for the period for current and deferred tax.

Current tax: the amount of income taxes payable in respect of the taxable profit for the period.

Deferred tax liabilities: the amounts of income taxes payable in future periods in respect of temporary timing differences.

Deferred tax assets: the amounts of income taxes recoverable in future periods in respect of

- deductible temporary differences;
- the carry forward of unused tax losses;
- the carry forward of unused tax credits.

Temporary differences: these are differences between the carrying amount of an asset or liability in the balance sheet and its tax base. They can be either:

- taxable temporary differences – these will result in taxable amounts in the future when the carrying amount of the asset or liability is settled;
- deductible temporary differences – these will result in deductible amounts in determining taxable profit when the carrying amount of the asset or liability is recovered or settled.

Tax base: the amount attributed to that asset or liability for tax purposes. A number of illustrations for both assets and liabilities are provided in Examples 8.1 and 8.2.

Example 8.1
Tax base of an asset

1. Machine costs €10,000. Capital allowances of €3,000 claimed to date. The tax base is now €7,000, as that can be deductible in the future.
2. Interest receivable has a carrying amount of €1,000. Interest is taxed on a receipt basis, thus the tax base is nil.
3. Trade debtors are €10,000. Revenue has already been included in taxable profits (as sales), thus the tax base is €10,000.
4. Dividends receivable from a subsidiary have a carrying value of €5,000, but the dividends are not taxable. The tax base is therefore €5,000.
5. A loan receivable has a carrying value of €1 m but the repayment will have no tax consequences, thus the tax base is €1 m.

Example 8.2
Tax base of a liability

1. There are accruals of €1,000 but expense is only allowed for tax when paid. The tax base is therefore nil. However, if it has already been deducted for tax purposes then the tax base would be €1,000.
2. There is interest received in advance of €10,000, but it is only taxed when received. The tax base is therefore nil.
3. There are accruals for disallowed expenditure of €100 (e.g. fines, penalties). The tax base is therefore €100.
4. A loan repayable has a carrying amount of €1 m but the repayment has no tax consequences. The tax base is therefore €1 m.

Where the tax base of an asset/liability is not immediately obvious, the fundamental principle is that a deferred tax liability or asset may only be recognised whenever recovery or settlement of the carrying amount of the asset/liability would make future tax payments larger or smaller than they would have been if such recovery or settlement were to have no tax consequences.

Recognition of current tax liabilities and current tax assets

Current tax for the current and prior periods should be recognised immediately as a liability. If the amount paid exceeds the amount due, then the excess should be recognised as an asset.

The benefit relating to a tax loss that can be carried back to recover current tax of a previous period should be recognised as an asset.

Recognition of deferred tax liabilities and deferred tax assets

Taxable timing differences

A deferred tax liability should be recognised for all taxable timing differences, unless it arises from:

1. Goodwill for which amortisation is not deductible for tax
2. The initial recognition of an asset/liability in a transaction which:
   - is not a business combination; and
   - at the time of the transaction does not affect accounting or taxable profit.

However, for taxable timing differences associated with investments in subsidiaries, associates and joint ventures, a deferred tax liability should be recognised.

Example 8.3 provides an illustration.

Example 8.3
Taxable timing differences

Asset	Cost	150	Book value	100
	Cumulative tax allowances	90	Tax rate	25%

Tax base: Cost $150 - 90 = 60 - 100$ NBV $= 40$ taxable timing difference
DT liability: $40 \times 25\% = 10$

Examples of similar temporary differences:
- interest revenue and interest received;
- depreciation and capital allowances;
- development costs capitalised and amortised but deducted for tax when incurred;
- cost of business acquisition is allocated to identifiable assets and liabilities *re* fair values but no equivalent adjustment is made for tax purposes;
- assets are revalued but no adjustment is made for tax;
- goodwill or negative goodwill on consolidation;
- non-taxable government grants;
- carrying amount of investments in subsidiaries, associates etc. which become different from the tax base of the investment.

Business combinations

In acquisitions when assets are revalued to fair value, temporary differences arise when the tax bases are left unaffected. In these cases a taxable temporary difference arise resulting in a deferred tax liability which also affects the value of goodwill.

Assets carried at fair value

Certain assets may be revalued (e.g. IAS 16 and IAS 25). The process does not affect taxable profit and the tax base remains the same. However, the future recovery of the carrying amount will result in a taxable flow of economic benefits to the enterprise, and thus the difference between the carrying amount and the tax base is a temporary difference and should give rise to a deferred tax liability or asset. This is true even if the entity has no intention of disposing the asset or is able to avail of rollover relief.

Goodwill

Amortisation is not allowable for tax and has a tax base of nil. Any difference between the carrying amount of goodwill and its tax base is a temporary timing difference. IAS 12, however, does not permit a deferred tax liability to be created, as goodwill is a residual and any tax would only increase goodwill.

Initial recognition of an asset or liability

A temporary difference may arise on the initial recognition of an asset or liability – e.g. when part of the cost of an asset is not deductible for tax. Its accounting treatment will depend on the nature of the transaction; for example:

- business combination – liability recognised and this will affect the amount of goodwill
- transaction affects accounting or taxable profit – liability recognised
- if neither of the above – liability or asset is not recognised.

Example 8.4 provides an illustration.

Example 8.4
Initial recognition of an asset or liability

Asset cost 100, no residual value, 5-year life, tax rate 40%. Depreciation is not allowed for tax and the capital gain is not taxable, nor any capital loss deductible. No recognition is therefore made initially.

Deductible temporary differences

A deferred tax asset should be recognised for all deductible temporary differences to the extent that it is probable that taxable profit will be available against which the deductible temporary difference can be utilised unless the deferred tax asset arises from:

. Negative goodwill – treated as income as per IFRS 3
. The initial recognition of an asset/liability in a transaction which:
  • is not a business combination; and
  • at the time of the transaction affects neither accounting nor taxable profit.

However, for deductible temporary differences associated with investments in subsidiaries, joint ventures and associates, a deferred tax asset should be recognised.

Example 8.5 provides an illustration.

Example 8.5
Deductible temporary differences

An enterprise recognises a liability of 100 for accrued warranty costs. These are not deductible for tax until paid.

The tax base is nil but the WDV of liability is 100, thus a temporary difference of 100 is created which, at 25%, results in a deferred tax asset of 25 provided it is probable that there will be sufficient taxable profits in the future to benefit from the costs.

The following are examples of deductible temporary differences which result in deferred tax assets:

- retirement benefit costs;
- research costs;
- cost of acquisition;
- certain assets revalued to fair value – deductible temporary difference arises if the tax base exceeds its carrying amount.

In all cases there must be sufficient future taxable profits available against which the deductible temporary differences can be utilised.

It is probable that there will be sufficient taxable profits when there are sufficient taxable temporary differences relating to the same tax authority and same taxable entity which are expected to reverse:

- in the same period as the expected reversal of the deductible temporary difference; o
- in periods into which a tax loss can be carried back or forward.

When there are insufficient taxable temporary differences, the deferred tax asset i recognised to the extent that:

- it is probable there will be sufficient taxable profit to the same tax authority and th same taxable entity in the same period as the reversal; or
- tax planning opportunities are available that will create taxable profit in appropriat periods – these might include electing to have interest income taxed on either received or receivable basis; deferring the claim for certain taxable deductions; the sal and leaseback of assets; selling an asset that generates non-taxable income (e.g. a gov ernment bond in order to purchase another investment that generates taxabl income).

Negative goodwill
No deferred tax asset is permitted for negative goodwill, as goodwill is a residual figure

Initial recognition of an asset or liability
Where a non-taxable capital grant is deducted from cost, a deductible temporary differ ences arises but no deferred tax asset should be set up. A similar result occurs for th deferred credit approach.

Unused tax losses and unused tax credits

A deferred tax asset should be recognised for the carry forward of unused tax losses and unused tax credits to the extent that it is probable that future taxable profit will be available against which the unused tax losses and unused tax credits can be utilised.

The rules are the same as for deductible temporary differences. However, the existence of unused tax losses is strong evidence that future taxable profits may not be available; thus a deferred tax asset may only be recognised to the extent that there is convincing other evidence that sufficient profits will be available. The following criteria should be considered in making that decision:

- whether there is sufficient taxable temporary differences relating to the same taxation authority and the same taxable entity to utilise the tax losses or credits;
- whether it is probable that the enterprise will have taxable profits before the unused tax losses or unused tax credits expire;
- whether the unused tax losses result from identifiable causes that are unlikely to recur;
- whether tax planning opportunities are available to create taxable profit in which the unused tax losses or credits can be utilised.

To the extent that it is not probable that taxable profit will be available then the deferred tax asset is not recognised.

Reassessment of unrecognised deferred tax assets

At each balance sheet date, a company should reassess unrecognised deferred tax assets – for example, if an improvement in trading occurs it may make it more probable that the company will be able to generate sufficient taxable profit in the future for the deferred tax asset to meet the recognition criteria.

Investments in subsidiaries, branches, associates and joint ventures

Temporary differences arise when the carrying amount of investments become different from the tax base (often cost). These differences may arise where:

there are undistributed profits;
changes occur in foreign exchange rates when a parent and its subsidiary are based in different countries; and
there is a reduction in the carrying amount of an investment in an associate to recoverable amount.

A company should recognise a deferred tax liability for all taxable temporary differences associated with these investments except to the extent that both of the following conditions are satisfied:

the parent can control the timing of the reversal of the temporary difference; and
it is probable that the temporary difference will not reverse in the foreseeable future.

As a parent controls the dividend policy of its subsidiary, it controls its timing. It is often impracticable to determine the amount of income taxes payable on reversal and thus if a parent determines that they cannot be distributed, no deferred tax liability should be recognised.

An investor in an associate does not control dividend policy, and thus a deferred tax liability should be recognised on temporary taxable differences. If it cannot be precise as to the amount, then a minimum amount should be recognised. Where a joint venturer can control the sharing of profits and it is probable that the profits will not be distributed in the foreseeable future, a deferred tax liability is not recognised.

A company should recognise a deferred tax asset only where it is probable that:

- the temporary difference will reverse in the foreseeable future; and
- taxable profit will be available against which the temporary difference can be utilised.

Measurement

Current tax liabilities (assets) should be based on tax rates enacted by the balance sheet date. They should be measured at tax rates that are expected to apply to the period when the asset is realised or liability settled.

Where different tax rates apply, average rates should be applied.

The measurement of deferred tax liabilities and assets should reflect the tax consequences that would follow from the manner in which the company expects, at the balance sheet date, to recover or settle the carrying amount of its assets and liabilities.

Illustrations are provided in Example 8.6.

Example 8.6
Measurement of deferred tax liabilities and assets

1. An asset has a carrying value of 100 and a tax base of 60. A tax rate of 20% applies if the asset is sold and 30% is applied to other income.
   Solution:
   A deferred tax liability of 8 (40 × 20%) is recognised if the entity expects to sell the asset, and a liability of 12 (40 × 30%) if it expects to retain the asset and recover from use.

2.

		NBV	**WDV**
Asset	Cost	100	100
	Depreciation	20	30
	Book value	80	70
	Revalued	150	150
	Capital gain	70	80

   Assume capital gains are not taxable.
   Solution:
   By using the asset: deferred tax is 80 × 30% = 24, but 30 cumulative tax depreciation is included in taxable income x.
   By selling the asset: deferred tax is 30% × 30 = 9.

3. The same details as above apply, except it should be assumed that capital gains are taxable at 40% after deducting an inflation adjusted cost of 110.

Solution:

By using the asset: the tax base (WDV) is 70 but 150 is taxable, thus timing difference is 80 and tax liability is $80 \times 30\% = 24$.

By selling the asset: the capital gain is 150 proceeds less the adjusted cost of	$110 = 40 \times 40\% = 16.$
The cumulative tax depreciation is	$30 \times 30\% = 9.$
Therefore, the total liability	$= 16 + 9 = 25.$

Deferred tax assets and liabilities should not be discounted

Discounting requires detailed scheduling of the timing of the reversal of each temporary difference. In many cases this process is impracticable or highly complex, therefore is inappropriate to require discounting. To permit discounting would result in deferred tax assets/liabilities not being comparable between enterprises.

The carrying amount of a deferred tax asset should be reviewed at each balance sheet date. The deferred tax asset should be reduced to the extent that it is no longer probable that sufficient taxable profit will be available to allow the asset to be utilised.

Recognition of current and deferred tax

Income statement

Current and deferred tax should be recognised as income/expenses except if it arises from a transaction directly recognised in equity or is a business combination that is an acquisition.

Items credited or charged directly to equity

Current and deferred tax should be charged directly to equity if the tax relates to items that are credited or charged directly to equity.

Examples of such items include:

a change resulting from a revaluation of fixed assets;
the correction of an error under IAS 8;
exchange differences arising on the translation of a foreign entity;
amounts arising on initial recognition of the equity component of a compound financial instrument.

Exceptionally it may be difficult to determine the tax that relates to equity, particularly where there are graduated rates of income tax and it is impossible to determine the rate at which a specific component of taxable profit has been taxed. It also occurs if there is a change in tax rate to an item previously charged or credited to equity, or where a deferred tax asset relates to an item previously charged or credited to equity. In such cases the tax should be pro rated on a reasonable basis.

Deferred tax arising from a business combination

Deferred tax assets or liabilities should be recognised on acquisitions at the date of acquisition, and these should affect the amount of goodwill calculated.

An acquiror may consider it probable that it will recover its own deferred tax asset via unused tax losses. In such cases a deferred tax asset should be recognised, and this should be taken into account when determining goodwill.

If a deferred tax asset is not recognised at the date of acquisition but is recognised subsequently, then the acquiror should adjust goodwill and related accumulated amortisation and also recognise the reduction in the net book value of goodwill as an expense. The acquiror, however, does not recognise negative goodwill nor does it increase the amount of negative goodwill in such cases (see Example 8.7).

Example 8.7
Deferred tax arising from a business combination

A company acquired a subsidiary with temporary deductible differences of 300. The tax rate was 30%. The deferred tax asset of 90 (300 × 30%) was not recognised in determining goodwill of 500. Goodwill is amortised over 20 years. Two years later, the company assumed that there would be sufficient taxable profits to recover the benefit of the deductible temporary differences.

The company should record a deferred tax asset of 90 and a deferred tax income of 90. It should reduce goodwill by 90 and accumulated amortisation by 9 (2 years). The balance of 81 is expensed in the income statement. Goodwill is now reduced to 410 (i.e. 500 − 90) less accumulated amortisation 41 (50 − 9).

If the tax rate increases to 40%, a deferred tax asset of 120 (i.e. 300 × 40%) and deferred tax income of 120 is created. If the tax rate decreases to 20%, a deferred tax asset of 60 (i.e. 300 × 20%) and deferred income of 60 is created. In both cases, goodwill is reduced by 90 and accumulated depreciation by 9.

Presentation

Tax assets and tax liabilities
Tax assets and liabilities should be presented separately from other assets and liabilities on the balance sheet. A distinction should be made between current and non-current assets and liabilities, but deferred tax assets should not be classified as current assets.

Offset
An enterprise should offset current tax assets and current tax liabilities if it has a legally enforceable right of set off and it intends to settle on a net basis. A legally enforceable right to set off normally exists when they relate to income taxes levied by the same taxation authority.

In consolidated accounts, a group offset is only allowed if there is a legally enforceable right to make or receive a single net payment and the enterprises intend to carry that out

Detailed scheduling may be required to establish reliably whether the deferred tax liability of one taxable entity will result in increased tax payments in the same period in which a deferred tax asset of another taxable entity will result in decreased payments by that second taxable entity.

Tax expense

The tax expense or income should be presented on the face of the income statement. Where exchange differences on deferred foreign tax liabilities or assets are recognised in the income statement, they may be classified as deferred tax expenses or incomes if that presentation is considered to be the most useful to users.

Disclosure

The major components of the tax expense or income should be disclosed separately. Disclosure may include:

1. Current tax expense or income
2. Adjustments for current tax of prior periods
3. The amount of deferred tax expense or income relating to the origination and reversal of temporary differences
4. The amount of deferred tax expense or income caused by changes in tax rates
5. The amount of the benefit arising from a previously unrecognised tax loss, tax credit or temporary difference of a prior period used to reduce current tax expense
6. The amount of the benefit from a previously unrecognised tax loss, tax credit or temporary difference of a prior period used to reduce deferred tax expense
7. Deferred tax expense arising from the write-down or reversal of a previous write-down of a deferred tax asset
8. The tax expense or income relating to changes in accounting policies or IAS 8 errors.

The following should also be disclosed separately:

1. The aggregate current and deferred tax charged directly to equity
2. The tax expense or income related to extraordinary items (now banned under IFRS 3)
3. An explanation of the relationship between tax expense and accounting profit via a numerical reconciliation between tax expense and the accounting profit multiplied by the current applicable tax rate or a reconciliation between the average effective tax rate and the applicable tax rate
4. An explanation of changes in applicable tax rates compared to previous years
5. The amount of deductible temporary differences, unused tax losses etc. for which no deferred tax asset is recognised
6. The aggregate amount of temporary differences associated with subsidiaries etc. for which no deferred tax liabilities have not been recognised
7. For each type of temporary difference:
   - the amount of deferred tax assets/liabilities recognised in the balance sheet
   - the amount of deferred tax income/expenses recognised in the income statement
8. For discontinued operations the tax expense relating to:
   - the gain or loss on discontinuance; and
   - the profit or loss from ordinary activities of discontinued activities together with corresponding amounts.

The enterprise should disclose the amount of a deferred tax asset and the nature of evidence supporting its recognition when both:

The utilisation of the deferred tax asset is dependent on future taxable profits in excess of profits arising from the reversal of existing taxable temporary differences
The enterprise has suffered a loss in either the current or preceding period in the tax jurisdiction to which the deferred tax asset relates.

Example 8.8 provides an illustration.

Example 8.8
Reconciliation of tax expense

In 2002 an enterprise has an accounting profit of 1,500 in country A (2001: 2,000) and in country B 1,500 (2001: 500). The tax rate is 30% in country A and 20% in country B. In country A, expenses of 100 (2001: 200) are not deductible for tax purposes.

Reconciliation of domestic tax rate:

		2001	**2002**	
Accounting profit	(2,000 + 500)	2,500	3,000	(1,500 + 1,500)
Tax at domestic rate of 30%		750	900	
Tax effect of expenses that are				
non-deductible for tax	(200 × 30%)	60	30	(100 × 30%)
Effect of lower tax rates in country B	(500 × 10%)	(50)	(150)	(1,500 × 10%)
Tax expense		760	780	

Reconciliation for each national jurisdiction:

Accounting profit			
Tax at domestic rates applicable to			
profits in the country concerned	((2,000 × 30%) +		((1,500 × 30%) +
	(500 × 20%)) 700		750 (1,500 × 20%))
Tax effect of expenses that are non			
deductible for tax	60		30
Tax expense	760		780

Illustrative disclosure

The amounts to be disclosed in accordance with IAS 12 are as follows.

Major components of tax expense (income)

	X5	**X6**
Current tax expense	3,570	2,359
Deferred tax expense relating to the origination and reversal		
of temporary differences	420	822
Deferred tax expense (income) resulting from a reduction		
in the tax base	–	(1,127)
Tax expense	3,990	2,054

Aggregate current and deferred tax relating to items
 charged or credited to equity

Deferred tax relating to revaluation of building	–	(11,130)

In addition, deferred tax of 557 was transferred in X6 from retained profits to revaluation reserve. This relates to the difference between the actual depreciation on the building and equivalent depreciation based on the cost of the building.

Explanation of the relationship between tax expense and accounting profit

There are two alternative methods for reconciling taxable income and accounting profit:

1. *Numerical reconciliation between tax expense/income and the product of accounting profit multiplied by the applicable tax rates.*

	X5	X6
Accounting profit	8,775	8,740
Tax at the applicable rate of 35% (X5: 40%)	3,510	3,059
Tax effect of expenses that are not deductible for tax:		
Charitable donations	200	122
Fines for environmental pollution	280	–
Reduction in opening deferred taxes caused by reduction in tax rate	–	(1,127)
Tax expense	3,990	2,054

The applicable tax rate is the aggregate of the national income tax rate of 30% (X5: 35%) and the local income tax rate of 5%.

2. *Numerical reconciliation between the average effective tax rate and the applicable tax rate, disclosing also the basis on which the applicable tax rate is computed.*

	X5	X6
	%	%
Applicable tax rate	40.0	35.0
Tax effect of expenses that are not deductible for tax:		
Charitable donations	2.3	1.4
Fines for environmental pollution	3.2	–
Effect on opening deferred taxes of reduction in tax rate	–	(12.9)
Average effective tax rate (tax expense divided by profit before tax)	45.5	23.5

The applicable tax rate is the aggregate of the national income tax rate of 30% (X5: 35%) and the local income tax rate of 5%.

Explanation of changes in the applicable tax rates compared to the previous accounting period

In X6 the government enacted a change in the national income tax rate from 35% to 30%.

In respect of each type of temporary difference, and in respect of each type of unused tax losses and unused tax credits, the following should be disclosed:

1. The amount of the deferred tax assets and liabilities recognised in the balance sheet for each period presented
2. The amount of the deferred tax income or expense recognised in the income statement for each period presented, if this is not apparent from the changes in the amounts recognised in the balance sheet.

		X5		X6
Accelerated depreciation for tax purposes	(24,300 × 40%)	9,720	10,322	(59,700 × 35%)
Liabilities for health care benefits that are deducted for tax only when paid	(2,000 × 40%)	(800)	(1,050)	(3,000 × 35%)
Product development costs deducted from taxable profit in earlier years	(250 × 40%)	100	–	
Revaluation, net of related depreciation (31,800 − 1,590 = 30,210 × 35%)		–	10,573	
Deferred tax liability		9,020	19,845	

SIC 21 *Income Taxes – Recovery of Revalued Non-Depreciable Assets* (June 2000)

Issue

Under IAS 12 the measurement of deferred tax liabilities and assets should reflect the tax consequences that would follow from the manner in which the entity expects, at the balance sheet date, to recover or settle the carrying amount of those assets and liabilities that give rise to temporary differences.

IAS 20 notes that revaluation does not always affect taxable profit in the period of revaluation and that the tax base of the asset may not be adjusted as a result of the revaluation. If the future recovery of the carrying value will be taxable, any difference between the carrying amount of the revalued asset and its tax base is a temporary difference and gives rise to a deferred tax liability or asset.

The issue is how to interpret the term 'recovery' in relation to an asset that is not depreciated and is revalued under IAS 16. It also applies to investment properties.

Consensus

The deferred tax liability or asset that arises from the revaluation of a non-depreciable asset under IAS 16 should be measured based on the tax consequences that would follow from recovery of the carrying amount of that asset through sale. That is regardless of the basis of measuring the carrying amount of that asset. Thus, if the tax law specifies a tax rate applicable to the taxable amount derived from the sale of an asset that differs from the tax rate applicable to the taxable amount derived from using the asset, the former rate is applied in measuring the deferred tax liability or asset related to a non-depreciable asset.

SIC 25 *Income Taxes – Changes in the Tax Status of an Enterprise or its Shareholders* (June 2000)

Issue

A change in tax status of an entity or of its shareholders may have consequences for an entity by increasing or decreasing its tax liabilities or assets. This may occur on the public listing of an entity's equity instruments or upon the restructuring of an entity's equity. It may also occur upon a controlling shareholder's move to a foreign country. As a result of such an event, an entity may be taxed differently; it may, for example, gain or lose tax incentives or become subject to a different rate of tax in the future.

A change in the tax status of an entity or its shareholders may have an immediate effect on the entity's current tax liabilities or assets. The change may also increase or decrease the deferred tax liabilities and assets recognised by the entity, depending on the effect the change in tax status has on the tax consequences that will arise from recovering or settling the carrying amount of the entity's assets and liabilities.

The issue is how an entity should account for the tax consequences of a change in its tax status or that of its shareholders.

Consensus

A change in tax status does not give rise to increases or decreases in amounts recognised directly in equity. The current and deferred tax consequences of a change in tax status should be included in net profit/loss for the period, unless those consequences relate to transactions and events that result, in the same or a different period, in a direct credit/charge to equity. Those tax consequences that relate to a change in equity in the same or a different period should be charged or credited directly to equity.

8.2   Examination questions

Question 8.1: H (CIMA)

(The first question in this chapter requires students to calculate the total tax charge, both current and deferred, that would appear in the financial statements of a reporting entity. In addition a discussion about the impact of retirement benefits on the likely set up of a deferred asset is covered, as well as the rationale for a reconciliation statement to be made between taxable and accounting profit.)

H is a major manufacturing enterprise. According to the enterprise's records, temporary differences of $2.00 million had arisen at 30 April 2002 because of differences between the carrying amount of non-current assets and their tax base. These had arisen because H had exercised its right to claim accelerated tax relief in the earlier years of the asset lives.

At 30 April 2001, the temporary differences attributable to non-current assets were $2.30 million.

H has a defined benefit retirement benefit scheme for its employees. The enterprise administers the scheme itself.

H's tax rate has been 30% in the past. On 30 April 2002, the directors of H were advised that the rate of tax would decrease to 28% by the time that the temporary differences on the non-current assets reversed.

The estimated tax charge for the year ended 30 April 2002 was $400,000. The estimated charge for the year ended 30 April 2001 was agreed with the tax authorities and settled without adjustment.

Required

(a) Prepare the notes in respect of current taxation and deferred tax as they would appear in the financial statements of H for the year ended 30 April 2002. (*Your answer should be expressed in $ million and you should work to two decimal places.*)

(b) The directors of H are concerned that they might be required to report a deferred tax asset in respect of their enterprise retirement benefit scheme. Explain why such an asset might arise.

(c) IAS 12 *Income Taxes* requires enterprises to publish an explanation of the relationship between taxable income and accounting profit. This can take the form of a numerical reconciliation between the tax expense and the product of accounting profit multiplied by the applicable tax rate. Explain why this explanation is helpful to the readers of financial statements.

Question 8.2: Payit (CIMA)

(The second question requires students to explain why the nil and partial provision bases have been rejected when developing IAS 12. There is also a short deferred tax calculation covering inter-company stock profits and tax losses of an overseas subsidiary.)

The problem of accounting for deferred tax is one that has been on the agenda of the standard setters around the world for some time. The International Accounting Standards Board last revised the International Accounting Standard dealing with deferred tax in 1996, when it published IAS 12 *Income Taxes*. This standard basically requires that the full provision basis be used to account for deferred tax, and therefore rejects the two alternative bases of accounting for deferred tax – the nil provision (or 'flow-through') basis and the partial provision basis. IAS 12 requires that (subject to certain exceptions) the full provision approach should be applied to all temporary differences. There is an alternative view (held, for example, by the Accounting Standards Board in the UK) that under the full provision approach, deferred tax is not required unless the temporary difference is a timing difference. Such an approach implies that enterprises are not normally required to provide for deferred tax on revaluation surpluses or fair value adjustments arising on consolidation of a subsidiary for the first time.

Required

(a) Explain why the IASB rejected the nil provision and partial provision bases when developing IAS 12.

(b) Discuss the logic underlying the IAS 12 approach to recognition of deferred tax and explain why this leads to deferred tax being provided on revaluation surpluses and fair value adjustments.

You are the management accountant of Payit. Your assistant is preparing the consolidated financial statements for the year ended 31 March 2002. However, he is unsure how to account for the deferred tax effects of certain transactions as he has not studied IAS 12. These transactions are given below.

Transaction 1:
During the year, Payit sold goods to a subsidiary for $10 million, making a profit of 20% on selling price. 25% of these goods were still in the inventories of the subsidiary at 31 March 2002. The subsidiary and Payit are in the same tax jurisdiction and pay tax on profits at 30%.

Transaction 2:
An overseas subsidiary made a loss adjusted for tax purposes of $8 million ($ equivalent). The only relief available for this tax loss is to carry it forward for offset against future taxable profits of the overseas subsidiary. Taxable profits of the overseas subsidiary suffer tax at a rate of 25%.

Required

(c) Compute the effect of BOTH the above transactions on the deferred tax amounts in the consolidated balance sheet of Payit at 31 March 2002. You should provide a full explanation for your calculations and indicate any assumptions you make in formulating your answer.

Question 8.3: Cohort (ACCA)

(The third question on the subject of taxation covers the deferred tax implications for a group of companies covering various topics such as the acquisition of a database, inter-company profit loading, the valuation of investments at market value, general loan provisions and unused tax losses.)

Cohort is a private limited company and has two 100% owned subsidiaries, Legion and Air, both themselves private limited companies. Cohort acquired Air on 1 January 2002 for $5 million when the fair value of the net assets was $4 million, and the tax base of the net assets was $3.5 million. The acquisition of Air and Legion was part of a business strategy whereby Cohort would build up the 'value' of the group over a 3-year period and then list its existing share capital on the Stock Exchange.

The following details relate to the acquisition of Air, which manufactures electronic goods:

(i) Part of the purchase price has been allocated to intangible assets because it relates to the acquisition of a database of key customers from Air. The recognition and measurement criteria for an intangible asset under IAS 22 *Business Combinations*/IAS 38 *Intangible Assets* do not appear to have been met, but the directors feel that the intangible asset of $0.5 million will be allowed for tax purposes and have computed the tax provision accordingly. However, the tax authorities could possibly challenge this opinion.

(ii) Air has sold goods worth $3 million to Cohort since acquisition and made a profit of $1 million on the transaction. The inventory of these goods recorded in Cohort's balance sheet at the year end of 31 May 2002 was $1.8 million.

(iii) The balance on the income statement of Air at acquisition was $2 million. The directors of Cohort have decided that, during the 3 years to the date that they intend to list the shares of the company, they will realise earnings through future dividend payments from the subsidiary amounting to $500,000 per year. Tax is payable on any remittance or dividends and no dividends have been declared for the current year.

Legion was acquired on 1 June 2001 and is a company which undertakes various projects ranging from debt factoring to investing in property and commodities. The following details relate to Legion for the year ending 31 May 2002:

(i) Legion has a portfolio of readily marketable government securities which are held as current assets. These investments are stated at market value in the balance sheet with any gain or loss taken to the income statement. These gains and losses are taxed when the investments are sold. Currently the accumulated unrealised gains are $4 million.

(ii) Legion has calculated that it requires a general provision of $2 million against its total loan portfolio. Tax relief is available when the specific loan is written off. Management feel that this part of the business will expand and thus the amount of the general provision will increase.

(ii) When Cohort acquired Legion it had unused tax losses brought forward. At 1 June 2001, it appeared that Legion would have sufficient taxable profit to realise the deferred tax asset created by these losses but subsequent events have proven that the future taxable profit will not be sufficient to realise all of the unused tax loss.

Amortisation of goodwill is not allowed as a deduction in determining taxable profit. The current tax rate for Cohort is 30% and for public companies is 35%.

Required

Write a note suitable for presentation to the partner of an accounting firm setting out the deferred tax implications of the above information for the Cohort Group of companies.

Question 8.4: DT (ACCA)

(The final question in the chapter requires students to discuss the balance sheet focus to providing for deferred tax, and the arguments for and against discounting deferred tax liabilities. The last section of the question requires a very detailed calculation of the deferred tax liability for a company incorporating tax losses, goodwill, revaluation of properties and other temporary differences.)

IAS 12 *Income Taxes* utilises a balance sheet focus in accounting for deferred taxation, which is calculated on the basis of temporary differences.

The methods used in IAS 12 can lead to accumulation of large tax assets or liabilities over a prolonged period, and this could be remedied by discounting these assets or liabilities. There is currently international disagreement over the discounting of deferred tax balances.

Required

(a) Explain what the terms 'Balance Sheet Focus' and 'Temporary Differences' mean in relation to deferred taxation.
(b) Discuss the arguments for and against discounting long-term deferred tax balances.

DT, a public limited company, has decided to adopt the provisions of the IASs for the first time in its financial statements for the year ended 30 November 2000. The amounts of deferred taxation provided and unprovided as set out in the notes of the group financial statements for the year ending 30 November 1999 were as follows:

	Provided $m	Unprovided $m
Tax depreciation in excess of accounting depreciation	38	12
Other timing differences	11	14
Liabilities for health care benefits	(12)	–
Losses available for offset against future taxable profits	(34)	(56)
Income tax on capital gains arising on the disposal of property which has been deferred	–	165
Tax that would arise if properties were disposed of at their revalued amounts	–	140
	3	275

The following notes are relevant to the calculation of the deferred tax provision as a 30 November 2000:

(i) DT acquired a 100% holding in an overseas company on 30 November 2000. The subsidiary does not propose to pay any dividends for the financial year t 30 November 2000 or in the foreseeable future. The carrying amount in DT' consolidated financial statements of its investment in the subsidiary at 30 November 2000 is made up as follows:

	$m
Carrying value of net assets acquired excluding deferred tax	76
Goodwill (before deferred tax and amortisation)	14
Carrying amount/cost of investment	90

The tax base of the net assets of the subsidiary at acquisition was $60 million. No deduction is available in the subsidiary's tax jurisdiction for the cost of goodwill.

Immediately after acquisition on 30 November 2000, DT had supplied the subsidiary with inventory amounting to $30 million at a profit of 20% on the selling price. This inventory had not been sold by the year end, and the tax rate applied to the subsidiary's profit is 25%. There was no significant difference between the fair values and carrying values on the acquisition of the subsidiary.

(ii) The carrying amount of the property, plant and equipment (excluding that of the subsidiary) is $2,600 million and their tax base is $1,920 million. The tax arising on the revaluation of properties, if disposed of at their revalued amounts, is the same at 30 November 2000 as at the beginning of the year. The revaluation of the properties is included in the carrying amount above.

Other taxable temporary differences (excluding the subsidiary) amount to $90 million as at 30 November 2000.

(iii) The liability for health care benefits in the balance sheet had risen to $100 million as at 30 November 2000 and the tax base is zero. Health care benefits are deductible for tax purposes when payments are made to retirees. No payments were made during the year to 30 November 2000.

(iv) Under the tax law of the country, tax losses can be carried forward for 3 years only. The taxable profits for the years ending 30 November were anticipated to be as follows:

2000	2001	2002
$m	$m	$m
110	100	130

The auditors are unsure about the availability of taxable profits in 2002 as the amount is based upon the projected acquisition of a profitable company. It is anticipated that there will be no future reversals of existing taxable temporary differences until after 30 November 2002.

(v) Income tax on the property disposed of becomes payable on 30 November 2003 under the deferral relief provisions of the tax laws of the country. There had been no sales or revaluations of property during the year to 30 November 2000.

(vi) Income tax is assumed to be 30% for the foreseeable future in DT's jurisdiction, and the company wishes to discount any deferred tax liabilities at a rate of 4% if allowed by IAS 12.

(ii) There are no other temporary differences other than those set out above. The directors of DT have calculated the opening balance of deferred tax using IAS 12 to be $280 million and not the total of the provided and unprovided amounts of $278 million at the beginning of the year.

Required

(c) Calculate the provision for deferred tax required by the DT Group at 30 November 2000 and the deferred tax expense in the Income Statement for the year ending 30 November 2000 using IAS 12, commenting on the effect that the application of IAS 12 will have on the financial statements of the DT Group.

9

Group accounting

9.1 IAS 27 *Consolidated and Separate Financial Statements* (December 2003)

Scope

This standard should be applied in the preparation and presentation of consolidated financial statements for a group of enterprises under the control of a parent.

IAS 27 should also be applied to accounting for investments in subsidiaries in a parent's separate financial statements.

The standard does not deal with:

- methods of business combinations (see IFRS 3);
- accounting for investments in associates (see IAS 28);
- accounting for investments in joint ventures (see IAS 31).

Key definitions

Control: power to govern the accounting and financial policies of another entity so as to obtain benefits from its activities.

Subsidiary: an entity that is controlled by another (the parent).

Parent: an entity that has one or more subsidiaries.

Consolidated financial statements: financial statements of a group presented as those of a single economic entity.

Minority interest: portion of the net results and net assets of a subsidiary attributable to interests not owned directly or indirectly by the parent.

Presentation of consolidated financial statements

A parent should present consolidated financial statements in which it consolidates its investments in subsidiaries in accordance with IAS 27.

However, a parent need not present consolidated financial statements if, and only, if:

the parent itself is a 100% owned subsidiary or is partially owned by another entity whose owners have been informed and do not object to the parent not preparing consolidated accounts; and

- the parent's debt or equity instruments are not traded publically; and
- the parent did not file nor is it in the process of filing its financial statements with a securities commission for the purpose of going on the public market; and
- the ultimate or any intermediate parent of the parent publishes consolidated financial statements available for public use that comply with IFRSs.

Scope of consolidated financial statements

A parent should consolidate all subsidiaries, foreign and domestic, other than those referred to below.

Control is presumed to exist when the parent owns over 50% of the voting power of an enterprise unless, in exceptional circumstances, it can be clearly demonstrated that such ownership does not constitute control.

Control also exists where there is:

- power over more than 50% of voting rights via an agreement with other investors; or
- power to govern the financial and operating policies under statute or agreement; or
- power to appoint or remove the majority of members of the board; or
- power to cast the majority of votes at meetings of the board of directors.

In making this judgement consideration should also be given to the existence and effect of potential voting rights held by another entity – e.g. share warrants, call options, convertible shares/debt etc.

A subsidiary should be excluded from consolidation when:

- control is only temporary as it is expected to be disposed in the near future (12 months); and
- management is actively seeking a buyer.

Such subsidiaries should be accounted for in accordance with IAS 39.

A subsidiary is not excluded just because its activities are dissimilar from those of the group nor if there are severe restrictions that impair its ability to transfer funds to the parent. Control must be lost for exclusion to occur. Better information is provided by full consolidation backed up by segment reporting, under IAS 14.

Consolidation procedures

The parent and its subsidiaries are combined on a line-by-line basis by adding together like items of assets, liabilities, equity, income and expenses. The following steps are then taken

1. The parent's investment in each subsidiary and the parent's portion of equity of each subsidiary are eliminated
2. Minority interests in the net income of subsidiaries are identified and adjusted against group income in order to arrive at the net income attributable to the parent
3. Minority interests in the net assets are identified and presented separately from liabilities. Minority interests in net assets consist of:
   - the amount at the date of the original combination as per IFRS 3; and
   - the minority's share of movements in equity since combination.

Where there are potential voting rights in existence, the proportions of profit or loss and changes in equity allocated to the parent and minority interests are determined on the basis of present ownership interests and they should not reflect the possible exercise or conversion of those potential voting rights.

Taxes should be computed in accordance with IAS 12.

Intra-group balances and transactions should be eliminated in full. Unrealised losses should also be eliminated unless their cost cannot be recovered. Unrealised profits on inventory and fixed assets should be eliminated in full and any timing differences dealt with in accordance with IAS 12.

The financial statements should be drawn up to the same reporting date for all entities in the group. However, if the financial statements are drawn up to different dates, adjustments should be made for the effects of significant transactions that occur between those dates. In any case, the difference between reporting dates should be no longer than 3 months.

Consistency dictates that the length of the reporting periods should be the same from period to period.

Uniform accounting policies must be adopted for like transactions and appropriate adjustments must be made in preparing the consolidated financial statements.

The subsidiary should be included in the consolidated accounts from the date of acquisition – i.e. the date control is effectively transferred to the buyer, in accordance with IFRS 3. The results of subsidiaries disposed are included in the consolidated income statement until the date of disposal – i.e. the date on which control ceases. The difference between the proceeds from disposal and carrying amount should be included in the income statement at the date of disposal. That includes the cumulative amount of any exchange differences that relate to the subsidiary recognised in equity in accordance with IAS 21 (i.e. recycling is compulsory).

An investment should be accounted for in accordance with IAS 39, from the date it ceases to fall within the definition of a subsidiary and does not become an associate under IAS 28. The carrying amount is regarded as its cost thereafter.

Minority interest must be presented within equity but separate from the parent shareholders' equity. Minority interests in the income statement should also be separately presented. The losses recorded may exceed the minority interest in the equity and this excess must be charged to the majority except to the extent that the minority has a binding obligation and is able to make good those losses. If the subsidiary subsequently reports profits, the majority interest is allocated all such profits until the minority's share of losses has been recovered.

If the subsidiary has cumulative preference shares held by a minority and classified as equity, the parent should compute its share of profits or losses after adjusting for the dividends on such shares, whether or not these dividends have been declared.

Accounting for investments in subsidiaries, jointly controlled entities and associates in separate financial statements

Where separate financial statements are prepared, investments in subsidiaries should be either:

carried at cost; or
accounted for as available for sale financial assets as per IAS 39.

The same accounting treatment should be applied for each category of investments.

Investments in subsidiaries, jointly controlled entities and associates that are accounted for in accordance with IAS 39 in the consolidated accounts should be accounted for in the same way as in the investor's separate financial statements.

Disclosure

The following disclosures should be made:

1. The fact that a subsidiary is not consolidated
2. Summarised financial information of subsidiaries, either individually or in groups, that are not consolidated, including the amounts of total assets, liabilities, revenues and profits or losses
3. The nature of the relationship between the parent and a subsidiary when the parent does not own, directly or indirectly through subsidiaries, more than 50% of the voting power
4. The reasons why ownership, directly or indirectly, of more than 50% of the voting power does not give control
5. The reporting date of a subsidiary, if different from the parent, and reason for using it
6. The nature and extent of any significant restrictions on the ability of subsidiaries to transfer funds to the parent via cash dividends or to repay loans or advances.

When separate financial statements are prepared for a parent that elects not to prepare consolidated financial statements, those separate financial statements should disclose:

1. The fact that the financial statements are separate; that the exemption from consolidation has been used; the name and country of incorporation or residence of the entity publishing consolidated accounts in accordance with IFRSs; and the address where consolidated accounts are available
2. A list of significant investments in subsidiaries, jointly controlled entities and associates, including the name, country of incorporation or residence, proportion of ownership interest and, if different, the proportion of voting power held
3. A description of the method used to account for the investments listed in (1).

When a parent, venturer or investor in an associate prepares separate financial statements, those statements must disclose:

1. The fact that the statements are separate and the reasons why prepared, if not by law
2. A list of significant investments in subsidiaries, jointly controlled entities and associates, including the name, country of incorporation or residence, proportion of ownership interest and, if different, proportion of voting power held
3. A description of the method used to account for the investments listed under (2).

SIC 12 *Consolidation – Special Purpose Entities* (November 1998)

Issue

An entity may be created to accomplish a narrow and well-defined objective, e.g. to effect a lease, research and development activities or a securitisation. Such a special purpose entity (SPE) may take the form of a corporation, trust, partnership or unincorporated entity. SPEs often include strict limits on their decision-making powers.

The sponsor frequently transfers assets to the SPE, obtains the right to use assets held by the SPE or performs services for the SPE, while other parties (capital providers) may provide the funding to the SPE. An entity that engages in transactions with an SPE may in substance control the SPE.

A beneficial interest in an SPE may take the form of a debt instrument, an equity instrument, a participation right, a residual interest or a lease. In most cases the sponsor retains a significant beneficial interest in the SPE's activities, even though it may own little or none of the SPE's equity.

IAS 27 does not provide explicit guidance on the consolidation of SPEs.

The issue is under what circumstances an entity should consolidate an SPE. It does not apply to post-employment benefit plans or equity compensation plans.

Consensus

An SPE should be consolidated when the substance of the relationship between an entity and an SPE indicates that the SPE is controlled by that entity.

In the context of an SPE, control may arise through the predetermination of the activities of the SPE (autopilot) or otherwise. Control may exist when less than 50% of the voting power rests with the reporting entity. Judgement is required to decide whether or not control exists in the context of all relevant factors.

In addition to IAS 27, the following circumstances may indicate a relationship in which an entity controls an SPE and consequently should consolidate the SPE:

- in substance, the activities of the SPE are being conducted on behalf of the entity according to its specific business needs so that the entity obtains benefits from the SPE's operation;

  in substance, the entity has the decision-making powers to obtain the majority of the benefits of the activities of the SPE or, by setting up an 'autopilot' mechanism, the entity has delegated these decision-making powers;

- in substance, the entity has rights to obtain the majority of the benefits of the SPE and therefore may be exposed to risks incident to the activities of the SPE; or

  in substance, the entity retains the majority of the residual or ownership risks related to the SPE or its assets in order to obtain benefits from its activities.

Predetermination of the ongoing activities of an SPE by an entity would not represent the type of restrictions referred to in IAS 27.

Some Indicators of Control over an SPE are provided in an appendix. These include:

- *Activities.* The activities are, in substance, being conducted on behalf of the reporting entity, and include situations where the SPE is principally engaged in providing a source of long-term capital to the entity or it provides a supply of goods and services consistent with the entity's major operations. Economic dependence of an entity on the reporting enterprise does not, by itself, lead to control.

- *Decision-making.* The reporting entity , in substance, has the decision-making powers to control or obtain control of the SPE or its assets, including certain decision-making powers coming into existence after the formation of the SPE. Such decision-making powers may have been delegated by establishing an 'autopilot' mechanism. Examples include the power to unilaterally dissolve an SPE, the power of change to the SPE's charter or the power to veto proposed changes of the SPE' s charter.

3. *Benefits.* The reporting entity, in substance, has rights to obtain a majority of the benefits of the SPE's activities through a statute, contract, agreement etc. Such rights may be indicators of control when they are specified in favour of an entity that is engaged in transactions with an SPE and that enterprise stands to gain those benefits from the financial performance of the SPE. Examples are rights to a majority of any economic benefits or rights to majority residual interests such as a liquidation.

4. *Risks.* An indication of control may be obtained by evaluating the risks of each party engaging in transactions with an SPE. This could be a guarantee to outside investors providing most of the capital to the SPE. Examples include when the capital providers do not have a significant interest in the underlying net assets of the SPE, the capital providers do not have rights to future economic benefits of the SPE, the capital providers are not substantively exposed to the inherent risks of the underlying net assets or operations of the SPE or in substance, or the capital providers receive mainly consideration equivalent to a lender's return through a debt or equity interest.

9.2 IFRS 3 *Business Combinations* (March 2004)

IAS 22 *Business Combinations* permitted two methods of accounting – the pooling of interests and the purchase method. Although IAS 22 restricted the use of pooling, analysts indicated that two methods impaired comparability and created incentives for structuring those transactions to achieve a particular accounting result.

This, combined with the prohibition of pooling by USA, Canada and Australia, prompted the IASB to seek harmonisation.

In addition, various jurisdictions dealt differently with goodwill, and IAS 22 permitted two methods of applying the purchase method – benchmark (combination of fair value of acquirer's ownership interest and pre-acquisition carrying amounts for minority interests) or allowed alternative to measure all assets at fair value.

The IASB seeks to ensure that similar transactions are not accounted for in dissimilar ways, as this impairs their usefulness.

The IFRS was an attempt to improve the quality of and seek international convergence on accounting for business combinations, including:

- the method of accounting for business combinations;
- the initial measurement of identifiable net assets acquired;
- the recognition of liabilities for terminating the activities of an acquiree;
- the treatment of any excess of an acquirer's interest in fair values of identifiable net assets acquired;
- the accounting treatment for goodwill and intangible assets.

Objective

The objective of IFRS 3 is to specify the financial reporting by an entity when it combines with one or more entities.

Scope

IFRS 3 should apply to all business combinations except for:

- joint ventures;
- business combinations under common control;
- business combinations involving two or more mutual entities; and
- business combination entities brought together by contract alone to form a reporting entity.

Identifying a business combination

A business combination is a bringing together of separate entities into one single reporting entity. It may be structured in a number of ways for legal, taxation or other reasons.

It may result in the creation of a parent–subsidiary relationship in which the acquirer is the parent and the acquiree the subsidiary. The acquirer should apply the IFRS to its consolidated statements. In its own accounts it records the investment under IAS 27 *Consolidated and Separate Financial Statements* as an investment in a subsidiary.

It may result in the purchase of net assets, including goodwill, but not the purchase of the entity itself. This does not result in a parent–subsidiary relationship.

Included within the IFRS are business combinations where one entity obtains control of another entity but the acquisition date does not coincide with the date of acquiring an ownership interest – e.g. a share buy-back arrangement. It does not apply to joint ventures (see IAS 31 *Financial Reporting of Interests in Joint Ventures*).

Business combinations involving entities under common control

These occur where all of the combining entities are ultimately controlled by the same party both before and after the date of business combination. A group of individuals are regarded as controlling an entity if, as a result of contractual arrangements, they collectively have the power to govern its financial and operating policies. These are outside the scope of the IFRS. The extent of minority interests is not relevant to determining whether or not the entity is under common control. They will be dealt with in a subsequent standard.

Method of accounting

All business combinations should be accounted for under the purchase method. This method recognises that the net assets are acquired by the acquirer and that the measurement of the acquirer's own net assets are not affected by the transaction.

Application of the purchase method

The following steps should be undertaken in the purchase method:

Identification of an acquirer
Measuring the cost of a business combination
Allocating, at the acquisition date, the cost to net assets acquired.

Identification of an acquirer

An acquirer should be identified for all business combinations. The acquirer is the entity that obtains control of the other combining entity. The purchase method always assumes an acquirer. Control is the power to govern the financial and operating policies of an entity in order to obtain benefits. Normally this requires more than 50% of an entity's voting rights. Even if this is not the case, the following could result in an acquirer:

- power over more than 50% of voting rights via an agreement with other investors; or
- power to govern the financial and operating policies of the other entity under statute or an agreement; or
- power to appoint or remove a majority of the board of directors; or
- power to cast a majority of votes at meetings of the board of directors.

Although it may be difficult to identify an acquirer, there are usually indications that one exists. For example:

- if the fair value of one of the combining entities is significantly greater than the other
- if there is an exchange of voting ordinary shares for cash
- if the management of one dominates the selection of the management team of the combined entity.

In a business combination via an exchange of equity, the entity that issues the equity shares is usually the acquirer. However, all pertinent facts must be considered in determining which of the combining entities has the power to govern the operating and financial policies of the other entity. In some business combinations, e.g. reverse acquisitions, the acquirer is the entity whose equity interests themselves have been acquired. That occurs when a private operating entity arranges to have itself acquired by a non-operating or dormant public entity as a means of obtaining a stock exchange listing. Although legally the public entity is the parent, the circumstances could indicate that the smaller entity has acquired a larger entity.

When a new entity is formed, one of the combining entities must be adjudged to be the acquirer on the evidence available.

Measuring the costs of a business combination

The acquirer shall measure the cost of a business combination as the aggregate of:

- the fair values of assets given (usually cash), liabilities incurred (e.g. loans) and equity issued by the acquirer in exchange for control of the acquiree; plus
- any costs directly attributable to business combination.

The acquisition date is the date when the acquirer effectively obtains control of the acquiree. When achieved through a single transaction, the date of exchange coincides with the acquisition date. However, if the entity is acquired in stages:

- the cost is the aggregate of individual transactions; and
- the date of exchange is the date of each exchange transaction whereas the acquisition date is the date on which an acquirer obtains control.

When settlement of any part of the cost is deferred, the fair value is determined by discounting the amounts payable to their present value at the date of exchange.

The published price at the date of exchange of a quoted equity provides the best evidence of the instrument's fair value. Other evidence should only be used in rare circumstances when the published price is unreliable and where that other evidence is a more reliable measure (e.g. thinness of the market). One example would be to use an estimate of their proportional interest in the fair value of the acquirer or by reference to their proportionate interest in the fair value of the acquiree obtained, whichever is more clearly evident. In any event, all aspects of the combination should be considered.

The cost of a combination includes liabilities incurred by the acquirer in exchange for control of the acquiree. However, future losses shall not be included as part of that cost. Costs should include professional fees incurred but not general administration expenses. The costs of arranging and issuing financial liabilities, however, are part of the cost of issuing the financial instrument, and are not part of the costs of the business combination. Similarly, the costs of issuing equity instruments are an integral part of the equity issue but they should not be included in the costs of a business combination.

Adjustments to the cost of a business combination contingent on future events (earn out clauses)

In these situations the acquirer should include an amount of the adjustment in the cost of combination if the contingency is probable and can be measured reliably. It could be paid after a specified level of income has been achieved in the future or on the market price being maintained. If the future events do not occur, then the cost can be adjusted accordingly. It should not be included if it is not probable or cannot be measured reliably, but if future events make it probable then it can be adjusted to the entity's cost of acquisition.

In some circumstances, the acquirer may be required to make a subsequent payment to the seller as compensation for a reduction in the value of assets given. This occurs if the acquirer has guaranteed the market price of equity or debt instruments issued. In such cases, no increase in the cost of the business combination is recognised. In the case of debt instruments, the additional payment is regarded as a reduction in the premium or an increase in the discount on the initial issue.

Allocating the cost of a business combination to the assets acquired and liabilities and contingent liabilities assumed

The acquirer, at acquisition date, should allocate the cost of a business combination by recognising the acquiree's identifiable net assets at fair value. Any difference between the cost of the combination and the acquirer's interest in the net fair value of identifiable assets should be accounted for as goodwill. However, non-current assets held for sale and discontinued operations are valued at fair value less costs to sell (as per IFRS 5).

The acquirer should recognise separately the acquiree's identifiable net assets at acquisition date only if they satisfy the following criteria:

. For an asset other than an intangible asset, it is probable that any associated future economic benefits will flow to the acquirer and it can be measured reliably
. For a liability other than contingencies, it is probable that an outflow of economic benefits will occur and its fair value can be reliably measured
. For intangible assets, their fair value can be measured reliably
. For contingent liabilities, their fair value can be reliably measured.

The acquirer's income statement shall incorporate the acquiree's post-acquisition profits and losses in the income statement. Expenses should be based on the cost of the business combination – for example, depreciation should be based on the fair values of those depreciable assets at the acquisition date (i.e. based on their cost to the acquirer).

It is not necessary for a transaction to be closed or finalised at law before the acquirer effectively obtains control. All pertinent facts should be considered in assessing when the acquirer has effectively obtained control.

Any minority interest in the acquiree should be stated at the minority's proportion of the net fair values of those items.

Acquiree's identifiable assets and liabilities

Only those identifiable net assets that existed at the acquisition date and satisfy the recognition criteria in (1) to (4) above may be recognised separately by the acquirer. Thus:

- the acquirer should recognise liabilities for terminating an acquiree only when the acquiree has an existing liability for restructuring recognised via IAS 37 *Provisions, Contingent Liabilities and Contingent Assets*; and
- the acquirer may not recognise liabilities for future losses.

A payment contractually agreed to be made to employees or suppliers, in the event it is acquired, is an obligation, but it is contingent until it becomes probable that a business combination will occur. The identifiable net assets might include some never recognised previously assets – e.g. tax benefit due to the acquiree's tax losses when the acquirer has adequate future taxable profits against which the losses can be offset.

Acquiree's intangible assets

An intangible asset of the acquiree may only be recognised if it meets the definition of an intangible asset under IAS 38 and its fair value can be reliably measured. A non-monetary asset must be identifiable and be separate from goodwill. Thus this can only happen if it:

- is separable, i.e. it is capable of being separated and sold, transferred, licensed, rented or exchanged; or
- arises from contractual or other legal rights.

Some examples are provided in the appendix to the standard, but these are not intended to be exhaustive (see Example 9.1).

Example 9.1
Intangible assets – separate from goodwill

An intangible asset must be a non-monetary asset without physical substance and be separate from goodwill – i.e. it must arise from contractual or other legal rights. Such assets include the following.

A. Marketing-related intangible assets

1. Trademarks, trade names, service marks, collective marks and certification marks
2. Internet domain names

3. Trade dress (unique colour, share or package design)
4. Newspaper mastheads
5. Non-competition agreements.

B. Customer-related intangible assets

1. Customer lists
2. Order or production backlogs
3. Customer contracts and the related customer relationships
4. Non-contractual customer relationships.

C. Artistic-related intangible assets

These normally arise from contractual or legal rights such as copyrights, and include:

1. Plays, operas and ballets
2. Books, magazines, newspapers and other literary works
3. Musical works
4. Pictures and photographs
5. Video material, including films, music videos, television programmes.

D. Contract-based intangible assets

1. Licensing, royalty agreements
2. Advertising contracts
3. Lease agreements
4. Construction permits
5. Franchise agreements
6. Operating and broadcasting rights
7. Drilling rights for water, air and minerals
8. Servicing and mortgage service contracts
9. Employment contracts.

E. Technology-based intangible assets

1. Patented technology
2. Computer software and mask works
3. Unpatented technology
4. Databases
5. Trade secrets (e.g. recipes).

Acquiree's contingent liabilities

These may only be recognised if their fair values can be measured reliably. If not, they would be disclosed in accordance with IAS 37.

After initial recognition, the acquirer should measure recognised contingent liabilities at the higher of:

the amount that would be recognised per IAS 37; and
the initial amount less cumulative amortisation per IAS 18.

The above does not apply to contracts under IAS 39. However, loan commitments excluded from IAS 39 are accounted for as contingent liabilities if it is not probable that an outflow will be required to settle the obligation or it cannot be reliably measured.

Goodwill

The acquirer should:

- recognise goodwill as an asset; and
- initially measure it at cost being the excess of cost over an acquirer's interest in the fair value of identifiable net assets.

Goodwill represents future economic benefits that are not capable of being individually identified and separately recognised. Goodwill is essentially the residual cost after allocating fair values to identifiable net assets taken over.

After initial recognition, the acquirer should measure goodwill at cost less accumulated impairment losses. It should not be amortised but instead tested annually for impairment, or more frequently if events indicate that it might be impaired, in accordance with IAS 36.

Excess of acquirer's interest in the net fair value of acquiree's identifiable assets, liabilities and contingent liabilities over cost (negative goodwill)

If the fair value of net assets acquired exceeds the cost, then the acquirer must:

- reassess the identification and measurement of the net assets acquired; and
- recognise immediately in profit or loss any excess remaining after that reassessment.

A gain in that situation could arise from the following:

- errors in measuring the fair value of the cost of the combination and the fact that future costs are not reflected correctly in the fair value of the acquiree's identifiable net assets;
- a requirement in an accounting standard to measure identifiable net assets at an amount that is not fair value but treated for this purpose as its fair value;
- a bargain purchase.

Business combination achieved in stages

Each exchange transaction should be treated separately by the acquirer to determine goodwill. This results in a step-by-step comparison of the cost of the individual investments with the acquirer's percentage interest in the fair values of the acquiree's identifiable net assets.

In that situation the fair values may be different at the date of each exchange transaction because:

- the acquiree's net assets are notionally restated to fair value at each exchange transaction; and
- the acquiree's identifiable assets must be valued at their fair values at acquisition date

Any adjustment to those fair values relating to previously held interests of the acquirer is a revaluation, but it does not signify that the acquirer has elected to apply a general policy of revaluation under IAS 16 *Property, Plant and Equipment*.

Initial accounting determined provisionally

Fair values need to be assigned to the acquiree's identifiable net assets initially. If these can only be determined provisionally at the end of the first reporting period, then these values may be adopted. However the acquirer should recognise any adjustments, after finalising the initial accounting, to those provisional values within 12 months of the acquisition date.

Also, any adjustments should be recognised from the acquisition date. Thus:

- the book value of adjusted net assets should be adjusted to fair value at that date;
- goodwill should be adjusted; and
- comparatives should be adjusted (e.g. additional depreciation).

Adjustments after the initial accounting is complete

Except for contingent consideration or finalisation of any deferred tax assets, adjustments to the initial accounting after an initial accounting is complete can only be recognised to correct an error in accordance with IAS 8 *Accounting Policies, Changes in Accounting Estimates and Errors*. In that case, a prior period adjustment should be recorded.

Recognition of deferred tax assets after the initial accounting is complete

If the potential benefit of the acquiree's income tax loss carry forwards did not satisfy the criteria for separate recognition, on initial accounting, but is subsequently realised, then in addition the acquirer should:

- reduce goodwill to an amount that would have been recognised if the deferred tax asset had been recognised as an identifiable asset from acquisition date; and
- recognise the reduction in the carrying amount of goodwill as an expense.

However, this procedure should not result in the creation of negative goodwill.

Disclosure

An acquirer should disclose sufficient information that enables users to evaluate the nature and financial effect of business combinations that were effected:

- during the reporting period; and
- after the balance sheet date but before the financial statements are authorised.

To achieve this, the following information should be provided for each business combination effected during the reporting period:

1. The names and descriptions of the combining entities
2. The date of acquisition
3. The percentage of voting equity instruments acquired
4. The cost of the combination and a description of the components of that cost; when equity instruments are issued the following should also be disclosed:
   - the number of equity instruments issued; and
   - the fair value of those instruments and the basis for determining that fair value (if no published price exists or that price has not been used as a reliable indicator, then that fact must be disclosed together with the reasons and the method and assumptions actually adopted as well as disclosing the aggregate amount of the difference between the value attributed to and the published price of equity instruments).
5. Details of operations that the entity has decided to dispose
6. The amounts recognised for each class of the acquiree's net assets at acquisition date together with their carrying amounts immediately prior to the combination

7. The amount of any excess recognised in profit or loss on the creation of negative goodwill
8. A description of the factors contributing to the recognition of goodwill
9. The amount of the acquiree's profit or loss since the acquisition date included in the acquirer's profit or loss for the period, unless impracticable; if impracticable, that fact must be disclosed.

The information above may be disclosed in aggregate for business combinations that are individually immaterial. If the initial accounting was only provisionally determined, that fact should also be disclosed together with an explanation of why this is the case.

The following should also be provided unless it would be impracticable:

1. The revenue of the combined entity for the period as though the acquisition date was at the start of the reporting period
2. The profit or loss of the combined entity for the period as though the acquisition date was at the start of the reporting period.

If it would be impracticable, that fact must be disclosed.

An acquirer should disclose information that enables users to evaluate the financial effects of gains, losses, error corrections and other adjustments recognised in the current period that relate to business combinations that were effected in the current or in previous periods. In that regard, the following should be disclosed:

1. The amount and explanation for any gain/loss recognised in the current reporting period that:
   - relates to the identifiable assets acquired or liabilities assumed in a business combination effected in a previous reporting period; and
   - is of such size, nature or incidence that disclosure is relevant to an understanding of the combined entity's financial performance.
2. If the initial accounting is provisional, the amounts and explanations of adjustments made to provisional values during the reporting period
3. Information about error corrections required to be disclosed under IAS 8.

An entity should disclose an intangible fixed asset schedule for goodwill which requires a reconciliation of goodwill between the start and end of the reporting period, showing separately:

1. The gross amount and accumulated impairment losses at the start of the period
2. Additional goodwill recognised in the period
3. Adjustments resulting in the subsequent recognition of deferred tax assets
4. Goodwill included in a disposal group (per IFRS 5) and derecognised in the period not included in a disposal group
5. Impairment losses recognised in accordance with IAS 36
6. Net exchange differences arising during the period (per IAS 21)
7. Any other changes in the carrying amount during the period
8. The gross amount and accumulated impairment losses at the end of the period.

Entities should also disclose any additional information as is necessary to meet the objectives of enabling users properly to evaluate the nature and financial effect of business combinations.

Transitional provisions and effective date

The IFRS applies to business combinations for which the agreement date is set on or after 31 March 2004. It should apply to:

goodwill arising from a business combination for which the agreement date is on or after 31 March 2004; or
any negative goodwill for an agreement date on or after 31 March 2004.

Previously recognised goodwill

The IFRS should apply on a prospective basis. Thus an entity must:

from the start of the first annual reporting period beginning on or after 31 March 2004, discontinue amortising goodwill for 'old' business combinations
from the start of the first annual reporting period on or after 31 March 2004, eliminate the carrying amount of accumulated amortisation with a corresponding reduction in goodwill; and
from the start of the first annual reporting period beginning on or after 31 March 2004, test goodwill for impairment in accordance with IAS 36 *Impairment of Assets*.

If goodwill was previously written off annually (per SSAP 22) an entity should not recognise that goodwill in the income statement when it disposes all or part of the business to which it relates or when a CGU is impaired.

Previously recognised negative goodwill

This should be derecognised starting on or after 31 March 2004, with a corresponding adjustment to opening retained earnings.

Previously recognised intangible assets

These should be reclassified as goodwill if that intangible asset does not, at 31 March 2004, meet the identifiability criterion in IAS 38.

Equity accounted investments

For equity accounted investments, the IFRS should apply in accounting for:

any goodwill included in the carrying amount of the investment
any negative goodwill, which should be treated as income.

For investments accounted for by applying the equity method and acquired before the IFRS was issued, it:

should be applied on a prospective basis and therefore should discontinue amortisation of goodwill
should derecognise any negative goodwill with a corresponding adjustment to retained earnings.

9.3 IAS 28 *Accounting for Investments in Associates* (December 2003)

Scope

IAS 28 should be applied by an investor in accounting for investments in associates.

Key definitions

Associate: an entity in which the investor has significant influence and which is neither subsidiary nor a joint venture of the investor.

Significant influence: the power to participate in the financial and operating policy decision of the investee, but without control over those policies.

The equity method: a method of accounting whereby the investment is initially recorded a cost and is adjusted thereafter for the post-acquisition change in the investor's share o net assets of the investee. The income statement reflects the investor's share of the resul of operations of the investee.

The cost method: the investment is recorded at cost. The income statement reflects incom only to the extent that the investor receives dividends from the investee subsequent to th date of acquisition.

Significant influence

If an investor holds, directly or indirectly, 20% or more of the voting power of th investee, it is presumed that it has significant influence unless it can be clearly demon strated that this is not the case. Conversely, if it holds less than 20% of the voting powe of the investee, the presumption is that the investor does not have significant influenc A majority shareholder by another investor does not preclude an investor having signif cant influence.

  Its existence is usually evidenced in one or more of the following ways:

* representation on the board of directors;
* participation in the policy-making processes;
* material transactions between the investor and the investee;
* interchange of managerial personnel; or
* the provision of essential technical information.

Equity method

The investment is initially recorded at cost and its carrying amount is increased/decrease to recognise the investor's share of profits/losses of the investee after the date of acquis tion. Dividends received from the investee reduce the carrying amount of the investmen

Cost method

The investment should be recorded at cost. Income should only be included to the extent that it receives dividends from post-acquisition profits. Dividends received in excess of such profits should be recorded as a reduction of the cost of the investment.

Consolidated financial statements

An investment in an associate should be accounted for in the consolidated accounts under the equity method except when:

- the investment is acquired and held exclusively with a view to its subsequent disposal in the near future; or
- it operates under severe long-term restrictions.

In these latter cases, the investments should be accounted for in accordance with IAS 39.

Dividends received may bear little relationship to the performance of the associate. As the investor has significant influence over the associate, the investor has a measure of responsibility for the associate's performance and it should account for this stewardship by extending the scope of consolidation to include the investor's share of results of such an associate. As a result, the application of the equity method provides more informative reporting of both net assets and net income of the investor.

An investor should discontinue the use of the equity method from the date that:

- it ceases to have significant influence but retains, either in part or in whole, its investment; or
- the use of the equity method is no longer appropriate as the associate operates under severe long-term restrictions.

The carrying value should be regarded as cost thereafter.

Separate financial statements of the investor

An investment in an associate, for an entity publishing consolidated accounts, should be:

carried at cost;
accounted for using the equity method as per IAS 28; or
accounted for as an 'available for sale financial asset' as per IAS 39.

An investment in an associate, for an entity not publishing consolidated accounts, should be:

carried at cost;
accounted for using the equity method if the equity method would be appropriate for the associate if the investor had issued consolidated accounts; or
accounted for under IAS 39 as an 'available for sale financial asset'.

Basically, an investor should provide the same information about its investments in associates as those entities that issue consolidated accounts.

Application of the equity method

Many of the procedures appropriate for applying equity accounting are similar to consolidation under IAS 27.

On acquisition, any difference between the cost of acquisition and the investor's share of the fair values of the net identifiable assets is accounted for under IFRS 3. Appropriate adjustments to post-acquisition share of profits are made to account for depreciation based on fair values.

The most recent available financial statements of the associate are used by the investor in applying the equity method, and they are usually drawn up to the same date as the investor's. When the dates differ, the associate often prepares statements specifically for the investor to the same date, but if this is impracticable then a different date may be used. However, the length of the reporting periods should be consistent from period to period.

When different dates have to be adopted, any adjustments for significant events occurring between the date of the associate's statements and the date of the investor's financial statements must be made.

Uniform accounting policies should be adopted and appropriate adjustments are made to the associate's statements, but if this is not practicable that fact must be disclosed.

If an associate has outstanding cumulative preferred shares held by outsiders, the investor must compute its share of profits/losses after adjusting for preferred dividends whether these are declared or not.

If an investor's share of losses exceeds the carrying amount of the investment, the investor should stop including its share of losses and instead report the investment at £nil. Additional losses are only provided to the extent that the investor has incurred obligations which it has guaranteed to the investee. If subsequently the associate does report profits, the investor can only resume inclusion of its share of the investee profits once its share of profits equals the share of losses not recognised.

Impairment losses

If there is an indication of impairment losses in an associate, an entity should apply IAS 36. In determining value in use, an entity estimates:

- its share of the present value of estimated future cash flows expected to be generated by the investee as a whole, including the proceeds on ultimate disposal; or
- the present value of estimated future cash flows expected to arise from dividends and from ultimate disposal.

Both methods give the same result, under appropriate assumptions. Any impairment loss is then allocated as per IAS 36. It must therefore be allocated first to goodwill.

The recoverable amount of an investment is assessed for each individual associate unless that associate does not generate independent cash flows.

Income taxes

Income taxes should be accounted for in accordance with IAS 12.

Contingencies

In accordance with IAS 37, an investor discloses:

- its share of contingent liabilities and capital commitments of an associate; and
- those contingent liabilities arising because the investor is severally liable for ALL the liabilities of the associate.

Disclosure

The following disclosures should be made:

1. An appropriate listing and description of significant associates, including the proportion of ownership interest and, if different, the proportion of voting power held
2. The methods used to account for such investments.

Investments in associates should be classified as long-term assets and disclosed separately in the balance sheet. The investor's share of profits/losses should be disclosed separately in the income statement.

9.4   IAS 31 *Interests in Joint Ventures* (December 2003)

Scope

This standard should be applied in accounting for interests in joint ventures and the reporting of joint venture assets, liabilities, income and expenses in the financial statements of venturers and investors, regardless of the structures under which the activities take place.

It does not apply, however, to interests held by venture capitalists or mutual funds/unit trusts classified as held for trading under IAS 39.

A venturer with an interest in a jointly controlled entity is exempted from proportional consolidation and equity accounting when it meets the following conditions:

- There is evidence that the interest is acquired and held exclusively with a view to disposal within 12 months from acquisition and management is actively seeking a buyer
- The exception in IAS 27 permitting a parent not to prepare consolidated accounts applies; or
- All of the following apply:
  - the venturer is 100% owned or the minority are aware and have given permission not to apply proportionate consolidation or the equity method;
  - the venturer's debt or equity are not traded in a public market;
  - the venturer did not file nor is in the process of filing its statements publically; and
  - the ultimate or intermediate parent publishes consolidated accounts.

Key definitions

Joint venture: a contractual agreement whereby two or more parties undertake an economic activity which is subject to joint control.

Joint control: the contractually agreed sharing of control over an economic activity.

Venturer: a party to a joint venture and having joint control over that joint venture.

Proportionate consolidation: a method of accounting and reporting whereby a venturer's share of each of the assets, liabilities, income and expenses of a jointly controlled entity is combined on a line-by-line basis with similar items in the venturer's financial statements or reported as separate line items.

Equity method: initially the investment is carried at cost and adjusted thereafter for the post-acquisition change in the venturer's share of net assets of the jointly controlled entity. The income statement reflects the venturer's share of results of operations of the jointly controlled entity.

Forms of joint venture

IAS 31 identifies three broad types of joint venture activity:

1. Jointly controlled operations
2. Jointly controlled assets
3. Jointly controlled entities.

They all have the common characteristics of having two or more joint venturers bound under contract and establishing joint control.

Joint control may be precluded when an investee is in legal reorganisation or in bankruptcy, or operates under severe long-term restrictions on its ability to transfer funds to the venturer.

Contractual arrangement

The existence of a contract distinguishes interests involving joint control from investments in associates in which an investor has significant influence.

The contract may be evidenced by way of a formal contract or minutes of discussion between the venturers. In some cases, it may be incorporated in the articles of the joint venture. It is usually in writing, and deals with such matters as:

- the activity, duration and reporting obligations of the joint venture;
- the appointment of the board of directors of the joint venture and voting rights of venturers;
- capital contributions by the venturers; and
- the sharing by the venturers of the output, income, expenses or results of the joint venture.

No single venturer is in a position unilaterally to control activity, but instead requires the consent of all the venturers to undertake essential decisions.

Jointly controlled operations

Some joint ventures involve the use of assets and other resources rather than the establishment of a corporation, partnership or other entity. Each venturer uses its own assets and incurs its own expenses, and raises its own finance.

The joint venture agreement usually provides a means by which revenue from the sale of the joint product and any expenses are shared among the venturers. An example might be a joint venture to manufacture, market and distribute jointly a particular product such as an aircraft. Different parts of the manufacturing process are carried out by each of the venturers, and each venturer takes a share of the revenue from the sale of the aircraft but bears its own costs.

A venturer should recognise in its financial statements the following:

- the assets it controls and the liabilities it incurs; and
- the expenses it incurs and its share of the income it earns from the sale of goods or services by the joint venture.

No adjustments or other consolidated procedures are required, as the elements are already included in the separate statements of the investor.

Separate accounting records may not be required for the joint venture, but the venturers may prepare management accounts in order to assess the performance of the joint venture.

Jointly controlled assets

Some joint ventures involve joint control by the venturers over one or more assets which are dedicated for the purposes of the joint venture. Each venturer may take a share of the output and bear an agreed share of the expenses incurred.

No corporation, however, is established. Many activities in oil and gas and mineral extraction involve jointly controlled assets (e.g. an oil pipeline). Another example is the joint control of property, with each taking a share of the rents received and bearing a share of the expenses.

A venturer should recognise in its financial statements:

its share of jointly controlled assets, classified according to their nature;
any liabilities it has incurred;
its share of any liabilities jointly incurred with other venturers;
any income from the sale or use of the share of the output of the joint venture together with its share of any expenses incurred;
any expenses incurred re its interest in the joint venture.

No adjustments or other consolidation adjustments are required, as the assets, liabilities, income and expenses are already recognised in the separate financial statements of the venturer.

The treatment of jointly controlled assets reflects the substance and economic reality and usually the legal form of the joint venture. Separate accounting records for the joint venture may be limited to those expenses incurred in common. Financial statements may not be prepared for the joint venture, but management accounts may be needed to assess performance.

Jointly controlled entities

In this case a corporation is established and operates as per other legal entities except that there is a contractual arrangement between the venturers that establishes joint control over the economic activity of the entity.

A jointly controlled entity controls the assets of the joint venture, incurs liabilities and expenses, and earns income. It may enter contracts in its own name and raise finance for itself, and each venturer is entitled to a share of the results of the jointly controlled entity.

An example is when two entities combine their activities in a particular line of business by transferring relevant assets and liabilities into a jointly controlled entity, or it could be a joint venture by establishing a joint entity with a foreign government.

In substance jointly controlled entities are often similar to jointly controlled operations or jointly controlled assets. However, a jointly controlled entity does maintain its own accounting records and prepare its financial statements in the same way as other normal entities in conformity with appropriate national regulations.

Each venturer usually contributes cash or other resources to the jointly controlled entity. These contributions are included in the accounting records of the venturer and are recognised in its financial statements as an investment in the jointly controlled entity.

Financial statements of a venturer

Proportionate consolidation

A venturer should report its interest in a jointly controlled entity using one of two reporting formats for proportionate consolidation, or using the equity method.

It is essential that a venturer reflects the substance and economic reality of the arrangement. The application of proportionate consolidation means that the consolidated balance sheet of the venturer includes its share of the assets it controls jointly, and its share of the liabilities for which it is jointly responsible. The consolidated income statement includes the venturer's share of the income and expenses of the jointly controlled entity. Many of the procedures are similar to consolidation procedures set out in IAS 27.

There are different reporting formats to give effect to proportionate consolidation. The first may combine the share of each of the assets, liabilities, income and expenses of the jointly controlled entity with similar items in the consolidated statements on a line-by-line basis (e.g. its share of inventory with inventory of the consolidated group). The second may include separate line items for a venturer's share of the jointly controlled entity's assets etc. – for example, it may show its share of a current asset of the jointly controlled entity separately as part of its current assets; it may show its share of the property etc. of the jointly controlled entity separately as part of property etc.

Both methods are acceptable under the standard and both result in identical profit being recorded, as well as the same overall value being placed on each major classification of assets. However, regardless of format, it is inappropriate to offset any assets or liabilities unless a legal right of set-off exists and the offsetting represents the expectation as to the realisation of the asset or settlement of the liability.

Proportionate consolidation should be discontinued from the date on which the venturer ceases to have joint control over a jointly controlled entity. This could happen when the venturer disposes of its interest, or when external restrictions mean that it can no longer achieve its goals.

Equity method

As an alternative, a venturer should report its interest in a jointly controlled entity using the equity method as per IAS 28. The equity method is supported by those who argue that it is inappropriate to combine controlled items with jointly controlled items. The standard does not recommend the use of the equity method because proportional consolidation better reflects the substance and economic reality of a venturer's interest in a jointly controlled entity. However, the standard does permit its adoption as an alternative treatment.

A venturer should discontinue the use of the equity method from the date it ceases to have joint control over or have significant influence in a jointly controlled entity.

Exceptions to proportional consolidation and equity method

A venturer should account for the following interests in accordance with IAS 39:

- an interest held exclusively with a view to its subsequent disposal in the near future;
- from the date on which a jointly controlled entity becomes a subsidiary of a venturer, the venturer accounts for its interest in accordance with IAS 27
- from the date on which a jointly controlled entity becomes an associate of a venturer, the venturer should account for its interest in accordance with IAS 28.

Separate financial statements of a venturer

In many countries, separate financial statements are presented by a venturer in order to meet legal or other requirements. These are provided for a variety of needs, but the standard does not indicate a preference for any particular treatment.

Transactions between a venturer and a joint venture

When a venturer contributes or sells assets to a joint venture, recognition of any portion of a gain or loss should reflect the substance of the transaction. While the assets are retained by the joint venture, and provided the venturer has transferred the significant risks and rewards of ownership, the venturer should recognise only that portion of the gain or loss which is attributable to the interests of the other venturers. The venturer should recognise the full amount of any loss when the sale provides evidence of a reduction in the NRV of current assets or an impairment loss.

When a venturer purchases assets from a joint venture, the venturer should not recognise its share of the profits of the joint venture until it resells the assets to an independent party. A venturer should recognise its share of the losses in the same way as profits except the losses should be recognised immediately when they represent a reduction in the NRV of current assets or an impairment loss under IAS 36.

Reporting interests in joint ventures in the financial statements of an investor

An investor in a joint venture which does not have joint control should report its interest in a joint venture in its consolidated accounts, under IAS 39 or, if it has significant influence, under IAS 28.

Operators of joint ventures

Operators or managers of a joint venture should account for any fees in accordance with IAS 18. The fees are accounted for by the joint venture as an expense.

Disclosure

A venturer should disclose the aggregate amount of each of the following contingent liabilities, unless the probability of loss is remote, separately:

1. Any contingent liabilities incurred in relation to its interest in joint ventures and its share in each contingent liability incurred jointly with other venturers
2. The venturer's share of contingent liabilities of the joint ventures for which it is contingently liable; and
3. Those contingent liabilities that arise because the venturer is contingently liable for the liabilities of the other venturers of a joint venture.

A venturer should disclose the aggregate amount of the following commitments *re* interests in joint ventures separately from other commitments:

1. Any capital commitments *re* joint ventures and its share in capital commitments incurred jointly with other venturers
2. Its share of capital commitments of the joint ventures themselves.

A venturer should disclose a listing and description of interests in significant joint ventures and the proportion of ownership interest held in jointly controlled entities. An entity that adopts line-by-line reporting for proportionate consolidation or the equity method should disclose the aggregate amounts of each of its current assets, long-term assets, current liabilities, long-term liabilities, income and expenses related to interests in joint ventures.

A venturer that does not publish consolidated accounts, because it has no subsidiaries should disclose the above information as well.

SIC 13 *Jointly Controlled Entities – Non-monetary Contributions by Venturers* (November 1998)

Issue

There is no explicit guidance in IAS 31 on the recognition of gains and losses resulting from contributions of non-monetary assets to jointly controlled entities (JCEs).

Contributions to a JCE are transfers of assets by venturers in exchange for an equity interest in the JCE. Such contributions may take various forms and can be made simultaneously by the venturers either upon setting up the JCE or subsequently. The consideration received by the venturer in exchange for assets contributed to the JCE may also include cash or other consideration that does not depend on future cash flows of the JCE.

The issues are:

- when the appropriate portion of gains or losses resulting from the contribution of non-monetary asset to a JCE in exchange for an equity interest in the JCE should be recognised by the venturer in the income statement;
- how additional consideration should be accounted for by the venturer; and

- how any unrealised gain or loss should be presented in the consolidated statements of the venturer.

The SIC deals with the venturer's accounting for non-monetary contributions to a JCE in exchange for an equity interest in the JCE that is accounted for using the equity method or proportionate consolidation.

Consensus

In applying IAS 31 to non-monetary contributions to a JCE in exchange for an equity interest in the JCE, a venturer should recognise in the income statement the portion of the gain or loss attributable to the equity interests of the other venturers except when:

- the significant risks and rewards of ownership of the contributed non-monetary assets have not been transferred to the JCE;
- the gain or loss on the non-monetary contribution cannot be reliably measured;
- the non-monetary assets contributed are similar to those contributed by the other venturers. (Non-monetary assets are similar to those contributed by other venturers when they have a similar nature, a similar use in the same line of business and a similar fair value. A contribution meets the similarity test only if all of the significant component assets thereof are similar to those contributed by the other venturers.)

Where any of the above apply, the gain/loss would be considered unrealised and therefore not recognised in income.

If, in addition to receiving an equity interest in the JCE, a venturer receives monetary or non-monetary assets dissimilar to those it contributed, an appropriate portion of gain/loss on the transaction should be recognised by the venturer in income.

Unrealised gains/losses on non-monetary assets contributed to JCEs should be eliminated against the underlying assets under the proportionate consolidation method or equity method. Such unrealised gains/losses should not be presented as deferred gains or losses in the venturer's consolidated balance sheet.

9.5   Examination questions

Question 9.1: Rod, reel and line (ACCA)

The first question in this series on group reporting incorporates the need to determine whether or not a subsidiary's holding in another entity should be considered on deciding whether or not a subsidiary exists. However, it also covers the normal consolidation adjustments for minority interests and pre-acquisition reserves. A special section on IAS 19 Employee Benefits is also included, as well as the decision to move from a policy of revaluation of fixed assets to one of retention of cost.)

The following draft balance sheets relate to Rod, a public limited company, Reel, a public limited company, and Line, a public limited company, as at 30 November 2002:

	Rod $m	Reel $m	Line $m
Non-current assets			
Tangible non-current assets – cost/valuation	1,230	505	256
Investment in Reel	640		
Investment in Line	160	100	
	2,030	605	256

Current assets			
Inventory	300	135	65
Trade receivables	240	105	49
Cash at bank and in hand	90	50	80
	630	290	194
Total assets	2,660	895	450
Capital and reserves			
Called up share capital	1,500	500	200
Share premium account	300	100	50
Revaluation reserve			70
Accumulated reserves	625	200	60
	2,425	800	380
Non-current liabilities	135	25	20
Current liabilities	100	70	50
Total equity and liabilities	2,660	895	450

The following information is relevant to the preparation of the group financial statements:

(i) Rod had acquired 80% of the ordinary share capital of Reel on 1 December 1999, when the accumulated reserves were $100 million. The fair value of the net assets of Reel was $710 million at 1 December 1999. Any fair value adjustment related to net current assets, and these net current assets had been realised by 30 November 2002. There had been no new issues of shares in the group since the current group was created.

(ii) Rod and Reel had acquired their holdings in Line on the same date as part of an attempt to mask the true ownership of Line. Rod acquired 40% and Reel acquired 25% of the ordinary share capital of Line on 1 December 2000. The accumulated reserves of Line on that date were $50 million and those of Reel were $150 million. There was no revaluation reserve in the books of Line on 1 December 2000. The fair values of the net assets of Line at 1 December 2000 were not materially different from their carrying values.

(iii) The group operates in the pharmaceutical industry and incurs a significant amount of expenditure on the development of products. These costs were formerly written off to the income statement as incurred but then reinstated when the related products were brought into commercial use. The reinstated costs are shown as 'Development Inventory'. The costs do not meet the criteria in IAS38 *Intangible Assets* for classification as intangibles, and it is unlikely that the net cash inflows from these products will be in excess of the development costs. In the current year, Reel has included $20 million of these costs in inventory. Of these costs, $5 million relates to expenditure on a product written off in periods prior to 1 December 1999. Commercial sales of this product had commenced during the current period. The accountant now wishes to ensure that the financial statements comply strictly with IAS/IFRS as regards this matter.

(iv) Reel had purchased a significant amount of new production equipment during the year. The cost before trade discount of this equipment was $50 million. The trade discount of $6 million was taken to the income statement. Depreciation is charged on the straight-line basis over a 6-year period.

v) The policy of the group is now to state tangible non-current assets at depreciated historical cost. The group changed from the allowed alternative treatment to the benchmark treatment under IAS16 *Property, Plant and Equipment* in the year ended 30 November 2002, and restated all of its tangible non-current assets to historical cost in that year except for the tangible non-current assets of Line, which had been revalued by the directors of Line on 1 December 2001. The values were incorporated in the financial records, creating a revaluation reserve of $70 million. The tangible non-current assets of Line were originally purchased on 1 December 2000 at a cost of $300 million. The assets are depreciated over 6 years on the straight-line basis. The group does not make an annual transfer from revaluation reserves to the accumulated reserve in respect of the excess depreciation charged on revalued tangible non-current assets. There were no additions or disposals of the tangible non-current assets of Line for the 2 years ended 30 November 2002.

i) During the year the directors of Rod decided to form a defined benefit pension scheme for the employees of the holding company, and contributed cash to it of $100 million. The following details relate to the scheme at 30 November 2002:

	$m
Present value of obligation	130
Fair value of plan assets	125
Current service cost	110
Interest cost – scheme liabilities	20
Expected return on pension scheme assets	10

The only entry in the financial statements made to date is in respect of the cash contribution, which has been included in Rod's trade receivables. The directors have been uncertain as to how to deal with the above pension scheme in the consolidated financial statements because of the significance of the potential increase in the charge to the income statement relating to the pension scheme. They wish to immediately recognise any actuarial gain.

vii) Goodwill is written off over 4 years on the straight-line basis.
iii) The group uses the allowed alternative treatment in IAS22 *Business Combinations* (now the only method permitted in IFRS 3) to allocate the cost of acquisition.

Required

a) Show how the defined benefit pension scheme should be dealt with in the consolidated financial statements.
b) Prepare a consolidated balance sheet of the Rod Group for the year ended 30 November 2002 in accordance with the standards of the International Accounting Standards Board.

Question 9.2: Hydrox (ACCA)

(The next question covers basic consolidation issues between a parent and subsidiary. However, a number of additional problems are introduced – e.g. the payment of dividends out of pre-acquisition reserves, the elimination of inter-company balances and unrealised profits/losses on inventories, fair value adjustments on acquisition, and minority interests. Section (b) covers going concern issues.)

Hydrox acquired 90% of Syntax's equity shares on 1 April 1998 for $30 million when Syntax's accumulated profits were $15 million. The balance sheets of the two companies at 31 March 2000 are shown below:

	Hydrox $000	Syntax $000
Non-current assets		
Property, plant and equipment at depreciated historic cost	26,400	16,200
Investment in Syntax	30,000	
Other quoted investments at cost	1,000	6,000
	57,400	22,200
Current assets		
Inventory	9,500	4,000
Accounts receivable	7,200	1,500
Bank	300	nil
	17,000	5,500
Total assets	74,400	27,700
Equity and liabilities		
Share capital and reserves		
Equity shares of $1 each	10,000	5,000
Reserves		
Accumulated profits	48,600	6,300
	58,600	11,300
Non-current liabilities		
12% Debenture	4,000	
Bank loan		6,000
Current liabilities		
Accounts payable	6,700	5,200
Provision for taxation	4,100	700
Proposed dividends	1,000	nil
Operating overdraft	nil	4,500
	11,800	10,400
Total equity and liabilities	74,400	27,700

The following information is relevant:

(i) The movements on the accumulated profits of Syntax plc since the date of acquisition have been:

	Losses after tax $000	Dividends paid $000	$000
Balance at acquisition, 1 April 1998			15,000
Year to 31 March 1999	(3,000)	nil	(3,000)
Year to 31 March 2000	(1,700)	(4,000)	(5,700)
Balance at 31 March 2000			6,300

Hydrox accounted for its share of Syntax's dividend as a credit to its income statement. The Group policy is that only dividends paid out of post-acquisition profits are credited to income.

(ii) At the date of acquisition the fair values of Syntax's net assets were approximately equal to their book values with the exception of two items:
- specialised plant of Syntax had a net replacement cost of $6 million in excess of its book value: it had an estimated remaining life of 5 years;
- the stock market value of Syntax's investments was $8 million; there have been no acquisitions or disposals of non-current assets since the date of acquisition.

(iii) The group accounting policy for goodwill is to write it off on a straight-line basis over a period of 6 years.

(iv) Three days before the current year end Hydrox processed the accounting entries in respect of a credit sale of goods to Syntax at a selling price of $600,000. Hydrox charges a standard mark-up on cost of 20% on all its sales. Syntax had not received the goods and therefore not included them in inventories; nor had it received the invoice for them by the year end. The agreed balance on Syntax's purchase ledger account with Hydrox prior to this transaction was $1.4 million.

(v) Hydrox uses the benchmark treatment in IAS 22 *Business Combinations* in respect of the allocation of the cost of acquisition as it affects fair values and minority interests.

Required

(a) Prepare the consolidated balance sheet of Hydrox as at 31 March 2000.

The auditor of the Hydrox Group is Brand and Company. Syntax is still audited by Greil and Company, its auditors prior to its acquisition by Hydrox. As a result of audit investigations including communication with Greil and Company, the following information has been ascertained:

(i) The stock market value of Syntax's investments has fallen sharply: their market value at 31 March 2000 was $2.5 million.

(ii) The bank overdraft limit of Syntax is set at $4 million, although the bank has allowed it to exceed this figure. The overdraft is unsecured and is not guaranteed by Hydrox. The bank loan is secured against Syntax's tangible fixed assets and is also underwritten by a guarantee from Hydrox.

(iii) The deterioration in the operating profits of Syntax has largely been caused by a shift in consumer confidence resulting from bad publicity relating to the specialist products manufactured by Syntax. This has prompted the Government to introduce new legislation in relation to these products. Without large-scale reorganisation and new investment, the trend of Syntax's losses is unlikely to be halted.

Required

(b) Describe the specific matters Brand and Company would consider in relation to the effect that the information in notes (i) to (iii) above may have on the financial statements (group and entity) of Hydrox. (*Note*: you are not required to amend your answer to (a) in respect of the information provided in (i)–(iii) above.)

Question 9.3: Hanford (ACCA)

(The third question in the series is a straightforward consolidation exercise, but it does exami.
preacquisition dividends as well as outlining when a reporting entity may legitimately avoid consolidation
Hanford acquired six million of Stopple's ordinary shares on 1 April 2001 for a
agreed consideration of $25 million. The consideration was settled by a shar
exchange of five new shares in Hanford for every three shares acquired in Stopple
and a cash payment of $5 million. The cash transaction has been recorded, bu
the share exchange has not. The draft balance sheets of the two companies a
30 September 2001 are:

	Hanford		Stopple	
	$000	$000	$000	$000
Assets				
Non-current assets				
Property, plant and equipment		78,540		27,180
Investment in Stopple		5,000		nil
		83,540		27,180
Current assets				
Inventory	7,450		4,310	
Accounts receivable	12,960		4,330	
Cash and bank	nil	20,410	520	9,160
Total assets		103,950		36,340
Equity and liabilities				
Capital and reserves				
Ordinary shares of $1 each		20,000		8,000
Reserves				
Share premium	10,000		2,000	
Accumulated profits:				
At 1 October 2000	51,260		6,000	
For the year to 30 September 2001	12,000	73,260	8,000	16,000
		93,260		24,000
Non-current liabilities				
8% Loan notes 2004		nil		6,000
Current liabilities				
Accounts payable and accruals	5,920		4,160	
Bank overdraft	1,700		nil	
Provision for taxation	1,870		1,380	
Proposed final dividend	1,200	10,690	800	6,340
Total equity and liabilities		103,950		36,340

The following information is relevant:

(i) The fair value of Stopple's land at the date of acquisition was $4 million in exce
of its carrying value. Stopple's financial statements contain a note of a continge
asset for an insurance claim of $800,000 relating to some inventory that w

damaged by a flood on 5 March 2001. The insurance company is disputing the claim. Hanford has taken legal advice on the claim and believes that it is highly likely that the insurance company will settle it in full in the near future.

The fair value of Stopple's other net assets approximated to their carrying values. Hanford uses the benchmark treatment in IAS 22 *Business Combinations* to recognise the fair values of acquired assets and liabilities.

ii) At the date of acquisition Hanford sold an item of plant that had cost $2 million to Stopple for $2.4 million. Stopple has charged depreciation of $240,000 on this plant since it was acquired.

ii) Hanford's current account debit balance of $820,000 with Stopple does not agree with the corresponding balance in Stopple's books. Investigations revealed that on 26 September 2001, Hanford billed Stopple $200,000 for its share of central administration costs. Stopple has not yet recorded this invoice. Inter-company current accounts are included in accounts receivable or payable as appropriate.

v) Stopple paid an interim dividend of $400,000 on 1 March 2001. The profit and total dividends (interim plus final) of Stopple are deemed to accrue evenly through-out the year. Stopple's retained profit of $8 million for the year to 30 September 2001 as shown in its balance sheet is after the deduction of both its interim and final dividends. Hanford's policy is to credit to income only those dividends received or receivable from post-acquisition profits. Hanford has not yet received or accounted for any dividends from Stopple. All proposed dividends were declared by the direc-tors before the relevant year ends.

v) Consolidated goodwill is written off on a straight-line basis over a 5-year life, with time apportionment in the year of acquisition.

Required

a) Prepare the consolidated balance sheet of Hanford at 30 September 2001.
b) Suggest reasons why a parent company may not wish to consolidate a subsidiary company, and describe the circumstances in which non-consolidation of subsidiaries is permitted by International Accounting Standards.

Question 9.4: Hydrate (ACCA)

Hydrate is a fairly straightforward group accounting question illustrating the differences between merger and acquisition accounting. However, it must be remembered that as from March 2004, under IFRS 3, merger or uniting of interests accounting will no longer be permitted and the purchase or acquisition method must be adopted for all future business combinations. There is still doubt as to whether merger accounting might be adopted in group reconstruction situations.)

Hydrate is a company operating in the industrial chemical sector. In order to achieve economies of scale, it has been advised to enter into business combinations with com-patible partner companies. As a first step in this strategy, Hydrate acquired all of the ordinary shares of Sulphate by way of a share exchange on 1 April 2002. Hydrate issued one of its own shares for every four shares in Sulphate. The market value of Hydrate's shares on 1 April 2002 was $6 each. The share issue has not yet been recorded i Hydrate's books. The summarised financial statements of both companies for the yea to 30 September 2002 are:

Income statement – year to 30 September 2002

	Hydrate $000	Sulphate $000
Sales revenue	24,000	20,000
Cost of sales	(16,600)	(11,800)
Gross profit	7,400	8,200
Operating expenses	(1,600)	(1,000)
Operating profit	5,800	7,200
Taxation	(2,000)	(3,000)
Profit after tax	3,800	4,200

Balance sheet – as at 30 September 2002

Non-current assets	$000	$000	$000	$000
Property, plant and equipment		64,000		35,000
Investment		nil		12,800
		64,000		47,800
Current assets				
Inventory	22,800		23,600	
Accounts receivable	16,400		24,200	
Bank	500	39,700	200	48,000
Total assets		103,700		95,800
Equity and liabilities				
Ordinary shares of $1 each		20,000		12,000
Reserves:				
Share premium	4,000		2,400	
Accumulated profits	57,200	61,200	42,700	45,100
		81,200		57,100
Non-current liabilities				
8% Loan note		5,000		18,000
Current liabilities				
Accounts payable	15,300		17,700	
Taxation	2,200	17,500	3,000	20,700
		103,700		95,800

The following information is relevant:

(i) The fair value of Sulphate's investment was $5 million in excess of its book value the date of acquisition. The fair values of Sulphate's other net assets were equal their book values.

(ii) Consolidated goodwill is deemed to have a 5-year life, with time apportione charges (treated as an operating expense) in the year of acquisition.

(iii) No dividends have been paid or proposed by either company.

Required

(a) Prepare the consolidated income statement and balance sheet of Hydrate for the year to 30 September 2002 using the purchase method of accounting (acquisition accounting).
(b) Prepare a consolidated income statement and the consolidated SHAREHOLDERS' FUNDS section of the balance sheet of Hydrate for the year to 30 September 2002 using the uniting of interests method of accounting (merger accounting).
(c) Describe the distinguishing feature of a uniting of interests, and discuss whether the business combination in (a) and (b) should be accounted for as a uniting of interests.

Question 9.5: Humbug (ACCA)

(The next question covers proportional consolidation, which is the benchmark treatment to be adopted in accounting for joint ventures. In addition, the question covers the normal consolidation adjustments in group accounting.)

Humbug acquired 80% of Spyder's $1 ordinary shares on 1 October 1999, paying $2.50 per share, and acquired half of its 10% loan notes at par on the same date. The balance on Spyder's accumulated profits at the date of its acquisition was $750,000, One year later, on 1 October 2000, Humbug acquired 50% of Juke Box's $1 ordinary shares for $3.00 per share. Juke Box specialises in the manufacture of musical equipment and was previously a wholly owned subsidiary of Music Man. From the date of Humbug's investment, Juke Box was managed as a joint venture by its two shareholders. The balance sheets of the three companies at 30 September 2001 are shown below.

	Humbug		Spyder		Juke Box	
	$000	$000	$000	$000	$000	$000
Non-current assets						
Property, plant and equipment		11,250		4,800		1,800
Investments		6,000		400		nil
		17,250		5,200		1,800
Current assets						
Inventory	1,120		640		600	
Accounts receivable	950		380		320	
Bank	180	2,250	nil	1,020	280	1,200
Total assets		19,500		6,220		3,000
Equity and liabilities						
Capital and reserves:						
Ordinary shares of $1 each		5,000		2,000		1,000
Reserves:						
Accumulated profits b/f	11,140		1,500		1,000	
Profit – year to 30 September 2001	1,500	12,640	900	2,400	500	1,500
		17,640		4,400		2,500
Non-current liabilities						
10% Loan notes		nil		500		nil
Current liabilities						
Accounts payable	1,300		850		400	
Taxation	560		350		100	
Overdraft	nil	1,860	120	1,320	nil	500
Total equity and liabilities		19,500		6,220		3,000

The following information is relevant:

(i) Fair value adjustments: at the date of acquisition, 1 October 1999, Spyder owned an item of plant that had a fair value of $700,000 in excess of its book value. The plant had a remaining life of 5 years. All plant and equipment is depreciated on the straight-line basis.

   At the same date Spyder also owned the copyright to the software of a computer game. The software had been fully written off, but sales of the game remain high. At the date of acquisition, Humbug expected strong sales of the game for a further 3 years and estimated the commercial value of the software to be $300,000. Humbug's expectations have not changed since acquisition.

   The fair value of Spyder's remaining net assets and all of Juke Box's net assets were equal to their book values at the relevant dates of acquisition.

   Humbug uses the benchmark treatment in IAS 22 *Business Combinations* to allocate the cost of acquisition.

(ii) On 1 October 2000 Humbug purchased some musical equipment from Juke Box for $200,000. It was sold at a mark up of 25% on cost. The equipment is in use by Humbug and is included in property, plant and equipment and being depreciated over a 4-year life.

(iii) All inter-company current account balances were settled prior to the year end.

(iv) The group accounting policy for goodwill is to write it off on a straight-line basis over a period of 5 years.

(v) Juke Box is to be treated under the benchmark treatment for jointly controlled entities in IAS 31 *Financial Reporting of Interests in Joint Ventures*. Humbug uses a 'line-by-line' presentation.

Required

(a) Prepare the consolidated balance sheet of Humbug as at 30 September 2001.
(b) Explain, with illustrations, the relevant features and accounting treatment of jointly controlled operations and jointly controlled assets in IAS 31.

Question 9.6: Holding (ACCA)

(Holding is a basic consolidation question requiring the student to incorporate the need to introduce uniform accounting policies and to comply with IAS 40. The elimination of inter company balances is also included as well as a discussion about the circumstances when brands may be incorporated on the balance sheet.)
Holding acquired 75% of Sandham's equity shares on 1 April 2001 when the accumulated retained profits of Sandham were $4 million. The draft balance sheets of the two companies at 31 March 2002 are:

	Holding		Sandham	
Assets	**$000**	**$000**	**$000**	**$000**
Non-current assets				
Property, plant and equipment		12,000		12,200
Investment property		6,000		nil
Investment in Sandham		8,850		nil
		26,850		12,200

Current assets				
Inventories	7,800		3,450	
Trade receivables	3,600		2,300	
Cash and bank	150	11,550	nil	5,750
Total assets		38,400		17,950

Equity and liabilities				
Ordinary shares of $1 each		5,000		2,000
Accumulated profits		27,150		5,000
		32,150		7,000
Non-current liabilities				
12% Loan note, 2005		nil		6,000
Current liabilities				
Trade payables	6,250		3,700	
Operating overdraft	nil	6,250	1,250	4,950
Total equity and liabilities		38,400		17,950

The following information is relevant:

(i) The 12% loan note of Sandham is repayable at par on 31 March 2005. The loan carries a fixed interest rate and cannot be redeemed without severe penalties. Since the loan was taken out, interest rates have fallen significantly. Because of this, Holding has estimated that the fair value of the liability for the loan at the date of acquisition was $6.6 million. Based on this liability, the interest charge for the year to 31 March 2002 in Sandham's income statement was overstated by $200,000.

   The fair value of Sandham's plant and equipment was $4 million in excess of its carrying value at the date of acquisition. It had a remaining estimated life of 4 years. Plant is depreciated on a straight-line basis. The fair values of Sandham's other net assets approximated to their carrying values.

ii) The investment property of Holding was acquired at a cost of $5 million on 1 April 1999. It had an estimated life of 20 years. Until the acquisition of Sandham the property had been let to a third party; however, from the date of acquisition it was let to Sandham on commercial terms. In its entity financial statements Holding has applied the fair value model in IAS 40 *Investment Properties*. The group policy for owner-occupied properties is to carry them at depreciated cost.

   Details of the movement in the fair value of the property are:

At 31 March 2000	5.2 million
At 31 March 2001	5.4 million
At 31 March 2002	6.0 million

i) During the year to 31 March 2002, Holding sold goods to Sandham for $3 million at a mark-up on cost of 20%. Sandham had half of these goods in its inventory at 31 March 2002. The reconciled inter-company current account balances at the year end showed Sandham owing $700,000 to Holding. Inter-company balances are included in trade payables and receivables as appropriate.

) Consolidated goodwill is written off on a straight-line basis over a 6-year life.

Required

(a) Prepare the consolidated balance sheet of Holding at 31 March 2002 using the allowed alternative treatment for the allocation of the purchase consideration in IAS 22 *Business Combinations*. Ignore taxation.

Shortly before the year end of 31 March 2002, the board of Holding discovered a report that had been commissioned by the previous board of Sandham. The report was dated only a short while prior to the acquisition and related to the valuation, made by independent consultants, of Sandham's main brand. The valuation of $3 million was essentially made on a multiple of earnings basis; Sandham had not included this brand in its balance sheet. The consultants had estimated that the remaining life of the brand was 30 years.

Required

(b) Discuss:
   (i) Whether the brand could have been recognised in Sandham's entity financial statements at the date of the report
   (ii) Whether it can be recognised by Holding in its consolidated financial statements at 31 March 2002, and, if so, describe its accounting treatment. *Note*: you are not required to amend your answer to (a) in respect of the information in part (b).

Question 9.7: Hyper (ACCA)

(Hyper covers the differences between accounting for full subsidiaries and adopting the equity method when accounting for associates. It also incorporates the balance sheet disclosures required for associates and the elimination of pre-acquisition dividends from the cost of the investment. The usual elimination of inter-company balances on consolidation is also covered.)

Hyper acquired 80% of Syphon's ordinary shares on 1 April 2002 at a cost of $8.70 per share. On the same date it also acquired 40% of Andean's ordinary shares at a cost of $6 per share. Both Hyper's and Andean's reporting year end is 30 September. Prior to its acquisition, Syphon had last reported for the year ended 30 June 2001. The following income statements of the three companies have been drafted.

	Hyper 12 months to 30 September 2002 $ million	Syphon 15 months to 30 September 2002 $ million	Andean 12 months to 30 September 200 $ million
Sales revenue	420	375	150
Cost of sales	(320)	(190)	(90)
Gross profit	100	185	60
Operating expenses	(40)	(30)	(10)
Interest payable	(12)	(10)	(2)
Dividend from Syphon	8	nil	nil
Profit before tax	56	145	48
Income tax	(20)	(35)	(12)
Profit after tax	36	110	36

The share capital and reserves of Syphon and Andean at 30 September 2002 were:

	Syphon			**Andean**	
	$ million	**$ million**		**$ million**	**$ million**
Ordinary shares of $1 each		30			20
Reserves:					
Accumulated profits:			Accumulated profits:		
At 30 June 2001	40		At 30 September 2001	14	
15 months to			Year to		
30 September 2002	110		30 September 2002	36	
Dividends paid (for					
15-month period)	(10)	140	Dividends paid	nil	50
Revaluation reserve (note (ii))		20	Revaluation reserve		nil
		190			70

The following information is relevant:

(i) In May 2002 Hyper sold $20 million of goods to Syphon at a mark-up on cost of 25%. Half of these goods had been processed and resold by Syphon by 30 September 2002.

(ii) The revaluation reserve of Syphon relates to a plot of land carried at its fair value on 30 June 2001. At the date of acquisition its fair value had increased by a further $5 million.

iii) At the date of acquisition, the fair value of Andean's plant was $18 million in excess of its book value and it had a remaining life of 3 years. Plant depreciation is charged to cost of sales.

iv) Assume that all income statement items accrue evenly throughout the period.

(v) Goodwill is to be amortised on a straight-line basis over a 5-year life using time apportionment in the year of acquisition.

vi) Dividends are deemed to accrue evenly on a time basis. Hyper treats any dividends paid out of pre-acquisition profits as a partial return of the cost of the investment.

Required

(a) Calculate the consolidated goodwill in respect of the acquisition of Syphon and Andean.

(b) Prepare the consolidated income statement of Hyper for the year to 30 September 2002.

(c) Calculate the carrying value of the investment in Andean at 30 September 2002.

Question 9.8: Pulp, fiction and truth (CIMA)

Pulp, Fiction and Truth is a basic group consolidated income statement question, but it does incorporate
the reassessment of a subsidiary as an associate after selling off 35% of its shares in a subsidiary, so it
has aspects of full consolidation and equity accounting in the question.)

You are the management accountant of Pulp plc, a company incorporated in the United Kingdom. Pulp plc prepares consolidated financial statements in accordance with International Accounting Standards. The company has a number of investments in other entities, but its two major investments are in Fiction Ltd and Truth Ltd. The income statements of all three companies for the year ended 31 December 2000 (the accounting reference date for all three) are given below.

	Pulp plc £000	Fiction Ltd £000	Truth Ltd £000
Turnover	30,000	32,000	28,000
Cost of sales	(15,000)	(16,000)	(14,000)
Gross profit	15,000	16,000	14,000
Other operating expenses	(8,000)	(8,500)	(6,000)
Operating profit	7,000	7,500	8,000
Investment income	2,850		
Interest payable	(1,000)	(1,200)	(1,000)
Profit before taxation	8,850	6,300	7,000
Taxation	(1,900)	(1,900)	(2,000)
Profit after taxation	6,950	4,400	5,000
Dividends paid 30 June 2000	(3,000)	(2,000)	(1,500)
Retained profit	3,950	2,400	3,500
Retained profit – 1 January 2000	9,500	8,900	9,000
Retained profit – 31 December 2000	13,450	11,300	12,500

The following notes are relevant:

(i) *Investment by Pulp plc in Fiction Ltd.* On 1 January 1995, Pulp plc purchased, for £13 million, 4 million £1 equity shares in Fiction Ltd. The balance sheet of Fiction Ltd at the date of the share purchase by Pulp plc (based on the carrying values in the financial statements of Fiction Ltd) showed the following balances:

	£000
Tangible fixed assets	7,000
Other net assets	3,000
	10,000
Share capital (£1 equity shares)	4,000
Share premium account	3,000
Profit and loss account	3,000
	10,000

Pulp plc carried out a fair value exercise on 1 January 1995, and concluded that the tangible fixed assets of Fiction Ltd at 1 January 1995 had a fair value of £8 million. All of these fixed assets were sold or scrapped prior to 31 December 1999. The fair values of all the other net assets of Fiction Ltd on 1 January 1995 were very close to their carrying values in Fiction Ltd's balance sheet.

(ii) *Investment by Pulp Plc in Truth Ltd.* On 1 January 1994, Pulp plc purchased, for £12 million, 6 million £1 equity shares in Truth Ltd. The balance sheet of Truth Ltd at the date of the share purchase by Pulp plc showed the following balances:

	£000
Share capital (1£ equity shares)	8,000
Share premium account	4,000
Profit and loss account	2,000
Net assets	14,000

Pulp plc carried out a fair value exercise on 1 January 1994 and concluded that the fair values of all the net assets of Truth Ltd were very close to their carrying values in Truth Ltd's balance sheet.

i) *Accounting policy regarding purchased goodwill.* Pulp plc amortises all purchased goodwill over its estimated useful economic life. For the acquisitions of Fiction Ltd and Truth Ltd, this estimate was 20 years.

v) *Sale of shares in Truth Ltd.* On 1 April 2000 Pulp plc sold 2.8 million shares in Truth Ltd for a total of £10 million. Taxation of £500,000 was estimated to be payable on the disposal. The profit and loss account of Pulp plc that is shown above does NOT include the effects of this disposal. The write-off by Pulp plc of goodwill on consolidation of Truth Ltd for the year ended 31 December 2000 should be based on the shareholding retained after this disposal. The profits of Truth Ltd accrued evenly throughout 2000.

v) *Administration charge.* Pulp plc charges Fiction Ltd an administration charge of £100,000 per quarter. This amount was also charged to Truth Ltd, but only until 31 March 2000. The charges are included in the turnover of Pulp plc and the other operating expenses of Fiction Ltd and Truth Ltd. Apart from these transactions and the payments of dividends, there were no other transactions between the three companies.

Our assistant normally prepares a first draft of the consolidated financial statements of the group for your review. He is sure that the change in the shareholding in Truth Ltd must have some impact on the method of consolidation of that company but is unsure exactly how to reflect it. He is similarly unsure how the proceeds of sale should be included in the consolidated financial statements. Pulp has 15 million equity shares.

Required

a) Prepare the consolidated income statement for the year ended 31 December 2000 for the Pulp group in accordance with International Financial Reporting Standards.
b) Prepare the statement of changes in equity for the year ended 31 December 2000 for the Pulp group.

Question 9.9: Harden (ACCA)

combination of accounting for subsidiaries and associates and the need to eliminate inter-company balances is the core topic of Harden, but it also incorporates the need to disclose, in narrative form, the accounting treatment of business combinations particularly contingent assets and deferred tax implications.) Harden acquired 800,000 of Solder's $1 equity shares on 1 October 1998 for $2.5 million. One year later, on 1 October 1999, Harden acquired 200,000 $1 equity shares in Active for $800,000. The balance sheets of the three companies at 30 September 2000 are shown below.

	Harden		Solder		Active	
	$000	$000	$000	$000	$000	$000
Non-current assets						
Property, plant and equipment		3,980		2,300		1,340
Patents		250		420		nil

Investments – in Solder	2,500					
– in Active	800					
– others	150	3,450		200		60
		7,680		2,920		1,400
Current assets						
Inventories	570		400		300	
Trade receivables	420		380		400	
Bank	nil	990	150	930	120	820
Total assets		8,670		3,850		2,220
Equity and liabilities						
Capital and reserves:						
Equity shares of $1 each		2,000		1,000		500
Reserves:						
Share premium	1,000		500		100	
Accumulated profits	4,500	5,500	1,900	2,400	1,200	1,300
		7,500		3,400		1,800
Non-current liabilities						
Deferred tax		200		nil		80
Current liabilities						
Trade payables	750		450		280	
Taxation	140		nil		60	
Overdraft	80	970	nil	450	nil	340
		8,670		3,850		2,220

The following information is relevant:

(i) The balances of the accumulated profits of the three companies were:

	Harden $000	**Solder** $000	**Active** $000
At 1 October 1998	2,000	1,200	500
At 1 October 1999	3,000	1,500	800

(ii) At the date of its acquisition the fair values of Solder's net assets were equal to their book values, with the exception of a plot of land that had a fair value of $200,000 in excess of its book value. The group adopts the benchmark treatment contained in IAS 22 (revised 1998) *Business Combinations* for accounting for the fair value of assets acquired and minority interests.

(iii) On 26 September 2000 Harden processed an invoice for $50,000 in respect of an agreed allocation of central overhead expenses to Solder. At 10 September 2000 Solder had not accounted for this transaction. Prior to this the current account between the two companies had been agreed at Solder owing $70,000 to Harden (included in trade receivables and trade payables respectively).

(iv) During the year Active sold goods to Harden at a selling price of $140,000, which gave Active a profit of 40% on cost. Harden had half of these goods in inventory at 30 September 2000.

(v) The group accounting policy for goodwill is to write it off on a straight-line basis over a period of 5 years.

Required

(a) Prepare the consolidated balance sheet of Harden as at 30 September 2000.

At the beginning of the following year, on 1 October 2000, the shareholders of Deployed accepted a bid from Harden to purchase the whole of its equity share capital. Harden is currently considering whether and at what value certain of Deployed's assets and liabilities should be recognised in the consolidated financial statements. The details are:

(i) Deployed has made an accounting and taxable loss of $200,000 in the year to 30 September 2000. This loss will be allowable for tax purposes for relief against any future trading profit that Deployed may make. Deployed has not recognised the loss as a deferred tax asset because the directors are not confident that the company will make sufficient profits in the near future to absorb the loss. The directors of Harden are firmly of the opinion that the profitability of the group is such that Deployed's tax losses can be utilised on a group basis. Assume an income tax rate of 30%.

(ii) Deployed is in dispute over an insurance claim relating to one of its buildings that has been damaged in a fire. The insurance company is disputing the claim on the basis that the use of the building was not properly disclosed when it was insured. A copy of the insurance proposal form has been obtained and sent to Deployed's lawyers. The lawyers have said that in their opinion the use of the building was adequately disclosed and in any event its use was not the cause of the fire, and therefore they believe the claim is valid. The cost of the damage caused by the fire has been provided for, but, as the claim is a contingent asset, the directors of Deployed have not recognised it in the financial statements.

Required

(b) Discuss how the directors of Harden should treat the above items when preparing consolidated financial statements to reflect the acquisition of Deployed.

Question 9.10: Horsefield (ACCA)

The next question covers the accounting treatment of associates, and requires students to present a narrative explanation of when an investment should be classified as an associate. It also covers the fair value exercise in computing goodwill for both subsidiaries and associates.)

Horsefield, a public company, acquired 90% of Sandfly's $1 ordinary shares on 1 April 2000, paying $3.00 per share. The balance on Sandfly's accumulated profits at this date was $800,000. On 1 October 2001, Horsefield acquired 30% of Anthill's $1 ordinary shares for $3.50 per share. The balance sheets of the three companies at 31 March 2002 are shown below:

	Horsefield		Sandfly		Anthill	
	$000	$000	$000	$000	$000	$000
Non-current assets						
Property, plant and equipment		8,050		3,600		1,650
Investments		4,000		910		nil
		12,050		4,510		1,650

Current assets					
Inventory	830		340		250	
Accounts receivables	520		290		350	
Bank	240	1,590	nil	630	100	700
Total assets		13,640		5,140		2,350
Equity and liabilities					
Capital and reserves:					
Equity shares of $1 each		5,000		1,200		600
Reserves:					
Accumulated profits b/f	6,000		1,400		800	
Profit year to 31 March 2002	1,300	7,300	800	2,200	600	1,400
		12,300		3,400		2,000
Non-current liabilities					
10% Loan notes		500		240		nil
Current liabilities					
Accounts payables	420		960		200	
Taxation	220		250		150	
Proposed dividends	200		100		nil	
Overdraft	nil	840	190	1,500	nil	350
		13,640		5,140		2,350

The following information is relevant:

(i) Fair value adjustments: on 1 April 2000 Sandfly owned an investment property that had a fair value of $120,000 in excess of its book value. The value of this property has not changed since acquisition.

Just prior to its acquisition, Sandfly was successful in applying for a 6-year licence to dispose of hazardous waste. The licence was granted by the government at no cost; however, Horsefield estimated that the licence was worth $180,000 at the date of acquisition.

(ii) In January 2002 Horsefield sold goods to Anthill for $65,000. These were transferred at a mark-up of 30% on cost. Two-thirds of these goods were still in the inventory of Anthill at 31 March 2002.

(iii) To facilitate the consolidation procedures, the group insists that all inter-company current account balances are settled prior to the year-end. However, a cheque for $40,000 from Sandfly to Horsefield was not received until early April 2002. Inter-company balances are included in accounts receivable and payable as appropriate.

(iv) The group accounting policy for goodwill is to write it off on a straight-line basis over a period of 5 years, with a proportionate charge where it arises part way through an accounting period.

(v) Anthill is to be treated as an associated company of Horsefield.

(vi) The directors of Horsefield and Sandfly declared the proposed dividends on 2? March 2002.

(vii) Horsefield uses the allowed alternative treatment in IAS 22 *Business Combinations* to allocate the cost of acquisition.

(viii) Horsefield has not accounted for any of Sandfly's proposed dividend.

Question 9.11: Portal (ACCA)

(Portal is an income statement question incorporating associates. It is complicated by the inclusion of a sale of shares in a subsidiary to turn it into an associate.)

Portal, a public limited company, acquired two subsidiary companies, Hub and Network, both public limited companies. The details of the acquisitions are as follows:

Subsidiary	Date of Acquisition	Ordinary share Capital of $1	Accumulated Reserves	Cost of investment	Ordinary share Capital acquired $1 shares	Fair value of net assets on acquisition
		$m	$m	$m	$m	$m
Hub	1 January 2000	400	200	565	300	700
Network	1 June 2000	300	100	410	240	450

The draft income statements for the year ended 31 May 2001 are:

	Portal $m	Hub $m	Network $m
Revenue	2000	1600	1250
Cost of sales	(1500)	(1400)	(1180)
Gross profit	500	200	70
Distribution costs	(120)	(40)	(26)
Administrative expenses	(100)	(36)	(34)
Profit from operations	280	124	10
Interest expense	(10)	(4)	(20)
Investment income (including inter company dividends)	50		
Profit/(loss) before taxation	320	120	(10)
Income tax expense	(90)	(36)	(6)
Net profit from ordinary activities	230	84	(16)
Accumulated profit at 1 June 2000	350	250	100

The following information is relevant to the preparation of the group financial statements:

) On 1 December 2000, Portal sold the following shareholdings in the subsidiary companies:

	Ordinary shares of $1 sold $m	Proceeds $m
Hub	60	140
Network	120	200

Portal maintains significant influence over Network after the disposal of shares.

(ii) Hub sold $100 million of goods to Portal during the year. The opening inventory of such goods held by Portal was $20 million and the closing inventory $30 million. The profit on these goods was 20% on selling price.

(iii) At the date of acquisition, the fair value of the tangible depreciable non-current assets of Hub was $10 million above their carrying value and that of non-depreciable land was $90 million above its carrying value. The fair value of the tangible non-current assets of Network was equivalent to its carrying value. Depreciation is charged on all group tangible non-current assets at 20% per annum on the carrying value of the asset with a full year's charge in the year of acquisition.

(iv) Portal is carrying out a review of the carrying value of goodwill as at 31 May 2001. This 'first year review' is based upon the following information:

- *Hub.* On acquisition, the management of Portal expected pre-tax profits in the year to 31 May 2001 to be $115 million. The policy of the group is to write off goodwill over 4 years where it is considered that the useful life of goodwill is not indefinite. A full year's charge is made in the year of acquisition.
- *Network.* On acquisition, it was anticipated that Network would be profitable for at least 5 years and that the useful life of goodwill was believed to be indefinite. At 31 May 2001, changes in business regulations have resulted in the net assets having a value in use of $460 million and an estimated net selling price of $430 million as at 31 May 2001 of Network as an income generating unit. The directors of Network are currently developing a new product which will hopefully increase the value in use of Network in future years.

(v) Portal had paid a dividend of $20 million and Hub had paid a dividend of $40 million in April 2001.

(vi) The fair value adjustments had not been incorporated into the subsidiaries' records, and the sales of shares had not been accounted for by Portal. Assume that profits accrue evenly and that there are no other items of income, expense or capital other than those stated in the question. Taxation on any capital gain can be ignored.

(vii) Depreciation and amortisation are charged to the income statement as part of cost of sales.

(viii) Candidates should ignore any inter-company profit in inventory when calculating the gain/loss on the disposal of shares.

Required

(a) Prepare a consolidated income statement for the Portal Group for the year ended 31 May 2001 in accordance with International Accounting Standards. (The amount of the consolidated profit dealt with in the holding company's accounts are not required.)

(b) Show the composition of the balance on the group accumulated reserves at 31 May 2001.

Question 9.12: Vitalise (ACCA)

(Vitalise is an excellent group accounting question requiring the preparation of both a consolidated income statement and balance sheet. However, it also incorporates the need to apply specific accounting standards – particularly IAS 33, IAS 32 and IAS 40 (fair value model). It also covers the demise of extraordinary items in IAS 8.)

The summarised draft financial statements of Vitalise to 30 September 2001 are shown below.

Vitalise Income Statement year to 30 September 2001:

	$000
Sales revenue	3,900
Cost of sales	(2,500)
Gross profit	1,400
Operating costs	(250)
	1,150
Finance costs	(65)
Profit before tax	1,085
Taxation	(260)
Profit after tax	825
Extraordinary items	(210)
Net profit for the period	615

Balance Sheet as at 30 September 2001:

Assets	$000	$000
Non-current assets		
Property, plant and equipment		3,810
Investment property		390
		4,200
Current assets		1,200
Total assets		5,400
Equity and liabilities		
Capital and reserves:		
Equity shares of $ 1 each		1,000
Reserves:		
Revaluation reserve (note (iii))	250	
Accumulated profits (note (vi))	1,850	2,100
		3,100
Non-current liabilities		
8% Convertible loan note (2004)		500
Current liabilities		1,800
		5,400

The following information is relevant to the draft financial statements:

i) Sales and repurchase agreement. Sales revenues include an amount of $250,000 for the sale of maturing goods to Easyfinance. The sale was made on 1 October 2000 and the goods had a cost of $100,000 at the date of sale. Vitalise has an option to repurchase the goods at anytime within the next 5 years. The repurchase price will be the original selling price plus interest at 10% per annum compounded annually. The above transaction has been treated as a normal sale by Vitalise.

(ii) Extraordinary item. This is the cost ($300,000 less tax relief of $90,000) of a failed takeover bid for Dunsters. A rival company of Vitalise eventually acquired Dunsters. As the cost of the attempted acquisition will never recur, it has been treated as an extraordinary item.

(iii) Property, plant and equipment. Property, plant and equipment contains an amount of $750,000 (SwF 3 million at an exchange rate of 4 to the $) for the purchase of a light aircraft on 1 July 2001. The aircraft was purchased from a company located in Switzerland and the purchase price of SwF 3 million is payable in French francs on 1 November 2001. The following exchange rates applied:

1 July 2001	SwF 6 to $1
30 September 2001	SwF 4 to $1

This is the only foreign currency transaction that Vitalise has entered into, and the company chose not to use any form of hedging. Ignore depreciation on the aircraft.

(iv) Properties. Vitalise owns two properties. One is used as the company's head office and is included in property, plant and equipment, and the other is an investment property that is leased to a third party on a 5-year operating lease. Vitalise's policy has been to revalue both properties each year and transfer the movements on them to a revaluation reserve. Relevant details of the cost and fair values of the properties are:

	Head office $	Investment property $
Cost	300,000	250,000
Valuation 30 September 2000	410,000	390,000
Valuation 30 September 2001	375,000	350,000

The valuations at the 30 September 2001 have not yet been incorporated into the financial statements. The management of Vitalise have become aware of the issue of IAS 40 *Investment Property*, and wish to apply the fair value model to its investment property for the current reporting period. Ignore depreciation.

(v) 8% Convertible loan note. On 1 October 2000 a convertible loan note with a nominal value of $500,000 was issued at par. It is redeemable on 30 September 2004 also at par, or it may be converted (at the option of the holder) into ordinary shares of Vitalise on the basis of 100 new shares for each $100 of loan note. An equivalent loan note without the conversion option would have carried a coupon rate of 12%. Interest of $40,000 has been paid and charged as a finance cost.

The present value of $1 receivable at the end of each year, based on discount rates of 8% and 12% should be taken as:

	8%	12%
End of year: 1	0.93	0.88
2	0.86	0.78
3	0.79	0.70
4	0.73	0.64

(vi) Bonus issue. On 30 October 2001 (i.e. 1 month after the year end), Vitalise made a bonus issue of one share for every five held. The company's financial statements had not been finalised by this date.

(vii) The balance of the accumulated profit is made up of:

	$000
Balance b/f 1 October 2000	1,500
Profit for the period	615
Dividends paid	(265)
	1,850

Required

(a) Redraft the financial statements, including a statement of changes in equity, of Vitalise for the year to 30 September 2001 to comply with relevant International Accounting Standards in relation to items (i) to (v) above. *Note*: ignore taxation on all of the above items other than item (ii).

(b) Calculate the basic and diluted Earnings Per Share for Vitalise in accordance with IAS 33. *Note*: assume only the actual loan interest paid is allowable as a tax deductible expense and the bonus issue does not affect the terms of the 8% convertible loan note. Ignore deferred tax.

Question 9.13: Inventure (ACCA)

The next question, Inventure, requires the finalisation of an income statement in accordance with IASs/IFRSs. In particular, it covers the adoption of pooling (formerly allowed in IAS 22), the accounting treatment of joint ventures under IAS 31, operating leases under IAS 17 and provisions under IAS 37.)

The directors of Inventure, a public limited company, are preparing the financial statements for the year ending 31 May 2002. The following extracts relate to those financial statements.

Group Income Statement for year ending 31 May 2002

	$000	$000
Revenue		5,740
Cost of sales		(3,215)
Gross profit		2,525
Distribution and administrative expenses (including depreciation $125,000)		(675)
Exceptional reorganisation costs	(240)	
Provision for retirement benefit cost	(50)	
Profit on disposal of non-current asset investments	70	
		(220)
Profit from operations		1,630
Finance cost		(60)
Profit before taxation		1,570
Income tax expense		(225)
Profit after taxation		1,345
Minority interests		(550)
Net profit for period		795

The directors have used the following accounting practices in arriving at the above financial statements, and wish your advice as to their acceptability:

(i) Inventure acquired the whole of the share capital of the Melia Group on 1 June 2001. The acquisition had been accounted for as a pooling of interests. The share-for-share exchange of ordinary shares was portrayed in the press as amounting to a purchase of the Melia Group by Inventure for 10 million ordinary shares of $1 in exchange for 5 million ordinary shares of $1 of Melia. The shares of Inventure were valued at $3.50 each. The market capitalisations at the time of the combination were Inventure $65 million and Melia $32 million. The book and fair value of the net assets of Inventure were $60 million and of Melia were $30 million respectively at the time of the acquisition. As part of the agreement between the parties, the board of directors of the combined company comprised entirely of the directors of Inventure. The policy of the group is to write off goodwill over 4 years.

(ii) The reorganisation costs in the income statement relate to the following item. Inventure had purchased 50% of the ordinary share capital of Caster, a limited company, for $30 million on 1 June 2001. The fair value and book value of the net assets of Caster at the date of acquisition were $58 million and $50 million respectively. Inventure's holding in Caster was subsequently sold to Melia on 1 January 2002, and the loss on sale was calculated at $240,000. This amount was then charged as reorganisation costs in the income statement. As Melia had been accounted for using pooling of interests accounting, then Caster was also accounted for using the same method. The regulatory framework normally requires the use of the allowed alternative treatment under IAS 31 *Financial Reporting of Interests in Joint Ventures*. The investment in Caster satisfied the definition of a joint venture, and its results for the year are as follows:

	$000
Revenue	1,500
Cost of sales	(700)
Gross profit	800
Distribution and administrative expenses	(100)
(including depreciation of $15,000)	
Operating profit	700
Income tax expense	(100)
Profit after tax	600

(iii) Inventure has paid an initial payment of $200,000 as a deposit under an operating lease. The payment has been capitalised as a non-current tangible asset, and is to be amortised over the 5-year life of the operating lease. The initial payment has substantially reduced the annual rental expense to $100,000 per annum.

(iv) Melia currently does not have a retirement benefit scheme for employees and, due to government legislation, is now obliged to provide such a scheme. The company has decided that it does not wish to provide a retirement benefit scheme for the employees of Melia and has provided for an amount of $50,000 for the fine which the government will levy if a scheme is not put in place by 30 September 2001. Inventure currently has a defined benefit scheme in place for its employees, but considering moving to a defined contribution scheme because of the current low returns on bonds and the current requirements of IAS19 *Employee Benefits*, and wish advice on this matter. The assets of the Inventure retirement benefit scheme are a mix of bonds and equities.

Required

(a) Discuss the nature and acceptability of the accounting practices set out in (i) to (iv) above, advising the directors on the correct accounting treatment or action that they should take.
(b) Show the revised group income statement for the year ending 31 May 2002.
(c) The directors have heard that alternative performance measures such as EBITDA (earnings before interest, tax, depreciation and amortisation) and enterprise value (market capitalisation plus debt) are being used by analysts, and are interested in your views on the use of these alternative performance measures. Comment briefly on the use of EBITDA and enterprise value as alternative measures of performance and the reasons why you feel that Inventure had utilised the accounting policies set out above.

Question 9.14: Bloomsbury (ACCA)

(The final question in the chapter covers joint venture reporting as its main topic. However, it also covers the subject areas of revenue recognition (agency v. principal), investment properties, revaluation of properties and the treatment of dividends in the financial statements.)

The following figures have been extracted from the accounting records of Bloomsbury on 30 September 2002.

	$000	$000
Sales revenue (note (i))		98,880
Cost of sales	56,000	
Joint venture account (note (ii))	1,200	
Operating expenses	14,000	
Loan interest paid	1,800	
Investment income		700
Investment property at valuation	10,000	
25-year leasehold factory at cost (note (iii))	50,000	
15-year leasehold factory at cost (note (iii))	30,000	
Plant and equipment at cost (note (iii))	49,800	
Depreciation 1 October 2001: – 25-year leasehold		10,000
– 15-year leasehold		10,000
– plant and equipment		19,800
Accounts receivable (note (i))	16,700	
Inventory – 30 September 2002	7,500	
Cash and bank	500	
Accounts payable		9,420
Deferred tax – 1 October 2001 (note (iv))		2,100
Ordinary shares of 25 cents each		40,000
10% Redeemable (in 2005 at par) preference shares of $1 each		10,000
2% Loan note (issued in 2000)		30,000
Accumulated profits – 1 October 2001		6,100
Investment property revaluation reserve – 1 October 2001		2,000
Interim dividends (note (iv))	1,500	
	239,000	239,000

The following notes are relevant:

(i) On 1 January 2002, Bloomsbury agreed to act as a selling agent for an overseas company, Brandberg. The terms of the agency are that Bloomsbury receives a commission of 10% on all sales made on behalf of Brandberg. This is achieved by Bloomsbury remitting 90% of the cash received from Brandberg's customers 1 month after Bloomsbury has collected it. Bloomsbury has included in its sales revenue $7.2 million of sales on behalf of Brandberg, of which there is 1 month's outstanding balances of $1.2 million included in Bloomsbury's accounts receivable. The cash remitted to Brandberg during the year of $5.4 million (i.e. 90% of $6 million) in accordance with the terms of the agency, has been treated as the cost of the agency sales.

(ii) The joint venture account represents the net balance of Bloomsbury's transactions in a joint venture with Waterfront which commenced on 1 October 2001. Each venturer contributes their own assets and pays their own expenses. The revenues for the venture are shared equally. The joint venture is not a separate entity.
Details of Bloomsbury's joint venture transactions are:

	$000
Plant and equipment at cost	1,500
Share of joint venture sales revenues	(800)
(50% of total sales revenues)	
Related cost of sales excluding depreciation	400
Accounts receivable	200
Accounts payable	(100)
Net balance of joint venture account	1,200

Plant and equipment should be depreciated in accordance with the company's policy in note (iii).

(iii) On 1 October 2001 Bloomsbury had its two leasehold factories revalued (for the first time) by an independent surveyor as follows:

25-year leasehold	$52 million
15-year leasehold	$18 million

Bloomsbury depreciates its leaseholds on a straight-line basis over the life of the lease
The directors of Bloomsbury are disappointed in the value placed on the 15-year leasehold. The surveyor has said that the fall in its value is due mainly to it unfavourable location, but in time the surveyor expects its value to increase. Th directors are committed to incorporating the revalued amount of the 25-year leasehold into the financial statements, but wish to retain the historic cost basis for th 15-year leasehold. Revaluation surpluses are transferred to accumulated realise profits in line with the realisation of the related assets.

Prior to the current year, Bloomsbury had adopted a policy of carrying its invest ment property at fair value, with the surplus being credited to reserves. For th current year, it will be applying the fair value method of accounting for investmen properties in IAS 40 *Investment Property*. The value of the investment property ha increased by a further $500,000 in the year to 30 September 2002.

Plant and equipment is depreciated at 20% per annum on the reducing balance basis.

(iv) A provision for income tax for the year to 30 September 2002 of $5 million is required. Temporary differences (related to the difference between the tax base of the plant and its balance sheet written down value) on 1 October 2001 were $7 million, and on 30 September 2002 they had declined to $5 million. Assume a tax rate of 30%. Ignore deferred tax on the property revaluations.

(v) The interim dividends paid include half of the full year's preference dividend. On 25 September 2002 the directors declared a final ordinary dividend of 3 cents per share.

Required

Prepare the financial statements for the year to 30 September 2002 for Bloomsbury in accordance with International Accounting Standards as far as the information permits. They should include:

- an income statement;
- a statement of changes in equity; and
- a balance sheet.

Notes to the financial statements are not required.

10

Disclosure standards

10.1   IAS 10 *Events After The Balance Sheet Date* (December 2003)

Introduction

As part of the ASB's convergence project, IAS 10 has been issued to replace IAS 10 *Events After The Balance Sheet Date* (revised 1999). The main change is the removal of dividends declared after the balance sheet date, as adjusting events. Instead they should be disclosed in the notes. They do not meet the definition of a liability under IAS 37 *Provisions, Contingent Liabilities and Contingent Assets*.

Similarly, dividends receivable from associates/subsidiaries, relating to a period prior to the balance sheet date, are now classified as non-adjusting.

There is also no exceptional provision in IAS 10 to use prudence to reclassify a non-adjusting event as adjusting.

Objectives

The objectives of IAS 10 are as follows:

1. To prescribe when an entity should adjust its financial statements for events after the balance sheet date, i.e. adjusting events
2. To prescribe the disclosures about the date of authorisation of the financial statements for both adjusting and non-adjusting events, and for non-adjusting events themselves.

IAS 10 also includes a requirement that an entity should not prepare its financial statements on a going concern basis if events after the balance sheet date indicate that it is no longer appropriate.

Scope

The standard should apply in accounting for and disclosure of events after the balance sheet date.

Key definition

Events after the balance sheet date: these occur between the balance sheet date and the date the financial statements are authorised for issue. There are two types:

1. Those providing evidence of conditions existing at the balance sheet date (adjusting)
2. Those that are indicative of conditions arising after the balance sheet date (non-adjusting).

If an entity submits its accounts to shareholders for approval AFTER the financial statements are issued, then the authorisation date is the date of original issuance – not the date of approval of the financial statements by the shareholders (see illustrations in Example 10.1).

Example 10.1
Events after the balance sheet date – authorisation date

1. Completion of draft financial statements	28 February 2002
Board reviews and authorises for issue	18 March 2002*
Profit announcement	19 March 2002
Available to shareholders	1 April 2002
AGM	15 May 2002
Filed with regulatory body	17 May 2002

*Correct date of authorisation for issue.

2. Management reviews and authorises for issue	18 March 2002*
Supervisory Board approves	26 March 2002
Available to shareholders	1 April 2002
AGM	15 May 2002
Filed with regulatory body	17 May 2002

*Correct date of authorisation for issue.

Events after the balance sheet date include all events up to the date when the financial statements are authorised for issue.

Recognition and measurement

Adjusting events after the balance sheet date

An entity should adjust the amounts recognised in its financial statements to reflect adjusting events after the balance sheet date.
  Examples include:

  settlement after the balance sheet date of a court case confirming a liability;
  receipt of information after the balance sheet date indicating that an asset was impaired at the balance sheet date (e.g. bankruptcy of customer, sale of inventories lower than cost);

- the determination, after the balance sheet date, of the cost of assets purchased or proceeds sold before the balance sheet date;
- the determination after the balance sheet date of the amount of profit/bonus payments provided there was a legal or constructive obligation at the balance sheet date;
- the discovery of fraud or error.

Non-adjusting events after the balance sheet date

An entity should not adjust the amounts recognised in the financial statements to reflect non-adjusting events after the balance sheet date.

An example would be a decline in the market value of investments. This reflects circumstances arising in the following period.

Dividends

If dividends are declared after the balance sheet date, no liability should be recognised at that date. Instead they should be disclosed in the notes as a contingent liability. They do not meet the definition of a liability under IAS 37.

Going concern

An entity cannot prepare its financial statements under the going concern basis if management intends to liquidate the business after the balance sheet date or ceases trading or has no realistic alternative to do so. IAS 1 outlines the required disclosure in such cases.

Disclosure

Disclosure should include:

1. The date of authorisation of issue
2. Who gave the authorisation
3. If the owners or others have powers to amend the financial statements after that date that fact.

Updating disclosure about conditions at the balance sheet date

If an entity receives information after the balance sheet date about conditions at the balance sheet date, the entity should update disclosures that relate to these conditions, in the light of any new information.

An example would be a contingent liability becoming a provision; then the disclosure re contingent liabilities need to be updated (as per IAS 37).

Non-adjusting events after the balance sheet date

If material, these could influence user decisions. Thus the following should be disclosed

1. The nature of the event
2. An estimate of such an event's financial effect, or a statement that such an estimate cannot be made.

Examples include:

- a major business combination/disposal after the balance sheet date;
- an announcement of a plan to discontinue an operation, or entering into binding agreements to sell;
- major purchases/disposals of assets or expropriations of major assets by government;
- the destruction of a major production plant by fire;
- the announcement or commencing of a major restructuring;
- major ordinary share and potential share transactions;
- abnormal large changes in asset prices or foreign exchange rates;
- changes in tax rates/laws enacted or announced after the balance sheet date;
- entering into significant commitments, e.g. guarantees;
- commencement of major litigation arising solely out of events that have occurred after the balance sheet date.

10.2   IAS 14 *Segment Reporting* (1997)

Objective

The objective of IAS 14 is to establish principles for reporting segment information, both products, services etc. and geographical. This is to help users:

better to understand past performance;
better to assess the entity's risks and returns; and
to make more informed judgements about the entity as a whole.

Consolidated data alone do not provide that information, and need to be disaggregated to achieve the objectives above.

Scope

IAS 14 should apply to the full financial statements that comply with IASs and be applied by entities whose equity or debt is publicly traded or are in the process of issuing those instruments in the public securities markets. Further voluntary disclosure, however, for other entities is encouraged, but they must comply in full with IAS 14.

Normally it is required only for consolidated accounts, but if a subsidiary is itself publicly traded then it must also be presented in its own separate financial report. Similar requirements also exist for associates or joint ventures.

Key definitions

Business segment: a distinguishable component of an entity that is engaged in providing an individual product or service or a group of related products/services and that is subject to risks and returns that are different from those of other business segments. Factors to consider include:

- the nature of the products/services;
- the nature of the production processes;

- the type or class of customer for the products or services;
- the methods used to distribute the products or provide the services; and
- if applicable, the nature of the regulatory environment, e.g. banking, insurance etc.

Geographical segment: a distinguishable component of an entity that is engaged in providing products or services within a particular economic environment and is subject to risks and returns that are different from those of components operating in other economic environments. Factors to consider include:

- similarity of economic and political conditions;
- relationships between operations in different geographical areas;
- proximity of operations;
- special risks associated with a particular area;
- exchange control regulations; and
- the underlying currency risks.

A geographical segment can be a single country, a group of two or more countries or even a region within a country.

Most organisations are organised and managed on the basis of predominant risks, thus an entity's organisational structure and internal financial reporting systems would be relevant in deciding the basis for identifying its segments.

Geographical segments may be based on either the location of an entity's operations (origin) or the location of its markets and customers (destination). The organisational structure should normally help to determine which is the more important of the two.

The determination of segments is judgemental, and must involve a consideration of the qualitative characteristics of relevance, reliability and comparability over time as well as its usefulness in assessing the risks and returns of the entity as a whole.

Segment revenue: represents revenue that is directly attributable to a segment and the relevant portion of enterprise revenue that can be allocated on a reasonable basis to a segment. That can arise from external sales or from internal segments of the same entity. It does not include extraordinary items, interest or dividend income unless it is a financial segment; nor should it include gains on the sale of investments or extinguishment of debt unless it is a financial segment.

It does include, however, an entity's share of profits/losses of associates and joint ventures accounted for under the equity method, as well as a joint venturer's share of the revenue of a jointly controlled entity that is accounted for by proportionate consolidation in accordance with IAS 31 *Financial Reporting of Interests in Joint Ventures*.

Segment expense: represents expenses that are directly attributable to a segment, and the relevant portion of an expense that can be allocated on a reasonable basis to the segment, including those relating to both external customers and internal segment. Segment expense does not include extraordinary items, interest unless a financial segment, losses on sale of investments unless a financial segment, losses on sale of investments, share of associates/joint venture losses, or income tax or general administration expenses that relate to the business as a whole. It does, however, include a joint venturer's share of expenses that are proportionately consolidated in accordance with IAS 31.

For a financial segment, interest income and expenses should be reported as a single net amount only if they are reported as such in the consolidated financial statements.

Segment result: the segment revenue less segment expense before any adjustments for minority interests.

Segment assets: operating assets employed by the segment for operating activities and are either directly attributable to the segment or can be allocated on a reasonable basis. If the segment result includes interest income, then segment assets should include the related income-producing assets.

Income tax assets are not included, and equity accounted investments are included only if the profit/loss from such investments is included within segment revenue. However, proportionately consolidated joint venture operating assets should be included. Examples include:

- current assets used in operating activities of the segment;
- property, plant and equipment;
- finance leases;
- intangible assets;
- share of operating assets used by two or more segments, provided a reasonable allocation can be made;
- goodwill directly attributable to a segment or allocated on a reasonable basis.

Revaluations and prior period adjustments to business combination segment assets must be reflected in segment disclosure.

Segment liabilities: operating liabilities that result from the operating activities of a segment and are either directly attributable to a segment or can be allocated to the segment on a reasonable basis. If the segment result includes interest expense, segment liabilities should include related interest-bearing liabilities. However, a joint venturer's share of the liabilities of a jointly controlled entity that is accounted for by proportionate consolidation under IAS 31 should be included. Income tax liabilities are excluded.

Examples include:

- trade and other payables;
- accrued liabilities;
- customer advances;
- product warranty provisions.

It is expected that the internal reporting system should enable reporting entities to identify attributable revenues, expenses, assets and liabilities to reporting segments. However, in some cases these could be argued to be arbitrary or difficult to understand by external users. Such an allocation would not be on a reasonable basis. Conversely, some items may not have been allocated internally but a reasonable basis for doing so exists, in which case they should be allocated.

Identifying reportable segments

Primary and secondary segment reporting formats

The dominant source and nature of an entity's risks and returns should govern whether a primary reporting format should be business or geographical segments. If they are affected predominantly by differences in the products/services it produces, then it primary format should be business segments with secondary information being reporte geographically, and *vice versa*.

An entity's internal organisational and management structure and its system of inter nal financial reporting should normally be the basis for identifying the predominan source and nature of risks and differing rates of return, and thus which reporting forma is primary – except in rare cases where:

- it is affected both by differences in products/services and geographically as evidence by a 'matrix approach' to managing the company and reporting internally, in whic case business segments should be primary and geographical secondary; and
- internal reporting is not based on either approach, in which case the directors shoul determine which is the more appropriate basis to adopt as the primary format.

IAS 14 does not require but it does not prohibit the adoption of a matrix presentatio (i.e. both treated as primary) if it is felt appropriate. In the first case above, the objectiv is to achieve a reasonable degree of comparability with other entities, enhance com parability and meet the expressed needs of investors, creditors and others for informa tion about product/service related and geographically related risks and returns.

Business and geographical segments

The business and geographical segments for external reporting should be in line wit internal reporting units that are used by the CEO and Directors to evaluate past perfor mance and make decisions about future allocations of resources within the entity.

If the internal reporting systems are based neither on products/services etc. nor o geography, the directors should choose either business segments or geographical segmen as the entity's primary segment reporting format based on their assessment of which for mat best reflects the primary source of the enterprise's risks and returns. The decisio should be based on the factors in the definitions of both consistent with the following:

- if one or more segments are based on the definition but others are not, in the case of thos not covered by the definitions management should look to the next lower level of intern segmentation that reports on product/geographical lines and if such a level meets th definition of a segment then it should be treated as an identifiable reportable segment itsel

This approach of looking to an enterprise's organisational and management structu and its internal reporting system to identify the entity's business and geographical se ments for external reporting purposes is sometimes called the 'management approach

Reportable segments

Two or more internally reported business segments or geographical segments that a substantially similar may be combined as a single business or geographical segment and only if:

- they exhibit similar long term financial performance;
- they are similar in all of the factors in the appropriate definition of either a busine or geographical segment.

A reportable segment should be identified if a majority of its revenue is earned from sales to external customers and:

- its revenue from sales to external customers and from other segments amounts to 10% or more of total revenue (internal and external); or
- its segment result is 10% or more of the combined result of all segments in profit or in loss whichever is greater; or
- its assets are 10% or more of total assets of all segments.

However, if an internally reported segment fails all of the above thresholds:

- it may be designated as a reportable segment despite its size;
- it may be combined into a separately reportable segment with one or more other similar segments that are also below the thresholds;
- if not treated as either of the above, it should be included as an unallocated reconciling item.

If total external revenue attributable to reportable segments is less than 75% of the total consolidated revenue, additional segments should be identified as reportable segments even if they fail the 10% thresholds until the 75% revenue threshold is met.

IAS 14 does not limit reporting segments to those that earn a majority of their revenue externally. For example, an oil company could report upstream activities (exploration and development) as a separate segment from downstream (refining and marketing) despite the fact that most of the upstream product is transferred internally. IAS 14 encourages voluntary disclosure along these lines with appropriate disclosure of the basis of pricing inter-segment transfers.

If an entity reports vertically integrated activities as separate segments and the entity does not choose to report them externally as business segments, the selling segment should be combined into the buying segment in identifying externally reportable business segments unless there is no reasonable basis for doing so, in which case the selling segment should be included as an unallocated reconciling item.

If a segment meets the threshold in a preceding period but not the current, then it should continue to be reported as a separate segment unless it is impracticable to do so.

Segment accounting policies

Segment information should be prepared in conformity with the accounting policies adopted for preparing and presenting the financial statements of the consolidated group.

IAS 14 does not prevent the disclosure of additional segment information prepared on a basis other than the accounting policies adopted for consolidated statements provided that:

- the information is reported internally to the board for making decisions on allocating resources; and
- the basis of measurement is clearly described.

Assets that are jointly used by two or more segments should be allocated only if their related revenues and expenses are also allocated to those segments. For example, an asset is included in segment assets only if the related depreciation or amortisation is deducted in measuring the segment result.

Disclosure

Primary reporting format

The disclosure requirements below should be applied to each reportable segment based on an entity's primary reporting format:

1. Segment revenue, with separate disclosure of external and internal
2. Segment result, with a clear description if accounting policies other than those for the consolidated financial statements are adopted (should normally be net profit/loss); if expenses cannot be allocated except arbitrarily, then gross margin on sales may be used
3. The total carrying amount of segment assets
4. Segment liabilities
5. Capital expenditure incurred on an accruals basis
6. Total depreciation and amortisation included in the segment result for the period
7. Entities are encouraged but not required to disclose the nature and amount of any items of segment revenue and expense that are of such size, nature or incidence that their disclosure is relevant to explain performance for the period, i.e. exceptional items; the decision *re* materiality should, however, be based on segments and not on the entity as a whole
8. Significant non-cash expenses other than depreciation and amortisation
9. Entities providing the voluntary segment disclosure under IAS 7 *Cash Flow Statement* need not disclose depreciation, amortisation or non cash expenses
10. Share of net profit/loss of associates, joint ventures etc. adopting the equity method if substantially all operations are within that single segment; if disclosed, then the aggregate investments in those associates/joint ventures should also be disclosed by the reportable segment
11. A reconciliation between the segmental information and the consolidated account is required – segment revenue to total, segment result to entity operating profit/loss as well as to net profit/loss, and segment assets and liabilities to entity total asset and liabilities.

Secondary segment information

If an entity's primary format for reporting segment information is business segments, it should also report the following information

1. Segment revenue from external customers by geographical area based on the geographical location of its customers for each segment which exceeds 10% or more total external sales

2. The total carrying amount of segment assets, for each geographical segment whose assets are 10% or more of total assets
3. The total cost incurred during the period to acquire segment fixed assets for each geographical segment that exceeds 10% or more of all geographical segments.

If an entity's primary format for reporting segment information is geographical segments (location of assets or of customers), it must also report the following secondary information for each business segment which exceeds 10% or more of total revenue or total assets:

1. Segment revenue from external customers
2. The total carrying amount of segment assets
3. The total cost incurred during the period to acquire segment fixed assets.

If an entity's primary format for reporting segment information is geographical segments (location of assets) and if location of its customers is different from the location of its assets, then the entity should also report revenue from sales to external customers for each customer based geographical segment whose revenue from sales to external customers is 10% or more of total entity revenue to external customers

If an entity's primary format for reporting segment information is geographical segments (location of customers) and if location of its assets is different from the location of its customers, then the following should be reported for each asset-based geographical segment whose revenue from external sales or segment assets is 10% or more of group amounts:

1. The total carrying amount of segment assets by geographical location
2. The total cost incurred in the period to acquire segment fixed assets, by location of assets.

Other disclosure matters

If a business segment for which information is reported to the CEO or Board is not a reportable segment because it earns a majority of its income from internal sales but still sells 10% or more of total entity revenue, the entity should disclose that fact and the amounts of revenue from (a) sales to external customers and (b) internal sales.

The basis of transfer pricing should be disclosed.

Changes in accounting policies adopted for segment reporting that have a material effect on segment information presented for comparative information should be restated unless it is impracticable to do so. Such disclosure should include a description of the nature of the change, the reasons for the change, the fact that comparative information has been restated or that it is impracticable to do so and the financial effect of the change, if reasonably determinable. If an entity changes the identification of its segments and it does restate prior periods, then the entity should report segment data for both the old and the new bases of segmentation in the year in which it changes the identification of its segments.

An enterprise should disclose the types of products/services included in each segment and indicate the composition of each reported geographical segment, *both primary and secondary,* if not otherwise disclosed in the financial report.

Table 10.1 Summary of required primary disclosures

Primary Format – Business	Primary Format – Geographic Location of Assets	Primary Format – Geographic Location of Customers
Revenue from external customers by business segment	Revenue from external customers by location of assets	Revenue from external customers by location of customers
Revenue from transactions with other segments by business segment	Revenue from transactions with other segments by location of assets	Revenue from transactions with other segments by location of customers
Segment result by business segment	Segment result by location of assets	Segment result by location of customers
Carrying amount of segment assets by business segment	Carrying amount of segment assets by location of assets	Carrying amount of segment assets by location of customers
Segment liabilities by business segment	Segment liabilities by location of assets	Segment liabilities by location of customers
Cost to acquire property, plant, equipment and intangibles by business segment	Cost to acquire property, plant, equipment, and intangibles by location of assets	Cost to acquire property, plant, equipment and intangibles by location of customers
Depreciation and amortisation by business segment	Depreciation and amortisation by location of assets	Depreciation and amortisation by location of customers
Non cash expenses by business segment	Non cash expenses by location of assets	Non cash expenses by location of customers
Share of net profit/ loss and investment in equity method associates or joint ventures by business segment (if substantially all within one segment)	Share of net profit/loss and investment in equity method associates or joint ventures by location of assets (if substantially all within one segment)	Share of net profit/loss and investment in equity method associates or joint ventures by location of customers (if substantially all within one segment)
Reconciliation of revenue, result, assets and liabilities by business segment	Reconciliation of revenue, result, assets and liabilities	Reconciliation of revenue, result, assets and liabilities

The latter should help users to assess the impact of changes in demand, changes in price of inputs, development of alternative products, the impact of changes in the economic and geographical environment etc.

Tables 10.1 and 10.2 provide summaries of required primary and secondary disclosures, respectively.

Table 10.2 Summary of required secondary disclosures

Primary Format – Business	Primary Format – Geographic Location of Assets	Primary Format – Geographic Location of Customers
Revenue from external customers by location of customers	Revenue from external customers by business segment	Revenue from external customers by business segment
Carrying amount of segment assets by location of assets	Carrying amount of segment assets by business segment	Carrying amount of segment assets by business segment
Cost to acquire property, plant, equipment and intangibles by location of assets	Cost to acquire property, plant, equipment and intangibles by business segment	Cost to acquire property, plant, equipment and intangibles by business segment
	Revenue from external customers by geographical customers if different from location of assets	
		Carrying amount of segment assets by location of assets if different from location of customers
		Cost to acquire property, plant, equipment and intangibles by location of assets if different from location of customers
Revenue for any business or geographical segment whose external revenue is more than 10% of entity revenue but that is not a reportable segment because a majority of its revenue is from internal transfers	Revenue for any business or geographical segment whose external revenue is more than 10% of entity revenue but that is not a reportable segment because a majority of its revenue is from internal transfers	Revenue for any business or geographical segment whose external revenue is more than 10% of entity revenue but that is not a reportable segment because a majority of its revenue is from internal transfers
Basis of pricing inter-segment transfers and any changes therein	Basis of pricing inter-segment transfers and any changes therein	Basis of pricing inter-segment transfers and any changes therein
Changes in segment accounting policies	Changes in segment accounting policies	Changes in segment accounting policies
Types of products and services in each business segment	Types of products and services in each business segment	Types of products and services in each business segment
Composition of each geographical segment	Composition of each geographical segment	Composition of each geographical segment

Illustrative layout

Information about business segments (£m)

	Paper products 2002	Paper products 2001	Office products 2002	Office products 2001	Publishing 2002	Publishing 2001	Other operations 2002	Other operations 2001	Eliminations 2002	Eliminations 2001	Consolidated 2002	Consolidated 2001
Revenue												
External sales	55	50	20	17	19	16	7	7				
Inter-segment sales	15	10	10	14	2	4	2	2	(29)	(30)		
Total revenue	70	60	30	31	21	20	9	9	(29)	(30)	101	90
Result												
Segment result	20	17	9	7	2	1	0	0	(1)	(1)	30	24
Unallocated corporate expenses											(7)	(9)
Operating profit											23	15
Interest expense											(4)	(4)
Interest income											2	3
Share of net profits of associates	6	5					2	2			8	7
Income taxes											(7)	(4)
Profit from ordinary activities											22	17
Extraordinary loss: uninsured earthquake damage to property		(3)									—	(3)
Net profit											22	14
Other information												
Segment assets	54	50	34	30	10	10	10	9			108	99
Investment in equity accounted associates	20	16					12	10			32	26
Unallocated corporate assets											35	30
Consolidated total assets											175	155
Segment liabilities	25	15	8	11	8	8	1	1			42	35
Unallocated corporate liabilities											40	55
Consolidated total liabilities											82	90
Capital expenditure	12	10	3	5	5		4	3				
Depreciation	9	7	9	7	5	3	3	4				
Non-cash expenses other than depreciation	8	2	7	3	2	2	2	1				

Note: Business and geographical segments

Business segments: for management purposes, the Company is organised on a worldwid[e] basis into three major operating divisions – paper products, office products and publishing each headed by a senior vice president. The divisions are the basis on which the Compan[y] reports its primary segment information. The paper products segment produces a broa[d] range of writing and publishing papers and newsprint. The office products segment man[u]ufactures labels, binders, pens and markers, and also distributes office products made b[y] others. The publishing segment develops and sells loose-leaf services, bound volumes an[d] CD-ROM products in the fields of taxation, law and accounting. Other operations inclu[de] development of computer software for specialised business applications for unaffiliate[d] customers, and development of certain former productive timberlands into vacation site[s.] Financial information about business segments is presented in Schedule A.

Geographical segments: although the Company's three divisions are managed on a worl[d]wide basis, they operate in four principal geographical areas of the world. In the Unit[ed]

Kingdom, its home country, the Company produces and sells a broad range of papers and office products. Additionally, all of the Company's publishing and computer software development operations are conducted in the United Kingdom, though the published loose-leaf and bound volumes and CD-ROM products are sold throughout the United Kingdom and Western Europe. In the European Union, the Company operates paper and office products manufacturing facilities and sales offices in the following countries: France, Belgium, Germany and the Netherlands. Operations in Canada and the United States are essentially similar, and consist of manufacturing papers and newsprint that are sold entirely within those two countries. Most of the paper pulp comes from company owned timberlands in the two countries.

Operations in Indonesia include the production of paper pulp, and the manufacture of writing and publishing papers and office products, almost all of which are sold outside Indonesia, both to other segments of the company and to external customers.

Sales by market: the following table shows the distribution of the company's consolidated sales by geographical market, regardless of where the goods were produced:

	Sales revenue by geographical market	
	2002	**2001**
United Kingdom	19	22
Other European Union countries	30	31
Canada and the United States	28	21
Mexico and South America	6	2
Southeast Asia (principally Japan and Taiwan)	18	14
	101	90

Assets and additions to property, plant, equipment and intangible assets by geographical area: the following table shows the carrying amount of segment assets, and additions to property, plant, equipment, and intangible assets, by geographical area in which the assets are located:

	Carrying amount of segment assets		**Additions to property, plant, equipment and intangible assets**	
	2002	**2001**	**2002**	**2001**
United Kingdom	72	78	8	5
Other European Union countries	47	37	5	4
Canada and the United States	34	20	4	3
Indonesia	22	20	7	6
	175	155	24	18

Segment revenue and expense: in Belgium, paper and office products are manufactured in combined facilities and are sold by a combined sales force. Joint revenues and expenses are allocated to the two business segments. All other segment revenue and expense is directly attributable to the segments.

Segment assets and liabilities: segment assets include all operating assets used by a segment and consist principally of operating cash, receivables, inventories and property, plant and equipment, net of allowances and provisions. While most such assets can be directly attributed to individual segments, the carrying amount of certain assets used jointly by two or more segments is allocated to the segments on a reasonable basis. Segment liabilities include all operating liabilities and consist principally of accounts, wages, and taxes currently payable and accrued liabilities. Segment assets and liabilities do not include deferred income taxes.

Inter-segment transfers: segment revenue, segment expenses and segment result include transfers between business segments and between geographical segments. Such transfers are accounted for at competitive market prices charged to unaffiliated customers for similar goods. Those transfers are eliminated in consolidation.

Unusual item: sales of office products to external customers in 2002 were adversely affected by a lengthy strike of transportation workers in the United Kingdom, which interrupted product shipments for approximately 4 months. The company estimates that sales of office products were approximately half of what they would have been during the 4-month period.

Investment in equity method associates: the company owns 40% of the capital stock of Europaper Ltd, a specialist paper manufacturer with operations principally in Spain and the United Kingdom. The investment is accounted for by the equity method. Although the investment and the company's share of Europaper's net profit are excluded from segment assets and segment revenue, they are shown separately in conjunction with data for the paper products segment. The company also owns several small equity method investments in Canada and the United States whose operations are dissimilar to any of the three business segments.

Extraordinary loss: the company incurred an uninsured loss of £3m caused by earthquake damage to a paper mill in Belgium in November 2001.

10.3 IAS 24 *Related Party Disclosures* (December 2003)

Objective

The objective of IAS 24 is to ensure that the disclosure of information about related party relationships draws attention to the possibility that the entity's financial position and performance may have been affected by the existence of related parties and by transactions and outstanding balances between an entity and its related parties.

Scope

The standard should apply in:

- identifying related party relationships, transactions and outstanding balances;
- identifying the circumstances in which disclosure is required in financial statements;
- determining the disclosures to be made.

Disclosure is also required of related party transactions and balances in the separate financial statements of a parent, venturer or investor as per IAS 27.

Purpose of related party disclosures

Related party relationships are a normal feature of commerce, but they could have a affect on profit/loss, financial position and cash flows. Related parties may enter contracts that unrelated parties may not – e.g. transfer of goods to a parent at cost.

The mere existence of a related party relationship may be sufficient to affect the transactions with other parties. One party may refrain from acting because of the significant influence of another; for example, a subsidiary may be instructed by a parent not to engage in research and development.

Thus knowledge of related party transactions, balances and relationships may affect assessments of an entity's operations, risks etc., and should be disclosed.

Key definitions

Related party: a party is related to an entity if it:

- directly, or indirectly through one or more intermediaries, controls, or is controlled by, or is under common control with the entity has an interest in the entity that gives it significant influence over that entity has joint control over the entity;
- is an associate as defined in IAS 28;
- is a joint venture as defined in IAS 31;
- is a member of the key management personnel of the entity or its parent;
- is a close member of the family of any individual referred to above;
  is an entity in which a controlling or jointly controlling interest over voting power is owned.
  is a post employment benefit plan.

Related party transaction: a transfer of resources, services or obligations between related parties, regardless of whether or not a price is charged.

Control: the power to govern the financial and operating policies of an entity to obtain benefits from its activities.

Joint control: contractually agreed sharing of control over an economic activity.

Significant influence: the power to participate in the financial and operating policy decisions, but not control. This can be achieved by share ownership, statute or agreement.

Close members: family members expected to influence or be influenced by an individual in their dealings with the entity. These include:

the individual's domestic partner and children;
children of the individual's domestic partner; and
dependants of the individual or individual's domestic partner.

In all cases attention is given to the substance of the relationship, not merely the legal form. The following are specifically mentioned as NOT being related parties:

two entities simply because they have common directors;
two venturers simply because they share joint control over a joint venture;
providers of finance, trade unions, public utilities and government departments;
economic dependent entities (e.g. major customers, suppliers, distributors, franchisers etc.).

Disclosure

Disclosure of control

Relationships between parents and subsidiaries should be disclosed irrespective of whether or not there have been transactions between those parties.

Where an entity is controlled by another party, the name of that party and, if different, the ultimate controlling party should be disclosed. If the ultimate party is not known, that fact should be disclosed. If neither the entity's parent nor the ultimate controlling party publishes financial statements for public use, then the most senior parent must be disclosed.

Disclosure of key management personnel compensation

Key management personnel compensation must be disclosed in total and for the each of the following:

1. Short-term employee benefits
2. Post-employment benefits
3. Other long-term benefits
4. Termination benefits
5. Equity compensation benefits.

Disclosure of transactions

The nature of the relationship between the parties should be disclosed, as well as the following MINIMUM information:

1. The amount of the transactions
2. The amount of outstanding balances and
   - their terms and conditions including details of security and nature of consideration
   - details of any guarantees provided or received
3. Provisions for doubtful debts
4. Bad debts written off.

The above must be disclosed separately for each of the following categories: the parent entities with joint control, subsidiaries, associates, joint ventures, key management, other related parties.

The following are examples of transactions that should be disclosed with a related party

- purchases and sale of goods;
- purchases and sales of property and other assets;
- rendering or servicing of services;
- leases;
- transfer of research and development;
- transfer under licence arrangements;
- transfer under finance arrangements;
- provision of guarantees or collateral;
- settlement of liabilities on behalf of the entity or by the entity on behalf of another party.

Disclosure that terms were on an arm's length basis should only be provided if the disclosures can be substantiated.

Similar items can be aggregated except if separate disclosure is necessary for a understanding of the effects of related party transactions on the financial statements.

10.4   Examination questions

Question 10.1 Portico (ACCA)

(The first of the three questions in this chapter covers the basics of segment reporting. It requires students to discuss the objectives and usefulness of providing such information as well as identifying the main problems encountered in delivering the information. The second part of the question requires a student to put theory into practice by asking him/her to identify the reportable segments for Portico and how certain specific items should be treated in the segment report.)

Consolidated financial statements effectively aggregate the results of members of the group. Whilst this achieves the objective of showing the results of the group as if it were a single entity, it does have the disadvantage of hiding the relative performance of the different components of the entity. The International Accounting Standards Board's solution to this problem is to require disclosures relating to the different segments of the entity.

Required

(a) Discuss the objectives and usefulness of reporting segment information.
(b) Define a reportable segment under IAS 14 *Segment Reporting*.
(c) Identify the main problems of providing segment information.

Portico has identified the following distinguishable business segments, together with their relative sizes:

Engineering	23%
Textiles	22%
Chemicals	20%
Travel agency	8%
House building	7%
Four others of 5% each	20%

None of the smaller segments are similar enough to be combined with other segments. The sizes above can be taken to relate to segment revenues, profits and assets.

The following additional information has been obtained:

(i) For cost control purposes, Portico's holding company is invoiced centrally and pays the utility costs (electricity and water) of each of its three reportable segments.

(ii) In its management accounts, central head office expenditure on research and development expenditure is allocated to reportable segments in relation to the relative turnover of each segment.

(iii) Certain assets, liabilities and expenses for the segments have been identified:

	$000	$000	$000
Leased assets at cost	12,000	25,000	18,000
Annual depreciation based on life of lease	1,200	1,250	1,500
Outstanding lease liability (at year end)	7,000	15,000	8,000
Lease interest for current year	800	1,300	600

Question 10.2 Global (CIMA)

(The second question in the group provides an already prepared segment report and requires students to try and interpret the information. As part of that process students are required to refer to any reservations they have on the information provided by the reporting entity.)

You are the Management Accountant of Global. Global has operations in a number of different areas of the world and presents segment information on a geographical basis in accordance with IAS 14 *Segment Reporting*. The segment information for the year ended 30 June 2002 is given below.

	Europe		America		Africa		Group	
	2002	2001	2002	2001	2002	2001	2002	2001
Revenue	$m	$m	$m	$m	$m	$m	$m	$m
External sales	700	680	600	550	400	200	1,700	1,430
Inter-segment sales	20	5	10	10	40	5	70	20
Total revenue	720	685	610	560	440	205	1,770	1,450
Result								
Segment result	70	69	90	90	(20)	(40)	140	119
Unallocated corporate expenses							(25)	(20)
Profit from operations							115	99
Interest expense							(22)	(18)
Interest income							4	3
Share of net profits of associates	10	9	12	5	–	–	21	
Income taxes								14
Net profit							(35)	(30)
							83	68
Other Information								
Segment asset	610	560	610	560	300	270	1,520	1,390
Investment in equity method associates	55	52	36	30	–	–	91	82
Unallocated corporate assets							200	175
Consolidated total assets							1,811	1,647
Segment liabilities	260	240	250	230	100	90	610	560
Unallocated corporate liabilities							80	5
Consolidated total liabilities							690	635

Your Chief Executive Officer has reviewed the segment information above and has expressed concerns about the performance of Global. He is particularly concerned about the fact that the Africa segment has been making losses ever since the initial investment in 2000. He wonders whether operations in Africa should be discontinued, given the consistently poor results.

Required

Prepare a report for the Chief Executive Officer of Global that analyses the performance of the three geographical segments of the business, based on the data that have been provided. The report can take any form you wish, but you should specifically refer to any reservations you may have regarding the use of the segment data for analysis purposes.

Question 10.3 Diversity (ACCA)

(The third question is mainly concerned with the actual preparation of a segment report, but it requires students to comment on the approach adopted by the management team in apportioning finance lease interest and consolidated goodwill. The first section is a general question identifying the main items of information that require to be disclosed under IAS 14.)

Consolidated financial statements effectively show the performance of a group as if it were a single entity. It is widely recognised that this information is of great value to many user groups, but consolidated financial statements also have been criticised. Many commentators have argued that to aggregate financial information relating to several subsidiaries that may operate in different industries and markets serves to produce information that may conceal important data and has the potential to confuse those who wish to analyse it. A defence of this point is that the financial statements of the individual companies within a group are often publicly available to those who would take the trouble to obtain them.

Required

(a) Identify the main items of information that require disclosure under IAS 14 (revised) *Segmental Reporting.*
(b) Bearing in mind the above comments:

(i) discuss the necessity for, and benefits of, segmental information; and
(ii) identify the problem areas relating to the provision of segmental information.

The following information has been extracted from the consolidated financial statements of Diversity for the year ended 31 March 2000. *Note*: the consolidated figures include inter-segment trading.

	$m
Sales revenue	900
Cost of sales	634
Distribution costs	87
Central administration	37
Amortisation of goodwill	20
Finance costs (lease 10, debenture 12)	22

Dividends	50
Consolidated goodwill	60
Non-current assets: – owned	370
– leased	150
Current assets	160
Current liabilities	90
Finance lease obligations	200
10% Debenture (issued in 1998)	120

The activities of Diversity relate to three operational segments: engineering, chemicals and a supermarket chain. Information relating to the segments is:

	Engineering	Chemicals	Supermarkets
Sales revenue	420	340	200
Gross profit margin on external sales	20%	40%	25%
Distribution and administration	24	38	25
Goodwill (see below)			
Owned fixed assets	150	120	100
Leased assets	60%	40%	nil
Current assets	70	60	30
Current liabilities	40	20	30
Lease obligations	50%	50%	nil

Notes:

(i) The segmental figures include the results of inter-segment trading; all figures (other than the percentages) are in $ million.

(ii) During the year the engineering division manufactured the steelwork for the super structure of several new supermarkets, this work was invoiced at cost ($20 million) to the supermarket division. The other inter-segment sales ($40 million) were from the chemical division to the engineering division at normal profit margins. There are n group unrealised profits.

(iii) The finance costs comprise of interest on finance leases and debenture interest. Th management of Diversity consider the debenture interest to be a common cost, bu not the interest on finance leases. This can be taken to accrue in proportion to th value of outstanding lease obligations.

(iv) The consolidated goodwill and its depreciation relate to a subsidiary that has bot engineering and chemical operations. Management assessed that, based on the re ative profitability at the time of acquisition, the goodwill should be allocated 30% t the engineering operations and 70% to the chemical operation.

(v) When preparing segment reports, Diversity uses its operating activities as the bas for its primary reporting format.

Required

(c) Prepare, as far as the information permits, a segment report for Diversity commenting on the merit of management's policy of apportioning the finance lease interest and the consolidated goodwill.

11

Employee benefits, pension schemes and share-based payment

11.1 IAS 19 *Employee Benefits* (December 1998, amended 2000)

Introduction

There are five categories of employee benefits:

1. Short-term, e.g. wages, salaries, paid leave, profit sharing, bonuses and non-monetary benefits such as medical care, housing, cars or subsidised goods
2. Post-employment benefits, e.g. pensions, medical care, life insurance
3. Other long-term employee benefits, e.g. long service leave, sabbaticals, long-term disability payments
4. Termination benefits, e.g. early retirement, redundancy payments
5. Equity compensation benefits.

Short-term employee benefits should be recognised when the employee has rendered service in exchange for the benefits.

Post-employment benefit plans are classified as defined contribution (DC) or defined benefit (DB). IAS 19 also covers multi-employer plans, state plans and plans with insured benefits.

Under DC, fixed contributions are paid into a fund – the employer has no further legal or constructive obligation to pay more into the fund if there are not sufficient assets to pay employee benefits. IAS 19 requires immediate expense of DC contributions when employees have rendered service in exchange for those contributions.

All other post-employment benefit plans are defined benefit plans. These may be unfunded, or wholly or partly funded. IAS 19 requires an enterprise to:

account for all legal and constructive obligations;

determine the present value of DB obligations and the fair value of any plan assets with sufficient regularity that the amounts recognised in the financial statements do not materially differ from the amounts that would be determined at the balance sheet date;

use the projected unit credit method;

accrue benefit to periods of service under the plan's benefit formula unless an employee's service in later years will lead to a higher level of benefits than in earlier years;

- use unbiased and mutually compatible actuarial assumptions re demographic and financial variables (financial assumptions should be based on market expectations at the balance sheet date);
- base the discount rate on high quality corporate bonds of a currency and term consistent with the currency and term of the post-employment benefit obligations.

Objective

The objective of IAS 19 is to prescribe the accounting treatment and disclosure for employee benefits (i.e. all forms of consideration given by an entity in exchange for services rendered by employees). The principle underlying all of the detailed requirements of the standard is that the cost of providing employee benefits should be recognised in the period in which the benefit is earned by the employee rather than when it is paid or payable.

Scope

IAS 19 applies to wages and salaries, paid vacation and sick leave, profit-sharing plans, medical and life assurance benefits during employment, housing benefits, free or subsidised goods or services given to employees, pension benefits, post-retirement medical and life insurance benefits, long service or sabbatical leave, deferred compensation programmes, termination benefits and equity compensation benefits.

Key definitions

Employee benefits: all forms of consideration given by an enterprise in exchange for services rendered by employees.

Short-term employee benefits: employee benefits (bar termination and equity compensation benefits) which fall wholly within 12 months after the end of the period in which the employees render the related service.

Post-employment benefits: employee benefits (bar termination and equity compensation benefits) which are payable after the completion of employment.

Defined contribution plans: post-employment benefit plans in which an enterprise pays fixed contributions into a separate entity fund. There are no legal or constructive obligation to pay further contributions if the fund is insufficient to pay all employee benefits.

Defined benefit plans: post-employment benefit plans other than defined contribution plans.

Multi-employer plans: DC or DB plans (other than state plans) that:

- pool the assets contributed by various enterprises not under common control; and
- use those assets to provide benefits to employees of more than one enterprise, on the basis that contribution and benefit levels are determined without regard to the identity of the enterprise that employs the employees concerned.

Other long-term employee benefits: employee benefits (other than post-employment benefits, termination and equity compensation benefits) which do not fall due within 12 months after the end of the period in which employees render the related service.

Termination benefits: employee benefits payable as a result of either:

- an enterprise's decision to terminate an employee's employment before normal retirement date; or
- an employee's decision to accept voluntary redundancy in exchange for those benefits.

Equity compensation benefits: employee benefits under which either:

- employees are entitled to receive equity financial instruments issued by the enterprise; or
- the amount of the enterprise's obligation to employees depends on the future price of equity financial instruments issued by the enterprise.

Current service costs: the increase in the present value of the DB obligation resulting from employee service in the current period.

Interest cost: the increase during a period in the present value of a DB obligation which arises because the benefits are one period closer to settlement.

Return on plan assets: interest, dividends and other revenue derived from the plan assets together with realised and unrealised gains or losses on the plan assets, less any cost of administering the plan and less any tax payable by the plan itself.

Post-service cost: the increase in the present value of the DB obligation for employee service in prior periods, resulting from the introduction of, or changes to, post-employment benefits or other long-term employee benefits. Can be positive or negative (i.e. benefits are improved or reduced).

Actuarial gains and losses: experience adjustments (i.e. differences between previous actuarial assumptions and what occurred), and the effects of changes in actuarial assumptions.

Short-term employee benefits

Accounting for short-term benefits is fairly simple as there are no actuarial assumptions to make and there is no requirement to discount future benefits.

Recognition and measurement

All short-term employee benefits

When an employee has rendered service the enterprise should recognise the undiscounted amount of short-term benefits expected to be paid in exchange for that service:

- as a liability (accrual) after deduction of amounts paid; if payments exceed benefits the excess should be treated as an asset (prepayment) to the extent that it will lead to a reduction in future payments or a cash refund;
- as an expense unless another IAS permits or requires the inclusion of employment costs as part of the cost of an asset (e.g. IAS 2 and IAS 16).

Short-term absences

An enterprise should recognise the expected cost of short-term employee benefits when:

- the employees render service that increases their entitlement to future compensated absences; and
- when the absences occur.

Examples include unused holiday leave which is expensed when employees render services. That is an accumulating entitlement (see Example 11.1).

Example 11.1
Short-term absence

An enterprise has 100 employees, who are each entitled to 5 working days of paid sick leave each year. Unused sick leave may be carried forward for 1 year. Sick leave is taken first out of the current year's entitlement and then out of any balance brought forward from the previous year (i.e. LIFO basis). At 31.12.2001, the average unused entitlement is 2 days per employee. Based on past experience, 92 employees will take no more than 5 days of paid sick leave in 2002 and the remaining 8 employees will take an average of 6.5 days each.

The enterprise expects to pay an additional 12 days of sick pay (8 employees × 1.5 days), thus a liability equal to 12 days sick pay should be accrued.

Other non-accumulating absences are only paid when they occur, but there is no accumulated entitlement. No liability or expense occurs until the time of the absence.

Profit-sharing and bonus plan

An enterprise should recognise the expected cost of profit-sharing and bonus payment only when both:

- the enterprise has a legal or constructive obligation to make such payments; and
- a reliable estimate of the obligation can be made.

Example 11.2 provides an illustration.

Example 11.2
Profit sharing

A profit-sharing plan requires an enterprise to pay a specified proportion of its net profit for the year to employees who serve throughout the year. If none leave, the total payments will be 3% of net profit. The enterprise estimates that staff turnover will reduce this to 2.5% of net profit.

The enterprise should recognise a liability and an expense of 2.5% of net profit.

---

constructive obligation can only exist if:

the formal terms of the bonus plan contain a formula for determining the size of the benefit;

the enterprise determines the amounts to be paid before the financial statements are authorised for issue;

past practice gives clear evidence of the amount of the obligation.

Disclosure

No specific disclosures are required *re* short-term employee benefits, but other IASs may require disclosures – e.g. IAS 24 *re* employee benefits for key management personnel and AS 1 *re* staff costs.

Post-employment benefits

Most employers provide post-employment benefits for their employees after they have retired. These include pension schemes but also post-employment death benefits and medical care. These benefit schemes are often referred to as 'plans'.

The plans receive regular contributions from employers (and sometimes employees) and the monies are invested in assets such as stocks and shares, bonds and property. The benefits are paid out of the income derived from the plan assets or the sale of some plan assets.

There are two types or categories of plans:

Defined contribution, where the contributions paid in are defined and the size of the benefit will depend on the performance of the plan assets – i.e. the risk is with the employee

Defined benefit, where the size of the benefits is determined in advance. The employer must contribute to meet those benefits, and if the assets are insufficient then any deficit must be made good by the employer by making additional contributions. If, however, there is a surplus, then an employer may take a contribution holiday or even obtain a refund from the fund. The risk, however, is clearly borne by the employer.

A clear distinction must be made between the funding of a pension scheme (i.e. actual cash contributions into the scheme) and its accounting treatment (i.e. cost to be charged the income and other performance statements).

Multi-employer plans

IAS 19 requires all multi-employer schemes to be classified as either DB or DC. If the scheme is DB, the entity should account for its proportionate share of the DB obligation, plan assets and costs in the same way as for other DB schemes, and provide full disclosure. However, where there is insufficient information (e.g. cannot get access to share plan assets/liabilities) then it should be accounted for as a DC scheme and provide additional disclosures that it is a DB scheme and the reasons why the information is not available.

In addition, to the extent that a surplus/deficit may affect the amount of future contributions, the following should be disclosed:

1. Any available information about the surplus/deficit
2. The basis used in determining the surplus/deficit
3. The implications, if any, for the enterprise.

Multi-employer plans must be distinguished from group administration plans. The latter is an aggregation of single employer plans combined to allow participating employers to pool their assets for investment purposes and reduce administration costs, but the claims of different employers are segregated. These, therefore, should be treated in the normal way for DB purposes.

State plans

These are established by legislation and operated by government. They cannot be controlled or influenced by the enterprise. They should therefore be treated in the same way as multi-employer schemes. In most state plans the enterprise has no legal or constructive obligation to pay future benefits, thus its only obligation is to pay the contributions as they fall due and if the enterprise ceases to employ the members of the state plan then there is no further obligation. They are usually, therefore, classified as DC schemes, but in rare cases they could be DB and the enterprise must follow the disclosure as per multi-employer schemes.

Insurance benefits

Insurance premiums should be treated as defined contributions to the plan unless the employer has a legal or constructive obligation to pay the benefits directly to the employees, or to make further payments in the event that the insurance company does not pay all the post-employment benefits for which the insurance has been paid.

Defined contribution schemes

These schemes are relatively straightforward as:

- the obligation is determined by the amount paid into the plan each period;
- there are no actuarial assumptions;
- there is no discounting involved, if the obligation is settled in the current period.

IAS 19 requires the following:

- contributions should be recognised as an expense in the period payable;
- any liability for unpaid contributions should be accrued as a liability;
- any excess contributions should be treated as prepayments, but only to the extent that they will lead to a refund or reduction in future payments.

If the contributions do not fall within 12 months, they should be discounted.

An enterprise must disclose a description of the plan as well as the amount recognised as an expense in the period.

Defined benefit plans

These are much more complex than DC schemes for the following reasons:

- the future benefits cannot be estimated exactly – actuarial assumptions are necessary;
- the obligations are payable in future years and therefore there is a need for these to be discounted to present value;
- if the actuarial assumptions change or experience differs from those assumptions, then actuarial gains and losses will arise.

These factors mean that the actual contributions paid into the fund in a particular period is not a fair charge for that period. DB plans may be funded or unfunded, and contributions are paid into a fund that is legally separate from the reporting enterprise.

Recognition and measurement

The following are the steps required in order for an employer to account for the expense and liability of a defined benefit plan:

. Actuarial assumptions must be used to make a reliable estimate of the amount of future benefits employees have earned from service in relation to the current and prior years – these include life expectancy, inflation, labour turnover, salary increases etc.
. The future benefits should be discounted using the projected unit credit method in order to provide a total present value of future benefit obligations arising from past and current periods of service
. The fair value of the plan assets should be established
. The total actuarial gain/loss should be determined, and the amount that should be recognised
. Where a plan has been improved, the additional cost arising from past service should be determined
. Where a plan has been curtailed or cancelled, the resulting gain or loss should be determined.

These procedures must be followed individually for each DB scheme the enterprise has. AS 19 makes it very clear that an entity must account for all constructive obligations; thus if it has an informal practice whereby the entity has no realistic alternative but to pay employee benefits, it should provide for those obligations – e.g. where a change in the enterprise's formal practices would cause unacceptable damage to its relationship with employees.

Projected unit credit method

Under this actuarial method it is assumed that each period of service by an employee gives rise to an additional unit of future benefits. The present value of that unit can be calculated and attributed to the period in which the service is given. The units, each measured separately, add up to the total overall obligation. The accumulated present value of discounted future benefits will incur interest over time, and thus an interest expense should be recognised (see Example 11.3).

Example 11.3
Projected unit credit method

Assume an employer pays a lump sum to employees when they retire. The lump sum is equal to 1% of their salary in the final year of service, for every year of service given.

- An employee is expected to work for 5 years (actuarial assumption)
- His/her salary is expected to rise by 8% per annum (actuarial assumption)
- His/her salary in 2001 is €10,000
- The discount rate is 10% per annum.

Based on a current salary of €10,000 and an annual rise of 8%, the salary in 2005 should be €13,605. An employee's lump sum entitlement is therefore expected to be €136 for each year's service, i.e. €680 in total.

Assuming no change in the actuarial assumptions and that no employees leave, the calculations are as follows:

Future benefit attributable to:	2001	2002	2003	2004	2005
	€	€	€	€	€
Prior years	0	136	272	408	544
Current year (1% of final salary)	136	136	136	136	136
Prior and current years total	136	272	408	544	680

The future benefit builds up to €680 over the 5 years, at the end of which the employee is expected to retire and the benefit is payable.

These figures, however, need to be discounted:

	2001	2002	2003	2004	2005
	€	€	€	€	€
Opening obligation	–	93	204	336	494
Interest at 10%	–	9	20	34	50
Current service cost	93	102	112	124	136
Closing obligation	93	204	336	494	680

Note that interest is the opening obligation multiplied by the discount rate.

Balance sheet

Under IAS 19, the following net total should be recognised as a defined benefit liabilit on the balance sheet:

- the present value of the defined benefit obligation at the balance sheet date;
- plus any actuarial gains, or minus any actuarial losses not yet recognised;
- minus any past service costs not yet recognised;
- minus the fair value of the assets in the plan out of which future obligations to curre and past employees will be directly settled.

The present value of DB obligations and plan assets should be determined with suf cient regularity that the amounts recognised in the financial statements do not diff materially from the amounts that would be determined at the balance sheet date. IAS does not require, but does encourage, the use of a qualified actuary in the measureme process.

If the total is negative, i.e. an asset, then it should be disclosed in the balance sheet as the lower of either the figure as calculated above, or the total of the present values of:

- any unrecognised actuarial losses and past service costs;
- any refunds expected from the plan;
- any reductions in future contributions, due to the surplus.

Example 11.4 provides an illustration.

Example 11.4
Balance sheet

A DB plan has the following characteristics:

Present value of the obligation	1,100
Fair value of plan assets	(1,190)
	(90)
Unrecognised actuarial losses	(110)
Unrecognised past service cost	(70)
Unrecognised increase in the liability on initial adoption of IAS 19	(50)
Negative amount determined	(320)
Present value of available future refunds and reductions in future contributions	100

The limit is computed as follows:

Unrecognised actuarial losses	(110)
Unrecognised past service costs	(70)
Present value of available future refunds and reductions in future contributions	(100)
Limit	(280)

As 280 is less than 320, the enterprise recognises an asset of 280 and discloses that the limit reduced the carrying amount of the asset by 40.

Income statement

The expense to be recognised in the income statement is the net total of the following:

the current service cost;
interest;
the expected return on plan assets and reimbursement rights;
actuarial gains and losses to the extent recognised;
past service costs to the extent recognised;
the effect of any curtailments or settlements.

Recognition and measurement: present value of defined benefit obligations and current service cost

There are many variables affecting the ultimate cost of a DB scheme – e.g. final salaries, labour turnover, mortality, medical cost trends etc. In order to measure the present value of the post-employment benefit obligations and related current service cost, it is necessary to:

- apply an actuarial valuation method, i.e. the projected unit credit method (see Example 11.3);
- attribute benefit to periods of service;
- make actuarial assumptions.

Attribute benefits to periods of service

These should be attributed under the plan's benefit formula. However, if an employee's service in later years will lead to a materially higher level of benefit than in earlier years, an enterprise should attribute benefit on a straight-line basis from the date when service by the employee first leads to benefits under the plan, until the date when further service by the employee will lead to no material amount of further benefits under the plan other than from further salary increases.

Example 11.5 provides an illustration.

Example 11.5
Present value of defined benefit obligations and current service cost

Assume a DB plan provides for an annual pension for former employees on retirement. The size of the pension is 2.5% of the employee's final salary for each year of service. The pension is payable from the age of 65.

The annual payment obligation of 2.5% should first be converted to a present value lump sum as at the date of retirement, using actuarial assumptions. The current service cost is the present value of that obligation (i.e. the present value of monthly pension payments of 2.5% of final salary, multiplied by the number of years of service to date). For example, if an employee is expected to earn €10,000 in his or her final year and to live for 15 years after retirement, the benefit payable for each year of employment would be the discounted value, as at retirement date, of €250 per annum for 15 years. This should then be converted to a present value to determine the current service cost for the year for that employee.

Probabilities should be taken into consideration. Assume a benefit of €1,000 for every year of service is payable to employees when they retire at 60, provided they remain with the employer until that time. Also assume an employee joins the company at the age of 40, with 20 years still to work.

The benefit attributable to each year of service is €1,000 × probability that the employee will remain with the employer until he or she is 60. Since the benefit is payable at retirement as a lump sum, it should be discounted – i.e. the present value of €40,000 (40 years × €1,000) multiplied by the same probability.

No added obligations arise after all significant post-employment benefits have vested. Suppose employees have an entitlement to a lump sum on retirement of €2,000 for every year they have worked, up to a maximum of 10 years (i.e. maximum of €20,000) and this vests after 10 years. A benefit of €2,000 should be attributed to each of the first 10 years of an employee's service. The current service cost in each of the 10 years should be the present value of €2,000. If an employee has 25 years to go before retirement, there should be a service cost in each of the first 10 years and none in the last 15 thereafter.

xample 11.6 provides a further example of how the rules should be applied.

Example 11.6
Inter Plc

Inter Plc's DB plan provides all employees with a paid lump sum retirement benefit of €100,000. They must be still employed aged 55 after 20 years of service, or still employed at he age of 65, no matter what their length of service.

For employees joining before age 35, service first leads to benefits at age 35 because they could leave at 30 and return at 33 with no effect on the amount/timing of benefits. Also, beyond age 55 no further benefits will arise. Inter Plc should allocate €100,000/20 = €5,000 o each year between the ages of 35 and 55.

For employees joining between the ages of 35 and 45, service beyond 20 years will lead to no further benefit. Inter Plc should therefore allocate €100,000/20 = € 5,000 to each of the irst 20 years.

Employees joining at 55 exactly will receive no further benefit past 65, so Inter Plc should allocate €100,000/10 years = €10,000 to each of the first 10 years.

Actuarial assumptions

These should be unbiased and mutually compatible. They are the enterprise's best estimate of the variables that will determine the ultimate cost of providing post-retirement benefits. They comprise:

demographic assumptions – mortality rates, employee turnover, disability and early retirement, proportion of members eligible for benefits and medical claim rates
financial assumptions – discount rate, future salary and benefit levels, future increase in medical costs, expected return on assets etc. – which should be based on market expectations, at the balance sheet date, for the period over which the obligations are to be settled.

The discount rate adopted should be determined by reference to market yields on high quality fixed rate corporate bonds, but in their absence yields on comparable government bonds should be used.

Actuarial gains and losses

These arise because of the following:

actual events differ from the actuarial assumptions;
actuarial assumptions are revised;
actual returns on plan assets differ from expected returns.

These are inevitable, and thus IAS 19 takes the view that they should not be recognised until they become significant. They are not recognised, however, if they fall within a tolerable range or 'corridor'.

IAS 19 requires that as a general rule, actuarial gains and losses should be recorded in the income statement as an expense/income and as part of the defined benefit liability/asset on the balance sheet. However, only a portion should be recognised if the net cumulative actuarial gains/losses exceed the greater of:

10% of the present value of the DB obligation (i.e. before deducting plan assets); and
10% of the fair value of the plan assets.

This must be carried out separately for each plan. The excess calculated as above should then be divided by the expected average remaining working lives of participating employees to arrive at the charge to go through the income statement.

IAS 19 does permit, however, any systematic method to be adopted if it results in faster recognition of actuarial gains and losses. The same basis must be applied to both gains and losses, and applied consistently from period to period.

Past service costs

Past service costs should be expensed on a straight-line basis over the average period until the benefits become vested. To the extent that the benefits are already vested immediately following the introduction of, or changes to, a defined benefit plan, an enterprise should recognise past service costs immediately (see Example 11.7).

Example 11.7
Past service costs

An enterprise operates a pension plan that provides for a pension of 2% of final salary for each year of service. On 1 January 2005 the enterprise improves the pension to 2.5% of final salary for each year of service starting from 1 January 2001. At the date of the improvement, the present value of the additional benefits for service from 1 January 2001 to 1 January 2005 is as follows:

Employees with more than 5 years service at 1.1.05	150
Employees with less than 5 years service at 1.1.05 (average vesting period: 3 years)	120
	270

The enterprise should recognise 150 immediately because those benefits are already vested. The enterprise should recognise 120 on a straight-line basis over 3 years from 1 January 2005.

Past service costs exclude:

- the effect of differences between actual and previously assumed salary increases;
- under/overestimates of discretionary pension increases where a constructive obligation exists;
- estimates of benefit improvements resulting from actuarial gains already recognised i the financial statements if the enterprise is obliged to use a surplus for the benefit (participants even if no award is formally made;
- the increase in vested benefits when employees complete vesting requirements;
- the effect of plan amendments that reduce benefits for future service (curtailments).

Recognition and measurement: plan assets

The contributions into a plan by the employer (and sometimes also employees) a invested in assets such as stocks and shares, property, bonds etc. The fair value of the plan assets is deducted from the defined benefits obligation in calculating the balan sheet liability.

Where no market price is available, the fair value is estimated by discounting futu cash flows using a discount rate that reflects both the risk and maturity of those asse

Unpaid contributions are excluded. Where plan assets include qualifying insurance policies that exactly match the amount and timing of some or all of the benefits payable under the plan, the fair value of those insurance policies is deemed to be the present value of the related obligations.

When it is virtually certain that another party will reimburse some or all of the expenditure required to settle a defined benefit obligation, an enterprise should recognise its right to reimbursement as a separate asset. This should be measured at fair value. In all other respects, an enterprise should treat that asset in the same way as plan assets. The expense should be presented net of any reimbursement (see Example 11.8).

Example 11.8
Recognition and measurement of plan assets

Present value of obligation	1,241
Unrecognised actuarial gains	17
Liability recognised on balance sheet	1,258

Rights under insurance policies that exactly match the amount and timing of some of the benefits payable under the plan (those benefits have a present value of 1,092)   1,092

The unrecognised actuarial gains of 17 are the net cumulative actuarial gains on the obligation and on the reimbursement rights.

Return on plan assets

The expected return on plan assets is one component of the expense recognised in the income statement. The difference between the expected return on plan assets and the actual return is an actuarial gain or loss. It is included with the actuarial gains/losses in determining the net amount that is compared with the limits of the 10% corridor.

The expected return is based on market expectations at the start of the period. Administration expenses are deducted in determining the expected and actual return on plan assets (see Example 11.9).

Example 11.9
Return on plan assets

At 1.1.2001, the fair value of plan assets was 10,000 and net cumulative unrecognised actuarial gains were 760. On 30.6.2001, the plan paid benefits of 1,900 and received contributions of 4,900. At 31.12.2001, the fair value of plan assets was 15,000 and the present value of the defined benefit obligation was 14,792. Actuarial losses for 2001 on the obligation were 60.

At 1.1.2001 the entity made the following estimates, based on market prices at that date:

	%
Interest and dividend income after tax	9.25
Realised and unrealised gains on plan assets after tax	2.00
Administration costs	(1.00)
Expected rate of return	10.25

For 2001 the expected and actual return on plan assets are as follows:

Return on 10,000 held for 12 months at 10.25%	1,025
Return on 3,000 held for 6 months at 5% (equivalent to 10.25%	
annually compounded every 6 months)	150
Expected return on plan assets for 2001	1,175
Fair value of plan assets at 31.12.2001	15,000
Less fair value of plan assets at 1.1.2001	(10,000)
Less contributions received	(4,900)
Add benefits paid	1,900
Actual return on plan assets	2,000

The difference between the expected return on plan assets (1,175) and the actual return on plan assets (2,000) is an actuarial gain of 825. Therefore, the cumulative net unrecognised gains are 1,525 (760 + 825 – 60). The limits of the corridor are set at 1,500 (greater of 10% × 15,000 and 10% of 14,792). In the following year (2002) the entity recognises in income an actuarial gain of 25 (1,525 – 1,500) divided by the expected average remaining life of the employees concerned.

Business combinations

For acquisitions, an entity should recognise the present value of the obligations less the present value of any plan assets arising from post-employment benefits. The present value includes the following, even if the acquiree has not recognised them at the date of acquisition:

- actuarial gains and losses that arose before the date of the acquisition;
- past service costs that arose from benefit changes before the date of acquisition; and
- amounts, under transitional arrangements, that the acquiree had not recognised.

Curtailments and settlements

Gains/losses should be recognised when the curtailment or settlement occurs, and a gain/loss should comprise:

- any resulting change in the present value of the plan assets;
- any resulting change in the fair value of plan assets;
- any related actuarial gains/losses and past service cost not previously recognised.

However, an entity should first determine the effect of a curtailment/settlement by remeasuring the obligation using current actuarial assumptions.

A curtailment occurs when there is a material reduction in the number of employees in the plan or when a plan is materially changed so that current employees no longer qualify for benefits or for reduced benefits (see Example 11.10). Curtailments are often linked to restructuring.

A settlement occurs when an entity eliminates all further legal or constructive obligations under a defined benefit plan.

When a curtailment relates to only some of the employees, the gain/loss includes proportionate share of the previously unrecognised past service cost and actuarial gains/losses. That is determined on the basis of the present value of obligations before and after curtailment or settlement unless another more rational basis is appropriate.

Example 11.10
Curtailment

A business segment is discontinued and employees will earn no further benefits. Using actuarial assumptions immediately prior to the curtailment, the net present value of the obligation is 1,000. Plan assets have a fair value of 820, and net cumulative unrecognised actuarial gains are 50. IAS 19 was adopted 1 year earlier and the net liability has risen by 100 (recognised over 5 years).

The effect of the curtailment is as follows:

	Before curtailment	Curtailment gain	After curtailment
Net present value of obligation	1,000	(100)	900
Fair value of plan assets	(820)	–	(820)
	180	(100)	80
Unrecognised actuarial gains	50	(5)	45
Unrecognised transitional amount (100 × 4/5)	(80)	8	(72)
Net liability recognised in balance sheet	150	(97)	53

Presentation

Offset

Only offset an asset on one plan against a liability on another plan if there is a legally enforceable right to use a surplus in one plan against a deficit on another, and the entity intends to settle its obligations on a net basis or to realise the surplus and settle its obligation simultaneously.

Current/non-current distinction

IAS 19 does not distinguish between current and non-current portions of assets and liabilities under post-employment benefit plans.

Financial components of post-employment benefit costs

IAS 19 does not specify whether an entity should present current service cost, interest cost and the expected return on plan assets as components of a single item of income/expense on the face of the income statement.

Disclosure

The following should be disclosed about defined benefit plans:

Accounting policy for recognising actuarial gains/losses
General description of the type of plan
Reconciliation of assets and liabilities recognised on balance sheet showing, at least:
- present value of defined benefit obligations wholly unfunded
- present value of defined benefit obligations wholly or partly funded
- fair value of any plan assets at the balance sheet date
- the net actuarial gains/losses not recognised in the balance sheet
- the past service cost not yet recognised on the balance sheet
- any amount not recognised as an asset

- the fair value of any reimbursement right recognised as an asset
- the other amounts recognised in the balance sheet.
4. The amounts included in the fair value of plan assets for:
   - each category of an entity's own financial instruments, and
   - any property occupied by, or other assets used by, the reporting entity
5. A reconciliation showing movements during the period in the net liability recognise
6. The total expense in income for:
   - current service cost
   - interest cost
   - expected return on plan assets
   - expected return on any reimbursement right recognised as an asset under 104(a)
   - actuarial gains and losses
   - past service costs, and
   - the effect of any curtailment or settlement
7. The actual return on plan assets and on any reimbursement right
8. The principal actuarial assumptions including;
   - the discount rates
   - the expected rates of return on plan assets
   - the expected rates of return for periods presented on any reimbursement right
   - the expected rates of salary increase
   - medical cost trend rates
   - any other material actuarial assumptions used.

Actuarial assumptions must be disclosed in absolute terms, not relative.

Other long-term employee benefits

These include:

- long-term compensated absences (e.g. sabbatical leave)
- jubilee or long-term benefits
- long-term disability benefits
- profit sharing and bonuses payable
- deferred compensation paid after more than 12 months.

These are not as complicated as post-employment benefits – they need a simple moc as their measurement is not usually subject to the same degree of uncertainty. T method differs from post-employment benefits as follows:

- actuarial gains and losses are recognised immediately – no 'corridor' is applied; anc
- all past service costs are recognised immediately.

Recognition and measurement

The liability should be the net total of the present value of defined benefit obligations the balance sheet date, minus the fair value at the balance sheet date of plan assets us to settle the obligations.

The liability should be measured as per DB schemes.

The net total should be expensed except to the extent that another IAS requires or permits their inclusion in the cost of an asset:

* current service cost;
* interest cost;
* expected return on plan assets and on any reimbursement right recognised as an asset;
* actuarial gains and losses which should be recognised immediately;
* past service cost recognised immediately; and
* the effect of any curtailments or settlements.

If there is a long-term disability benefit, the obligation arises when the service is rendered and the measurement of that obligation reflects the probability that payment will be required and the length of time for which it will be paid.

Disclosure

No specific disclosures are required, but under IAS 24 an entity should disclose information about other long-term employee benefits for key management personnel.

Termination benefits

An entity should recognise termination benefits as a liability and an expense when, and only when, the entity is demonstrably committed to either:

terminating the employment of an employee/s before the normal retirement date; or providing termination benefits as a result of an offer made to encourage voluntary redundancy.

An entity is demonstrably committed to a termination date when the entity has a detailed formal plan for the termination. The plan should include, as a minimum:

the location, function and approximate number of employees of termination; the termination benefits for each job; the time at which the plan will be implemented.

Termination benefits are usually lump sum payments, but also include:

enhancement of retirement benefits; and salary until the end of a specified notice period if the employee does not render further service.

As these benefits do not provide an entity with future economic benefits, they are therefore expensed immediately.

If the benefits fall due after more than 12 months, they should be discounted. The measurement of a voluntary redundancy programme should be based on the expected number of employees expected to accept the offer.

Disclosure

Where uncertainty exists, a contingent liability should be disclosed under IAS 37. Under IAS 8, the nature and amount of an expense, if exceptional, should be disclosed, as well as termination benefits for key management personnel, under IAS 24.

Equity compensation benefits

These include such benefits as:

- shares, share options and other equity issued to employees at less than fair value; and
- cash payments whose amount depends on the future market price of the shares.

There are no specific recognition and measurement requirements in the standard on equity compensation payments (but see IFRS 2).

Equity compensation benefits may affect:

- an entity's financial position by having to issue equity; and
- an entity's performance and cash flows by reducing cash or increasing expenses.

An entity should disclose:

1. The nature and terms of equity compensation plans
2. The accounting policy for equity compensation plans
3. The amounts recognised for equity compensation plans
4. The number and terms of equity instruments that are held by equity compensation plans at the start and end of the period (the extent to which the employees' entitlements to those instruments are vested at the start and end of the year should be specified)
5. The number and terms of equity instruments issued by the entity to equity compensation plans or to employees during the period and the fair value of any consideration received from the equity compensation plans or the employees
6. The number, exercise dates and exercise prices of share options exercised under equity compensation plans during the period
7. The number of share options held by equity compensation plans or held by employees under the plans that lapsed during the period
8. The amount, and principal terms of any loans or guarantees granted by the entity to or on behalf of equity compensation plans.

In addition, the entity should also disclose:

1. The fair value at start and end of the period of the entity's own equity instrument held by equity compensation plans
2. The fair value, at date of issue, of the entity's own equity instruments issued by the entity to equity compensation plans or to employees, or by equity compensation plans to employees during the period.

If it is not practicable to determine the fair value of equity instruments, that fact should be disclosed.

If there is more than one equity instrument, the disclosures can be carried out individually or in suitable groupings. If the latter, disclosures should be provided in the form of weighted averages or of relatively narrow ranges. It might be useful to distinguish 'out of the money' options separately.

Additional disclosures may be required under IAS 24 if an entity:

- provides equity compensation benefits to key management personnel;
- provides equity compensation benefits via instruments issued by the entity's parent; or
- enters into related party transactions with equity compensation plans.

Transitional provisions

On first adoption of IAS 19, the transitional liability for DB schemes is determined as:

- the present value of the obligation at date of adoption;
- minus the fair value, at date of adoption, of plan assets out of which obligations will be settled;
- minus any past service cost that should be recognised in later periods.

If the liability is larger than the previous accounting policy the entity should recognise irrevocably the increase as:

- immediate as per IAS 8; or
- as an expense on a straight-line basis up to 5 years from the date of adoption, but the entity must apply the limit in para. 58 in measuring the asset, disclose the amount still unrecognised and the amount recognised in the period, and limit the actuarial gain only to the extent that net cumulative unrecognised actuarial gains exceed the unrecognised part of the transitional liability; it must also include the related part of the unrecognised transitional liability in determining any subsequent gain or loss on settlement or curtailment.

Any decreases should be recognised immediately under IAS 8.

Example 11.11 provides an illustration.

Example 11.11
Transitional provisions

At 31.12.1998 a pension liability of 100 exists on the balance sheet. IAS 19 is adopted from 1.1.1999, when the present value of the obligation is 1,300 and the fair value of plan assets is 1,000. On 1.1.1993 the entity improved pensions (cost for non-vested benefits 160; average remaining period 10 years).

The transitional effect is as follows:

Present value of the obligation	1,300
Fair value of plan assets	(1,000)
Less past service cost to be recognised in later periods (160 × 4/10)	(64)
Transitional liability	236
Liability already recognised	100
Increase in liability	136

The entity may choose to recognise the increase of 136 immediately or over up to 5 years, but the choice is irrevocable.

At 31.12.1999 the present value of the obligation is 1,400 and the fair value of plan assets 1,050. Net cumulative unrecognised actuarial gains since adopting the standard is 120. The expected average working life of employees in the plan was 8 years. The policy is to recognise all actuarial gains and losses immediately.

The effect of the limit is as follows:

Net cumulative unrecognised actuarial gains	120
Unrecognised part of the transitional liability (136 × 4/5)	(109)
Maximum gain to be recognised	11

Illustrative example

The following information is provided about a defined benefit plan. To keep interest simple, all transactions are assumed to occur at the year end. The present value of the obligation and the fair value of the plan assets were both 1,000 at 1.1.2001. Net cumulative unrecognised actuarial gains at that date were 140.

	2001	2002	2003
Discount at start of the year	10.0%	9.0%	8.0%
Expected rate of return on plan assets at start of year	12.0%	11.1%	10.3%
Current service cost	130	140	150
Benefits paid	150	180	190
Contributions paid	90	100	110
Present value of obligation at 31 December	1,141	1,197	1,295
Fair value of plan assets at 31 December	1,092	1,109	1,093
Expected average remaining working lives of employees (years)	10	10	10

In 2002 the plan was amended to provide additional benefits with effect from 1.1.2002. The present value as at 1.1.2002 of additional benefits for employee service before 1.1.2002 was 50 for vested benefits and 30 for non-vested benefits. As at 1 January 2002 the enterprise estimated that the average period until the non-vested benefits would become vested was 3 years; the past service cost arising from additional non-vested benefits is therefore recognised on a straight-line basis over 3 years. The past service cost arising from additional vested benefits is recognised immediately. The enterprise has adopted a policy of recognising actuarial gains and losses under the minimum requirements of IAS 19.

Changes in the present value of the obligation and in the fair value of the plan assets

The first step is to summarise the changes in fair value of the obligation and in the fair value of the plan assets and use this to determine the amount of the actuarial gains or losses for the period. These are as follows:

	2001	2002	2003
Present value of obligation, 1 January	1,000	1,141	1,197
Interest cost (10%, 9%, 8%)	100	103	96
Current service cost	130	140	150
Past service cost – non-vested benefits	–	30	–
Past service cost – vested benefits	–	50	–
Benefits paid	(150)	(180)	(190)
Actuarial (gain)/loss on obligation (balancing figure)	61	(87)	42
Present value of obligation, 31 December	1,141	1,197	1,295
Fair value of plan assets, 1 January	1,000	1,092	1,109
Expected return on plan assets	120	121	114
Contributions	90	100	110
Benefits paid	(150)	(180)	(190)
Actuarial gain/(loss) on plan assets (balancing figure)	32	(24)	(50)
Fair value of plan assets, 31 December	1,092	1,109	1,093

Limits of the corridor

The next step is to determine the limits of the corridor and then compare these with the cumulative unrecognised actuarial gains and losses in order to determine the net actuarial gain or loss to be recognised in the following period. The limits are set at the greater of:

- 10% of the present value of the obligation before deducting plan assets; and
- 10% of the fair value of any plan assets.

These limits and the recognised and unrecognised actuarial gains and losses are as follows:

	2001	2002	2003
Net cumulative unrecognised actuarial gains (losses) at 1 January	140	107	170
Limits of corridor at 1 January	100	114	120
Excess (a)	40	–	50
Average expected remaining working lives (years) (b)	10	10	10
Actuarial gain (loss) to be recognised (a/b)	4	–	5
Unrecognised actuarial gains (losses) at 1 January	140	107	170
Actuarial gain (loss) for year – obligation	(61)	87	(42)
Actuarial gain (loss) for year – plan assets	32	(24)	(50)
Subtotal	111	170	78
Actuarial gain (loss) recognised	(4)	–	(5)
Unrecognised actuarial gains (losses) at 31 December	107	170	73

Amounts recognised in the balance sheet and income statement, and related analyses

The final step is to determine the amounts to be recognised in the balance sheet and income statement, and the related analyses to be disclosed under paragraphs 120(c), (e), (f) and (g) of the standard. These are as follows:

	2001	2002	2003
Present value of the obligation	1,141	1,197	1,295
Fair value of plan assets	(1,092)	(1,109)	(1,093)
	49	88	202
Unrecognised actuarial gains (losses)	107	170	73
Unrecognised past service cost – non-vested benefits	–	(20)	(10)
Liability recognised in balance sheet	156	238	265
Current service cost	130	140	150
Interest cost	100	103	96
Expected return on assets	(120)	(121)	(114)
Net actuarial (gain) loss recognised in year	(4)	–	(5)
Past service cost – non-vested benefits	–	10	10
Past service cost – vested benefits	–	50	–
Expense recognised in income statement	106	182	137

Movements in the net liability recognised in the balance sheet, to be disclosed unde paragraph 120(e):

Opening net liability	140	156	238
Expense as above	106	182	137
Contributions paid	(90)	(100)	(110)
Closing net liability	156	238	265

Actual return on plan assets, to be disclosed under paragraph 120(g):

Expected return on assets	120	121	114
Actuarial gain (loss) on plan assets	32	(24)	(50)
Actuarial return on plan assets	152	97	64

Illustrative disclosures

Employee benefit obligations

The amounts recognised in the balance sheet are as follows:

	Defined benefit pension plans		Post-employmer medical benefit	
	2002	2001	2002	2001
Present value of funded obligations	12,310	11,772	2,819	2,721
Fair value of plan assets	(11,982)	(11,188)	(2,480)	(2,415
	328	584	339	306
Present value of unfunded obligations	6,459	6,123	5,160	5,094
Unrecognised actuarial gains (losses)	(97)	(17)	31	72
Unrecognised past service cost	(450)	(650)	–	–
Net liability in balance sheet	6,240	6,040	5,530	5,472
Amounts in the balance sheet:				
Liabilities	6,451	6,278	5,530	5,472
Assets	(211)	(238)	–	–
Net liability in balance sheet	6,240	6,040	5,530	5,472

The pension plan assets include ordinary shares issued by the enterprise with a fair valu of 317 (2001: 281). Plan assets also include property occupied by the enterprise with fair value of 200 (2001: 185).

The amounts recognised in the income statement are as follows:

	Defined benefit pension plans		Post-employmeı medical benefit	
	2002	2001	2002	200
Current service cost	1,679	1,554	471	41
Interest on obligation	1,890	1,650	819	70
Expected return on plan assets	(1,392)	(1,188)	(291)	(26
Net actuarial losses (gains) recognised in year	90	(187)	–	–
Past service cost	200	200	–	–
Losses (gains) on curtailments and settlements	221	(47)	–	–
Total, included in 'staff costs'	2,688	1,982	999	85
Actual return on plan assets	1,232	1,205	275	25

Movements in the net liability recognised in the balance sheet are as follows:

	Defined benefit pension plans		Post-employment medical benefits	
	2002	**2001**	**2002**	**2001**
Net liability at start of year	6,040	5,505	5,472	5,439
Net expense recognised in the income statement	2,688	1,982	999	850
Contributions	(2,261)	(1,988)	(941)	(817)
Exchange differences on foreign plan	(227)	221	–	–
Liabilities acquired in business combinations	–	320	–	–
Net liability at end of year	6,240	6,040	5,530	5,472

Principal actuarial assumptions at the balance sheet date (expressed as weighted averages):

	2002	**2001**
Discount rate at 31 December	10.0%	9.1%
Expected return on plan assets at 31 December	12.0%	10.9%
Future salary increases	5.0%	4.0%
Future pension increases	3.0%	2.0%
Proportion of employees opting for early retirement	30.0%	30.0%
Annual increase in health care costs	8.0%	8.0%
Future changes in maximum state healthcare benefits	3.0%	2.0%

The group also participates in an industry-wide defined benefit plan which provides pension benefits linked to final salaries and is funded on a pay-as-you-go basis. It is not practicable to determine the present value of the group's obligation or the related current service cost, as the plan computes its obligations on a basis that differs materially from the basis used in the enterprise's financial statements. On that basis, the plan's financial statements to 30 June 2000 show an unfunded liability of 27,525. The unfunded liability will result in future payments by participating employers. The plan will result in future payments by participating employers. The plan has approximately 5,000 members, of whom approximately 5,000 are current or former employees of the enterprise or their dependants. The expense recognised in the income statement, which is equal to contributions due for the year, and is not included in the above amounts, was 230 (2001: 215). The group's future contributions may be increased substantially if other enterprises withdraw from the plan.

1.2 IAS 26 *Accounting and Reporting by Retirement Benefit Plans* (1994)

Objective

The objective of IAS 26 is to specify measurement and disclosure principles for the reports of retirement benefit plans. All plans should include in their reports a statement of changes in net assets available for benefits, a summary of significant accounting policies, and a description of the plan and the effect of any changes in the plan during the period.

Scope

This standard should be applied in the reports of retirement benefit plans where such reports are prepared.

The plan should be separate from the employer's. It covers reporting by the plan to all participants, not to individuals. It complements IAS 19, which applies to the cost of retirement plans in an employer's own financial statements.

The plans may be defined contribution or defined benefit. They may require the creation of separate funds to which contributions are made and from which retirement benefits are paid. IAS 26 applies regardless of whether or not a fund is created. Similarly, funds invested through insurance companies are also covered.

It does not cover employment termination indemnities, long service leave benefits, special early retirement or redundancy plans, health and welfare plans etc.

Key definitions

Retirement benefit plans: arrangements whereby an entity provides benefits for its employees on or after termination of service when such benefits can be determined or estimated in advance of retirement from the provisions of a document or from the entity's practices.

Defined contribution plans: retirement benefit plans under which retirement benefits are determined by contributions to a fund together with investment earnings thereon.

Defined benefit plans: retirement benefit plans under which retirement benefits are determined by reference to a formula usually based on employees' earnings and years of service.

Funding: the transfer of assets to a fund separate from the employer's entity to meet future obligations for the payment of retirement benefits.

Most plans are based on formal agreements, but some plans permit employers to limit their obligations under the plans although it is usually difficult to cancel a plan if the employees are to be retained. The same accounting should apply to both formal and informal plans.

Any hybrid plans should be considered to be defined contribution for the purpose of IAS 26.

Defined contribution plans

The report of a defined contribution plan should contain a statement of net assets available for benefits, and a description of the funding policy.

Future benefits are determined by the contributions paid by the employer and investment earnings thereon. There is no need for actuarial advice, and the employer's obligation is a closed end liability. However, an employer is interested in the efficient and fair operation of the plan and participants are concerned about proper control being exercised to protect their rights.

The objective of reporting by a DC plan is periodically to provide information about the plan and the performance of its investments. That is achieved by providing a report including the following:

- a description of significant activities for the period and the effect of any changes relating to the plan, its membership and terms and conditions;
- statements reporting on the transactions and investment performance for the period and the financial position of the plan at the end of the period; and
- a description of the investment policies.

Defined benefit plans

The report of a DB plan should contain either a statement that shows:

- the net assets available for benefits;
- the actuarial present value of promised retirement benefits, distinguishing between vested benefits and non vested benefits; and
- the resulting excess or deficit

or a statement of net assets available for benefits including either:

- a note disclosing the actuarial present value of promised retirement benefits, distinguishing between vested benefits and non vested benefits; or
- a reference to this information in an accompanying actuarial report.

If an actuarial valuation has not been prepared at the date of the report, the most recent valuation should be used as a base and the date of the valuation disclosed.

The actuarial present value should be based on the benefits promised under the terms of the plan based on service to date using either current or projected salary levels, with disclosure of the basis. The effect of any changes in actuarial assumptions having a significant effect on the actuarial present value of promised benefits should also be disclosed.

The report should explain the relationship between the actuarial present value of promised actuarial benefits and net assets available, and the policy for funding.

The payment of promised benefits depends on the financial position of the plan and the ability to make future contributions, as well as investment performance and operating efficiency. It requires actuarial advice to assess the financial position, review the assumptions and recommend future contribution levels.

The objective of reporting by a DB plan is periodically to provide information about the financial resources and activities of the plan that is useful in assessing the relationships between the accumulation of resources and plan benefits over time. The objective usually achieved by providing a report including the following:

- a description of significant activities for the period and the effect of any changes relating to the plan, its membership and terms and conditions;
- statements reporting on the transactions and investment performance for the period and the financial position of the plan at the end of the period;
- actuarial information either as part of the statements or by way of a separate report; and
- a description of the investment policies.

Actuarial present value of promised retirement benefits

The present value of future expected payments may be calculated using either current or expected salary levels.

The reasons for adopting a current salary approach include the following:

- the actuarial present value can be calculated more objectively than with projected salary levels as it involves fewer assumptions;
- increases in benefits due to salary increases become an obligation of the plan at the time of the salary increase; and
- the amount of the actuarial present value is more closely related to the amount payable in the event of a termination or discontinuance of the plan.

The reasons for adopting a projected salary approach include the following:

- financial information should be prepared on a going concern basis, irrespective of the assumptions and estimates made;
- under final pay schemes, benefits are determined by reference to salaries at or near retirement date – salaries, contribution levels and rates of return must be projected; and
- failure to incorporate salary projections may result in an apparent overfunding.

The actuarial value of benefits based on current salaries is disclosed in the report of a plan to indicate the obligation for benefits earned to the date of the report. The actuarial value of benefits based on projected salaries is disclosed to indicate the magnitude of the potential obligation on a going concern basis.

In addition, sufficient explanation may need to be given to indicate clearly the context in which the actuarial valuation should be read. It may take the form of providing information on the adequacy of future funding and of the funding policy based on salary projections. This can be provided in the financial information or in the actuary's report.

Frequency of actuarial valuations

In many countries, actuarial valuations are obtained every 3 years. If not prepared at the date of the report, the most recent valuation should be used as the base and the date of valuation disclosed.

Report content

For defined benefit plans, the information should be provided in one of the following formats:

1. A statement in the report showing the net assets, the actuarial present value of benefits and the excess/deficit. The report should also contain statements of changes in net assets and in the actuarial present value of benefits. It may include a separate actuary report supporting the actuarial present value of promised retirement benefits.
2. A report that includes a statement of net assets and a statement of changes in those benefits. The actuarial present value of benefits is disclosed in the notes. The report may also include a report from an actuary supporting the actuarial present value of promised benefits.

3. A report that includes a statement of net assets and a statement of changes in net assets with the actuarial value of promised retirement benefits contained in a separate actuarial report.

In each format, a trustee's report and an investment report may accompany the statements.

All plans

Valuation of plan assets

Investments should be valued at fair value – for marketable securities, that is market value. If the fair value is not possible, disclosure should be made of the reason why it is not adopted.

Disclosure

The following information should also be provided:

1. A statement of changes in net assets available for benefits
2. A summary of significant accounting policies
3. A description of the plan and the effect of any changes in the plan during the period.

Net assets

There should be a statement of net assets available for benefits disclosing:

1. Assets at the end of the period suitably classified
2. The basis of valuation of assets
3. Details of any single investment exceeding 5% of the net assets available for benefits
4. Details of any investment in the employer
5. Liabilities other than the actuarial present value of promised retirement benefits.

There should be a statement of changes in net assets available for benefits disclosing:

1. Employer contributions
2. Employee contributions
3. Investment income – interest and dividends
4. Other income
5. Benefits paid or payable
6. Administration expenses
7. Other expenses
8. Taxes on income
9. Profits and losses on disposal of investments and changes in their value
10. Transfers to and from other plans.

description of the funding policy

For defined benefit plans, this should include the actuarial present value of promised retirement benefits based on benefits promised, service rendered to date and using either current salary levels or projected salary levels.

For defined benefit plans, there should be a description of the significant actuarial assumptions made and the method used to calculate the actuarial present value of promised retirement benefits.

There should be a description of the plan, either as part of the financial information or in a separate report, including:

1. The names of the employers and groups concerned
2. The number of participants receiving benefits and the number of other participants, classified as appropriate
3. The type of plan – defined contribution or defined benefit
4. A note as to whether participants contribute to the plan
5. A description of the retirement benefits promised
6. A description of any plan termination terms
7. Changes in items (1) to (6) during the period covered by the report.

11.3   IFRS 2 *Share-Based Payment* (April 2004)

Share options are a common feature of employee remuneration. In addition, some entities issue share options to suppliers. However, until this IFRS was issued, there was no IFRS on the subject.

Objective

The objective of this IFRS is to specify the financial reporting by an entity when it undertakes a share-based payment transaction particularly its impact in profit or loss and financial position.

Scope

An entity shall apply this IFRS for all share-based payment transactions including:

- equity-settled share-based payment transactions;
- cash-settled share-based payment transactions; and
- transactions in which the entity receives or acquires goods or services and the terms provide a choice of settling in cash or by issuing equity.

Transfers of an entity's equity instruments by its shareholders to suppliers are share-based payment transactions.

A transaction with an employee in his or her capacity as a holder of equity of the entity is not a share-based payment transaction.

'Goods' includes inventories, consumables, property, plant and equipment, intangible assets and other non-financial assets. However, IFRS 2 does not apply to a business combination (see IFRS 3 *Business Combinations*). Hence, equity issued in a business combination in exchange for control of the acquiree is not within the scope of this IFRS. However, equity granted in the capacity as employees (e.g. in return for continued service) is within the scope of this IFRS.

This IFRS does not apply to a contract within the scope of paras 8–10 of IAS 32 *Financial Instruments: Disclosure and Presentation* or paras 5–7 of IAS 39 *Financial Instruments: Recognition and Measurement*.

Key definitions

Cash-settled share-based payment transaction: a share-based payment transaction in which the entity acquires goods or services by incurring a liability to transfer cash or other assets to the supplier of those goods or services for amounts that are based on the price (or value) of the entity's shares or other equity instruments of the entity.

Equity instrument: a contract that evidences a residual interest in the assets of an entity after deducting all of its liabilities.

Equity-settled share-based payment transaction: a share-based payment transaction in which the entity receives goods or services as consideration for equity instruments of the entity (including shares or share options).

Grant date: the date at which the entity and another party (including an employee) agree to a share-based payment arrangement, being when the entity and the counterparty have a shared understanding of the terms and conditions of the arrangement. At grant date the entity confers on the counterparty the right to cash, other assets, or equity instruments of the entity, provided the specified vesting conditions, if any, are met. If that agreement is subject to an approval process (for example, by shareholders), grant date is the date when that approval is obtained.

Intrinsic value: the difference between the fair value of the shares to which the counterparty has the (conditional or unconditional) right to subscribe or which it has the right to receive, and the price (if any) the counterparty is (or will be) required to pay for those shares. For example, a share option with an exercise price of £15, on a share with a fair value of £20, has an intrinsic value of £5.

Market condition: a condition upon which the exercise price, vesting or exercisability of an equity instrument depends and that is related to the market price of the entity's equity instruments, such as attaining a specified share price or a specified amount of intrinsic value of a share option, or achieving a specified target that is based on the market price of the entity's equity instruments relative to an index of market prices of equity instruments of other entities.

Measurement date: the date at which the fair value of the equity instruments granted is measured for the purposes of this IFRS. For transactions with employees and others providing similar services, the measurement date is the grant date. For transactions with parties other than employees (and those providing similar services), the measurement date is the date the entity obtains the goods or the counterparty renders service.

Reload feature: a feature that provides for an automatic grant of additional share options whenever the option holder exercises previously granted options using the entity's shares, rather than cash, to satisfy the exercise price.

Reload option: a new share option granted when a share is used to satisfy the exercise price of a previous share option.

Share-based payment transaction: a transaction in which the entity receives goods or service as consideration for equity instruments of the entity (including shares or share options or acquires goods or services by incurring liabilities to the supplier of those goods o services for amounts that are based on the price of the entity's shares or other equit instruments of the entity.

Share option: a contract that gives the holder the right, but not the obligation, to subscrib to the entity's shares at a fixed or determinable price for a specified period of time.

Vest: to become an entitlement. Under a share-based payment arrangement, a counter party's right to receive cash, other assets, or equity instruments of the entity vests upo satisfaction of any specified vesting conditions.

Vesting conditions: the conditions that must be satisfied for the counterparty to becom entitled to receive cash, other assets or equity instruments of the entity, under a share based payment arrangement. Vesting conditions include service conditions, whic require the other party to complete a specified period of service, and performance con ditions, which require specified performance targets to be met (such as a specifie increase in the entity's profit over a specified period of time).

Vesting period: the period during which all the specified vesting conditions of a share-base payment arrangement are to be satisfied.

Recognition

An entity must recognise the goods or services received or acquired in a share-base payment transaction when it obtains the goods or as the services are received. The enti must recognise a corresponding increase in equity if the goods or services were receive in an equity-settled share-based payment transaction, or a liability if the goods c services were acquired in a cash-settled share-based payment transaction.

When the goods or services received do not qualify as assets, they must be expense Typically, an expense arises from the consumption of goods or services. Services ar typically consumed immediately, in which case an expense is recognised as the counte party renders service. Goods might be consumed over a period of time, in which case a expense is recognised when the goods are consumed or sold. However, sometimes it necessary to recognise an expense before the goods or services are consumed or sol because they do not qualify for recognition as assets. For example, an entity might acqui goods as part of the research phase of a project. Although those goods have not bee consumed, they might not qualify for recognition as assets under the applicable IFRS.

Equity-settled share-based payment transactions

Overview

For equity-settled share-based payment transactions, the entity must measure the goo or services received, and the corresponding increase in equity, directly, at the fair valu of the goods or services received, unless that fair value cannot be estimated reliably. the entity cannot estimate reliably the fair value of the goods or services received, th entity must measure their value, and the corresponding increase in equity, indirectly, l reference to the fair value of the equity instruments granted.

For transactions with employees and others providing similar services, the fair value of the services received is referred to the fair value of the equity granted, as it is not possible to estimate reliably the fair value of the services received. The fair value of equity should be measured at grant date.

Typically, share options are granted to employees as part of their remuneration package. Usually, it is not possible to measure directly the services received for particular components of the employee's remuneration package. It might also not be possible to measure the fair value of the total remuneration package independently, without measuring directly the fair value of equity instruments granted, as share options are sometimes granted as part of a bonus arrangement (e.g. as an incentive to the employees to remain in the entity's employ, or to reward them for their efforts in improving the entity's performance). By granting shares or share options, the entity is paying additional remuneration to obtain additional benefits. Estimating the fair value of those additional benefits is likely to be difficult. Because of the difficulty of measuring directly the fair value of the services received, the entity must measure the fair value of the employee services received by reference to the fair value of the equity instruments granted.

For parties other than employees, there is a rebuttable presumption that the fair value of the goods or services received can be estimated reliably. It is measured at the date the entity obtains the goods or the counterparty renders service. In rare cases, if the entity rebuts this presumption because it cannot estimate reliably the fair value of the goods or services received, the entity must measure the goods or services received, and the corresponding increase in equity, indirectly, by reference to the fair value of the equity instruments granted. These should be measured at the date the entity obtains the goods or the counterparty renders service.

Transactions in which services are received

If the equity vests immediately, the services rendered are assumed to have been received. In this case, on grant date, the entity must recognise the services received in full, with a corresponding increase in equity.

If the equity does not vest until the counterparty completes a specified period of service, the services will be received in the future, during the vesting period. The entity must account for those services as they are rendered by the counterparty during the vesting period, with a corresponding increase in equity. For example:

If an employee is granted share options conditional upon completing 3 years' service, over that 3-year vesting period.

If an employee is granted share options conditional upon, say, a condition being satisfied, and the length of the vesting period varies, the entity must presume that the services rendered by the employee as consideration will be received in the future, over the expected vesting period. The entity must estimate the length of the expected vesting period at grant date, based on the most likely outcome of the performance condition. If the performance condition is a market condition, the estimate of the length of the expected vesting period shall be consistent with the assumptions used in estimating the fair value of the options granted, and shall not be subsequently revised. If the performance condition is not a market condition, the entity must revise its estimate of the length of the vesting period, if necessary, if subsequent information indicates that the length of the vesting period differs from previous estimates (see Example 11.12).

Example 11.12
Equity-settled share-based payment transactions

Background
An entity grants 100 options to each of its 500 employees. Each is conditional on the employee working for the entity over the next 3 years. Assume the fair value is £15. Based on weighted average probability, 20% of employees will leave during the 3-year period and thus forfeit their rights. The total fair value of options granted = 500 × 100 options × £15 × 80% = £600,000.

The entity also estimates that the departures will occur evenly over three years.

Application

1. Scenario 1:

		Cumulative	Expense
If everything turns out as expected			
Year 1	50,000 options × 80% × £15 × 1/3 year	200,000	200,000
Year 2	50,000 options × 80% × £15 × 2/3 years	400,000	200,000
Year 3	50,000 options × 80% × £15 × 3/3 years	600,000	200,000
Total over 3 years			600,000

2. Scenario 2:
During year 1, 20 employees leave and the entity revises its estimate of total departures from 20% to 15%. During year 2, 22 employees leave and the entity revises its estimate of total departures from 15% to 12%. During year 3, 15 employees leave. Thus 57 in total have forfeited their rights, leaving 443 × 100 options vested.

		Cumulative	Expense
Year 1	50,000 options × 85% × £15 × 1/3 year	212,500	212,500
Year 2	50,000 options × 88% × £15 × 2/3 years	440,000	227,500
Year 3	44,300 options × £15 × 3/3 years	664,500	224,500
Total over 3 years			664,500

Transactions measured by reference to the fair value of the equity instruments granted
Determining the fair value of equity instruments granted   The fair value of equity instru ments granted at the measurement date is based on market prices if available, takin into account the terms and conditions upon which those equity instruments wei granted.

If market prices are not available, the entity shall estimate the fair value of the equi using a valuation technique to estimate what the price of those equity instruments wou have been on the measurement date in an arm's length transaction between knowledg able, willing parties. The valuation technique shall be consistent with generally accepte valuation methodologies for pricing financial instruments, incorporating all factors ar assumptions that knowledgeable, willing market participants would consider in settin the price.

Treatment of vesting conditions   A grant of equity instruments might be condition upon satisfying specified vesting conditions – such as the employee remaining in t entity's employ for a specified period of time. There might be performance conditions that must be satisfied (e.g. achieving a specified growth in profit or specified increase in the entity's share price). Vesting conditions should not be taken into account when estimating the fair value at the measurement date. Instead, vesting conditions are used to adjust the number of equity instruments included in the measurement of the transaction amount so that, ultimately, the amount recognised for goods or services received as consideration for the equity instruments granted shall be based on the number of equity instruments that eventually vest. Hence, on a cumulative basis, no amount is recognised for goods or services received if the equity instruments granted do not vest because of failure to satisfy a vesting condition – for example, the counterparty fails to complete a specified service period, or a performance condition is not satisfied, subject to the requirements of para. 21.

The entity should recognise an amount for the goods/services received during the vesting period based on the best available estimate of the number of equity instruments expected to vest, and it must revise that estimate if subsequent information indicates that the number of equity instruments expected to vest differs from previous estimates. On vesting date, the entity must revise the estimate to equal the number of equity instruments that ultimately vested.

Market conditions, such as a target share price, must be taken into account when estimating the fair value of the equity instruments granted.

Treatment of a reload feature   A reload option should be accounted for as a new option grant when a reload option is subsequently granted.

After vesting date   No subsequent adjustment must be made to total equity after vesting date. No reversal occurs if the vested equity instruments are later forfeited or not exercised. However, the entity may transfer within equity, i.e. a transfer from one component of equity to another.

If the fair value of the equity instruments cannot be estimated reliably   In rare cases, the entity may be unable to estimate reliably the fair value of the equity instruments granted at the measurement date. In these cases, the entity shall instead:

. Measure the equity instruments at their intrinsic value, initially at the date the entity obtains the goods or the counterparty renders service and subsequently at each reporting date and at the date of final settlement, with any change in intrinsic value recognised in profit or loss. For a grant of share options, the share-based payment arrangement is finally settled when the options are exercised, are forfeited (e.g. upon cessation of employment) or lapse (e.g. at the end of the option's life).

Recognise the goods or services received based on the number of equity instruments that ultimately vest or (where applicable) are ultimately exercised. The amount recognised for goods or services received during the vesting period shall be based on the number of share options expected to vest. The entity shall revise that estimate, if necessary, if subsequent information indicates that the number of share options expected to vest differs from previous estimates. On vesting date, the entity shall revise the estimate to equal the number of equity instruments that ultimately vested.

After vesting date, the entity shall reverse the amount recognised for goods or services received if the share options are later forfeited, or lapse at the end of the share option's life.

Modifications to the terms and conditions on which equity instruments were granted, including cancellations and settlements

If an entity reduces the exercise price of options granted to employees (i.e. reprices the options), it increases the fair value of those options. IFRS 2 shall also be applied equally to share-based payment transactions with parties other than employees that are measured by reference to the fair value of the equity instruments granted.

As a minimum, the services received should be measured at the grant date fair value of the equity instruments granted, unless those equity instruments do not vest because of failure to satisfy a vesting condition (other than a market condition) that was specified at grant date. This applies irrespective of any modifications or a cancellation or settlement of that grant of equity instruments. In addition, the entity shall recognise the effects of modifications that increase the total fair value of the share-based payment arrangement or are otherwise beneficial to the employee.

If the entity cancels or settles a grant of equity during the vesting period (other than forfeiture):

1. The entity shall account for the cancellation/settlement as an acceleration of vesting, and therefore recognise immediately the amount that otherwise would have been recognised for services received over the remainder of the vesting period.
2. Any payment made to the employee on the cancellation or settlement of the grant shall be accounted for as a repurchase of an equity interest, i.e. as a deduction from equity, except to the extent that the payment exceeds the fair value of the equity instruments granted, measured at the repurchase date. Any such excess is recognised as an expense.
3. If new equity is granted to the employee, and on grant date the entity identifies the new equity as replacement equity for the cancelled equity, the entity must account for replacement equity in the same way as a modification of the original grant. The incremental fair value granted is the difference between the fair value of the replacement equity instruments and the net fair value of the cancelled equity instruments, at the date replacement equity instruments are granted. The net fair value of the cancelled equity instruments is their fair value, immediately before the cancellation less the amount of any payment made to the employee on cancellation of the equity that is accounted for as a deduction from equity in accordance with (2) above. If the entity does not identify new equity granted as replacement equity for the cancelled equity instruments, the entity must account for the new equity as a new grant of equity instruments.

If an entity repurchases vested equity, the payment made to the employee shall be accounted for as a deduction from equity, except to the extent that the payment exceeds the fair value of the equity repurchased, measured at the repurchase date. Any excess should be expensed.

Examples 11.13 and 11.14 provide illustrations.

Example 11.13
***Equity-settled share-based payment transactions (performance
condition – vesting period varies)***

Background

At the start of year 1 an entity grants 100 shares to 500 employees conditional on staying for vesting period. Shares vest at end of year 1 if earnings increase by more than 18%. Shares vest at end of year 2 if earnings increase by more than an average of 13% p.a. over 2-year period. Shares vest at end of year 3 if earnings increase by more than an average of 10% p.a. over 3-year period.

Fair value at start of year 1 is £30 per share, and no dividends are expected over the 3 years.

At the end of year 1, earnings increased by 14% and 30 employees left. Earnings are expected to increase similarly in year 2, and thus shares vest at the end of year 2. However, a further 30 employees are expected to leave.

At the end of year 2, earnings increased by only 10% and 28 employees left during the year. A further 25 are expected to leave during year 3. Earnings are expected to rise by a further 6% and thus achieve an average of 10% p.a.

At the end of year 3, 23 employees had left and earnings rose by 8% – an average of 10.67% over 3 years. At the end of the year, 419 employees received 100 shares.

Application

		Cumulative	**Expense**
Year 1	440 employees × 100 shares × £30 × 1/2 year	660,000	660,000
Year 2	417 employees × 100 shares × £30 × 2/3 years	834,000	174,000
Year 3	419 employees × 100 shares × £30 × 3/3 years	1,257,000	423,000
Total charged during the 3-year period			1,257,000

Example 11.14
***Equity-settled share-based payment transactions (performance
condition – number of equity instruments varies)***

Background

At the start of year 1, A grants options to 100 employees to vest after 3 years provided employees stay for period and sales volumes increase by 5% p.a.

If sales volumes are between 5% and 10%, employees receive 100 options. If sales volumes are between 10% and 15%, employees receive 200 options. If sales volumes exceed 15%, employees receive 300 options.

The fair value at date of grant is £20 per option.

Grant date – assume growth between 10% and 15%, and that 20% of employees will leave.

At the end of year 1, 7 employees left but 20 in total are still expected to leave by the end of year 3. Sales increased by 12%, and this is expected to continue.

At the end of year 2, 5 employees left and only 3 more are expected to leave. Sales increased by 18% – an average of 15% over 2 years – but a 15% plus growth is expected over a 3-year period.

At the end of year 3, 2 employees left. Sales growth was 16% over the 3-year period.

Application

		Cumulative	**Expense**
Year 1	80 employees × 200 options × £20 × 1/3 year	106,667	106,667
Year 2	85 employees × 300 options × £20 × 2/3 years	340,000	233,333
Year 3	86 employees × 300 options × £20 × 3/3 years	516,000	176,000
Total expense over the 3 years			516,000

Cash-settled share-based payment transactions

Goods or services acquired and the liability incurred should be measured at the fair value of the liability. Until the liability is settled, it should be remeasured at each reporting date and at the date of settlement, with any changes in fair value being recognised in profit or loss.

Share appreciation rights to employees as part of their remuneration package is popular, whereby the employees will become entitled to a future cash payment based on the increase in the entity's share price from a specified level over a specified period of time. Alternatively, an entity might grant its employees a right to receive a future cash payment by granting them a right to shares (including shares to be issued upon the exercise of share options) that are redeemable, either mandatorily (e.g. upon cessation of employment) or at the employee's option.

An entity should recognise services received and a liability, as the employees render service. Some share appreciation rights vest immediately, and the employees are therefore not required to complete a specified period of service to become entitled to the cash payment. In the absence of evidence to the contrary, the entity should presume that the services rendered by the employees in exchange for the share appreciation rights have been received. Thus, the entity shall recognise immediately the services received and a liability to pay for them. If the share appreciation rights do not vest until the employee have completed a specified period of service, the entity shall recognise the services received, and a liability to pay for them, as the employees render service during that period.

The liability should be measured, initially and each reporting date until settled, at the fair value of the share appreciation rights, by applying an option pricing model, taking into account the terms and conditions on which the share appreciation rights were granted and the extent to which the employees have rendered service to date (see Example 11.15).

Example 11.15
Cash-settled share-based payment transactions

Background
An entity grants 100 cash share appreciation rights (SARs) to each of its 500 employees as long as an employee stays 3 years.

During year 1, 35 employees leave. The entity estimates that a further 60 will leave during years 2 and 3. During year 2, 40 employees leave and the entity estimates a further 25 will leave during year 3. During year 3, 22 employees leave. At the end of year 3, 150 employees exercise their SARs; another 140 exercise at the end of year 4 and the remaining 113 at the end of year 5.

	Fair value	Intrinsic value
Year 1	£14.40	
2	£15.50	
3	£18.20	£15.00
4	£21.40	£20.00
5		£25.00

Application			**Cumulative**	**Expense**
Year 1	Expense for services received and consumed, and the year end liability (500 − 95 employees × 100 SARs × £14.40 × 1/3)		194,400	194,400
Year 2	(500 − 100 employees × 100 SARs × £15.50 × 2/3)		413,333	218,933
Year 3	(500 − 97 left − 150 exercised × 100 SARs × £18.20 × 3/3	460,460		
	150 exercised × 100 exercised × £15	225,000	685,460	272,127
Year 4	150 exercised × 100 SARs × £15	225,000		
	140 exercised × 100 SARS × £20	280,000		
	(500 − 97 left − 290 exercised × 100 SARs × £21.40	241,820	746,820	61,360
Year 5	150 exercised × 100 SARs × £15	225,000		
	140 exercised × 100 SARs × £20	280,000		
	113 exercised × 100 SARs × £25	282,500	787,500	40,680
Total charged over the 5 years				787,500

Share-based payment transactions with choice of settlement

For transactions which provide either the entity or the counterparty with the choice of whether the entity settles in cash or by issuing equity, the entity should account for that transaction as a cash-settled share-based payment transaction if it has incurred a liability to settle in cash, or as an equity-settled transaction if no such liability has been incurred.

Where the entity has granted a compound financial instrument which includes a debt and an equity component

For transactions with parties other than employees, the entity should measure the equity component of the compound as the difference between the fair value of the goods or services received and the fair value of the debt component, at the date when the goods or services are received.

For other transactions, including those with employees, the entity should measure the fair value of the compound instrument at the measurement date, taking into account the terms and conditions on which the rights to cash or equity instruments were granted.

The entity must first measure the fair value of the debt component, and then the fair value of the equity component. The fair value of the compound financial instrument is the sum of the fair values of the two components. However, share-based payment transactions in which the counterparty has the choice of settlement are often structured so that the fair value of one settlement alternative is the same as the other – for example, the counterparty might have the choice of receiving share options or cash-settled share appreciation rights. In such cases, the fair value of the equity component is zero, and thus the fair value of the compound instrument is the same as the fair value of the debt component. Conversely, if the fair values of the settlement alternatives differ, the fair value of the equity component usually will be greater than zero, in which case the fair value of the compound instrument will be greater than the fair value of the debt component.

Any goods/services received or acquired in respect of each component of the compound instrument should be accounted for separately. For the debt component, the goods/services acquired and liability to pay for those goods/services should be reported as the counterparty supplies goods or renders service, in accordance with cash-settled transactions. For the equity component (if any), the entity should recognise the goods/services received, and an increase in equity, as the counterparty supplies goods or renders service, in accordance with the requirements applying to equity-settled transactions.

At the date of settlement, the liability should be remeasured to fair value. If the entity issues equity on settlement rather than paying cash, the liability should be transferred direct to equity, as the consideration for the equity instruments issued.

If the entity pays in cash on settlement rather than issuing equity, that payment should be applied to settle the liability in full. Any equity component previously recognised shall remain within equity. By electing to receive cash, the counterparty forfeited the right to receive equity. However, this does not preclude the entity from recognising a transfer within equity, i.e. a transfer from one component of equity to another.

Share-based payment transactions in which the terms of the arrangement provide the entity with a choice of settlement

Where the terms provide an entity with the choice of whether to settle in cash or by issuing equity, the entity must determine whether it has a present obligation to settle in cash and account for it accordingly. The entity has a present obligation to settle in cash if the choice of settlement in equity has no commercial substance or the entity has a past practice or a stated policy of settling in cash, or generally settles in cash whenever the counterparty asks for cash settlement.

If the entity has a present obligation to settle in cash it must account for the transaction in accordance with cash-settled transactions, but if no such obligation exists it should be accounted for as an equity-settled share-based payment transaction. Upon settlement:

1. If the entity elects to settle in cash, the cash payment shall be accounted for a repurchase of an equity interest, i.e. as a deduction from equity, except as noted in (3 below
2. if the entity elects to settle by issuing equity, no further accounting is required (other than a cross-equity transfer), except as noted in (3) below
3. If the entity elects the settlement alternative with the higher fair value, as at the date of settlement, the entity shall recognise an additional expense for the excess value given, i.e. the difference between the cash paid and the fair value of the equity that would otherwise have been issued, or the difference between the fair value of the equity issued and the amount of cash that otherwise would have been paid whichever is applicable.

Example 11.16 provides an illustration.

Example 11.16
Share-based payment arrangements with cash alternatives

Background
An entity grants employees a choice of 1,000 phantom shares (cash), or 1,200 shares conditional on 3 years' service. If they choose the latter, they must hold the shares for a further 3 years after vesting date.

At grant date the share price is £50, and at end of years 1, 2 and 3 it is £52, £55 and £60 respectively. No dividends are expected to be paid out during the 3 years.

After taking into account the effects of post-vesting transfer restrictions, the entity estimates that the grant date fair value of the share alternative is £48 per share.

At the end of year 3, the employee chooses (1) cash or (2) equity.

Application
Fair value of equity is £57,600 (1,200 shares × £48). Fair value of cash is £50,000 (1,000 phantom shares × £50). Fair value of equity component of compound is £7,600.

			Cumulative liability	Cumulative equity	Expense
Year 1	Liability	(1,000 × £52 × 1/3 year)	17,333		17,333
	Equity	(£7,600 × 1/3 year)		2,533	2,533
Year 2	Liability	(1,000 × £55 × 2/3 years)	36,666		19,333
	Equity	(£7,600 × 2/3 years)		5,066	2,533
Year 3	Liability	(1,000 × £60 × 3/3 years)	60,000		23,334
	Equity	(£7,600 × 3/3 years)		7,600	2,534
Total expense under both scenarios					67,600

		Cumulative liability	Cumulative equity	Expense
Scenario (1)				
End Year 3	Paid	(60,000)		
		Nil		
Scenario (2)				
End Year 3		(60,000)	60,000	
		Nil	67,600	

Disclosures

Information must be provided to enable users to understand the nature and extent of share-based payment arrangements.

At least the following should be disclosed:

A description of each type of share-based payment, including general terms and conditions

The number and weighted average exercise prices of share options for each of the following groups of options:
• outstanding at the beginning of the period
• granted during the period
• forfeited during the period

- exercised during the period
- expired during the period
- outstanding at the end of the period
- exercisable at the end of the period

3. For share options exercised, the weighted average share price at the date of exercise
4. For share options outstanding at the end of the period, the range of exercise prices and weighted average remaining contractual life. If the range is wide, the options should be divided into meaningful ranges for assessing the number and timing of additional shares that may be issued or cash that may be received on exercise.

Further information that enables users to understand how the fair value of the goods or services received, or the fair value of equity granted was determined should be provided, including the option pricing model adopted, the expected volatility and how other features of option grants were incorporated into fair value. Details of any modifications and the overall expense must also be provided.

11.4 Examination questions

Question 11.1: Klondike (ACCA)

(The first question covers the accounting treatment for pension costs under a defined benefit scheme in order to comply with IAS 19. It initially requires students to outline the relevant features of the two main type of pension schemes – defined contribution and defined benefit – and then requires the production of the extracts from the financial statements once the defined benefit rules in IAS 19 are put into place.)

IAS 19 *Employee Benefits* was issued in February 1998. Amongst other things, the standard deals with the treatment of post-employment benefits such as pensions and other retirement benefits. Post-employment benefits are classified as either defined contribution or defined benefit plans.

Required

(a) Describe the relevant features and required accounting treatment of defined contribution and defined benefit plans under IAS 19.

Klondike operates a defined benefit post-retirement plan for its employees. The plan reviewed annually. Klondike's actuaries have provided the following information:

	At 31 March 2001 $000	At 31 March 200 $000
Present value obligation	1,500	1,750
Fair value of plan assets	1,500	1,650
Current service cost – year to 31 March 2002		160
Contributions paid – year to 31 March 2002		85
Benefits paid to employees – year to 31 March 2002		125
Net cumulative unrecognised gains at 1 April 2002	200	
Expected return on plan assets at 1 April 2001	12%	
Discount rate for plan liabilities at 1 April 2001	10%	

The average remaining working lives of Klondike's employees at 31 March 2001 is 10 years.

Required

(b) Prepare extracts of Klondike's financial statements for the year to 31 March 2002 in compliance with IAS 19 *Employee Benefits* in so far as the information permits.

Question 11.2: A (ACCA)

(The next question concentrates solely on defined benefit schemes, and requires the four key issues to be listed in determining the method of accounting to be adopted. It then requires those issues to be applied to a specific company and the resulting financial statement extracts to be presented.)

Accounting for retirement benefits remains one of the most challenging areas in financial reporting. The values being reported are significant, and the estimation of these values is complex and subjective. Standard-setters and preparers of financial statements find it difficult to achieve a measure of consensus on the appropriate way to deal with the assets and costs involved. IAS 19 *Employee Benefits* formerly focused on the income statement, viewing employee benefits as an operating expense. However, the revised standard concentrates on the balance sheet and the valuation of the pension fund. The philosophy and rationale of the two statements are fundamentally different.

Required

(a) Describe four key issues in the determination of the method of accounting for retirement benefits in respect of defined benefit plans.

(b) Discuss how IAS 19 *Employee Benefits* deals with these key issues and to what extent it provides solutions to the problems of accounting for retirement benefits.

A, a public limited company, operates a defined benefit plan. A full actuarial valuation y an independent actuary revealed that the value of the liability at 31 May 2000 was 1,500 million. This was updated to 31 May 2001 by the actuary and the value of the ability at that date was $2,000 million. The scheme assets comprised mainly bonds and quities, and the fair value of these assets was as follows:

	31 May 2000 $m	31 May 2001 $m
Fixed interest and index linked bonds	380	600
Equities	1,300	1,900
Other investments	290	450
	1,970	2,950

he scheme had been altered during the year with improved benefits arising for the nployees, and this had been taken into account by the actuaries. The increase in the ctuarial liability in respect of employee service in prior periods was $25 million (past rvice cost). The increase in the actuarial liability resulting from employee service in the rrent period was $70 million (current service cost). The company had not recognised y net actuarial gain or loss in the income statement to date.

The company had paid contributions of $60 million to the scheme during the period. The company expects its return on the scheme assets at 31 May 2001 to be $295 million and the interest on pension liabilities to be $230 million.

The average expected remaining working lives of the employees is 10 years, and the net cumulative unrecognised gains at June 2000 were $247 million.

Required

(c) Calculate the amount which will be shown as the net plan asset in the balance sheet of A as at 31 May 2001, showing a reconciliation of the movement in the plan surplus during the year and a statement of those amounts which would be charged to operating profit.

Question 11.3: G (CIMA)

(The third question is really a normal income statement presentation question which could have been included in Chapter 1. However, as part of the adjustments to be made to the draft trial balance there is a defined benefit pension scheme to be incorporated under IAS 19.)

G is a large manufacturing company. It is listed on its national stock exchange. The company's shares are widely held by a very large number of individual shareholders, and its activities are heavily reported in the business press.

G's trial balance at 31 December 2000 is shown below:

	$ million	$ million
Administrative expenses	130	
Bank	10	
Cost of sales	240	
Deferred taxation		200
Dividend – interim paid	40	
Goodwill – net book value	1,900	
Interest	95	
Inventory at 31 December 2000	110	
Interest-bearing borrowings		1,100
Reserves – accumulated profits		1,875
Property, plant and equipment – net book value	2,400	
Revenue (sales)		1,000
Selling and distribution costs	100	
Share capital		500
Reserves – share premium		400
Tax		10
Trade and other payables		30
Trade and other receivables	90	5,115
	5,115	5,115

Notes:

(i) The company has a funded, defined benefit pension scheme. The company mak⁣ regular payments to the insurance company that operates the scheme on its beha⁣

These payments are treated as an employment cost and included under cost of sales in the trial balance.

During the year ended 31 December 2000, G received a report on the fund. This indicated that it was under-funded by $20 million. The actuaries who prepared the report recommended that the company should pay an additional $5 million into the fund each year for the next 4 years. These payments would be in addition to the regular payments to the fund.

During the year ended 31 December 2000, G paid the first instalment of $5 million to supplement the pension fund. The company also paid $8 million as its routine annual contribution into the fund.

The actuaries who prepared the report estimated the average service life of the company's work force at 10 years. The directors have decided to amortise the actuarial loss of $20 million over that period. The figures in the trial balance have not yet been updated to reflect the actuaries' report.

Pension costs are included in the cost of sales figure.

(ii) The directors estimate the tax charge on the year's profits at $120 million. The balance on the taxation account represents the balance remaining after settling the amount due for the year ended 31 December 1999.

(iii) The balance on the provision for deferred taxation should be increased to $280 million.

(iv) The directors have proposed a final dividend of $60 million. The company did not pay a dividend during the year ended 31 December 1999.

(v) G's share capital is made up of $1 shares, all of which are fully paid up. The company issued 100 million shares on 29 February 2000. These were sold for their full market price of $1.40 per share. This sale has been included in the figures shown in the trial balance.

(vi) A major customer went into liquidation on 16 January 2001, owing G $8 million. G's directors are of the opinion that this mount is material.

(vii) A member of the public was seriously injured on 24 January 2001 while using one of G's products. The company lawyer is of the opinion that the company will have to pay $2 million in compensation. G's directors are of the opinion that this amount is material.

Required

(a) Prepare G's income statement for the year ended 31 December 2000 and its balance sheet at that date. These should be in a form suitable for publication, and should be accompanied by notes as far as you are able to prepare these from the information provided. Do NOT prepare a statement of accounting policies, a statement of total recognised gains and losses, a statement of changes in equity or calculate earnings per share.

(b) Calculate G's earnings per share (EPS) in accordance with the requirements of IAS 33 *Earnings per Share*.

(c) It has been suggested that the EPS ratio is unique in that its calculation is the subject of detailed Accounting Standards. Explain why it has been necessary to provide such detailed guidance on the calculation of EPS.

(d) Identify what is meant by 'diluted' earnings per share and explain the reasons why companies should be required to disclose this figure.

Question 11.4: SNOB (CIMA)

(The final question covers a number of issues including how to account for share based schemes und *IFRS 2 and off balance sheet finance. It is fairly general in nature, but does cover some of the curre. topical issues in accounting.)*

You report to a manager who does not have a detailed knowledge of recent develop ments in financial reporting. However, the manager does have a reasonable basic know edge of financial accounting. Your manager has recently attended a course at which number of recent developments were discussed. He has sent you a note requiring clar fication of a number of issues:

(i) *Issue (a) Share-based payment*

We were told that when enterprises issue shares or share options to their employees, the they should make a charge to the income statement. It doesn't seem logical to me make a charge to income when an enterprise issues shares – surely that's not wh: normally happens? When you extend this principle to share options this seems even le logical – the options may never be exercised. Please explain where my thinking fal down on this. Has a new Accounting Standard been issued that has escaped my notic

(ii) *Issue (b) Non-financial disclosures*

We were told that more and more enterprises are voluntarily giving information abo social and environmental policies in their annual reports. Surely annual reports shou focus on financial matters. How can non-financial information such as social and env ronmental policies add value to corporate reports? I can't believe our shareholders nec to know about this type of issue. The annual reports are for the shareholders aren't the or have I got it wrong?

(iii) *Issue (c) Off balance sheet finance*

The course leader kept using this term. She stated that standard-setters around tl world are developing new standards to ensure that all financial obligations are report on the balance sheet. I don't really understand what off balance sheet finance mear Please explain it to me. Surely the finance that an enterprise has is a matter of fact. W would they want to keep finance off balance sheet anyway? I would have thought th showing all the finance on the balance sheet would make the balance sheet stronger.

I would also be interested to know about current International Accounting standar that deal with off balance sheet finance. If new standards are planned, then what a the likely implications for our group? I overheard someone saying that current dev opments in this area have potentially wide-ranging implications for enterprises th lease (rather than purchase) properties. As you know that describes our situation a this concerned me.

Required

Draft an appropriate reply to the note by your manager that explains the issues that have bee raised.

Financial instruments

12.1 IAS 30 *Disclosures in Financial Statements of Banks and Similar Institutions* (reformatted 1994)

Background

Users need relevant, reliable and comparable information to help make economic decisions. They also need information about the special characteristics of the operations of a bank. Disclosures must be sufficiently comprehensive.

A bank is exposed to liquidity risk, foreign currency risks, interest rate movements and changes in market price. Users would have a better understanding if a commentary were provided by management which describes the way in which the bank manages and controls its risks.

Objective

The objective of IAS 30 is to prescribe appropriate presentation and disclosure standards for banks and similar financial institutions, which supplement the requirements of other standards. The intention is to provide users with appropriate information to assist them in evaluating the financial position and performance of banks, and to enable them to obtain a better understanding of the special characteristics of the operations of banks.

Scope

The standard should be applied to the financial statements of banks and similar financial institutions. These are involved in taking deposits and lending within the banking legislation.

Users are particularly concerned about the liquidity and solvency of banks, and these special needs must be met. IAS 30 supplements other IASs which also apply to banks as well as to both individual and consolidated financial statements.

Accounting policies

The following policies need to be disclosed to improve comparability:

- the recognition of the principal types of income;
- the valuation of investment and dealing securities;

- the distinction between those transactions and other events that result in the recognition of assets and liabilities on the balance sheet and those transactions and other events that only give rise to contingencies and commitments;
- the basis for the determination of losses on loans and advances and for writing off uncollectable loans and advances;
- the basis for the determination of charges for general banking risks and the accounting treatment of such charges.

Income statement

A bank should present an income statement which groups income and expenses by nature, and discloses the amounts of the principal types of income and expenses.

In addition to other IASs, the following income and expenses should be disclosed in the income statement or in the notes:

1. Interest and similar income
2. Interest expense and similar charge
3. Dividend income
4. Fee and commission income
5. Fee and commission expense
6. Gains less losses arising from dealing securities
7. Gains less losses arising from dealing in foreign currencies
8. Other operating income
9. Losses on loans and advances
10. General administrative expenses
11. Other operating expenses.

Each type of income is separately disclosed so that users can assess the bank's performance. This is in addition to IAS 14 *Segment Reporting*. The principal types of expenses are also disclosed for the same reason.

Income and expense items should not be offset except for those relating to hedges and to assets and liabilities which have been offset in accordance with the balance sheet offset rules. Users need to assess the separate activities.

Gains and losses on the following are normally reported net:

- disposals and changes in the carrying amount of dealing securities;
- disposals of investment securities;
- dealings in foreign currencies.

Interest income and expense are separately disclosed to give a better understanding of the composition of and the reasons for changes in net interest. A commentary about average interest rates, average interest earning assets and average interest bearing liabilities for the period should also be provided.

Balance sheet

A bank should present a balance sheet that groups assets and liabilities by nature and lists them in order of their relative liquidity.

In addition to other IASs, the disclosures in the balance sheet or notes should include, but are not limited to, the following assets and liabilities.

Assets:

1. Cash and balances with the central bank
2. Treasury bills and other bills eligible for rediscounting with the central bank
3. Government and other securities held for dealing purposes
4. Placements with, and loans and advances to, other banks
5. Other money market placements
6. Loans and advances to customers
7. Investment securities.

Liabilities:

1. Deposits from other banks
2. Other money market deposits
3. Amounts owed to other depositors
4. Certificates of deposit
5. Promissory notes and other liabilities evidenced by paper
6. Other borrowed funds.

The classification is based on nature and on order of liquidity, but current/non-current items are not presented separately because most assets/liabilities of a bank can be realised or settled in the near future. It is also important to distinguish balances between other banks and the money market, as they may be dependent on those markets.

The amount at which any asset/liability is stated should not be offset unless there is a legal right of offset and the offsetting represents the expectation as to the realisation or settlement of the asset or liability.

A bank should disclose the fair values of each class of assets and liabilities as required by IAS 32 and IAS 39. There are four classifications of financial assets: loans and receivables originated by the entity; held-to-maturity investments; financial assets held for trading; and available-for-sale financial assets.

Contingencies and commitments including off balance sheet items

A bank should disclose the following contingent liabilities and commitments:

The nature and amount of commitments to extend credit that are irrevocable because they cannot be withdrawn at the discretion of the bank without the risk of incurring significant penalty or expense

The nature and amount of contingent liabilities and commitments arising from off balance sheet items including those relating to:

- direct credit substitutes including general guarantees of indebtedness, bank acceptance guarantees and standby letters of credit serving as financial guarantees for loans and securities
- certain transaction related contingent liabilities including performance bonds, bid bonds, warranties and standby letters of credit related to particular transactions

- short-term self-liquidating trade-related contingent liabilities arising from the movement of goods, such as documentary credits where the underlying shipment is used as security
- those sale and repurchase agreements not recognised in the balance sheet
- interest and foreign exchange rate related items including swaps, options and futures
- other commitments, note issuance facilities and revolving underwriting facilities.

Although IAS 37 *Provisions, Contingent Liabilities and Contingent Assets* covers this topic, banks are engaged in many types of contingent liabilities and commitments and they also enter into transactions that are presently not recognised as assets/liabilities but do give rise to contingencies and commitments. Users must know about off balance sheet items as these may add to or reduce other risks, and therefore it is important to provide adequate disclosure about the nature and amount of off balance sheet transactions undertaken by a bank.

Maturities of assets and liabilities

A bank should disclose an analysis of assets and liabilities into relevant maturity groupings based on the remaining period at the balance sheet date to the contractual maturity date.

The matching and controlled mismatching of the maturities and interest rates of assets and liabilities is fundamental to the management of a bank. Matching will never be perfect, since unmatched positions can enhance profitability as well as increase the risk of losses.

The maturity of assets and liabilities and the ability to replace, when mature, is an important factor in assessing the liquidity of a bank and its exposure to changes in interest rates and exchange rates.

The maturity groupings differ between banks, but examples could include the following

- up to 1 month
- from 1 to 3 months
- from 3 months to 1 year
- from 1 year to 5 years
- 5 years and over.

Frequently the periods are combined, and each instalment should be allocated to the period in which it is contractually agreed to be paid or received.

The maturity periods should be the same for assets and liabilities, and should be expressed in terms of the remaining period to the repayment date, the original period to the repayment date or the remaining period to the next date when interest rates will be changed.

Management may also provide in its commentary information about interest rate exposure and how it controls and manages such exposures.

In many countries bank deposits may be withdrawn on demand, but in practice they are often maintained for long periods without withdrawal. However, the disclosure should be based on contractual maturities.

Disclosures may need to be supplemented by information as to the likelihood repayment within the remaining period. Management may comment about the way manages and controls the risks and exposures associated with different maturity and interest rate profiles.

Concentrations of assets, liabilities and off balance sheet items

A bank should disclose any significant concentrations of its assets, liabilities and off balance sheet items. Such disclosures should be made in terms of geographical areas, customer or industry groups, or other concentrations of risk. A bank should also disclose the amount of significant net foreign exchange exposures.

These disclosures are in addition to those in IAS 14. The disclosures should provide users with a useful indication of the potential risks inherent in the realisation of assets and the funds available to the bank.

Losses on loans and advances

A bank should disclose the following:

1. The accounting policy which describes the basis on which uncollectable loans and advances are recognised as an expense and written off
2. Details of the movements in the provision for losses on loans and advances during the period; it should disclose separately the amount expended in the period for losses on uncollectable loans and advances, the amount charged in the period for loans and advances written off, and the amount credited in the period for loans and advances previously written off that have been recovered
3. The aggregate amount of provision for losses on loans and advances at the balance sheet date
4. The aggregate amount included on balance sheet for loans and advances on which interest is not being accrued, and the basis used to determine the carrying amount of such loans and advances.

Any amounts set aside for losses on loans and advances in addition to those losses that have been specifically identified or potential losses which experience indicates are present in the portfolio of loans and advances should be accounted for as appropriations of retained earnings. Any credits resulting from the reduction of such amounts result in an increase in retained earnings and are not included in determining net profit or loss for the period.

Local legislation may require or allow a bank to set aside amounts for losses and advances in addition to those losses which have been specifically identified and those potential losses which experience indicates are present in the portfolio of loans and advances. Any amounts set aside are appropriations and not expenses in computing income.

Users of a bank need to know the impact that losses on loans/advances have had on the financial position and resources of the bank – it helps users to judge the effectiveness of how the bank has employed its resources. Thus the bank discloses the aggregate amount of provision for losses on loans and advances and movements in the provision during the year.

Banks have different policies as regards writing off loans and advances, thus it is important to disclose its policy for such write-offs.

General banking risks

Any amounts set aside for general banking risks, including future losses and other unforeseeable risks or contingencies, should be separately disclosed as appropriations of retained earnings. Any credits resulting from the reduction of such amounts result in an increase in retained earnings and should not be included in the determination of net profit or loss for the period.

These do not qualify as provisions under IAS 37, and must be treated as appropriations in order to avoid the overstatement of liabilities. The balance sheet cannot provide relevant and reliable information if it includes overstated liabilities.

Assets pledged as security

A bank should disclose the aggregate amount of secured liabilities and the nature and carrying amount of assets pledged as security.

These can be substantial, and thus have a significant impact on the assessment of the financial position of a bank.

Trust activities

Provided the bank is legally acting as a trustee, any assets placed on their behalf must not be included in the bank's balance sheet. Disclosure of significant trust activities should be made, however, because of their potential liabilities if the bank fails in its fiduciary duties.

Related party transactions

Certain transactions between related parties may be effected on different terms from those with unrelated parties – for example, a bank may advance a larger sum or charge lower interest rates. Information about such transactions is relevant to user needs, and should be disclosed as per IAS 24.

The nature of the relationship, the types of transactions as well as any element necessary for an understanding, including lending policy to related parties, should be disclosed. In particular, the following should be included:

1. Loans and advances, deposits and acceptances and promissory notes – aggregate amounts at the start and the end of period as well as changes during the period
2. Each of the principal types of income, interest expense and commissions paid
3. The amount of expense recognised in the period for losses on loans and advances and the amount of the provision at the balance sheet date
4. Irrevocable commitments and contingencies and those arising from off balance sheet items.

12.2   IAS 32 *Financial Instruments: Disclosure and Presentation* (revised 2003)

Objective

The dynamic nature of international financial markets has led to a widespread use of a variety of financial instruments, ranging from primary to various forms of derivatives. The objective of IAS 32 is to enhance users' understanding of the significance of financial instruments to an entity's position, performance and cash flows.

IAS 32 prescribes requirements for presentation and the information that must be disclosed. It classifies instruments between equity and liabilities, and details how to present and disclose related interest, dividends, losses and gains. The disclosure includes factors that affect the amount, timing and certainty of an entity's future cash flows relating to financial instruments. It also covers information about the nature and extent of an entity's use of financial instruments, their associated risks and management's policies for controlling those risks.

Scope

IAS 32 applies to all financial statements giving a true and fair view, except that paras 42–95 on disclosure should only apply to banks and PLCs having capital instruments listed.

IAS 32 should be applied to all types of financial instruments except:

   those interests in subsidiary, quasi subsidiary and associated undertakings, partnerships and joint ventures accounted for under IAS 27 and IAS 28 (it should be applied to subsidiaries held exclusively for resale);
   employers' rights and obligations under IAS 19 and IAS 26;
   rights and obligations under insurance contracts (see IFRS 4);
   contracts for contingent consideration in a business combination;
   contracts requiring a payment based on climatic, geological or other physical variables.

It applies to both recognised and unrecognised financial instruments.

Other standards specific to particular types of financial instruments contain additional presentation and disclosure requirements – e.g. IAS 17 *Leases*, IAS 19 *Employee Benefits*.

IAS 32 should be applied to those contracts to buy or sell a non-financial item that can be settled net in cash or by some other financial instrument as if they were financial instruments. Examples include contracts to buy or sell commodities at a fixed price at a future date.

Definitions

Financial instrument: any contract giving rise to both a financial asset of one entity and a financial liability or equity instrument of another entity.

Financial asset: any asset that is

   cash;
   a contractual right to receive cash or another financial asset from another entity;

- a contractual right to exchange financial instruments with another entity under conditions that are potentially favourable; or
- an equity instrument of another entity.

Financial liability: a contractual obligation

- to deliver cash to another entity;
- to exchange financial instruments with another entity under conditions that are potentially unfavourable.

Equity instrument: any contract evidencing a residual interest in the assets of an entity after deducting all of its liabilities.

Fair value: the amount for which an asset could be exchanged in an arm's length transaction.

Market value: the amount obtainable from the sale or payable of a financial instrument in an active market.

Financial instruments include both primary and derivative instruments. Derivatives create rights and obligations that transfer one or more of the financial risks inherent in an underlying primary financial instrument between the parties to the instrument. They do not result in a transfer of the underlying primary instrument, and a transfer does not necessarily occur on maturity of the contract.

Physical and intangible assets (patents/trademarks) are not financial assets, nor are prepayments or deferred revenue as the latter are associated with the delivery of goods and services. Income taxes are not financial liabilities. They are created as a result of statutory requirements.

Commitments to buy or sell non-financial items do not meet the definition of a financial instrument, nor do operating leases for the use of a physical asset that can be settled only by the receipt or delivery of non-financial assets.

Minority interest is neither a financial liability nor an equity instrument of the parent

Presentation

Liabilities and equity

An issuer must classify a financial instrument, on initial recognition, as a liability or as equity in accordance with the substance of the contract and the definitions of a financial liability and an equity instrument.

Some financial instruments take the legal form of equity but are liabilities in substance and others combine features of both. Their classification should be based on substance, and that classification continues at each reporting date until the instrument is derecognised.

The critical feature in differentiating a financial liability from equity is the existence of a contractual obligation of one party to a financial instrument either to deliver cash to the other party or to exchange another financial instrument under conditions that are potentially unfavourable to the issuer.

When a financial instrument does not give rise to a contractual obligation it should be classified as equity. When a preferred share provides for mandatory redemption by the issuer for a fixed or determinable amount at a fixed or determinable future date (or giv the holder the right to require the issuer to redeem the share at a particular date or amount), then the instrument meets the definition of a financial liability and is classified as such.

Where an entity issues a financial instrument to be settled by cash or other financial assets depending on the occurrence/non-occurrence of certain uncertain future events, e.g. consumer price index, it should be classified as a financial liability. The issuer does not have an unconditional right to avoid settlement.

If an entity issues a 'puttable instrument' (i.e. it gives the holder the right to put the instrument back to the issuer for cash based on an index), even if its legal form gives the holder the right to the residual interest, the inclusion of the option meets the definition of a financial liability.

An entity may have a contract of a fixed amount or a variable amount that fluctuates in response to an external variable. If the entity can settle by delivery of its own equity instruments, it is still a financial liability of the entity.

If the number of an entity's own shares required to settle an obligation varies with changes in their fair value, it is still a financial liability.

Classification of compound instruments by the issuer

An issuer of a financial instrument containing both a liability and an equity element must classify the component parts separately.

It is a matter of form, not substance, that a single instrument can represent both equity and debt features. An issuer recognises separately the component parts of a financial instrument (e.g. convertible loan) that:

create a financial liability of the issuer (to deliver cash); and
grant an option to convert it into equity (a call option to convert into shares).

The economic effect is the same as issuing simultaneously a debt instrument with an early settlement provision and warrants to purchase common shares.

Classification is not revised as a result of a change in the likelihood that a conversion option will be exercised. The issuer's obligation remains outstanding until extinguished through conversion, maturity or other transaction.

A financial instrument may contain components that are neither financial liabilities nor equity – e.g. the right to receive in settlement a non-financial asset such as a commodity and an option to exchange that right for a fixed number of shares of the issuer. The equity instrument should be disclosed separately from the liability element, whether the liabilities are financial or non-financial.

Equity instruments represent a residual interest and should be assigned the residual amount after deducting from the total the amount separately determined for the liability. The sum assigned to the liability and equity components on initial recognition is always equal to the carrying amount ascribed to the instrument as a whole. No gain or loss arises on initial recognition.

The issuer of a convertible bond, therefore, must first determine the carrying amount of the liability. The carrying amount of the equity instrument, represented by the option to convert the instrument into shares, is calculated by deducting the carrying amount of the financial liability from the amount of the compound instrument as a whole.

Transactions in an entity's own equity instruments

Treasury shares

If an entity reacquires its own equity, those 'treasury shares' should be deducted from equity. No gain or loss is recognised, and any consideration paid or received is recognised directly in equity. The amount of treasury shares should be disclosed separately in the notes or on the balance sheet itself.

Derivatives based on an entity's own equity instruments

A derivative should be classified as equity if it is settled by the exchange of a fixed number of an entity's own equity instruments for a fixed amount of cash. Any consideration received is added directly to equity. Any consideration paid is deducted directly from equity. Changes in the fair value of a derivative in that case are not recognised.

A derivative is not classified as equity solely because it may result in the receipt or delivery of an entity's own equity instruments. A derivative that requires to be settled on a net basis in cash is a derivative asset or liability. Similarly, a derivative that requires settlement on a net basis in an entity's own equity instruments is a derivative asset/liability.

If a derivative has more than one settlement alternative (e.g. cash, equity or exchange of equity for cash), the contract is a derivative asset/liability unless the entity:

- has an unconditional right and ability to settle by exchanging a fixed number of its own equity for a fixed amount of cash;
- has an established practice of settling such contracts by exchanging a fixed number of its own equity for a fixed amount of cash; and
- intends to settle the contract by exchanging a fixed number of its own equity for a fixed amount of cash.

In these situations, the contract should be classified as equity.

Where an entity enters into a derivative contract, e.g. a forward contract that requires settlement by cash, that instrument ceases to meet the definition of equity and is therefore a financial liability. Its cost (the present value of the redemption amount) is reclassified from equity to debt. If the contract expires without delivery of cash, it is then reclassified to equity.

A derivative whose fair value fluctuates in response to changes in external variables is clearly not equity and must be classified as a derivative asset/liability.

Interest, dividends, losses and gains

All of the above relating to financial liabilities should be recognised in the income statement as expenses/incomes. However, dividends paid to equity holders must be charged direct to equity, and any transaction costs deducted from equity net of any tax benefit. The latter must, however, be incremental external costs directly attributable to the equity transaction.

Transaction costs for hybrids must be allocated to the components in proportion to the allocation of proceeds, and if related to more than one transaction they must be allocated on a rational and consistent basis. Those costs deducted from equity must be disclosed separately.

Dividends can be disclosed separately or with interest, but if there are significant tax differences between the two then separate disclosure is desirable.

It is the classification of instruments between equity/liabilities that determines where related interest/expenses are charged.

Offsetting of a financial asset and a financial liability

A financial asset and a financial liability shall be offset and the net amount reported in the balance sheet when, and only when, both the following occur:

1. An entity has a legally enforceable right of set off
2. An entity intends to settle on a net basis or to realise the asset and settle the liability simultaneously.

Offsetting differs from ceasing to recognise a financial asset or liability. The latter not only removes items from the balance sheet; it may also result in the recognition of a gain or loss.

The existence of a legal right of setoff affects the rights and obligations associated with a financial asset and a financial liability, and may significantly affect an entity's exposure to credit and liquidity risk. The existence of the right itself, however, is not a sufficient basis for offsetting. In the absence of an intention to exercise, the right to settle means that the amount of the entity's future cash flows are not affected. Where the intention is to exercise, the presentation on a net basis reflects more appropriately the amounts and timing of the expected future cash flows, as well as the risks to which the cash flows are exposed. An intention to settle net without a legal right to do so is not sufficient to justify offsetting, because the rights and obligations remain unaltered.

Intentions may reflect normal business practice, the needs of the financial markets, and any other circumstances that could limit the ability to settle net or simultaneously (i.e. at the same moment).

Offsetting is usually inappropriate when:

several different financial instruments are used to emulate the features of a single financial instrument (a 'synthetic instrument');
financial assets and liabilities arise from instruments having the same primary risk exposure (e.g. portfolio of forward contracts) but involving different counterparties;
financial or other assets are pledged as collateral for non-recourse financial liabilities;
financial assets are set aside in trust by a debtor to discharge an obligation without those assets having been accepted by the creditor in settlement; or
obligations are incurred by events giving rise to losses expected to be recovered from a third party via an insurance policy claim.

'master netting arrangement', providing for a single net settlement of all financial instruments covered by the agreement in the event of a default, commonly creates a right of set-off that becomes enforceable only following a specified event of default or other circumstances not normally expected in the normal course of business.

Normally a master netting arrangement does not provide a basis for offsetting unless both the criteria (1) and (2) at the start of this section are satisfied. If not offset, then details of credit risk exposure must be provided.

Disclosure

The purpose of the disclosures in IAS 32 is to provide information to enhance a understanding of the significance of financial instruments to an entity's financial pos tion, performance and cash flows that will assist in assessing the amounts, timing an certainty of future cash flows associated with those instruments.

In particular, the required disclosure is to help assess the following risks relating t financial instruments as follows.

1. Market risk:
   - currency risk – value fluctuates due to changes in foreign exchange rates
   - fair value interest risk – value fluctuates due to changes in interest rates
   - price risk – value fluctuates due to changes in market prices, whether specific (affecting all securities traded in the market
2. Credit risk: the risk that one party will fail to discharge an obligation and cause tl other party to incur a financial loss
3. Liquidity risk: the risk encountered in raising funds to meet commitments
4. Cash flow interest rate risk: the risk that future cash flows will fluctuate due i changes in interest rates.

Format and location

IAS 32 does not prescribe either the location or the format of the information requir under the standard. If it is disclosed on the face of the financial statements, it does nee to be repeated in the notes. The format may contain both a quantitative and a narrati element, as appropriate.

The extent of detail of disclosure requires judgement and an ability to strike a be ance between providing excessive detail and obscuring significant information by to much aggregation. Details of individual instruments may be important if they represe a significant component of an entity's capital structure, but similar instruments may we be combined.

Classification distinguishing between cost and fair value items would seem preferab

Risk management policies and hedging activities

An entity should describe its financial risk management objectives and policies, includii its policy for hedging each major type of forecast transaction for which hedge accountii is used.

These will include policies on matters such as hedging of risk exposures, avoidan of undue concentration of risk, and requirements for collateral to mitigate credit ris This is a valuable independent perspective from that gathered from the specific instr ments held.

The following should be disclosed separately for designated fair value hedges, ca flow hedges and hedges of a net investment in a foreign operation as per IAS 39:

1. A description of the hedge
2. A description of the financial instruments designated as hedging instruments a their fair values at the balance sheet date

. The nature of the risks being hedged
. For hedges of forecast transactions, the periods in which the forecast transactions are expected to occur, when they are expected to enter into the determination of profit or loss, and a description of any forecast transaction for which hedge accounting had previously been used but which is no longer expected to occur.

gains/losses on derivative and non-derivative financial assets and liabilities designated as edging instruments in cash flow hedges have been recognised, by remeasuring the hedging strument an entity must disclose the amount so recognised during the period and provide n explanation of how the gains/losses have been dealt with in the financial statements.

erms, conditions, and accounting policies

or each class of financial asset, financial liability and equity instrument, an entity ould disclose:

, Information about the extent and nature of the financial instruments, including significant terms and conditions that might affect the amount, timing and certainty of future cash flows
The accounting policies and methods adopted, including the criteria for recognition and the basis of measurement applied.

erms and conditions of contracts are very important in assessing future cash flows. hese should be disclosed for individual contracts, if significant, but the information ay be presented by reference to appropriate groupings of like instruments.
If financial instruments create a potentially significant exposure to risks, then the rms and conditions that should be disclosed include:

1. The principal on which future payments are based
2. The date of maturity, expiry or execution
3. Early settlement options, including the period when they can be exercised and their prices
4. Options held to convert instruments into others, including the period of exercise and the exchange ratio
5. The amount and timing of scheduled cash flows of the principal amount
6. The stated rate of interest, dividend or other return on principal
7. Collateral held or pledged
8. For instruments denominated in a foreign currency other than presentation, that currency
9. For exchanges, items (1) to (8)
10. Any condition which would significantly alter the other terms of the contract.

here the presentation differs from the legal form, the entity should explain, in the tes, the nature of the instrument.
Any relationship between individual instruments that can affect the amount, timing or rtainty of future cash flows would be useful – e.g. hedging relationships.
All significant accounting policies should be disclosed, including the general principles opted in applying the principles to significant transactions. Disclosures include:

The criteria applied in determining when to recognise a financial asset or liability and when to derecognise it

2. The basis of measurement applied to financial assets and liabilities initially and subsequently
3. The basis on which income and expenses arising from financial assets and liabilities are recognised and measured.

If IAS 39 is not being applied, it would be particularly important, to provide adequate information for users, to disclose for cost-based instruments:

1. Costs of acquisition
2. Premiums/discounts on monetary financial assets and liabilities
3. Changes in the estimated determinable future cash flows associated with a monetary instrument such as an indexed-linked bond
4. Changes in circumstances resulting in significant uncertainty about the timely collection of amounts due from monetary assets
5. Declines in the fair value of financial assets below their carrying amount
6. Restructured financial liabilities.

For fair value instruments, an entity should disclose whether they are determined from quoted market prices, independent appraisals, discounted cash flow analysis or another appropriate method, as well as disclosing any significant assumptions.

The basis of reporting unrealised gains, losses and interest should be provided, and this includes information about the basis on which income and expenses arising from financial instruments, held for hedging, are recognised. If income and expenses are presented net even though corresponding assets and liabilities have not been offset, the reason for that presentation should be disclosed, if significant.

Interest rate risk

For each class of financial assets and liabilities, an entity must disclose information about its exposure to interest rate risk, including:

1. Contractual repricing or maturity dates, whichever are earlier
2. Effective interest rates, when applicable.

It is important that exposure to the effects of future changes in the prevailing level of interest rates and how changes in market rates affect cash flows be provided.

Information *re* maturity dates provides useful information as to the length of time that rates are fixed and the levels at which they are fixed. Disclosure provides users with a basis for evaluating the fair value interest rate risk to which an entity is exposed, and thus the potential for gain or loss.

To supplement the above, an entity may elect to disclose information about repricing or maturity dates if those dates differ significantly from the contractual dates. Such information is particularly relevant when predicting the amount of fixed rate mortgage loans that will be repaid prior to maturity, and the information is used as the basis for managing its interest rate risk exposure.

An entity indicates which of its financial assets/liabilities are:

• exposed to fair value interest rate risk;
• exposed to cash flow interest rate risk, e.g. floating rates; and
• not directly exposed to interest rate risk, e.g. investments in equity securities.

An entity may become exposed to interest rate risk – e.g. a commitment to lend funds at a fixed rate. The entity should disclose information that permits users to understand the nature and extent of its exposure. That normally includes the stated principal, interest rate, and term to maturity of the amount to be lent, and the significant terms of the transaction giving rise to the exposure to risk.

Exposure to interest rate risk can be presented in tables, in narrative form or as a combination of the two. If the entity has a significant number of instruments exposed to fair value or cash flow interest rate risk, it may adopt one or more of the following approaches to presenting information.

1. The carrying amounts exposed to interest rate risk may be presented in tabular form, grouped by those contracted to mature or be repriced in the following periods after the balance sheet date:
   - not later than 1 year
   - later than 1 year and not later than 2 years
   - later than 2 years and not later than 3 years
   - later than 3 years and not later than 4 years
   - later than 4 years but not later than 5 years, and
   - later than 5 years.
2. Where performance is significantly affected by exposure to interest rate risk, more details are required. A bank, for example, may disclose separate groupings of instruments to mature or be repriced:
   - within 1 month of the balance sheet date
   - more than 1 month and less than 3 months from the balance sheet date, and
   - more than 3 months and less than 12 months from the balance sheet date.
3. Similar cash flow interest rate risk exposure may be provided indicating groups of floating rate financial assets/liabilities maturing within various future time periods.
4. Interest rate information may be disclosed for individual instruments or weighted average rates, or a range of rates may be presented for each class of instrument.

In some cases, the effects of hypothetical changes in market interest rates on fair values and future earnings/cash flows would be useful. Such interest rate sensitivity, when disclosed, should indicate the basis on which it has prepared the information, including any significant assumptions.

Credit risk

For each class of financial asset and other credit exposures, an entity should disclose information about its exposure to credit risk, including:

the amount that best represents its maximum credit risk exposure at the balance sheet date, without taking account of the fair value of any collateral, in the event of other parties failing to perform their obligations under financial instruments; and significant concentrations of credit risk.

The first requirement of ignoring collateral is to provide users with a consistent measure of the amount exposed to risk and to take into account the possibility that the maximum exposure to loss may differ from the carrying value of the financial assets.

Where an entity has entered one or more master netting arrangements that serve to mitigate its exposure to credit loss and this significantly reduces the credit risk associated, an entity must provide additional information indicating that:

- the credit risk is eliminated only to the extent that financial liabilities due to the same counterparty will be settled after the assets are realised; and
- the extent to which an entity's overall exposure to credit risk is reduced through a master netting arrangement; the disclosure of terms may also be useful.

Concentrations of credit risk should be disclosed if they are not apparent from other disclosures about the nature of the business and financial position of the entity and result in a significant exposure to loss in the event of default by other parties. Identification of significant concentrations requires judgement by management taking into account the circumstances of the entity and its debtors. IAS 14 may provide guidance in this regard.

Characteristics giving rise to significant concentrations of credit risk include the nature of the activities undertaken by debtors, such as the industry in which it operates, the geographical area in which activities take place and the level of creditworthiness of groups of borrowers (e.g. bank lending to less developed nations).

Disclosure of credit risk includes a description of the shared characteristic that identifies each concentration and the amount of the maximum credit risk exposure associated with all financial assets sharing that characteristic.

Fair value

For each class of financial assets and liabilities, an entity should disclose the fair value of that class of assets and liabilities in such a way that it permits it to be compared with the corresponding amount in the balance sheet. IAS 39 provides guidance on how the fair value should be determined.

If IAS 39 is being applied and unquoted investments are valued at cost (no reliable fair value), that fact should be disclosed together with a description of the instruments their carrying amount, an explanation of why fair value cannot be measured reliably and, if possible, the range of estimates within which fair value is highly likely to lie. If these financial assets are then sold, that fact, their carrying value at date of sale and the amount of gain/loss should be disclosed.

An entity should disclose:

1. The methods and significant assumptions applied in determining fair values of financial assets and liabilities separately for significant classes
2. The extent to which fair values are determined directly via market prices or are estimated using a valuation technique
3. The extent to which fair values are determined in full or in part using a valuation technique based on assumptions that are not supported by observable market prices
4. If a fair value estimated using a valuation technique is sensitive to valuation assumptions that are not supported by observable market prices, a statement of this fact and the effect on the fair value of using a range of reasonably possible alternative assumptions
5. The total amount of the change in fair value estimated using a valuation technique that was recognised in profit or loss during the period.

Fair values are widely used in business, and provide relevant information to users as well permitting comparisons of financial instruments having the same economic characteristic regardless of their purpose and when or by whom they are issued. If fair values are not included within the balance sheet, they should be disclosed as supplementary disclosures.

Disclosure of fair value information includes disclosure of the method used to determine fair value and any significant assumptions made – e.g. prepayment rates, discount rates, rates of estimated credit losses.

For financial instruments such as short-term trade receivables and payables, no disclosure of fair value is required when their carrying value approximates fair value.

Fair values should only be grouped into classes and offset to the extent that their related carrying amounts are offset in the balance sheet.

Other disclosures

The following should also be disclosed for financial instruments:

1. Significant incomes, expenses, gains and losses resulting from financial assets and liabilities, whether included in the performance statements or on the balance sheet; in particular, the following should be disclosed:
   - total interest income and interest expense for financial assets and liabilities not designated as held for trading (historic cost basis)
   - for available for sale financial assets, the amount of any gain or loss recognised directly in the performance statement during the period, and
   - the amount of any interest income accrued on impaired loans
2. If the entity has sold or transferred a financial asset, but it does not qualify for derecognition in full or in part:
   - the nature of the assets transferred
   - the nature of the continuing involvement in the assets transferred
   - the extent of such transfers, and
   - information about the risks retained in any portion of a transferred asset that the transferor continues to recognise
. If the entity has entered into a securitisation agreement and has a continuing involvement in all or a portion of the securitised financial assets at the balance sheet date, for each major asset type:
   - the nature of the assets transferred
   - the extent of such transactions, including quantitative information about the key assumptions used in calculating fair values, and
   - the total principal amount outstanding, any portion derecognised, and the portion that continues to be recognised

If IAS 39 forces the entity to reclassify a financial asset at cost rather than at fair value, the reason for that reclassification

The nature and amount of any impairment loss recognised for a financial asset, separately for each significant class

The carrying amount of financial assets pledged as collateral for liabilities, the carrying amount of financial assets pledged as collateral for contingent liabilities, and any significant terms and conditions relating to pledged assets

When an entity has accepted collateral:
- the fair value of collateral that it is permitted to sell or repledge in the absence of default
- the fair value of collateral that it has sold and has an obligation to return, and
- any significant terms and conditions associated with its use of collateral

8. If the entity has designated non-derivative financial liabilities as held for trading, the difference between their carrying amount and the amount the entity would be contractually required to pay to the holders of the obligations at maturity
9. If the entity has issued an instrument containing both a liability and an equity amount and the instrument has multiple embedded derivative features whose values are interdependent, the existence of these features and the effective yield on the liability element
10. With respect to defaults of principal, interest, sinking fund, or redemption provisions during the period on loans payable recognised at the balance sheet date, and any other breaches during the period of loan agreements when those breaches can permit the lender to demand repayment:
    - details of those breaches
    - the amount recognised at the balance sheet date in respect of loans payable on which the breaches occurred; and, with respect to these amounts, whether the default has been remedied or the terms of the loans payable renegotiated before the date the financial statements were authorised for issue.

12.3 IAS 39 *Financial Instruments: Recognition and Measurement* (revised March 2004)

Objective

The objective of IAS 39 is to establish principles for recognising and measuring financial assets and liabilities.

Scope

IAS 39 applies to all financial instruments giving a true and fair view and prepared under fair value accounting.

It applies to all types of financial instruments except for:

- interest in subsidiaries, quasi subsidiaries and associated undertakings; those investments, however, held exclusively with a view to subsequent disposal are included;
- leases under IAS 17;
- employers' rights and obligations under IAS 19;
- insurance contracts (but it does apply to derivatives embedded in insurance contracts
- equity instruments issued by the entity including options and warrants;
- financial guarantee contracts including letters of credit made to reimburse the holde for a loss it incurs because a specified debtor fails to pay;
- contracts for contingent consideration in a business combination;
- contracts that require a payment based on climatic, geological or other physical var ables, as the payout is unrelated to the amount of an insured entity's loss;
- loan commitments that cannot be settled net in cash.

Sometimes a 'strategic investment' is made, and if under IAS 28/31 the equity methc is not applied then the entity must apply IAS 39. It must also be applied to contracts buy or sell a non-financial item that can be settled net in cash. The exception is those contracts entered into for the purpose of receipt or delivery of a non-financial item in accordance with the entity's expected purchase, sale or usage requirements.

Definitions

Most of the key definitions are covered in IAS 32. However, a number of other definitions are also provided:

Derivatives

Derivative: a financial instrument with all three of the following characteristics:

- its value changes in response to the change in an underlying specified interest rate, security price, commodity price, foreign exchange rate;
- it requires no initial net investment or an initial net investment that is smaller than would be expected to changes in market factors;
- it is settled at a future date.

Financial instruments

Financial asset or liability held for trading: a financial instrument is classified as held for trading if it:

is acquired or incurred principally for the purpose of selling or repurchasing it in the near future;

is part of a portfolio of identified financial instruments that are managed together and for which there is evidence of a recent actual pattern of short-term profit-taking; or

is a derivative, except if used as a hedging instrument.

Held to maturity investments: financial assets with fixed or determinable payments and fixed maturity that an entity has positive intent and ability to hold to maturity other than those the entity elects to designate as held for trading or meet the definition of loans and receivables.

Loans and receivables originated by the entity: financial assets created by the entity to provide money, goods or services directly to a debtor other than those originated with the intent of sale immediately or in the short term and designated as held for trading.

Available for sale financial assets: financial assets that are not classified as:

loans and receivables originated by the entity;

held to maturity investments; or

held for trading.

Definitions relating to measurement

Amortised cost of a financial asset or liability: the initial recognition minus principal repayments, plus or minus the cumulative amortisation using the effective interest method and minus any write-down for impairment.

Effective interest method: a method of calculating amortised cost using the effective interest rate of a financial asset or liability. It is the rate that exactly discounts future cash payments or receipts through maturity or the next market-based repricing date to the net carrying amount of the financial asset or liability. The computation includes all fees, and the rate is based on the estimated stream of cash receipts. The effective rate is sometimes termed the 'level yield to maturity or next repricing'.

Transaction costs: incremental external costs directly attributable to the acquisition or disposal of a financial asset or liability.

Firm commitment: a binding agreement for the exchange of a specified quantity of resources at a specified price on a specified future date or dates.

Definitions relating to hedge accounting

Hedged item: an asset, liability or commitment that exposes the entity to risk of changes in fair value or future cash flows and is designated as being hedged.

Hedging instrument: a designated derivative whose fair value or cash flows are expected to offset changes in the fair value of a hedged item.

Hedging effectiveness: the degree to which offsetting changes in fair value or cash flows attributable to a hedged risk are achieved by the hedging instrument.

Elaboration on the definitions

Derivatives

Typical examples are futures and forward, swap and option contracts. A derivative usually has a notional amount, but the holder is not required to invest or receive the notional amount at the inception of the contract. Alternatively a derivative could require a fixed payment as a result of some future event unrelated to a notional amount – e.g. a fixed payment of 1,000 if 6-month LIBOR increases by 100 basis points.

It includes contracts that are settled gross by delivery of the underlying item. It may have a contract to buy or sell non-financial items that can be settled net in cash.

One of the defining characteristics of a derivative is that it has an initial net investment that is smaller than would be required for other types of contracts. An option qualifies as the premium is less than the value of the investment that would be required to obtain the underlying financial instrument to which the option is linked. A currency swap also qualifies as it has a zero initial net investment. Forward contracts also meet the definition.

Transaction costs

These include fees and commissions paid to agents; levies by regulatory authorities, and transfer taxes and duties. However, they do not include debt premiums or discounts and any financing or internal administration expenses.

Financial assets and financial liabilities held for trading

These are used with the objective of generating a profit from short-term price fluctuations. However, designated trading items are not precluded simply because the entity does not intend to sell or repurchase in the near future. Under IAS 39, any financial instrument may be designated initially as 'held for trading'.

Financial liabilities held for trading include:

- derivative liabilities not accounted for as hedging instruments;
- obligations to deliver securities borrowed by a short seller;
- financial liabilities incurred with an intention to repurchase them in the near future

- financial liabilities that are part of a portfolio managed together and for which there is evidence of a recent actual pattern of short-term profit trading; and
- other financial liabilities designated as held for trading.

If an entity elects to designate as 'held for trading' instruments that are not for short-term profit, then it should present them as 'financial instruments at fair value' rather than as 'held for trading'.

Loans and receivables originated by the entity

An acquisition of an interest in a pool of loans/receivables, e.g. securitisation, is a purchase and not an origination, as the entity did not provide money, goods or services directly to the underlying debtors. In addition, a transaction that is, in substance, a purchase of a loan that was previously originated is not a loan originated by the entity. A loan acquired by an entity in a business combination is regarded as originated provided it was similarly classified by the acquired entity.

Any financial asset with fixed or determinable payments could potentially meet the definition. However, financial assets quoted in an active market do not qualify. In addition, financial assets that are purchased by an entity after origination are not classified as loans or receivables originated by the entity. If they do not meet the definition, they may be classified as 'held to maturity investments' if they meet the conditions for that classification.

Embedded derivatives

These are components of hybrid instruments that also include non-derivative host contracts. A derivative that is attached to a financial instrument but is contractually transferable independently is not an embedded derivative, but a separate financial instrument. IAS 39 does not address whether an embedded derivative shall be presented separately on the face of the financial statements.

An embedded derivative shall be separated from the host contract and accounted for as a derivative under IAS 39 if, and only if, all of the following conditions are met:

the economic characteristics and risks of the embedded derivative are not closely related to those of the host contract;

a separate instrument with the same terms as the embedded derivative would meet the definition of a derivative; and

the hybrid is not measured at fair value with changes in fair value reported in profit or loss.

If an embedded derivative is separated, the host contract should be accounted for under IAS 39 if it is a financial instrument.

If an entity is required to separate an embedded derivative from its host contract but unable to measure the embedded derivative, it shall treat the entire combined contract as a financial instrument held for trading.

Measurement

Initial measurement of financial assets and financial liabilities

When a financial asset/liability is recognised initially an entity should measure it at cost, which is the fair value of consideration given or received. Transaction costs that are directly attributable are included in the initial measurement.

Fair value should be referenced to the transaction price or other market prices. If these are not available, then fair value should be the sum of all future cash payments/receipts discounted using prevailing market rates for similar instruments.

Subsequent measurement of financial assets

After initial recognition, an entity should measure financial assets at fair value without deduction for transaction costs, except for the following:

- loans and receivables originated by the entity must be measured at amortised cost using the effective interest method;
- held to maturity investments must be measured at amortised cost using the effective interest method;
- investments in equity instruments that do not have a quoted market price in an active market and whose fair value cannot be reliably measured, and derivatives linked to and settled by delivery of such unquoted equity instruments, must be measured at cost.

Financial assets designated as hedged items are subject to hedge accounting, and all financial assets, other than those fair valued, are subject to impairment review.

If a financial asset is measured at fair value and its fair value is below zero, it should be accounted for as a financial liability.

Example 12.1 provides an illustration.

Example 12.1
Measurement of financial assets

Assume an asset is acquired for 100 + commission of 2. Initially the asset should be recognised at 102. Next year the market price is 100 but a commission of 3 would be paid, thus the asset is measured at 100 and a loss of 2 reported in profit and loss.

Loans and receivables originated by an entity are measured at amortised cost without regard to the entity's intention to hold them until maturity.

For floating rate financial assets, periodic re-estimation of cash flows to reflect movements in market rates should take place with any changes therein being recognised over the remaining term of the asset or the period to the next repricing date.

Held to maturity investments

An entity does not have a positive intention to hold to maturity a financial asset if ANY one of the following conditions is met:

- the entity intends to hold the asset for an undefined period;
- the entity stands ready to sell the asset in response to interest rate changes, liquidity needs, changes in yield on alternative investments or changes in foreign exchange risk;
- the issuer has a right to settle at an amount significantly below its amortised cost.

Most equity securities cannot be said as being 'held to maturity', either due to their indefinite life or because the amount a holder may receive can vary. Similarly, if the terms of a perpetual debt instrument provide for interest for an indefinite period then that instrument cannot be classified as 'held to maturity', as there is no maturity date.

A financial asset that is puttable cannot be classified as 'held to maturity', as this is inconsistent with an intention to hold until maturity.

Any financial assets which an entity has sold or reclassified more than an insignificant amount of held to maturity investments during the year or previous 2 years may not be classified as held for maturity. However, a number of exceptions exist:

- sales/reclassifications so close to maturity that changes in market rates would not significantly affect the asset's fair value;
- sales/reclassifications occurring after the entity has already collected substantially all of the asset's original principal (e.g. 90%); or
- sales/reclassifications due to an isolated event beyond the entity's control, is non-recurring and could not have been reasonably anticipated by the entity.

Fair value is more appropriate than amortised cost for most financial assets; however, 'held to maturity' is an exception but only if the entity has a positive intention to hold the investment to maturity.

A 'disaster scenario' (e.g. run on a bank) is not an event that should be considered in deciding whether or not there is a positive intention to hold to maturity.

Sales before maturity do not raise a question about 'intention to hold' if they are due to:

a significant deterioration in the issuer's credit worthiness – e.g. sale following a downgrade in credit rating;
a change in tax law eliminating or significantly reducing the tax exempt status of interest;
a major business combination necessitating the sale or transfer of held to maturity investments to maintain the entity's existing interest rate risk position or credit risk policy;
a change in statutory requirements causing an entity to dispose of a held to maturity investment;
a significant increase in capital needs causing the entity to downsize by selling 'held to maturity' investments; or
a significant increase in the risk weights of 'held to maturity' investments used for regulatory risk based capital purposes.

An entity does not have an ability to 'hold to maturity' a financial asset if either of the following conditions is met:

it does not have the financial resources to continue to finance until maturity; or
it is subject to existing legal constraints that could frustrate its intention to hold the asset to maturity.

There could be other circumstances which do not have a positive intention to hold to maturity, and an entity needs to assess its intention not only when initially recognised but also at each subsequent balance sheet date.

Subsequent measurement of financial liabilities

After initial recognition an entity should measure all financial liabilities, other than those held for trading and derivatives, at amortised cost using the effective interest rate method. Financial liabilities held for trading and fair value derivatives, except for a derivative liability linked to and settled by delivery of an unquoted equity instrument whose fair value cannot be reliably measured, should be kept at cost. Financial liabilities designated as hedged items are subject to separate hedge accounting rules.

Reclassifications

Because the designation of a financial asset/liability held for trading is made on initial recognition, an entity shall not reclassify a financial instrument into or out of trading while it is held.

If it is no longer appropriate to carry a 'held to maturity' investment at amortised cost, it should be reclassified into the 'available for sale' category and remeasured at fair value, with any difference between carrying amount and fair value accounted for in accordance with fair value measurement considerations.

Similarly, if a reliable measure becomes available for a financial asset/liability for which there was no previously available fair value, then it should be remeasured at fair value and the difference accounted for in accordance with fair value measurement considerations.

If, due to a change in intention, a reliable measure is no longer available or two preceding years have passed, it is appropriate to carry a financial asset at cost or amortised cost rather than at fair value, with the fair value on that date becoming its new cost. If a previous gain or loss has gone directly to the equity statement, no adjustment should be made on the reclassification of the financial asset.

Fair value measurement considerations

In determining the fair value, an entity should presume that it is a going concern and is not to be valued as a forced transaction.

Active market: quoted price

The existence of published price quotations in an active market is the best evidence of fair value, and this is usually the current bid price. When current bid prices are unavailable, the price of the most recent transaction is sufficient evidence provided there has not been a significant change in economic circumstances between the transaction date and the reporting date. If a published price quotation in an active market does not exist in its entirety, but active markets exist for its component parts, fair value is determined on the basis of relevant market prices for its component parts.

No active market: unquoted price

If the market is not active, the best evidence of fair value is recent market transactions between willing parties in an arm's length transaction.

No active market: valuation technique

If an entity has to use a valuation technique to assess fair value, this must:

- incorporate all the factors to be considered in setting a price; and
- be consistent with accepted economic theory for pricing.

Valuation techniques that are well established include reference to the current market value of another instrument that is substantially the same, discounted cash flow analysis, and option pricing models.

If a measure is used commonly to price instruments, then that measure should be adopted.

In applying discounted cash flow analysis, the discount rate should be equal to the prevailing rate of return for instruments having substantially the same terms and characteristics, including the creditworthiness of the debtor, the remaining term, and the currency in which payments are made. When the terms extend beyond the period for which market prices are available, the valuation technique uses current market prices and extrapolates those prices for later periods.

The initial acquisition or origination of a financial asset or incurrence of a financial liability is a market transaction that provides a foundation for estimating fair value. A debt instrument can be valued by referring to the market conditions that existed at its acquisition or origination date and current market conditions or interest rates.

Alternatively, provided there is no change in credit risk, an estimate of the current market interest rate may be derived by using a benchmark interest rate reflecting a better credit quality than the underlying debt instrument and adjusting for the change in the benchmark interest rate from the origination date.

No active market: equity instruments

For equity instruments, with no quoted market prices and which must be settled by delivery of an unquoted equity instrument, a reliable measure can be found if:

the variability in the range of reasonable fair value estimates is not significant; or
the probabilities can be reasonably assessed.

Gains and losses

A recognised gain or loss arising from a change in fair value of a financial asset/liability that is not part of a hedging relationship should be recognised as follows:

a gain or loss on a financial asset/liability held for trading should be recognised in profit or loss for the period in which it arises;
a gain or loss on an available for sale financial asset should be recognised in the change in equity statement; however, the amortisation charge, using the effective interest method, of any difference between the amount initially recognised and the maturity amount represents interest and is recognised in profit or loss.

For financial assets and liabilities carried at amortised cost, a gain or loss is recognised in profit or loss when the financial asset/liability is derecognised or impaired, as well as through the amortisation process.

An entity should apply IAS 21 *The Effect of Changes in Foreign Exchange Rates* to monetary items denominated in a foreign currency. An exception is a derivative designated as a hedging instrument.

Where financial assets are not classified as monetary items, any changes in fair value are accounted for as per the fair value approach. If hedging exists between a non-derivative monetary asset and a non-derivative monetary liability, changes in the foreign currency component should be recognised in profit or loss.

Impairment and uncollectability of financial assets

An entity should assess, at every balance sheet date, whether there is any objective evidence that a financial asset or group of assets is impaired. If so, the entity must apply 'amortised cost' or treat them as 'available for sale financial assets'.

Objective evidence exists if there is:

- significant financial difficulty for the issuer;
- a breach of contract – e.g. default in interest or principal;
- the granting by the lender to the borrower of a concession that the lender would not otherwise consider;
- a high probability of bankruptcy of the issuer;
- recognition of an impairment loss on that asset in a prior period;
- the disappearance of an active market for the financial asset due to financial difficulties;
- an historical pattern of collections of groups of financial assets indicating that the entity will not be able to collect all amounts due (principal and interest).

The disappearance of an active market is not evidence of impairment, nor is a downgrade of credit rating or a decline in the fair value of a financial asset below cost. An adverse change in the technological, market, economic or legal environment may indicate that the asset may not be recovered. A significant and prolonged decline in fair value of an equity investment below cost is also objective evidence of impairment.

Financial assets carried at amortised cost

If there is objective evidence of impairment and it is probable that an entity will not be able to collect all amounts due (principal and interest), an impairment has occurred. The loss is the difference between the asset's carrying amount and the present value of expected future cash flows discounted at the original effective interest rate. The carrying amount of the asset shall be reduced to its estimated recoverable amount either directly or through use of an allowance account. The loss should go through profit and loss.

An entity first assesses whether or not there is objective evidence of impairment either individually or collectively. If there is no objective evidence of individual impairment, the asset must be included in a group of financial assets with similar credit risk characteristics that can be collectively assessed. Assets assessed individually for impairment are not included in the collective assessment for impairment.

Impairment of a financial asset carried at amortised cost should be measured at the instrument's original effective interest rate, as discounting at current market rates would impose fair value measurement. If a loan has a variable interest rate, the discount rate should be the current effective interest rate determined under the contract. As a practical expedient, a creditor may measure impairment using an observable market price.

For collective evaluation of impairment, financial assets are grouped on the basis of similar credit risk characteristics.

Impairment losses recognised on a group basis represent an interim step pending the identification of impairment losses on individual assets. As soon as information is available to identify losses individually, the assets must be removed from the group.

Expected cash flows for a group should be based on the contractual cash flows of the assets in the group and historical loss experience for assets with similar risk characteristics.

to the group. If there is insufficient experience, entities should use peer group experience for comparable groups. Historical loss experience is adjusted to reflect current conditions. Estimates of changes in expected cash flows reflect changes in related observable data from period to period – e.g. unemployment rates, property prices etc. The methodology and assumptions must be reviewed regularly.

In discounting groups of financial assets, an entity uses a weighted average of the original effective interest rates of the group assets. For example, if the original contractual rate is 12% and past experience is 10%, then the original effective rate should be the expected rate of 10%.

If subsequently the impairment decreases and this can be related objectively to an event occurring after the write down, the write down shall be reversed either directly or by adjusting an allowance account. The reversal must not result in a carrying amount of the financial asset exceeding what the amortised cost would have been had the impairment not been recognised.

Interest income after impairment recognition

Once impaired, interest income is thereafter based on the rate of interest used to discount the future cash flows for the purpose of measuring the recoverable amount. Additionally, the entity reviews the asset for further impairment.

Financial assets carried at cost

If there is objective evidence of impairment of an unquoted equity instrument that is not carried at fair value because its fair value cannot be objectively determined, the loss is the difference between the carrying amount of the asset and the present value of expected future cash flows discounted at the current market rate of interest for similar assets. Such losses shall not be reversed.

Available for sale financial assets

A decline in the fair value of an available for sale financial asset that has been recognised in the change in equity statement should not subsequently be recognised in profit and loss if and when objective evidence of impairment is discovered.

Impairment losses recognised in profit or loss should not be reversed as long as the instrument is recognised.

Hedging

Hedging instruments

Qualifying instruments

IAS 39 does not restrict the circumstances in which a derivative may be designated as a hedging instrument provided the conditions listed in (1) to (5) (see p. 352) are met. However, a non-derivative financial asset may be designated as a hedging instrument only for a hedge of a foreign currency risk.

The potential loss on an option could be significantly greater than the potential gain in value of a related hedged item, i.e. a written option is not effective in reducing exposure and thus does not qualify unless designated as an offset to a purchased option. In contrast, a purchased option has potential gains equal to or greater than losses and thus has the potential to reduce profit or loss exposure from changes in fair values or cash flows. Therefore it can qualify.

Held to maturity investments carried at amortised cost may be effective hedging instruments with respect to risks from changes in foreign currency exchange rates.

An investment in an unquoted equity instrument that is not carried at fair value, as that value cannot be reliably measured, cannot be designated as a hedging instrument.

An entity's own equity securities cannot be designated as hedging instruments.

For hedge accounting, only derivatives involving a party external to the entity can be designated as hedging instruments. Although individual entities within a group may enter hedging transactions with other entities in the group, any gains or losses are eliminated on consolidation. Therefore inter-company hedging transactions do not qualify for hedge accounting on consolidation.

Designation of hedging instruments

Normally there is a single fair value measure for a hedging instrument in its entirety. The only exceptions permitted are:

- separating the intrinsic value and the time value of an option and designating only the change in the intrinsic value of an option as the hedging instrument; and
- separating the interest element and the spot price on a forward contract.

These are permitted only because the intrinsic value and the premium on the forward contract can be measured separately.

A proportion of the entire hedging instrument may be designated as the hedging instrument in a hedging relationship. However, a hedging relationship may not be designated for only a portion of the time period during which the time period remains outstanding.

A single hedging instrument may be designated as a hedge of more than one type of risk provided that:

- the risks hedged can be identified clearly;
- the effectiveness of the hedge can be demonstrated; and
- it is possible to ensure that there is specific designation of the hedging instrument and different risk positions.

Two or more derivatives may be viewed in combination. However, where a written option component is combined with a purchased option it does not qualify as a hedging instrument if it is, in effect, a net written option.

Hedged items

Qualifying items

A hedged item can be a recognised asset or liability, an unrecognised firm commitment, an uncommitted but highly probable anticipated future transaction, or a net investment in a foreign operation. The hedged item can be:

- a single asset, liability, commitment; or
- a group of assets, liabilities, commitments with similar characteristics.

A held to maturity investment cannot be a hedged item with respect to interest or prepayment risk because designation requires an intention to hold the investment until maturity without regard to changes in the fair value or cash flows. It can be a hedged item, however, with respect to foreign exchange and credit risks.

A firm commitment to acquire a business in a business combination cannot be a hedged item, except for foreign exchange risk, because other risks being hedged cannot be specifically identified and measured.

An equity method investment cannot be a hedged item in a fair value hedge, as it recognises in profit the investor's share of the associate's accrued profit or loss rather than fair value changes. For similar reasons, an investment in a consolidated subsidiary cannot be a hedged item in a fair value hedge.

Designation of financial items as hedged items

If the hedged item is a financial asset/liability, it may be a hedged item with respect to the risks associated with only a portion of its cash flows provided that effectiveness can be measured – for example, an identified and separately measurable portion of the interest rate exposure of an interest bearing asset may be designated as the hedged risk.

Designation of non-financial items as hedged items

If the hedged item is a non-financial liability, it shall be designated as a hedged item either (a) for foreign currency risks or (b) in its entirety for all risks, because of the difficulty of isolating and measuring the appropriate portion of the cash flows or fair value changes attributable to specific risks other than foreign currency risks.

If there is a difference between the terms of the hedging instrument and the hedged item (e.g. hedge of the forecast purchase of Brazilian coffee using a forward contract to purchase Colombian coffee), it may qualify provided the conditions are expected to be highly effective. However, the hedging relationship might result in ineffectiveness that would be recognised in profit or loss during the term of the hedging relationship.

Designation of groups of items as hedged items

If similar assets or liabilities are aggregated and hedged as a group, the change in fair value attributable to the hedged risk for each individual item in the group is expected to be approximately proportional to the overall change in fair value attributable to the hedged risk of the group.

For example, if a bank has 100 of assets and 90 of liabilities with risks and terms of a similar nature and hedges the net 10 exposure, it can designate 10 of those assets as the hedged item. This designation can be used if at fixed rates (fair value hedge) or at variable rates (cash flow hedge).

Similarly, if an entity has a firm commitment to purchase in a foreign currency of 100 and a firm commitment to make a sale in a foreign currency of 90, it can hedge the net amount of 10 by acquiring a derivative and designating it as a hedging instrument associated with 10 of the firm purchase commitment of 100.

Hedge accounting

Hedge accounting recognises the offsetting effects on profit or loss of changes in the fair values of the hedging instrument and the hedged item.

Hedging relationships are of three types:

1. *Fair value hedge*: a hedge of the exposure to changes in fair value of a recognised asset or liability or a previously unrecognised firm commitment to buy or sell an asset at a fixed price, or an identified portion that is attributable to a particular risk and could affect reported profit or loss
2. *Cash flow hedge*: a hedge of the exposure to variability in cash flows that:
   - is attributable to a particular risk or a forecast transaction, and
   - could affect profit or loss
3. *Hedge of a net investment in a foreign operation*: these hedges are defined in IAS 21.

An example of a fair value hedge is a hedge of exposure to changes in the fair value of fixed rate debt as a result of changes in interest rates.

An example of a cash flow hedge is the use of a swap to change floating rate debt to fixed rate debt.

A hedge of a firm commitment (e.g. a hedge by an airline to purchase an aircraft for a fixed amount of a foreign currency, or a hedge of a change in fuel price relating to an unrecognised contractual commitment by an electric utility to purchase fuel at a fixed price) is a hedge of an exposure to a change in fair value, and thus it is accounted for as a fair value hedge.

Under IAS 39, a hedging relationship qualifies for hedge accounting if, and only if, all of the following conditions are met:

1. At the inception of the hedge there is formal documentation of the hedging relationship and the entity's risk management objective and strategy for undertaking the hedge. That includes identifying the hedging instrument, the related hedged item the nature of the risk being hedged and how the entity will assess the hedging instruments's effectiveness.
2. The hedge is expected to be highly effective in achieving offsetting changes in fair value or cash flows attributable to the hedged risk.
3. For cash flow hedges, a forecast transaction must be highly probable and present an exposure to cash flow variations that could ultimately affect reported profit or loss.
4. The effectiveness of the hedge can be reliably measured.
5. The hedge is assessed on an ongoing basis and is determined to have been highly effective throughout the financial reporting period.

Assessing hedge effectiveness

A hedge is normally highly effective if, at inception and throughout its life, the entity can expect changes in the fair value or cash flows of the hedged item to be almost fully offset by changes in the fair value or cash flows of the hedging instrument, and if actual results are within a range of 80% to 125% (see Example 12.2).

Example 12.2
Assessing hedge effectiveness

If the loss on the hedging instrument is 120 and the gain on the cash instrument is 100, offset can be measured by 120/100 (120%) or by 100/120 (83%). It is therefore highly effective.

The method adopted for assessing hedge effectiveness depends on its risk management strategy, and there could be different methods for different types of hedges. If the terms of the hedging instrument and hedged item are the same, the changes in fair values and cash flows may be likely to offset each other – e.g. an interest rate swap is likely to be effective if the notional and principal amounts, term, repricing dates, dates of interest and principal receipts/payments, and basis for measuring interest rates are the same for both hedging instrument and hedged item.

Sometimes a hedge is only partially effective, for example in different currencies not moving in tandem.

To qualify for hedge accounting, the hedge must relate to a specific and designated risk, not merely to overall business risks, and must ultimately affect the entity's profit or loss. A hedge of the risk of obsolescence or expropriation of property by government would not be eligible for hedge accounting, as the risks are not reliably measured.

Hedge effectiveness may be assessed by preparing a maturity schedule for financial assets and liabilities showing the net interest rate exposure for each time period. There is no single method for assessing hedge effectiveness, so an entity must document its procedures. As a minimum, effectiveness should be computed at every interim and final year end. If the critical terms are the same for both hedged instrument and hedged item, then an entity could conclude that changes in fair values/cash flows are expected to offset each other fully at inception and on an ongoing basis. A forecast purchase of a commodity with a forward contract will be highly effective and there will be no ineffectiveness to be recognised in profit or loss if:

> the forward contract is for the purchase of the same quantity of the same commodity at the same time and location as the hedged forecast purchase;
> the fair value of the forward contract at inception is zero;
> either the change in discount/premium on the forward contract is excluded from the assessment of effectiveness and included directly in profit or loss or the change in expected cash flows on the forecast transaction is based on the forward price for the commodity.

The time value of money should be considered. There is no need for perfect matching or either fixed or variable rates between the hedging instrument and hedged item.

Fair value hedges

If a fair value hedge meets the conditions of hedging it should be accounted for as follows:

> the gain or loss from remeasuring the hedging instrument at fair value (for a derivative) or the foreign currency component of its carrying amount (for a non-derivative) should be recognised immediately in profit or loss; and
> the gain or loss on the hedged item attributable to the hedged risk shall adjust the carrying amount of the hedged item and be recognised immediately in profit or loss. This applies even if a hedged item is measured at fair value with changes in fair value recognised in the changes in equity statement. That also applies if the hedged item is measured at cost.

An entity shall discontinue prospectively the hedge accounting noted above if any one of the following occurs:

> the hedging instrument expires or is sold, terminated or exercised; or
> the hedge no longer meets the criteria for hedge accounting.

An adjustment to the carrying amount of a hedged interest bearing financial instrument should be amortised to profit or loss. Amortisation may start as soon as an adjustment exists, and no later than when the hedged item ceases to be adjusted for changes in its fair value attributable to the risk being hedged. The adjustment is based on a recalculated effective interest rate at the date amortisation begins, and should be amortised fully by maturity.

Cash flow hedges

If a cash flow hedge meets the conditions for hedging during the period, it should be accounted for as follows:

- the portion of the gain or loss on the hedging instrument that is determined to be an effective hedge should be reported on the balance sheet and described as 'gains and losses arising on effective cash flow hedges not yet recognised in the profit and loss'; and
- the ineffective portion of the gain or loss on the hedging instrument should be recognised immediately in profit or loss.

If a hedge of a forecast transaction subsequently results in the recognition of an asset or liability, then the associated gains or losses that were reported on the balance sheet shall be reclassified into profit or loss in the same period during which the asset acquired or liability incurred affects profit or loss. However, if an entity expects that all or a portion of a net loss reported amongst assets and liabilities will not be recovered, it should recognise the amount not expected to be recovered immediately into profit and loss.

All cash flow hedges, other than those above, reported on the balance sheet should be included in profit and loss in the same period during which the hedged forecast transaction affects profit or loss.

An entity should discontinue prospectively the hedge accounting specified above if any one of the following occurs:

1. The hedging instrument expires, is sold, terminated or exercised. The cumulative gain or loss on the hedging instrument that was initially reported in the balance sheet when the hedge was effective should remain until the forecast transaction occurs. When the transaction occurs, the above accounting treatment will apply.
2. The hedge no longer meets the criteria for hedge accounting. The cumulative gain or loss initially reported on the balance sheet when the hedge was effective should remain until the forecast transaction occurs. When the transaction occurs, the above accounting treatment will apply.
3. The forecast transaction is no longer expected to occur, in which case any related cumulative gain or loss that had been reported on the balance sheet should be recognised in profit and loss for the period. A forecast that is no longer highly probable may still be expected to occur.

Hedges of a net investment

Hedges of a net investment in a foreign operation, including a hedge of a monetary item that is accounted for as part of the net investment, should be accounted for as follows

- the portion of the gain or loss on the hedging instrument that is determined to be an effective hedge should be recognised in the changes in equity statement;

- The ineffective portion should be recognised immediately in profit or loss if the hedging instrument is a derivative; or (in accordance with Gains and losses section earlier in this chapter) in the limited circumstances in which the hedging instrument is not a derivative.

The amount of the gain or loss on the hedging instrument relating to the effective portion of the hedge that has been recognised in the changes in equity statement should not be reversed or adjusted at the disposal of the foreign operation.

Hedges that do not qualify for hedge accounting

If a hedge does not qualify for hedge accounting as it fails to meet the criteria, gains and losses arising from changes in the fair value of a hedged item that is measured at fair value after initial recognition are recognised in one of two ways (see Gains and losses section earlier in this chapter). Fair value adjustments of a hedging instrument that is a derivative would be recognised in profit or loss.

12.4   Examination questions

Most of the questions on the subject of financial instruments concentrate on the overview of the process rather than the practical implementation of the standards. That is because of their particularly specialised nature which really requires expert treasury knowledge of those instruments.

Question 12.1: IAS 32/39 issues (CIMA)

The first question covers the need for financial instruments to be fair valued rather than being maintained at historic cost, and why the disclosure standard IAS 32 was not sufficient to satisfy user needs in the area.)
One of the issues dealt with by the International Accounting Standards Committee in its Framework for the Preparation and Presentation of Financial Statements is the measurement of assets and liabilities in financial statements. The Framework notes that the historical cost system is the one most widely used in financial statements at present. However, the Framework suggests that other models and concepts, apart from the historical cost system, may be more appropriate in order to meet the objective of providing useful information.

Developments in financial reporting over the last decade suggest that a mixed measurement system may well evolve, in which some assets and liabilities are measured based on historical cost while others are measured based on current values. The use of current values is already accepted practice for measuring certain categories of non-current asset, particularly properties.

In 1998, the IASC issued IAS 39 *Financial Instruments: Recognition and Measurement*. This standard required that certain categories of financial instruments be measured at their current values and allowed hedge accounting in certain circumstances. Previous practice as set out in IAS 32 *Financial Instruments: Disclosure and Presentation*) tended to focus on the disclosure of information regarding fair values.

Recent developments suggest that further international harmonisation in accounting for financial instruments is appropriate. A recent proposal from the IASB suggests measuring virtually all financial instruments at current values, rather than (as required by IAS 39) measurement of certain categories only at current values and (as required by IAS 32) extensive disclosure in the notes to the financial statements. The same proposal also suggests that hedge accounting should be prohibited.

Required

(a) Identify the strengths and weaknesses of using a historical cost system of measurement for assets and liabilities.
(b) Explain why a current value measurement system is more appropriate for financial instruments than a historical cost system.
(c) Explain why the disclosure requirements of IAS 32 were insufficient on their own to satisfy the needs of users.
(d) Discuss the likely effect on current international accounting practice should the recent IASB proposal be implemented.

Question 12.2: Tall (CIMA)

(This question, taken from a pilot CIMA paper, first requires students to identify the problems associated with accounting for financial instruments and then, using a more specific example, looks at how to present these instruments in order to accord with IAS 32. It also mixes in a discussion about the appropriateness of adopting the uniting of interests method of consolidation rather than the purchase method.)
Two standards have been published by the IASB to deal with the complex area of financial instruments:

- IAS 32 *Financial Instruments: Disclosure and Presentation*
- IAS 39 *Financial Instruments: Recognition and Measurement.*

Required

(a) What are the problems with the way that financial instruments have been accounted for in the past that these standards were issued to correct?

You are the management accountant of Tall. The company is planning a number c acquisitions in 20x0 and so you are aware that additional funding will be needec Today's date is 30 November 20x9. The balance sheet of the company at 30 Septembe 20x9 (the financial year end of Tall) showed the following balances.

	$m
Equity share capital	100.0
Share premium account	35.8
Income statement	89.7
	225.5
Net assets	225.5

On 1 October 20x9, Tall raised additional funding as follows:

(i) Tall issued 15 million $1 bonds at par. The bonds pay no interest but are redeemable on 1 October at $1.61 – the total payable on redemption being $24.15m. As an alternative to redemption, bondholders can elect to convert their holdings into $1 equity shares on the basis of one equity share for every bond held. The current price of a $1 share is $1.40, and it is reckonable that this will grow by at least 5% per annum for the next 5 years.

(ii) Tall issued 10 million $1 preferred shares at $1.20 per share, incurring costs of $100,000. The preferred shares carry no dividend and are redeemable on 1 October 20x5 at $2.35 per share – the total payable on redemption being $23.5m.

Your assistant is unsure how to reflect the additional funding in the financial statements of Tall. He expresses the opinion that both the new capital instruments should logically be reflected in the shareholders' funds section of the balance sheet. He justifies this by saying that:

• the preferred shares are legally shares and so shareholders' funds is the appropriate place to present them;

• the bonds and the preferred shares seem to have similar terms of issue and it is quite likely that the bonds will *become* shares in 5 years' time, given the projected growth in the equity share price.

He has no idea how to show the finance costs of the capital instruments in the income statement. He is aware that IAS 39 *Financial Instruments: Recognition and Measurement* has recently been issued, but is unaware of the details.

Your assistant has also queried the method of financing that is being proposed for the acquisitions. He considers that it would be better to finance the acquisition by issuing new equity shares, because the uniting of interests method of consolidation could then be used. This method, according to your assistant, would lead to higher reported profits.

Required

(b) Write a memorandum to your assistant which evaluates the comments he has made regarding the presentation of the financial instruments and explaining the correct treatment where necessary. Your memorandum should refer to the provisions of relevant accounting standards. Next:

(i) Explain and evaluate the relevant positions of IAS 39 regarding the computation of the finance cost of capital instruments such as bonds and preferred shares. You are NOT required to compute the finance costs for either of the instruments mentioned in this question.

(ii) Evaluate your assistant's comments regarding the use of the uniting of interests method of consolidation. You should refer to the provision of relevant accounting standards.

13

Sundry financial reporting standards

13.1   IAS 34 *Interim Financial Reporting* (1998)

Objective

The objective of IAS 34 is to prescribe the minimum content of an interim financial report and to prescribe the principles for recognition and measurement in interim reports.

Scope

The standard is not mandatory, but instead strongly recommends to regulators that interim financial reporting should be a requirement for publicly traded securities. Specifically they are encouraged to:

- publish an interim report for at least the first 6 months of their financial year;
- ensure that it is available no later than 60 days after the end of the interim report.

Key definitions

Interim period: a financial reporting period shorter than a full financial year.

Interim financial report: a financial report containing either a complete set of financial statements or a set of condensed financial statements.

Content of an interim financial report: IAS 34 defines the minimum content of an interim report, which should contain condensed financial statements together with selected explanatory notes, but should focus on new activities and events. Obviously entities can disclose the following minimum content if they wish:

- condensed balance sheet;
- condensed income statement;
- condensed statement of all changes in equity or changes in equity other than those arising from capital transactions with owners and distributions to owners;
- condensed cash flow statement; and
- selected explanatory notes.

The condensed statements should include each of the headings and subtotals that were included in its most recent annual financial statements. Additional line items should be included if their omission would make the condensed interim statements misleading.

Basic and diluted EPS should be presented on the face of an income statement for an interim period.

Selected explanatory notes

IAS 34 is not concerned with relatively minor changes from its most recent annual financial statements. However, the notes to the interim report should include the following information (unless the information is contained elsewhere in the report):

- a statement that the same accounting policies and methods of computation are followed in the interim statements as compared with the most recent annual statements or, if changed, a description of the nature and effect of the change;
- explanatory comments about the seasonality or cyclicality of interim operations;
- the nature and amount of unusual items affecting assets, liabilities, incomes and expenses because of their nature, size or incidence;
- the nature and amount of changes in estimates, if they have a material effect in the current interim period;
- the issue or repurchase of equity or debt securities;
- dividends paid, separately for ordinary and other shares;
- segmental results for the primary basis of reporting (i.e. either geographical or business);
- material events since the end of the interim period;
- the effect of business combinations during the interim report;
- changes in contingent liabilities or contingent assets since the last annual balance sheet date.

Examples of the above include:

- writedowns of inventories to NRV and reversals;
- acquisitions, disposals, impairments of property, plant etc. and reversals;
- litigation settlements;
- corrections of material errors;
- related party transactions.

Disclosure of compliance

the interim report is in compliance with IAS 34, that fact should be disclosed.

Periods covered

Balance sheet data at the end of the current interim period and comparative data at the end of the most recent financial year

Income statements for the current interim period and cumulative data for the current year to date together with comparative income statements for the comparable interim periods of the immediately preceding year

3. Cash flow statement cumulatively for the current financial year to date with a comparative statement for the comparable year to date period of the immediately preceding financial year

4. Changes in equity statement cumulatively for the current financial year to date with a comparative statement for the comparable year to date period of the immediately preceding financial year.

Materiality

Materiality should be assessed in relation to the interim period financial data. It should be recognised that interim measurements rely to a greater extent on estimates than do annual financial data.

Disclosure in annual financial statements

If an estimate of an amount reported in an interim report has changed significantly during the final interim report and a separate financial report has not been published for that period, then the nature and amount of that change in estimate should be disclosed in a note to the annual financial statements for that financial year.

Recognition and measurement

Use the same accounting policies as for annual statements

The same accounting policies should be adopted in the interim report as are applied in the annual statements, except for accounting policy changes made after the date of the most recent annual financial statements that will be reflected in the next set of annual statements.

The guiding principle for recognition and measurement is that an enterprise should use the same recognition and measurement principles in its interim statements as it does in its annual financial statements – for example, a cost would not be classified as an asset in the interim report if it would not be classified as such in the annual report.

Revenues received occasionally, seasonally or cyclically

Revenue which is received occasionally or seasonally should not be anticipated or deferred in interim reports. The principles of revenue recognition should be applied consistently to interim and annual reports.

Costs incurred unevenly during the financial year

These should only be anticipated or deferred if it would be appropriate to anticipate or defer the expense in the annual financial statements. It would be inappropriate, for example, to anticipate part of the cost of a major advertising campaign later in the year for which no expenses have yet been incurred.

Appendix – Examples of Application of Recognition and Measurement Principles

Employer payroll taxes and insurance contributions

In some countries these are assessed on an annual basis but paid at an uneven rate during the year. It is therefore appropriate, in this situation, to adopt an estimated average annual tax rate for the year in an interim statement, not the actual tax paid. Taxes are an annual assessment but payment is uneven.

Cost of a planned major periodic overhaul

The cost of such an event must not be anticipated unless there is a legal or constructive obligation to carry out the work. A mere intention to carry out work later in the year is not sufficient justification to create a liability.

Year-end bonus

This should not be provided in the interim report unless there is a constructive obligation to pay such a bonus and it can be reliably measured.

Intangible asset

IAS 34 must follow IAS 38 *Intangible Assets*, and thus it would be inappropriate in an interim report to defer a cost in the expectation that it will eventually be part of a non-monetary intangible asset that has not yet been recognised.

Holiday pay

If holiday pay is an enforceable obligation on the employer, then any unpaid accumulated holiday pay may be accrued in the interim report.

Tax on income

An expense for tax should be included in the interim report and the tax rate should be the estimated average annual tax rate for the year (see Example 13.1).

Example 13.1
Tax on income

Assume a quarterly reporting entity expects to earn 10,000 pre-tax each quarter and operates in a tax jurisdiction with a tax rate of 20% on the first 20,000 and 30% on all additional earnings. Actual earnings match expectations. The tax reported in each quarter is as follows:

Tax expense	2,500	2,500	2,500	2,500	10,000

Total estimate 40,000 (20,000 × 20% = 4,000 + 20,000 × 30%
= 6,000, i.e. 10,000 / 4
= 2,500)

Assume a quarterly reporting entity expects to earn 15,000 pre-tax in Q1 but losses of 5,000 in Q2–4. The tax rate is still 20%. The tax reported in each quarter is as follows:

Tax expense	3,000	(1,000)	(1,000)	(1,000)	Nil

Assume year end is 30 June and taxable year end is 31 December. Assume pre-tax earnings of 10,000 each quarter and an average tax rate of 30% in Year 1 and 40% in Year 2. The tax reported in each quarter is as follows:

Tax expense	3,000	3,000	4,000	4,000	14,000

Some countries give enterprises tax credits against the tax payable based on amounts of capital expenditure on research and development. These are usually awarded on an annual basis, thus it is appropriate to include anticipated tax credits within the estimated average tax rate for the year and apply this to calculate the tax on income for interim periods. However, if it relates to a one-off event it should be recognised in the interim period in which the event occurs.

Inventory valuations
These should be valued in the same way as for year-end accounts, but it will be necessary to rely more heavily on estimates for interim reports.

Depreciation
Depreciation should only be charged in the interim statement on assets that have been owned during the period but not on assets that will be acquired later in the financial year.

Foreign currency translation gains and losses
These should be calculated using the same principles as at the end of the year, in accordance with IAS 21.

Appendix – Use of Estimates

Although accounting information must be reliable and free from material error, it may be necessary to sacrifice some accuracy and reliability for the sake of timeliness and costs/benefits. This is particularly the case in interim reporting, where estimates must be used to a greater extent.

Some examples provided in the Appendix are:

1. Inventories – there is no need for a full inventory count but it is sufficient to estimate inventory values using sales margins
2. Provisions – it is inappropriate to bear the cost of experts to advise on the appropriate amount of a provision or an expert valuer to value fixed assets at the interim date
3. Income taxes – it is sufficient to apply an estimated weighted average tax rate to income earned in all jurisdictions; there is no need to calculate the tax rate in each country separately.

13.2   IAS 41 *Agriculture* (February 2001)

Objective

This specialised standard has been published because agriculture is very important in developing countries, as well as the developed world, in terms of GDP.

The main problem in developing such a standard is the great diversity in practice of accounting that exists in agriculture. It is also very difficult to apply traditional accounting methods to agricultural activities.

The main problems are as follows:

1. When and how should entities account for critical events associated with biological transformation (growth, procreation, production and degeneration) which alter the substance of biological assets?
2. Balance sheet classification is made difficult by the variety and characteristics of the living assets of agriculture.
3. The nature of management of agricultural activities means that the unit of measurement is difficult to determine.

Scope

IAS 41 applies to the three elements that form part of, or result from, agricultural activity:

1. Biological assets (see Table 13.1)
2. Agricultural produce at the point of harvest (see Table 13.1)
3. Government grants.

The standard does not apply to agricultural land (see IASs 16 and 40) or intangible assets (see IAS 38). Also, after harvest, IAS 2 *Inventories* applies.

Key definitions

Agricultural activity: the management by an enterprise of the biological transformation of biological assets for sale, into agricultural produce or into additional biological assets.

Agricultural produce: the harvested product of an enterprise's biological assets.

Biological asset: a living animal or plant.

Biological transformation: the processes of growth, degeneration, production and procreation that cause qualitative and quantitative changes in a biological asset.

Group of biological assets: an aggregation of similar living animals or plants.

Harvest: the detachment of produce from a biological asset or the cessation of a biological asset's life processes.

Table 13.1   Biological assets, agricultural produce, and products resulting from post-harvest processing

Biological assets	Agricultural produce	Products that are the result of processing after harvest
Sheep	Wool	Yarn, carpet
Trees in a plantation forest	Logs	Lumber
Plants	Cotton Harvested cane	Thread, clothing sugar
Dairy cattle	Milk	Cheese
Pigs	Carcass	Sausages, cured hams
Bushes	Leaf	Tea, cured tobacco
Vines	Grapes	Wine
Fruit trees	Picked fruit	Processed fruit

Biological assets

Biological assets are the core income producing assets of agricultural activity, held for their transformation abilities (see Table 13.1). Biological transformation leads to various different outcomes:

- asset changes – growth (increase in quantity and/or quality) and degeneration (decrease in quantity and/or quality);
- creation of new assets – production (separable non-living products) and procreation (separable living animals).

Asset changes are critical to the flow of future economic benefits both in and beyond the current accounting period, but their relative importance depends on the purpose of the agricultural activity.

The IAS distinguishes between two broad categories of agricultural production:

1. Consumable – animals/plants harvested
2. Bearer – animals/plants that bear produce for harvest.

Biological assets are usually managed in groups of animal or plant classes with characteristics which permit sustainability in perpetuity, and land often forms an integral part of the activity itself.

Recognition of biological assets

The recognition criteria are very similar to those for other assets, as these may not be recognised unless the following conditions are met:

- the enterprise controls the asset as a result of past events;
- it is probable that the future economic benefits will flow to the enterprise;
- the fair value or cost can be measured reliably.

Measurement of biological assets

IAS 41 requires that, at each balance sheet date, all biological assets should be measured at fair value less estimated point of sale costs.

The IAS permits an alternative method of valuation if a fair value cannot be determined because market prices are not available. In that case it can be measured at cost less accumulated depreciation and impairment losses.

The alternative basis is only permitted on initial recognition. Fair value has greater relevance, reliability, comparability and understandability as a measure of future economic benefits.

Determining fair value

The primary indicator of fair value should be net market value, as this provides the best evidence of fair value when an active market exists. Markets generally differentiate between differing qualities and quantities.

Recognition

The change in the carrying amount for a group of biological assets should be allocated between:

* the change attributable to differences in fair value; and
* the physical change in biological assets held.

The total change in carrying value between the opening and closing periods thus consists of two components. IAS 41 insists that the separate disclosure of each is fundamental to appraising current period performance and future prospects. That is because they will not be reported in the same way in the financial statements.

The change in carrying amount attributable to the physical change must be recognised as income or expense, and described as the change in biological assets. This should enable management performance to be evaluated, and thus should be included in the 'operating' part of the change in carrying amount.

The change in carrying amount attributable to differences in fair value should be recognised in the statement of non-owner movements in equity, and presented in equity under the heading of surplus/(deficit) on fair valuation of biological assets. This is the 'holding' part of the change in the carrying amount.

In the balance sheet, the biological assets must be recorded at fair value after incorporating the consequences of all biological transformations. These assets, together with differing risk and return characteristics, should be identified clearly.

The recommended method of separating the above components is to calculate the change attributable to the differences in fair value by restating biological assets on hand at the opening balance sheet, using end of period fair values, and comparing this with the closing carrying amount.

There are exceptions to this approach – for example, where the production cycle is less than 1 year (broiler chickens, mushroom growing, cereal crops etc.). In these cases the total change in carrying amount should be reported in the income statement as a single item of income or expense.

Any other events giving rise to a change in biological assets of such a size, nature or incidence that their disclosure is relevant to explain the entity's performance should be included in the change in biological assets recognised as an income or expense. They should be recorded as a separate item in the reconciliation required to determine the change attributable to biological transformation.

Presentation and disclosure

Balance sheet

Biological assets should be classified as a separate class of assets falling under neither current nor non-current classifications (unlimited life on a collective basis); it is the total exposure to the type of asset that is important.

Biological assets should also be sub-classified as follows:

Class of animal or plant
Nature of activities (consumable or bearer)
Maturity or immaturity for intended purpose.

Where activities are consumable the maturity criterion will be the attainment of harvestable specifications, whereas in bearer activities it will be the attainment of sufficient maturity to sustain economic harvests.

In the income statement, an analysis of income and expenses based on their nature should be presented rather than the cost of sales method.

IAS 41 also requires detailed disclosures to include the measurement base used for fair value, the details of the reconciliation of the change in carrying value for the year etc.

Agricultural produce

This is recognised at the point of harvest, e.g. detachment from the biological asset (see Table 13.1). It is either incapable of biological process or such processes are dormant. Recognition ends once the produce enters trading activities or production processes within integrated agribusinesses.

Measurement and presentation

Agricultural produce should be measured at fair value at each balance sheet date. The change in the carrying amount of agriculture produce held at two balance sheet dates should be recognised as income or expenses in the income statement. This will be rare, as such produce is usually sold or processed within a short time.

Agricultural produce that is harvested for trading or processing activities within integrated agricultural operations should be measured at fair value at the date of harvest, and this amount is the deemed cost for application of IAS 2 to consequential inventories.

Presentation on the balance sheet

Agricultural produce should be classified as inventory in the balance sheet and disclosed separately either on the face of the balance sheet or in the notes.

Government grants

An unconditional government grant related to a biological asset measured at fair value less estimated point of sale costs should be recognised as income when, and only when the grant becomes receivable.

If a grant requires an enterprise not to engage in agricultural activity, an enterprise should only recognise the grant as income when the conditions are met.

IAS 20 normally does not apply to agricultural grants. However, if a biological asset is measured at cost less accumulated depreciation and impairment losses, then IAS 2 does apply.

Overall disclosure

An enterprise should disclose the aggregate gain or loss arising during the current period on initial recognition of biological assets and agricultural produce and from the change in fair value less estimated point of sale costs of biological assets, as well as a description of each group of biological assets.

If not disclosed elsewhere, the following should also be disclosed:

1. The nature of its activities involving each group of biological assets
2. Non-financial measures or estimates of the physical quantities of:
   - each group of the enterprise's biological assets at the end of the period, and
   - output of agricultural produce during the period.

The methods and significant assumptions applied in determining the fair value of each group of agricultural produce at the point of harvest and each group of biological assets should also be disclosed.

The fair value less estimated point of sale costs of agricultural produce harvested during the period, determined at the point of harvest, should be disclosed.

An enterprise should also disclose:

1. The existence and carrying amounts of biological assets whose title is restricted, and the carrying amounts of biological assets pledged as security for liabilities
2. The amount of commitments for the development or acquisition of biological assets
3. Financial risk management strategies related to agricultural activity.

A reconciliation should be provided of changes in the carrying amount of biological assets between the start and the end of the current period, and this should include:

the gain or loss arising from changes in fair value less estimated point of sale costs;
increases due to purchases;
decreases due to sales;
decreases due to harvest;
increases resulting from business combinations;
net exchange differences arising from the translation of financial statements of a foreign entity; and
other changes.

Additional disclosures for biological assets where fair value cannot be reliably measured

These should include:

. A description of the biological assets
An explanation of why fair value cannot be reliably measured
If possible, the range of estimates within which fair value is highly likely to lie
The depreciation method used
The useful lives or the depreciation rates adopted
The gross carrying amount and the accumulated depreciation at the start and the end of the period.

during the current period, an enterprise measures biological assets at their cost less any accumulated depreciation and accumulated impairment losses, an enterprise should disclose any gain or loss recognised on disposal of such biological assets and the reconciliation required above should disclose amounts related to such biological assets separately.

In addition, the reconciliation should include the following amounts included in the net profit or loss related to those biological assets:

- impairment losses;
- reversals of impairment losses;
- depreciation.

If a previously measured biological asset at cost now becomes reliably measured at fair value, the following should be disclosed for those assets;

1. A description of the biological assets
2. An explanation of why fair value has become reliably measurable
3. The effect of the change.

Government grants
The following should be disclosed:

1. The nature and extent of government grants recognised in the financial statements
2. Unfulfilled conditions and other contingencies attached to the grants
3. Significant decreases expected in the level of government grants.

Illustrative example

XYZ Dairy Ltd

Balance sheet

	Notes	31 December 2001	31 December 2000
ASSETS			
Non-current assets:			
Dairy livestock – immature		52,060	47,730
Dairy livestock – mature		372,990	411,840
Biological assets	3	425,050	459,570
Property, plant and equipment		1,462,650	1,409,800
Total non-current assets		1,887,700	1,869,370
Current assets:			
Inventories		82,950	70,650
Trade and other receivables		88,000	65,000
Cash		10,000	10,000
Total current assets		180,950	145,650
Total assets		2,068,650	2,015,020
EQUITY AND LIABILITIES			
Equity:			
Issued capital		1,000,000	1,000,000
Accumulated profits		902,828	865,000
Total equity		1,902,828	1,865,000
Current liabilities:			
Trade and other payables		165,822	150,020
Total current liabilities		165,822	150,020
Total equity and liabilities		2,068,650	2,015,020

Income statement

	Notes	31 December 2001	31 December 2000
Fair value of milk produced			518,240
Gains arising from changes in fair value less estimated point of sale costs of dairy livestock	3		39,930
			558,170
Inventories used			(137,523)
Staff costs			(127,283)
Depreciation expense			(15,250)
Other operating expenses			(197,092)
			(477,148)
Profit from operations			81,022
Income tax expense			(43,194)
Net profit for the period			37,828

Statement of changes in equity

	Share capital	Accumulated profits	Year ended 31 December 2001
Balance at 1 January 2001	1,000,000	865,000	1,865,000
Net profit for the period		37,828	37,828
Balance at 31 December 2001	1,000,000	902,828	1,902,828

Cash flow statement

	Notes	Year ended 31 December 20x1
Cash flows from operating activities:		
Cash receipts from sales of milk		498,027
Cash receipts from sales of livestock		97,913
Cash paid for supplies and to employees		(460,831)
Cash paid for purchases of livestock		(23,815)
		111,294
Income taxes paid		(43,194)
Net cash flow from operating activities		68,100
Cash flows from investing activities:		
Purchase of property, plant and equipment		(68,100)
Net cash used in investing activities		(68,100)
Net increase in cash		0
Cash at beginning of period		10,000
Cash at end of period		10,000

Notes to the financial statements

Operations and principal activities

XYZ Dairy Ltd ('the Company') is engaged in milk production for supply to various customers. At 31 December 20x1, the Company held 419 cows able to produce milk (mature assets) and 137 heifers being raised to produce milk in the future (immature assets). The Company produced 157,584kg of milk with a fair value less estimated point-of-sale costs of 518,240 (that is determined at the time of milking) in the year ended 31 December 2001.

2. Accounting policies

Livestock and milk: livestock are measured at their fair value less estimated point-of-sale costs. The fair value of livestock is determined based on market prices of livestock of similar age, breed, and genetic merit. Milk is initially measured at its fair value less estimated point-of-sale costs at the time of milking. The fair value of milk is determined based on market prices in the local area.

3. Biological assets

Reconciliation of carrying amounts of dairy livestock	**2001**
Carrying amount at 1 January 2001	459,570
Increases due to purchases	26,250
Gain arising from changes in fair value less estimated point-of-sale costs attributable to physical changes	15,350
Gain arising from changes in fair value less estimated point-of-sale costs attributable to price changes	24,580
Decreases due to sales	(100,700)
Carrying amount at 31 December 2001	425,050

4. Financial risk management strategies

The Company is exposed to financial risks arising from changes in milk prices. The Company does not anticipate that milk prices will decline significantly in the foreseeable future and, therefore, has not entered into derivative or other contracts to manage the risk of a decline in milk prices. The Company reviews its outlook for milk prices regularly in considering the need for active risk management.

Physical change and price change

(The following example illustrates how to separate physical change and price change. Separating the change in fair value less estimated point-of-sale costs between the portion attributable to physical changes and the portion attributable to price changes is encouraged but not required by the standard.)

A herd of 10 2-year-old animals was held at 1 January 2001. One animal aged 2.5 years was purchased on 1 July 2001 for 108, and one animal was born on 1 July 2001. No animals were sold or disposed of during the period. Per unit fair values less estimated point-of-sale costs were as follows:

2 year old animal at 1 January 2001	100
Newborn animal at 1 July 2001	70
2.5-year-old animal at 1 July 2001	108
Newborn animal at 31 December 2001	72
0.5-year-old animal at 31 December 2001	80
2-year-old animal at 31 December 2001	105
2.5-year-old animal at 31 December 2001	111
3-year-old animal at 31 December 2001	120

Fair value less estimated point-of-sale costs of herd at 1 January 2001	(10 × 100)	1,000
Purchase on 1 July 2001	(1 × 108)	108

Increase in fair value less estimated point-of-sale costs due to price change:

$10 \times (105 - 100)$	50	
$1 \times (111 - 108)$	3	
$1 \times (72 - 70)$	2	
		55

Increase in fair value less estimated point-of-sale costs due to physical change:

$10 \times (120 - 105)$	150	
$1 \times (120 - 111)$	9	
$1 \times (80 - 72)$	8	
1×70	70	
		237

Fair value less estimated point-of-sale costs of herd at 31 December 2001:

11×120	1,320	
1×80	80	
		1,400

13.3   IFRS 4 *Insurance Contracts* (March 2004)

Objective

IFRS 4 was introduced to prescribe the financial reporting required for insurance contracts by any entity issuing such contracts.

Scope

It is applied to insurance contracts issued, reinsurance contracts held and financial instruments issued with a discretionary participation feature.

However, it does not apply to the following:

product warranties (covered by IAS 18 and IAS 37);
employers' assets and liabilities under employee benefit plans (see IASs 19 and 26);
contractual rights that are contingent on the future use of or right to use a non-financial item and a lessee's residual value guarantees on finance leases (see IASs 17, 18 and 38);
financial guarantees entered into within the scope of IAS 39;
contingent consideration re business combination (see IFRS 3);
direct insurance contracts that an entity holds as a policyholder.

Key points

IFRS 4 is only the first phase on the project on insurance contracts. The main points in the standard are as follows:

It prohibits the recognition of a liability for provisions for future claims under insurance contracts that are not in existence at the reporting date (e.g. catastrophe and equalisation provisions)

It requires an assessment to be made of the adequacy of recognised insurance liabilities and the recognition of any impairment of reinsurance assets

3. It requires an entity to keep insurance liabilities on the balance sheet until they are discharged or cancelled or expired, and to ensure that insurance liabilities are presented without any offsetting against related reinsurance assets.

An entity is only permitted to change its accounting policies for insurance contracts if, as a result, its financial statements are more relevant or more reliable and no less relevant than previously. In particular, an entity must not introduce any of the following practices, although, if currently adopted, it may continue to use them:

- measuring insurance liabilities on an undiscounted basis;
- measuring contractual rights to future investment management fees at an amount that exceeds their fair value as implied by a comparison with current fees charged by other market participants for similar services;
- using non-uniform accounting policies for the insurance contracts of subsidiaries;
- measuring insurance liabilities with excessive prudence.

There is a rebuttable presumption that an insurer's financial statements will become less relevant and reliable if it introduces an accounting policy that reflects future investment margins in measuring insurance contracts. When an insurer changes its accounting policies for insurance liabilities, it may reclassify some or all of its financial assets as 'at fair value through profit or loss'.

Sundry issues

IFRS 4 also specifies the following:

1. An entity need not account for an embedded derivative separately at fair value if the embedded derivative meets the definition of an insurance contract
2. An entity is required to unbundle deposit components of some insurance contracts
3. An entity may apply 'shadow accounting' (i.e. account for both realised and unrealised gains or losses on assets in the same way relative to the measurement of insurance liabilities)
4. Discretionary participation features contained in insurance contracts or financial instruments may be recognised separately from the guaranteed element and classified as a liability or as a separate component of equity.

Disclosures

IFRS 4 requires disclosure of the amounts in an entity's financial statements that arise from insurance contracts and the amount, timing and uncertainty of future cash flow from insurance contracts.

13.4 Examination questions

(There is only one question in this chapter, as questions on interim reporting are fairly rare since they not impact on the annual report. In addition, the content of the interim report is fairly factual and the leaves little room for subjective judgements to the extent there would be in other subject areas.

As the topic of insurance contracts is very specialised, it is unlikely that questions would be asked, other than in general terms, about the broad thrust of the document. As it is only a very recent document, there are no questions to date on the subject.

The topic of agriculture, however, has emerged with the publication of IAS 41, and it will have substantial impact within parts of Europe which rely heavily on agriculture. The question below was taken from the ACCA examinations and requires students to advise a client on how to account for their biological assets in relation to the fair value approach adopted in IAS 41.)

Question 13.1: The Lucky Dairy (ACCA)

The Lucky Dairy, a public limited company, produces milk for supply to various customers. It is responsible for producing 25% of the country's milk consumption. The company owns 150 farms, and has a stock of 70,000 cows and 35,000 heifers which are being raised to produce milk in the future. The farms produce 2.5 million kilograms of milk per annum and normally hold an inventory of 50,000 kilograms of milk. (Extracts from the draft accounts to 31 May 2002.)

The herds comprise at 31 May 2002:

- 70,000 × 3-year-old cows (all purchased on or before 1 June 2001)
  25,000 × heifers (average age $1\frac{1}{2}$ years old, purchased 1 December 2001)
  10,000 × heifers (average age 2 years, purchased 1 June 2001).

There were no animals born or sold in the year. The per unit values less estimated point of sale costs were as follows:

	$
2-year-old animal at 1 June 2001	50
1-year-old animal at 1 June 2001 and 1 December 2001	40
3-year-old animal at 31 May 2002	60
$1\frac{1}{2}$-year-old animal at 31 May 2002	46
2-year-old animal at 31 May 2002	55
1-year-old animal at 31 May 2002	42

The company has had a difficult year in financial and operating terms. The cows had contracted a disease at the beginning of the financial year, which had been passed on in the food chain to a small number of consumers. The publicity surrounding this event had caused a drop in the consumption of milk, and as a result the dairy was holding 90,000 kilograms of milk in storage.

The government had stated, on 1 April 2002, that it was prepared to compensate farmers for the drop in the price and consumption of milk. An official government letter was received on 6 June 2002 stating that $1.5 million will be paid to Lucky on 1 August 2002. Additionally, on 1 May 2002 Lucky had received a letter from its lawyer saying that legal proceedings had been started against the company by the persons affected by the disease. The company's lawyers have advised them that they feel that it is probable that they will be found liable and that the costs involved may reach $2 million. The lawyers, however, feel that the company may receive additional compensation from a government fund if certain quality control procedures had been carried out by the company. However, the lawyers will only state that the compensation payment is 'possible'.

The company's activities are controlled in three geographical locations: Dale, Shire and Ham. The only region affected by the disease was Dale, and the government has decided that it is to restrict the milk production of that region significantly. Lucky estimates that the discounted future cash income from the present herds of cattle in the region amounts to $1.2 million, taking into account the government restriction order. Lucky was not sure that the fair value of the cows in the region could be measured reliably at the date of purchase because of the problems with the diseased cattle. The cows in this region amounted to 20,000 in number and the heifers 10,000 in number. All of the animals were purchased on 1 June 2001. Lucky has had an offer of $1 million for all of the animals in the Dale region (net of point of sale costs), and $2 million for the sale of the farms in the region. However, there was a minority of directors who opposed the planned sale and it was decided to defer the public announcement of sale pending the outcome of the possible receipt of the government compensation. The Board had decided that the potential sale plan was highly confidential but a national newspaper had published an article stating that the sale may occur and that there would be many people who would lose their employment. The Board approved the planned sale of Dale farms on 31 May 2002.

The directors of Lucky have approached your firm for professional advice on the above matters.

Required

Advise the directors on how the biological assets and produce of Lucky should be accounted for under IAS 41 *Agriculture*, and discuss the implications for the published financial statements of the above events. (Candidates should produce a table which shows the changes in value of the cattle stock for the year to 31 May 2002 due to price change and physical change, excluding the Dale region, and the value of the herd of the Dale region as at 31 May 2002. Ignore the effects of taxation. Heifers are young female cows.)

Exposure drafts and statements of the International Financial Reporting Interpretations Committee (IFRIC formerly SIC)

14.1 IFRS 6 Exploration for and Evaluation of Mineral Resources (December 2004) (ED 6 January 2004)

Background

The IASB are concerned about the divergent practices portrayed by mineral resource companies, so they have published an interim exposure draft to try to ensure better comparability between entities whilst postponing a more comprehensive review until a fuller consideration of the accounting issues has taken place.

Objectives

The objectives of IFRS 6 are:

to make limited improvements to accounting practices for the exploration and evaluation of mineral resources;
to require impairment testing in accordance with IAS 36 via either a general CGU or, alternatively, via a specialised CGU for exploration and evaluation assets;
to disclose information about exploration and evaluation assets, how impairment has been assessed and details of any impairment losses.

Scope

The draft is applicable to all entities engaged in exploration and evaluation expenditures.

Recognition of exploration and evaluation assets

An entity applying this IFRS may elect to continue to recognise and measure exploration and evaluation assets in accordance with its existing policies, with the exception that once technical feasibility and commercial viability are established no further amounts may be capitalised nor should any administration costs be included as an asset.

Measurement of exploration and evaluation assets

Measurement at recognition

Exploration and evaluation assets must be measured at cost.

Elements of exploration and evaluation assets

The following may be included in the measurement of an asset:

- acquisition of rights to explore;
- topographical, geological, geochemical and geophysical studies;
- exploratory drilling;
- trenching;
- sampling; and
- activities to evaluate the technical feasibility and commercial viability of extracting mineral resources.

However, administration costs and development costs post-technical feasibility/commercial viability are not permitted. An entity must also apply IAS 37 to the costs of removal and restoration incurred in the exploration and evaluation of mineral resources.

Measurement after recognition

An entity may apply the cost or revaluation model in accordance with IAS 16 and IAS 38.

Changes in accounting policies

If an entity elects to continue with its existing policies, those may only be changed if the change makes the financial statements more relevant for decision-making purposes.

Impairment

Exploration and evaluation assets must be reviewed for impairment annually, and any loss recognised as per IAS 38.

IAS 38 identifies external sources as guidelines on when an impairment might arise. These are supplemented by the following:

- the period of right to explore in a specific area has expired and is unlikely to be renewed;
- further exploration in the area is neither budgeted nor planned for;

- significant adverse changes to the main assumptions (e.g. prices, exchange rates) have occurred in the specific area;
- the decision not to develop the mineral resource in the specific area has been made;
- the entity plans to dispose of the asset at an unfavourable price; and
- the entity does not expect the assets to be recovered from successful development of the specific area or by sale.

Cash generating unit for exploration and evaluation assets

Impairment of exploration and evaluation assets may be tested on a 'CGU' or a 'CGU for exploration and evaluation assets' basis.

Disclosure

The following should be disclosed:

1. Accounting policies adopted including the recognition of exploration and evaluation assets
2. Amounts of assets, liabilities, incomes and expenses arising from exploration and evaluation of mineral resources
3. The level at which an entity tests exploration and evaluation assets for impairment.

4.2   Standards Interpretations Committee (extant interpretations)

Over the years the Standing Interpretations Committee (now IFRIC) has issued a number of statements which are part and parcel of providing a fair presentation of the financial statements. The following is a brief summary of those that were still extant as at 31 October 2004.

IFRIC 1 *Changes in Existing Decommissioning, Restoration and Similar Liabilities* (May 2004)

IFRIC 1 contains guidance on accounting for changes in decommissioning, restoration and similar liabilities that have previously been recognised both as part of the cost of an item of property, plant and equipment under IAS 16 and as a provision (liability) under IAS 37. An example would be a liability that was recognised by the operator of a nuclear power plant for costs that it expects to incur in the future when the plant is shut down (decommissioned). The interpretation addresses subsequent changes to the amount of the liability that may arise from (a) a revision in the timing or amount of the estimated decommissioning or restoration costs, or (b) a change in the current market-based discount rate.

IAS 37 requires the amount recognised as a provision to be the best estimate of the expenditure required to settle the obligation at the balance sheet date. This is measured at its present value, which IFRIC 1 confirms should be measured using a current market-based discount rate. The interpretation deals with three kinds of change in an existing liability for such costs.

The two main kinds of change dealt with in IFRIC 1 are those that arise from:

- the revision of estimated outflows of resources embodying economic benefits – for example, the estimated costs of decommissioning a nuclear power plant may vary significantly both in timing and amount; and
- revisions to the current market-based discount rate.

Most entities account for their property, plant and equipment using the cost model. Where this is so, these changes are required to be capitalised as part of the cost of the item and depreciated prospectively over the remaining life of the item to which they relate. This is consistent with the treatment under IAS 16 of other changes in estimate relating to property, plant and equipment.

In the spirit of convergence, the IFRIC considered the US GAAP approach in Statement of Financial Accounting Standard No. 143 *Accounting for Asset Retirement Obligations*. The interpretation treats changes in estimated cash flows in a similar way to SFAS 143. However, SFAS 143 does not require any adjustment to the cost of the item, or to the provision, to reflect the effect of a change in the current market-based discount rate. The IFRIC did not choose this approach because IAS 37, unlike US GAAP requires provisions to be measured at the current best estimate, which should reflect current discount rates. Also, IFRIC considered it important that both kinds of change should be dealt with in the same way.

Where entities account for their property, plant and equipment using the fair value model, a change in the liability does not affect the valuation of the item for accounting purposes. Instead, it alters the revaluation surplus or deficit on the item, which is the difference between its valuation and what would be its carrying amount under the cost model. The effect of the change is treated consistently with other revaluation surpluses or deficits. Any cumulative deficit is taken to profit or loss, but any cumulative surplus is credited to equity.

The third kind of change dealt with by IFRIC 1 is an increase in the liability that reflects the passage of time – also referred to as the unwinding of the discount. This is recognised in profit or loss as a finance cost as it occurs as per IAS 37.

SIC 7 *Introduction of the Euro* (May 1998)

SIC 7 addresses how the introduction of the euro, resulting from the European Economic and Monetary Union (EMU), affects the application of IAS 21, *The Effects of Changes Foreign Exchange Rates*. SIC 7 states that the requirements of IAS 21 should be strictly applied. This means that monetary assets and liabilities should continue to be translated the spot rate. Where an enterprise has an existing accounting policy of deferring exchange gains and losses related to anticipatory hedges, an enterprise should continue to account for such deferred exchange gains and losses notwithstanding the changeover to the euro.

Cumulative differences classified as equity relating to foreign entities should continue to be recognised as income or expenses only on the disposal of the foreign entity

The allowed alternative treatment of IAS 21 regarding exchange differences resulting from severe devaluations does not apply to currencies participating in EMU.

SIC 10 *Government Assistance – No Specific Relation to Operating Activities* (July 1998)

In some countries, government assistance to enterprises can be aimed at encouragement or long-term support of business activities either in certain regions or in industry sectors. Conditions to receive such assistance may not be specifically related to the operating activities of the enterprise. The issue is whether such government assistance is 'a government grant' within the scope of IAS 20 and should therefore be accounted for in accordance with this standard.

Under SIC 10, government assistance to enterprises that is aimed at encouragement or long-term support of business activities either in certain regions or in industry sectors meets the definition of government grants in IAS 20. Such grants should therefore not be credited directly to shareholders' interests.

SIC 12 *Consolidation – Special Purpose Entities* (November 1998)

SIC 12 addresses when a special purpose entity should be consolidated by a reporting enterprise under the consolidation principles in IAS 27. The SIC agreed that an enterprise should consolidate a special purpose entity (SPE) when, in substance, the enterprise controls the SPE.

Examples of SPEs include entities set up to effect a lease, a securitisation of financial assets, or R&D activities. The concept of control used in IAS 27 requires having the ability to direct or dominate decision making accompanied by the objective of obtaining benefits from the SPE's activities. The interpretation provides example indications of when control may exist in the context of an SPE. The examples involve activities of the SPE on behalf of the reporting enterprise, the reporting enterprise having decision-making powers over the SPE, and the reporting enterprise having rights to the majority of benefits and exposure to significant risks of the SPE.

Some enterprises may also need separately to evaluate the topic of de-recognition of assets, for example, related to assets transferred to an SPE. In some circumstances such transfer of assets may result in those assets being de-recognised and accounted for as a sale. Even if the transfer qualifies as a sale, the provisions of IAS 27 and SIC 12 may mean that the enterprise should consolidate the SPE. SIC 12 does not address the circumstances in which sale treatment should apply for the reporting enterprise, or the elimination of the consequences of such a sale upon consolidation.

SIC 13 *Jointly Controlled Entities – Non-Monetary Contributions by Venturers* (November 1998)

SIC 13 clarifies the circumstances in which the appropriate portion of gains or losses resulting from a contribution of a non-monetary asset to a jointly controlled entity (JCE) in exchange for an equity interest in the JCE should be recognised by the venturer in the income statement.

SIC 13 indicates that under IAS 31 recognition of gains or losses on contributions of non-monetary assets is appropriate unless:

- the significant risks and rewards related to the non-monetary asset are not transferred to the jointly controlled entity;
- the gain or loss cannot be measured reliably; or
- similar assets are contributed by the other venturers.

Non-monetary assets contributed by venturers are similar when they have a similar nature, a similar use in the same line of business, and a similar fair value. A contribution meets the similarity test only if all significant component assets included in the contribution are similar to each of the significant component assets contributed by the other venturers. A gain should also be recognised if, in addition to the equity interest in the jointly controlled entity, the venturer receives consideration in the form of either cash or other assets which are dissimilar to the non-monetary assets contributed.

SIC 15 *Operating Leases – Incentives* (July 1999)

In SIC 15, the SIC clarifies the recognition of incentives related to operating leases by both the lessee and lessor. The interpretation indicates that lease incentives (such as rent-free periods or contributions by the lessor to the lessee's relocation costs) should be considered an integral part of the consideration for the use of the leased asset. IAS 17 requires an enterprise to treat incentives as a reduction of lease income or lease expense. As they are an integral part of the net consideration agreed for the use of the leased asset, incentives should be recognised by both the lessor and the lessee over the lease term, with each party using a single amortisation method applied to the net consideration.

SIC 21 *Income Taxes – Recovery of Revalued Non-Depreciable Assets* (July 2000)

SIC 21 deals with cases where a non-depreciable asset (freehold land) is carried at revaluation under IAS 16. No part of the carrying amount of such an asset is considered to be recovered through its use. Therefore, SIC 21 concludes that the deferred tax liability or asset that arises from revaluation must be measured based on the tax consequences that would follow from the sale of the asset rather than through use. In some jurisdictions, this will result in the use of a capital gains tax rate rather than the rate applicable to corporate earnings.

SIC 25 *Income Taxes – Changes in the Tax Status of an Enterprise or its Shareholders* (July 2000)

A change in the tax status of an enterprise or its shareholders does not give rise to increases or decreases in the pre-tax amounts recognised directly in equity. Therefore SIC 25 concludes that the current and deferred tax consequences of the change in tax status should be included in net profit or loss for the period. However, where a transaction or event does result in a direct credit or charge to equity (for example the revaluation property, plant or equipment under IAS 16), the related tax consequence would still be recognised directly in equity.

SIC 27 *Evaluating the Substance of Transactions in the Legal Form of a Lease* (October 2000)

SIC 27 addresses issues that may arise when an arrangement between an enterprise and an investor involves the legal form of a lease. Among the provisions of SIC 27 are the following:

1. Accounting for arrangements between an enterprise and an investor should reflect the substance of the arrangement. All aspects of the arrangement should be evaluated to determine its substance, with weight given to those aspects and implications that have an economic effect.

   In this respect, SIC 27 includes a list of indicators that individually demonstrate that an arrangement may not, in substance, involve a lease under IAS 17. If an arrangement does not meet the definition of a lease, SIC 27 addresses whether a separate investment account and lease payment obligation that might exist represent assets and liabilities of the enterprise; how the enterprise should account for other obligations resulting from the arrangement; and how the enterprise should account for a fee it might receive from an investor. SIC 27 includes a list of indicators that collectively demonstrate that, in substance, a separate investment account and lease payment obligations do not meet the definitions of an asset and a liability and should not be recognised by the enterprise. Other obligations of an arrangement, including any guarantees provided and obligations incurred upon early termination, should be accounted for under IAS 37or IAS 39, depending on the terms. Further, it agreed that the criteria in IAS 18 should be applied to the facts and circumstances of each arrangement in determining when to recognise a fee as income that an enterprise might receive.

. A series of transactions that involve the legal form of a lease is linked, and therefore should be accounted for as one transaction, when the overall economic effect cannot be understood without reference to the series of transactions as a whole.

IC 29 *Disclosure – Service Concession Arrangements* July 2001)

IC 29 prescribes the information that should be disclosed in the notes to the financial atements of a concession operator and a concession provider when the two parties are ined by a service concession arrangement. A service concession arrangement exists hen an enterprise (the concession operator) agrees with another enterprise (the conssion provider) to provide services that give the public access to major economic and cial facilities.

Examples of service concession arrangements involve water treatment and supply cilities, motorways, car parks, tunnels, bridges, airports and telecommunication networks. camples of arrangements that are not service concession arrangements include an terprise outsourcing the operation of its internal services (for instance, an employee feteria, building maintenance, and accounting or information technology functions).

Under SIC 29, the following should be disclosed in each period:

1. A description of the arrangement
2. Significant terms of the arrangement that may affect the amount, timing and certainty of future cash flows (such as the period of the concession, repricing dates, and the basis on which repricing or re-negotiation is determined)
3. The nature and extent (quantity, time period, or amount, as appropriate) of:
   - rights to use specified assets
   - obligations to provide or rights to expect provision of services
   - obligations to acquire or build items of property, plant and equipment
   - obligations to deliver or rights to receive specified assets at the end of the concession period
   - renewal and termination options
   - other rights and obligations (for instance, major overhauls), and
   - changes in the arrangement occurring during the period.

SIC 31 *Revenue – Barter Transactions Involving Advertising Services* (July 2001)

Under IAS 18, revenue cannot be recognised if the amount of revenue is not reliably measurable. SIC 31 deals with the circumstances in which a seller can reliably measure revenue at the fair value of advertising services received or provided in a barter transaction. Under SIC 31, revenue from a barter transaction involving advertising cannot be measured reliably at the fair value of advertising services received. However, a seller can reliably measure revenue at the fair value of the advertising services it provides in a barter transaction by reference only to non-barter transactions that:

- involve advertising similar to the advertising in the barter transaction;
- occur frequently;
- represent a predominant number of transactions and amount when compared to all transactions to provide advertising that is similar to advertising in the barter transaction
- involve cash and/or another form of consideration (such as marketable securities non-monetary assets, and other services) that has a reliably measurable fair value; and
- do not involve the same counterparty as in the barter transaction.

SIC 32 *Intangible Assets – Website Costs* (July 2001)

SIC 32 concludes that a website developed by an enterprise using internal expenditure whether for internal or external access, is an internally generated intangible asset that subject to the requirements of IAS 38 *Intangible Assets*. SIC 32 identifies the followin stages of website development:

1. Planning
2. Application and infrastructure development
3. Content development
4. Operating.

SIC 32 addresses the appropriate accounting treatment for internal expenditure on each of those stages of development and operation as follows.

1. A website arising from development should be recognised as an intangible asset if, and only if, in addition to complying with the general requirements described in IAS 38 for recognition and initial measurement, an enterprise can satisfy the requirements in IAS 38. In particular, an enterprise may be able to satisfy the requirement to demonstrate how its website will generate probable future economic benefits under IAS 38 when, for example, the website is capable of generating revenues, including direct revenues from enabling orders to be placed. An enterprise is not able to demonstrate how a website developed solely or primarily for promoting and advertising its own products and services will generate probable future economic benefits, and consequently all expenditure on developing such a website should be recognised as an expense when incurred.

2. Any internal expenditure on the development and operation of an enterprise's own website should be accounted for in accordance with IAS 38. The nature of each activity for which expenditure is incurred (e.g. training employees and maintaining the website) and the website's stage of development or post-development should be evaluated to determine the appropriate accounting treatment. For example:

   • *Planning.* The planning stage is similar in nature to the research phase in IAS 38. Expenditure incurred in this stage should be recognised as an expense when it is incurred.

   • *Application and infrastructure development.* The application and infrastructure development stage, the graphical design stage and the content development stage, to the extent that content is developed for purposes other than to advertise and promote an enterprise's own products and services, are similar in nature to the development phase in IAS 38. Expenditure incurred in these stages should be included in the cost of a website recognised as an intangible asset in accordance with this interpretation when the expenditure can be directly attributed, or allocated on a reasonable and consistent basis, to preparing the website for its intended use. For example, expenditure on purchasing or creating content (other than content that advertises and promotes an enterprise's own products and services) specifically for a website, or expenditure to enable use of the content (such as a fee for acquiring a licence to reproduce) on the website, should be included in the cost of development when this condition is met. However, in accordance with IAS 38, expenditure on an intangible item that was initially recognised as an expense in previous financial statements should not be recognised as part of the cost of an intangible asset at a later date (for instance, when the costs of a copyright have been fully amortised, and the content is subsequently provided on a website).

   • *Content development.* Expenditure incurred in the content development stage, to the extent that content is developed to advertise and promote an enterprise's own products and services (such as digital photographs of products), should be recognised as an expense when incurred in accordance with IAS 38. For example, when accounting for expenditure on professional services for taking digital photographs of an enterprise's own products and for enhancing their display, expenditure should be recognised as an expense as the professional services are received during the process, not when the digital photographs are displayed on the website.

- *Operating.* The operating stage begins once development of a website is complete. Expenditure incurred in this stage should be recognised as an expense when it is incurred unless it meets the criteria in IAS 38.
3. A website that is recognised as an intangible asset under SIC 32 should be measured after initial recognition by applying the requirements of IAS 38. The best estimate of a website's useful life should be short.

14.3   IFRICs developed after 31st October 2004

IFRIC 2 *Member's Shares in Co-operative Entities and Similar Instruments* (November 2004)

Shares for which a member has the right to request redemption are normally classified as liabilities. However, they are equity if:

1) The entity has an unconditional right to refuse redemption, or
2) Local law or custom imposes restriction on redemption.

IFRIC 3 *Emission Rights* (December 2004)

In cap and trade agreements where government imposes a cap on pollution but enables and entity to trade 'spare licenses' in an open market, the following rules apply:

1) Rights and allowances to pollute are assets under IAS 38; and
2) If allowances are issued below fair value, the difference is regarded as a government grant and treated under IAS 20; and
3) As a company pollutes it creates an obligation under IAS 37.

IFRIC 4 *Determine Whether an Arrangement Contains a Lease* (December 2004)

Certain arrangements may look like leases (outsourcing pay contracts, etc.). These should be treated as leases if fulfilment depends on a specific asset and the arrangement conveys a right to a control the use of the underlying asset by operation, physical access etc., or there is only a remote possibility that parties other than the purchaser will take more than an insignificant amount of the output of the asset.

IFRIC 5 *Rights to Interests Arising from Decommissioning Restoration and Environmental Rehabilitation Funds* (December 2004)

If an entity contributes to a fund to most decommissioning liabilities it should apply IAS 27, SIC 12, IAS 28 and IAS 31 to determine how to account for fund. If the fund is not consolidated, proportionary consolidated or equity accounted, an obligation under IAS 37 should be set up. Similarly, any additional contributions should be accounted for under IAS 37.

Printed and bound by CPI Group (UK) Ltd, Croydon, CR0 4YY

08/05/2025

01864859-0002